THE NEW INTERNATIONAL
WEBSTER'S
THESAURUS

TRIDENT
PRESS
INTERNATIONAL

Published by
Trident Press International
2002 Edition

ISBN 1582793964

Printed in Peru

A

abandon, v. SYN.-abdicate, abjure, relinquish, renounce, resign, surrender, vacate, waive; desert, forsake, leave, quit. ANT.-defend, maintain, uphold; stay, support.

abase, v. SYN.-debase, degrade, demote, humble, lower.

abate, v. SYN.-assuage, decrease, diminish, lessen, lower, moderate, reduce, suppress. ANT.-amplify, enlarge, increase, intensify, revive.

abbey, n. SYN.-cloister, convent, hermitage, monastery, nunnery, priory.

abbreviate, v. SYN.- abridge, condense, contract, curtail, diminish, lessen, limit, reduce, restrict. ANT.-elongate, extend, lengthen.

abbreviation, n. SYN.-abridgement, contraction, reduction, shortening. ANT.-amplification, enlargement, expansion, extension.

abdicate, v. SYN.-abandon, abjure, relinquish, renounce, resign, surrender, vacate, waive; desert, forsake, leave, quit. ANT.-defend, maintain, uphold; stay, support.

aberrant, a. SYN.-abnormal, capricious, devious, eccentric, irregular, unnatural, unusual, variable. ANT.-fixed, methodical, ordinary, regular, usual.

abet, v. SYN.-aid, assist, encourage, help, incite. ANT.-discourage, hinder, oppose, resist.

abhor, v. SYN.-abominate, despise, detest, dislike, hate, loathe. ANT.-admire, approve, cherish, like, love.

abhorrence, n. SYN.-antipathy, aversion, disgust, disinclination, dislike, distaste, dread, hatred, loathing, repugnance, repulsion,

reluctance animosity, detestation, enmity, hostility, ill will, malevolence, rancor. ANT.-affection, attachment, devotion, enthusiasm attraction, friendship, love.

abide, v. SYN.-continue, dwell, endure, live, remain, room, wait, withstand.

ability, n. SYN.-aptitude, aptness, capability, capacity, dexterity, efficiency, faculty, power, qualification, skill, talent. ANT.-disability, incapacity, incompetence, unreadiness.

abject, a. SYN.-contemptible, debased, despicable, disheartening, groveling, ignoble, low, mean, vile, worthless, wretched. ANT.-attractive, decent, laudable; upright.

able, a. SYN.-apt, agile, adept, capable, clever, competent, efficient, experienced, fitted, gifted, qualified, skillful, versatile. ANT.-inadequate, incapable, incompetent, unfitted.

ablution, n. SYN. bath, cleansing, washing; ceremony, rite.

abnormal, a. SYN.-aberrant, capricious, devious, eccentric, irregular, unnatural, unusual, variable. ANT.-fixed, methodical, ordinary, regular, usual.

abode, n. SYN.-dwelling, home, house.

abolish, v. SYN.-destroy, end, eradicate, obliterate, overthrow; abrogate, annul, cancel, invalidate, revoke. ANT.-continue, establish, promote, restore, sustain.

abominable, a. SYN.-detestable, execrable, foul, hateful, loathsome, odious, revolting, vile. ANT.-agreeable, commendable, delightful, pleasant.

aboriginal, a. SYN.-ancient, antiquated, early, old, primary, primeval, primitive primordial, pristine. ANT.-civilized, late, modern, modish, sophisticated.

abound, *v.* SYN.-copious, full, overflow, rich, plenty, plentiful, teem.

above, *a.* SYN.-aloft, beyond, higher, over, overhead, raised, superior. ANT.-low, below, beneath, under.

abrade, *v.* SYN.-rub, scrape, wear.

abridge, *v.* SYN.-abbreviate, condense, contract, curtail, diminish, lessen, limit, reduce, restrict shorten. ANT.-elongate, extend, lengthen.

abridgement, *n.* SYN.-abbreviation, contraction, reduction, shortening. ANT.-amplification, enlargement, expansion, extension.

abrogate, *v.* SYN.-cancel, cross out, delete, eliminate, erase, expunge, obliterate; abolish, annul, invalidate.

abrupt, *a.* SYN.-hasty, precipitate, sudden, unannounced, unexpected; blunt, brusque, curt, rude; craggy, harsh, precipitous, rough, rugged, sharp, steep. ANT.-anticipated, expected; courteous, gradual, smooth.

absent, *a.* SYN.-abroad, away, departed; absent-minded, abstracted, distracted, inattentive, preoccupied. ANT.-attending, present; attentive, watchful.

absolute, *a.* SYN.-actual, complete, entire, perfect, pure, ultimate, unconditional, unqualified, unrestricted; arbitrary, authoritative, despotic, tyrannous. ANT.-accountable, conditional, contingent, dependent, qualified.

absolve, *v.* SYN.-acquit, clear, condone, excuse, forgive, overlook, pardon, release, remit. ANT.-accuse,

chastise, condemn, convict, punish.

absorb, *v.* SYN.-assimilate, consume, digest, engulf, imbibe, swallow up; engage, engross, occupy. ANT.-discharge, dispense, emit, expel, exude.

abstain, *v.* SYN.-avoid, decline, desist, fast, forbear, forgo, refrain, renounce, shun, withhold. ANT.-continue, indulge, persist.

abstention, *n.* See **abstinence.**

abstinence, *n.* SYN.-abstention, continence, denial, fasting, forbearance, moderation, self-denial, sobriety, temperance. ANT.-excess, gluttony, greed, intoxication, self-indulgence.

abstract, *v.* SYN.-draw from, part, remove, separate, appropriate, purloin, steal; abridge, summarize; ideal, intellectual. ANT.-add, replace, restore, return, unite.

absurd, *a.* SYN.-foolish, inconsistent, irrational, nonsensical, preposterous, ridiculous, self-contradictory, silly, unreasonable. ANT.-consistent, rational, reasonable, sensible, sound.

abundance, *n.* SYN.-affluence, bounty, overflowing, plenty, profusion, wealth. ANT.-lack, need, want.

abundant, *a.* SYN.-ample, bountiful, copious, overflowing, plenteous, plentiful, profuse, rich, teeming. ANT.-deficient, insufficient, scant, scarce.

abuse, *n.* SYN.-aspersion, defamation, desecration, dishonor, disparagement, insult, invective, maltreatment, misuse, outrage, perversion, profanation, reproach, reviling, upbraiding. ANT.-approval, commendation, laudation, plaudit, respect.

abuse, *v.* SYN.-asperse, defame, disparage, ill-use, malign, revile, scandalize, traduce, vilify; misapply, misemploy, misuse. ANT.-cherish, honor, praise, protect, respect.

academic, *a.* SYN.-bookish, erudite, formal, learned, pedantic, scholarly, scholastic, theoretical. ANT.-common-sense, ignorant, practical, simple.

accede, *v.* SYN.-accord, allow, concede, grant, permit; abdicate, acquiesce, capitulate, cede, quit, relent, relinquish, resign, submit, succumb, surrender, waive, yield. ANT.-deny, dissent, oppose, refuse; assert, resist, strive, struggle.

accelerate, *v.* SYN.-dispatch, expedite, facilitate, forward, hasten, hurry, push, quicken, rush, speed. ANT.-block, hinder, impede, retard, slow.

accent, *n.* SYN.-beat, emphasis, inflection, intonation.

accept, *v.* SYN.-acknowledge, admit, agree, allow, assent, concede, confess, get, grant, permit, receive, take, welcome. ANT.-bestow, deny, dismiss, give, impart, reject, discharge, shun, turn away.

acceptable, *a.* SYN.-agreeable, amiable, charming, gratifying, pleasant, pleasing, pleasurable, suitable, welcome. ANT.-disagreeable, obnoxious, offensive, unpleasant.

access *n.* SYN.-accessibility, admission, admittance; approach, entrance, passage, path.

accessible, *a.* SYN.-available handy, obtainable, prepared, ready, usable. ANT.-inaccessible, unavoidable.

accessory, *n.* SYN.-abettor, accomplice, ally, assistant, associate, confederate. ANT.-adversary, enemy, opponent, rival.

accident, *n.* SYN.-calamity, casualty, contingency, disaster, fortuity, misfortune, mishap. ANT.-calculation, design, intention, purpose.

accidental, *a.* SYN.-casual, chance, contingent, fortuitous, incidental, undesigned, unintended. ANT.-calculated, decreed, intended, planned, willed.

acclaim, *v.* SYN.-applaud, approve, cheer, hail.

accommodate, *v.* SYN.-adapt, adjust, aid, assist, benefit, conform, fit, gratify, help, serve, suit. ANT.-disturb, misapply, misfit.

accompany, *v.* SYN.-associate with, attend, chaperone, consort with, convoy, escort, go with. ANT.-abandon, avoid, desert, leave, quit.

accomplice, *n.* SYN.-abettor, accessory, ally, assistant, associate, confederate. ANT.-adversary, enemy, opponent, rival.

accomplish, *v.* SYN.-achieve, attain, complete, consummate, do, effect, execute, finish, fulfill, perfect, perform. ANT.-block, defeat, fail, frustrate, spoil.

accord, *v.* SYN.-agree, grant, harmonize.

accordance, *n.* SYN.-agreement, coincidence, concord, concurrence, harmony, understanding, unison, bargain, compact, contract, covenant, pact, stipulation. ANT.-difference, disagreement, discord, dissension, variance.

account, *n.* SYN.-chronicle, description, detail, history, narration, narrative, recital, relation; computation, reckoning, record. ANT.-caricature, confusion, distortion, misrepresentation.

account, *v.* SYN.-believe, chronicle,

consider, deem, esteem, estimate, hold, judge, rate, reckon, regard, think, view; elucidate, explain, expound.

accountability, *n.* SYN.-amenability, liability, obligation, responsibility, trustworthiness; duty, trust.

accountable, *a.* SYN.-amenable, answerable, exposed to, liable, reliable, responsible, trustworthy, subject to. ANT.-exempt, careless, negligent, free, immune, independent, irresponsible.

accumulate, *v.* SYN.-accrue, amass, collect, gather, heap, hoard, increase, store. ANT.-diminish, disperse, dissipate, scatter, waste.

accuracy, *n.* SYN.-constancy, exactness, fidelity, precision. ANT.-carelessness, imprecision.

accurate, *a.* SYN.-correct, definite, distinct, exact, faultless, impeccable, precise, proper, right, strict. ANT.-careless, erroneous, false, faulty, untrue, wrong.

accusation, *n.* SYN.-arraignment, charge, imputation, incrimination, indictment. ANT.-exculpation, exoneration, pardon.

accuse, *v.* SYN.-arraign, censure, charge, incriminate, indict. ANT.-absolve, acquit, exonerate, release, vindicate.

accustom, *v.* SYN.-acclimate, familiarize, inure, train. ANT.-ignore, neglect, overlook.

accustomed, *a.* SYN.-customary, habitual, usual.

ache, *n.* SYN.-pang, pain, paroxysm, throe, twinge; agony, anguish, distress, grief, suffering. ANT.-comfort, ease, relief, happiness, pleasure, solace.

achieve, *v.* SYN.-accomplish, acquire, do, effect, execute, gain,

obtain, realize, win. ANT.-fail, fall short, lose, miss.

achievement, *n.* SYN.-deed, exploit, feat, accomplishment, attainment, completion, performance, realization. ANT.-neglect, omission; defeat, failure.

acid, *a.* SYN.-biting, sharp, sour, tart.

acknowledge, *v.* SYN.-accept, admit, agree, allow, assent, avow, certify, concede, confess, grant, identify, own, permit, recognize, welcome. ANT.-deny, dismiss, reject, shun.

acquaintance, *n.* SYN.-cognizance, companionship, familiarity, fellowship, friendship, intimacy, knowledge. ANT.-ignorance, inexperience, unfamiliarity.

acquiesce, *v.* SYN.-allow, concede, grant, permit; abdicate, accede, acquiesce, capitulate, cede, quit, relent, relinquish, resign, submit, succumb, surrender, waive, yield. ANT.-deny, dissent, oppose, refuse; assert, resist, strive, struggle.

acquire, *v.* SYN.-assimilate, attain, earn, gain, get, obtain, procure, secure, win. ANT.-forego, forfeit, lose, miss, surrender.

acquisition, *n.* SYN.-award, donation, earnings, fortune, gain, gift, income, purchase, proceeds, profit, riches, salary, wages.

acquit, *v.* SYN.-absolve, condone, excuse, forgive, overlook, pardon, repay, release, remit, return. ANT.-accuse, chastise, condemn, convict, punish.

acquittal, *n.* SYN.-absolution, amnesty, pardon, forgiveness, remission. ANT.-conviction, penalty, punishment, sentence.

acrid, *a.* SYN.-biting, bitter, caustic, distasteful, galling, grievous, harsh, painful, poignant, pungent, sardonic, severe, sharp, sour, tart. ANT.-bland, delicious, gentle, mellow, pleasant, sweet.

act, *n.* SYN.-accomplishment, action, deed, doing, execution, feat, operation, performance, transaction; decree, edict, law, statute. ANT.-cessation, deliberation, inactivity, inhibition, intention.

act, *v.* SYN.-affect, assume, bear, behave, carry, comport, conduct, demean, deport, feign, interact, manage, operate, pretend, profess, sham, simulate.

action, *n.* SYN.-achievement, activity, deed, exercise, exploit, feat, motion, movement, performance, play, procedure. ANT.-idleness, inactivity, inertia, repose, rest.

activate, *v.* SYN.-begin, initiate, stimulate.

active, *a.* SYN.-operative, working; busy, industrious; agile, alert, brisk, lively, nimble, quick, sprightly, supple. ANT.-dormant, inactive; indolent, lazy, passive.

activity, *n.* SYN.-action, agility, briskness, energy, enterprise, exercise, intensity, liveliness, motion, movement, quickness, rapidity, vigor. ANT.-dullness, idleness, inactivity, inertia, sloth.

actor, *n.* SYN.-character, entertainer, ham, mime, mimic, performer, player, tragedian.

actual, *a.* SYN.-authentic, certain, genuine, positive, real, substantial, true, veritable. ANT.-apparent, fictitious, imaginary, supposed, unreal.

actuate, *v.* SYN.-agitate, drive, impel, induce, instigate, move, persuade, propel, push, shift, stir. ANT.-deter, halt, rest, stay, stop.

acute, *a.* SYN.-intense, keen, penetrating, poignant, sharp, shrill; crucial, decisive, important, sensitive, vital.

adamant, *a.* SYN.-firm, hard, immovable, insistent, positive, unyielding.

adage, *n.* SYN.-aphorism, apothegm, byword, maxim, motto, proverb, saw, saying.

adapt, *v.* SYN.-accommodate, adjust, conform, fit, suit. ANT.-disturb, misapply, misfit.

add, *v.* SYN.-adjoin, affix, append, attach, augment, increase, sum, total. ANT.-deduct, detach, reduce, remove, subtract.

addiction, *n.* SYN.-fixation, inclination, obsession.

address, *v.* SYN.-accost, approach, greet, hail, speak to. ANT.-avoid, pass by.

adept, *a.* SYN.-able, accomplished, clever, competent, cunning, expert, ingenious, practiced, proficient, skilled, skillful, versed. ANT.-awkward, bungling, clumsy, inexpert, untrained.

adequate, *a.* SYN.-ample, capable, commensurate, enough, fitting, satisfactory, sufficient, suitable. ANT.-deficient, lacking, scant.

adherent, *n.* SYN.-devotee, disciple, follower, supporter, votary; learner, pupil, scholar, student.

adjacent, *a.* SYN.-abutting, adjoining, adjunct, bordering, close, contiguous, immediate, impending, near, nearby, neighboring, tangent, touching. ANT.-afar, distant, faraway, removed.

adjoin, *v.* SYN.-abut, append, border, connect, join, unite. ANT.-divide, separate.

adjourn, *v.* SYN.-defer, delay, move, postpone, suspend. ANT.-continue, expedite, hasten.

adjunct, *n.* SYN.-accessory, assistant, helper, modifier. ANT.-thing. primary, principal.

adjust, *v.* SYN.-accommodate, adapt, arrange, conform, fit, harmonize, modify, refashion, suit. ANT.-disturb, misapply, misfit.

adjutant, *n.* SYN.-aide, assistant.

administer, *v.* SYN.-direct, manage, supervise; apply, dispense, dole, give, minister, tender, treat.

administration, *n.* SYN.-government, management, supervision; directors, executives, officers, supervisors.

admirable, *a.* SYN.-eminent, fair, honest, honorable, noble, respectable, true, trusty, upright, virtuous; creditable, esteemed, proper, reputable. ANT.-disgraceful, ignominious, infamous, shameful.

admire, *v.* SYN.-adore, appreciate, approve, esteem, regard, respect, revere, venerate, wonder. ANT.-abhor, despise, dislike.

admissible, *a.* SYN.-allowable, fair, justifiable, permissible, probable, tolerable, warranted. ANT.-inadmissible, irrelevant, unsuitable.

admit, *v.* SYN.-accept, acknowledge, agree, allow, assent, concede, confess, grant, permit, welcome. ANT.-deny, dismiss, reject, shun.

admonition, *n.* SYN.-advice, caution, counsel, exhortation, instruction, recommendation, suggestion, warning; information, intelligence, notification.

adopt, *v.* SYN.-accept, appropriate, assume, choose, espouse, select, take.

adore, *v.* SYN.-esteem, honor, love, respect, revere, venerate, worship. ANT.-despise, hate, ignore.

adorn, *v.* SYN.-beautify, bedeck, decorate, embellish, garnish, gild, ornament, trim. ANT.-deface, deform, disfigure, mar, spoil.

adroit, *a.* SYN.-apt, clever, dexterous, quick, quick-witted, skillful, talented, witty; bright, ingenious, sharp, smart. ANT.-awkward, bungling, clumsy, slow, unskilled; dull, foolish, stupid.

adult, *a.* SYN.-developed, grown, mature.

adulterate, *v.* SYN.-abase, alloy, corrupt, debase, defile, degrade, deprave, depress, humiliate, impair, lower, pervert, vitiate. ANT.-enhance, improve, raise, restore, vitalize.

advance, *v.* SYN.-aggrandize, elevate, forward, further, promote, adduce, allege, assign, bring forward, offer, propose, propound, improve, proceed, progress, rise, thrive, augment, enlarge, increase. ANT.-hinder, oppose, retard, retreat, withhold.

advantage, *n.* SYN.-edge, mastery, superiority; benefit, good, profit, service, utility. ANT.-detriment, handicap, harm, impediment, obstruction.

advantageous, *a.* SYN.-beneficial, good, helpful, profitable, salutary, serviceable, useful, wholesome. ANT.-deleterious, destructive, detrimental, harmful, injurious.

adventure, *n.* SYN.-experience, happening, story, tale.

adventurous, *a.* SYN.-bold, chivalrous, daring, enterprising, foolhardy, precipitate, rash. ANT.-cautious, hesitating, timid.

adversary, *n.* SYN.-antagonist, competitor, enemy, foe, opponent, rival. ANT.-accomplice, ally, comrade, confederate, friend, teammate.

adverse, *a.* SYN.-antagonistic, contrary, hostile, opposed, opposite; counteractive, disastrous, unfavorable, unlucky. ANT.-benign, favorable, fortunate, lucky, propitious.

adversity, *n.* SYN.-accident, affliction, calamity, catastrophe, disaster, distress, hardship, misfortune, mishap, ruin. ANT.-blessing, comfort, prosperity, success.

advertise, *v.* SYN.-announce, communicate, declare, display, exhibit, proclaim, publicize.

advertisement, *n.* SYN.- announcement, bulletin, declaration, notification, promulgation. ANT.-hush, muteness, silence, speechlessness.

advice, *n.* SYN.-admonition, caution, counsel, exhortation, guidance, instruction, recommendation, suggestion, warning; information, intelligence, notification.

advise, *v.* SYN.-acquaint, apprise, enlighten, impart, inform, instruct, notify, recommend, teach, tell, warn. ANT.-conceal, delude, distract, mislead.

aesthetic, *a.* SYN.-appreciative, creative, inventive, spiritual.

affable, *a.* SYN.-affable, civil, communicative, friendly, gregarious, hospitable, outgoing, sociable, social. ANT.-antisocial, disagreeable, hermitic, inhospitable.

affair, *n.* SYN.-concern, duty, interest, matter, obligation, pursuit, responsibility.

affect, *v.* SYN.-alter, change, influence, modify, transform; concern, interest, regard; impress, melt, move, soften, subdue, touch; adopt, assume, feign, pretend.

affected, *a.* SYN.-artificial, ceremonious, dramatic, histrionic, melodramatic, showy, stagy, theatrical. ANT.-modest, subdued, unaffected, unemotional.

affection, *n.* SYN.-attachment, endearment, fondness, kindness, love, tenderness; disposition, emotion, feeling, inclination. ANT.-aversion, hatred, indifference, repugnance, repulsion.

affidavit, *n.* SYN.-affirmation, testimony, statement.

affiliate, *v.* SYN.-ally, associate, combine, conjoin, connect, join, link, mingle, mix. ANT.-disrupt, divide, estrange, separate.

affinity, *n.* SYN.-attraction, closeness, fondness, liking.

affirm, *v.* SYN.-assert, aver, declare, maintain, protest, state, swear. ANT.-contradict, demur, deny, dispute, oppose.

affix, *v.* SYN.-adjoin, administer, allot, annex, append, apply, appropriate, assign, attach, avail, connect, devote, direct, employ, use; bear, pertain, refer, relate; appeal, petition, request, join, stick, unite; associate, attribute. ANT.-detach, disengage, separate, unfasten, untie.

afflict, *v.* SYN.-burden, encumber, load, oppress, overload, tax, trouble, weigh. ANT.-alleviate, console, ease, lighten, mitigate.

affluence, *n.* SYN.-abundance, fortune, luxury, money, opulence, plenty, possessions, riches, wealth. ANT.-indigence, need, poverty, want.

affluent, *a.* SYN.-abundant, ample, bountiful, copious, costly, luxurious, opulent, plentiful, prosperous, rich, sumptuous, wealthy, well-to-do. ANT.-beggarly, destitute, indigent, needy, poor.

affront, n. SYN.-abuse, defiance, indignity, insolence, insult, offense. ANT.-apology, homage, salutation

afraid, a. SYN.-apprehensive, fainthearted, fearful, frightened, scared, timid, timorous. ANT.-assured, bold, composed, courageous, sanguine.

afterward, a. SYN.-after, eventually, later, subsequently, ultimately.

against, a. SYN.-adverse, facing, opposed, toward, versus.

age, n. SYN.-adolescence, adulthood, dotage, senescence, senility, seniority, youth; antiquity, date, duration, epoch, era, generation, period, span, time. ANT.-childhood, infancy, youth.

agency, n. SYN.-bureau, company, firm, office, representative.

agent, n. SYN.-apparatus, channel, device, instrument, means, medium, tool, utensil, vehicle. ANT.-hindrance, impediment, obstruction, preventive.

aggravate, v. SYN.-heighten, increase, intensify, magnify; annoy, chafe, embitter, exasperate, inflame, irritate, nettle, provoke, vex. ANT.-appease, mitigate, palliate soften, soothe.

aggregate, n. SYN.-amount, collection, conglomeration, entirety, sum, total, whole. ANT.-element, ingredient, part, particular, unit.

aggression, n. SYN.-assault, attack, battle, incursion, invasion, offensive, raid, threat, war.

agile, a. SYN.-active, alert, brisk, deft, flexible, lively, nimble, quick, spirited, sprightly, spry, supple. ANT.-awkward, clumsy, heavy, inert, slow, sluggish.

agitate, v. SYN.-arouse, disconcert, disturb, excite, jar, perturb, rouse, ruffle, shake, trouble. ANT.-calm, ease, placate, quiet.

agitated, a. SYN.-disquieted, disturbed, irresolute, restless, sleepless, uneasy, unquiet; active, roving, transient, wandering. ANT.-at ease, peaceable, quiet, tractable.

agony, n. SYN.-ache, anguish, distress, misery, pain, suffering, throe, torment, torture, woe. ANT.-comfort, ease, mitigation, relief.

agree, v. SYN.-accede, acquiesce, assent, comply, consent; coincide, concur, conform, tally. ANT.-contradict, differ, disagree, dissent, protest.

agreeable, a. SYN.-acceptable, amiable, charming, gratifying, pleasant, pleasing, pleasurable, suitable, welcome. ANT.-disagreeable, obnoxious, offensive, unpleasant.

agreement, n. SYN.-accordance, coincidence, concord, concurrence, harmony, understanding, unison; bargain, compact, contract, covenant, pact, stipulation. ANT.-difference, disagreement, discord, dissension, variance.

agriculture, n. SYN.-agronomy, cultivation, farming, gardening, horticulture, husbandry, tillage.

ahead, a. SYN.-before, first, leading, preceding.

aid, n. SYN.- alms, assistance, backing, comfort, furtherance, help, patronage, relief, succor, support. ANT.-antagonism, counteraction, defiance, hostility, resistance.

aid, v. SYN.-abet, back, further, help, promote, serve, support, sustain, assist, succor, uphold; facilitate, mitigate, relieve, remedy. ANT.-hamper, hinder, impede, prevent resist, thwart; afflict.

ailment, n. SYN.-complaint, disease,

disorder, illness, infirmity, malady, sickness. ANT.-health, healthiness, soundness, vigor.

aim, *n.* SYN.-ambition, aspiration, design, emulation, end, goal, incentive, intent, intention, object, objective, purpose. ANT.-accident, contentment, indifference, indolence, resignation, satisfaction.

aim, *v.* SYN.-level, point, train; conduct, direct, govern, guide, manage, regulate, rule; bid, command, instruct, order. ANT. -deceive, distract, misdirect, misguide.

aimless, *a.* SYN.-blind, careless, capricious, drifting, erratic, pointless, purposeless, rambling, unplanned, unpredictable, wandering. ANT.-considered, directed, purposeful, planned.

air, *n.* SYN.-atmosphere, breeze, draft, oxygen, ventilation, wind.

air, *v.* SYN.-cool, freshen, open, ventilate; broadcast, disclose, expose, reveal.

aisle, *n.* SYN.-corridor, course, opening, passage, passageway, path, walk, way.

ajar, *a.* SYN.-agape, unclosed, uncovered, unlocked, unobstructed, available, open, accessible, exposed, public, unrestricted.

alarm, *n.* SYN.-affright, apprehension, consternation, dismay, fear, fright, signal, terror, warning. ANT.-calm, composure, quiet, security, tranquillity.

alarm, *v.* SYN.-affright, appall, astound, daunt, dismay, frighten, horrify, intimidate, scare, startle, terrify, terrorize. ANT.-allay, compose, embolden, reassure, soothe.

alert, *a.* SYN.-alert, anxious, attentive, careful, cautious, circumspect, observant, vigilant, wakeful,

wary, watchful. ANT.-careless, inattentive, lax, neglectful, oblivious.

alibi, *n.* SYN.-assertion, defense, excuse, explanation, reply.

alien, *a.* SYN.-adverse, contrasted, exotic, extraneous, foreign, irrelevant, remote, strange, unconnected. ANT.-akin, germane, kindred, relevant.

alienate, *v.* SYN.-divide, estrange, separate, withdraw.

alike, *a.* SYN.-akin, allied, analogous, comparable, correlative, correspondent, corresponding, like, parallel, similar. ANT.-different, dissimilar, divergent, incongruous, opposed.

alive, *a.* SYN.-animate, breathing, conscious, existing, growing, living, mortal. ANT.-dead, inanimate, lifeless.

all, *n.* SYN.-collection, ensemble, entire, everyone, everything, group, total. ANT.-nobody, none, nothing.

allege, *v.* SYN.-advance, affirm, assign, cite, claim, declare, maintain. ANT.-contradict, deny, disprove, gainsay, refute.

allegiance, *n.* SYN.-constancy, devotion, faithfulness, fealty, fidelity. ANT.-disloyalty, falseness, perfidy, treachery.

alleviate, *v.* SYN.-abate, allay, assuage, diminish, extenuate, mitigate, relieve, soften, solace, soothe. ANT.-aggravate, agitate, augment, increase, irritate.

alliance, *n.* SYN.-association, coalition, combination, confederacy, entente, federation, league, partnership, union; compact, covenant, marriage, treaty. ANT.-divorce, schism, separation.

allocate, *v.* See **allot.**

allot, *v.* SYN.-apportion, deal, dispense, distribute, divide, mete; allocate, appropriate, assign, give, grant, measure. ANT.-confiscate, keep, refuse, retain, withhold.

allotment, *n.* SYN.-apportionment, division, fragment, moiety, part, piece, portion, scrap, section, segment, share. ANT.-entirety, whole.

allow, *v.* SYN.-let, permit, sanction, suffer, tolerate; authorize, give, grant, yield; acknowledge, admit, concede. ANT.-forbid, object, protest, refuse, resist.

allowable, *a.* SYN.-admissible, fair, justifiable, permissible, probable, tolerable, warranted. ANT.-inadmissible, irrelevant, unsuitable.

allowance, *n.* SYN.-alimony, annuity, bequest, commission, gift, grant, legacy, pay, stipend, subsidy, wages.

allude, *v.* SYN.-advert, hint, imply, insinuate, intimate, refer, suggest. ANT.-declare, demonstrate, specify, state.

alluring, *a.* SYN.-attractive, bewitching, captivating, charming, enchanting, engaging, fascinating, winning. ANT.-repugnant, repulsive, revolting.

alone, *a.* SYN.-abandoned, deserted, desolate, isolated, lonely, secluded, unaccompanied, unaided; lone, only, single, sole, solitary. ANT.-accompanied, attended, surrounded.

aloof, *a.* SYN.-distant, far, faraway, remote, removed; cold, reserved, stiff, unfriendly. ANT.-close, near, nigh; cordial, friendly.

also, *adv.* SYN.-besides, furthermore, in addition, likewise, moreover, similarly, too.

alter, *v.* SYN.-change, exchange, substitute; convert, modify, shift, transfigure, transform, vary, veer.

ANT.-retain; continue, establish, preserve, settle, stabilize.

alteration, *n.* SYN.-change, modification, mutation, substitution, variation, variety, vicissitude. ANT.-monotony, stability, uniformity.

alternate, *n.* SYN.-agent, deputy, lieutenant, proxy, representative, substitute, understudy. ANT.-head, master, principal, sovereign.

alternative, *n.* SYN.-election, option, choice, preference, selection.

altitude, *n.* distance, elevation, height.

always, *adv.* SYN.-constantly, continually, eternally, ever, evermore, forever, incessantly, perpetually, unceasingly. ANT.-fitfully, never, occasionally, rarely, sometimes.

amass, *v.* SYN.-accumulate, assemble, gather, collect, congregate, convene, muster; cull, garner, glean, harvest, pick, reap; conclude, deduce, infer, judge. ANT.-disband, disperse, distribute, scatter, separate.

amateur, *n.* SYN.-apprentice, beginner, dabbler, dilettante, learner, neophyte, novice. ANT.-adept, authority, expert, master, professional.

amazement, *n.* SYN.-astonishment, awe, bewilderment, curiosity, surprise, wonder, wonderment. ANT.-triviality; apathy, expectation, indifference.

ambiguity, *n.* SYN.-distrust, doubt, hesitation, incredulity, scruple, skepticism, suspense, suspicion, unbelief, uncertainty. ANT.-belief, certainty, conviction, determination, faith.

ambiguous, *a.* SYN.-dubious, enigmatical, equivocal, obscure, uncertain, vague. ANT.-clear, explicit, obvious, plain, unequivocal.

ambition, n. SYN.-aspiration, eagerness, emulation, goal, incentive, pretension. ANT.-contentment, indifference, indolence, resignation, satisfaction.

ambush, n. SYN.-net, pitfall, ruse, snare, stratagem, trap, trick, wile.

amend, v. SYN.-correct, mend, rectify, reform, right; admonish, discipline, punish. ANT.-aggravate, ignore, spoil; condone, indulge.

amiable, a. SYN.-agreeable, engaging, friendly, good-natured, gracious, pleasing. ANT.-churlish, disagreeable, hateful, ill-natured, surly.

amicable, a. SYN.-affable, companionable, friendly, genial, kindly, neighborly, sociable, social. ANT.-antagonistic, cool, distant, hostile, reserved.

amid, prep. See **among.**

among, prep. SYN.-amid, amidst, between, betwixt, mingled, mixed, within.

amount, n. SYN.-aggregate, number, product, quantity, sum, total, whole.

ample, a. SYN.-broad, extensive, great, large, spacious, wide; abundant, bountiful, copious, full, generous, liberal, plentiful, profuse, rich. ANT.-constricted, limited, small; insufficient, lacking, meager.

amplify, v. SYN.-accrue, augment, enhance, enlarge, expand, extend, grow, heighten, increase, intensify, magnify, multiply, raise, wax. ANT.-atrophy, contract, decrease, diminish, reduce.

amusement, n. SYN.-diversion, entertainment, fun, game, pastime, play, recreation, sport. ANT.-bore-

dom, labor, toil, work.

analogous, a. SYN.-akin, alike, allied, comparable, correlative, correspondent, corresponding, like, parallel, similar. ANT.-different, dissimilar, divergent, incongruous, opposed.

analyze, v. SYN.-assess, audit, check, contemplate, dissect, examine, inquire, interrogate, notice, question, quiz, review, scan, scrutinize, survey, view, watch. ANT.-disregard, neglect, omit, overlook.

anarchy, n. SYN.-chaos, disorder, lawlessness, turmoil.

ancestry, n. SYN.-clan, folk, lineage, nation, people, race, stock, strain, tribe.

anchor, n. SYN.-ballast, mooring, protection, safeguard, security, tie.

ancient, a. SYN.-aged, antiquated, antique, archaic, obsolete, old, old-fashioned, venerable. ANT.-modern, new, young, youthful.

anecdote, n. SYN.-account, anecdote, chronicle, fable, fabrication, falsehood, fiction, history, narration, narrative, novel, report, story, tale, yarn.

angelic, a. SYN.-beautiful, devout, good, heavenly, lovely, pure, radiant, saintly. ANT.-bad, evil, ugly.

anger, n. SYN.-animosity, choler, exasperation, fury, indignation, ire, irritation, passion, petulance, rage, resentment, temper, wrath. ANT.-conciliation, forbearance, patience, peace, self-control.

angry, a. SYN. enraged, exasperated, furious, incensed, indignant, irate, maddened, provoked, wrathful, wroth. ANT.-calm, happy, pleased, satisfied.

anguish, n. SYN.-agony, distress, grief, misery, suffering, torment, torture. ANT.-comfort, joy, relief, solace.

animosity, *n.* SYN.-bitterness, enmity, grudge, hatred, hostility, malevolence, rancor, spite. ANT.-friendliness, good will, love.

angular, *a.* SYN.-bent, crooked, crotched, forked, jagged, rectangular, staggered, triangular, zig-zag.

animated, *a.* SYN.-active, alive, expressive, gay, lively, spirited.

animosity, *n.* SYN.-abhorrence, dislike, hatred,

annihilate, *v.* SYN.-demolish, destroy, devastate, eradicate, exterminate, extinguish, obliterate, ravage, raze, ruin, wreck. ANT.-construct, establish, make, preserve, save.

announce, *v.* SYN.-advertise, declare, give out, herald, make known, notify, proclaim, promulgate, publish, report. ANT.-bury, conceal, stifle, suppress, withhold.

announcement, *n.* SYN.-advertisement, bulletin, declaration, notification, promulgation. ANT.-hush, muteness, silence, speechlessness.

annoy, *v.* SYN.-bother, chafe, disturb, inconvenience, irk, irritate, molest, pester, tease, trouble, vex. ANT.-accommodate, console, gratify, soothe.

annoying, *a.* SYN.-bothersome, distressing, disturbing, irksome, troublesome, trying, vexatious. ANT.-accommodating, amusing, gratifying, pleasant.

annul, *v.* SYN.-destroy, end, eradicate, obliterate, overthrow; abrogate, cancel, invalidate, revoke, cross out, delete, eliminate, erase, expunge, abolish, nullify, quash, repeal, rescind, ANT.-continue, establish, promote, restore, sustain,

confirm, enact, enforce, perpetuate

answer, *n.* SYN.-rejoinder, reply, response, restatement, result, retort, retaliation, solution, total; defense, rebuttal. ANT.-inquiry, questioning, summoning; argument.

antagonistic, *a.* SYN.- contrary, hostile, opposed, opposite; counteractive, disastrous, unfavorable, unlucky adverse, inimical, unfriendly, warlike. ANT.-benign, favorable, fortunate, lucky, propitious amicable, cordial.

antic, *n.* SYN.-caper, frolic, trick.

anticipation, *n.* SYN.-contemplation, expectation, foresight, forethought, hope, preconception, prescience, presentiment. ANT.-doubt, dread, fear, worry.

antipathy, *n.* SYN.-animosity, antagonism, enmity, hatred, hostility, ill-will, invidiousness, malignity. ANT.-affection, cordiality, friendliness, good will, love.

antiquated, *a.* SYN.-ancient, archaic, obsolescent, obsolete, old, out-of-date, venerable. ANT.-current, extant, fashionable, modern, recent.

anxiety, *n.* SYN.-apprehension, care, concern, disquiet, fear, solicitude, trouble, worry, ANT.-assurance, confidence, contentment, equanimity, nonchalance.

anxious, *a.* SYN.-ardent, avid, enthusiastic, eager, fervent, hot, impassioned, impatient, keen, yearning. ANT.-apathetic, indifferent, unconcerned, uninterested.

apart, *a.* SYN.-alone, disconnected, distant, far, isolated, separated.

apathy, *n.* SYN.-disinterestedness, impartiality, indifference, insensibility, neutrality, unconcern. ANT.-affection, ardor, fervor, passion.

apex, *n.* SYN.-acme, climax, consummation, culmination, height, peak, summit, zenith. ANT.-anticlimax, base, depth, floor.

apology, *n.* SYN.-alibi, confession, defense, excuse, explanation, justification. ANT.-accusation, complaint, denial, dissimulation.

apparatus, *n.* SYN.-agent, channel, device, instrument, means, medium, tool, utensil, vehicle. ANT.-hindrance, impediment, obstruction, preventive.

apparel, *n.* SYN.-array, attire, clothes, clothing, drapery, dress, garb, garments, raiment, vestments, vesture. ANT.-nakedness, nudity.

apparent, *a.* SYN.-clear, evident, manifest, obvious, palpable, plain, self-evident, transparent, unambiguous, unmistakable, visible; illusory, ostensible, seeming. ANT.-ambiguous, dubious, indistinct, real, uncertain.

appeal, *n.* SYN.-beg, entreaty, petition, plea, prayer, request, supplication.

appear, *v.* SYN.-look, seem; arise, arrive, emanate, emerge, issue. ANT.-be, exist; disappear, vanish, withdraw.

appearance, *n.* SYN.-advent, apparition, arrival, air, aspect, demeanor, look, manner, mien, fashion, guise, pretense, semblance.

appease, *v.* SYN.-allay, alleviate, assuage, calm, compose, lull, pacify, placate, quell, quiet, relieve, satisfy, soothe, still, tranquilize. ANT.-arouse, excite, incense, inflame.

appetite, *n.* SYN.-hunger, relish, stomach, thirst, zest; craving, desire, inclination, liking, longing, passion. ANT.-disgust, distaste, re-

nunciation, repugnance, satiety.

apply, *v.* SYN.-administer, affix, allot, appropriate, assign, attach, avail, devote, direct, employ, use; bear, pertain, refer, relate; appeal, petition, request.

appoint, *v.* SYN.-call, denominate, designate, entitle, mention, name, specify. ANT.-hint, miscall, misname.

apportion, *v.* SYN.-allot, appropriate, assign, dispense, distribute, divide, parcel, partake, partition, portion, share. ANT.-aggregate, amass, combine, condense.

appraise, *v.* SYN.-assign, assess, calculate, compute, estimate, evaluate, fix, levy, reckon, tax.

appreciate, *v.* SYN.-admire, cherish, enjoy, esteem, prize, regard, value, appraise, estimate, evaluate, rate, apprehend, comprehend, understand, go up, improve, rise. ANT.-belittle, degrade, depreciate, misapprehend, misunderstand.

appreciative, *a.* SYN.-beholden, grateful, indebted, obliged, thankful. ANT.-thankless, unappreciative.

apprehend, *v.* SYN.-arrest, capture, catch, clutch, grasp, grip, lay hold of, seize, snare, trap. ANT.-liberate, lose, release, throw.

apprehension, *n.* SYN.-anxiety, concern, disquiet, fear, trouble, uneasiness, worry. ANT.-contentment, equanimity, peace, satisfaction.

apprehensive, *a.* SYN.-afraid, fainthearted, fearful, frightened, scared, timid, timorous. ANT.-assured, bold, composed, courageous, sanguine.

apprentice, *n.* SYN.-amateur, beginner, learner, student.

approach, *v.* SYN.-advance, approximate, come, gain, near, touch. ANT.-

depart, leave, recede.

appropriate, *a.* SYN.-applicable, apt, becoming, fitting, particular, proper, suitable. ANT.-contrary, improper, inappropriate.

appropriation, *n.* SYN.-allowance, benefaction, bequest, boon, bounty, donation, endowment, gift, grant, subsidy.

approval, *n.* SYN.-approbation, assent, commendation, consent, endorsement, praise, sanction, support. ANT.-censure, reprimand, reproach, stricture.

approve, *v.* SYN.-appreciate, commend, like, praise; authorize, confirm, endorse, ratify, sanction. ANT.-criticize, disparage; condemn, nullify.

approximate, *a.* SYN.-about, almost, guess, imprecise, inexact, rough. ANT.-exact, precise, sure.

apropos, *a.* SYN.-applicable, apposite, appropriate, apt, fit, germane, material, pertinent, related, relating, relevant, to the point. ANT.-alien, extraneous, foreign, unrelated.

aptitude, *n.* SYN.-ability, adroitness, aptness, capability, capacity, cleverness, deftness, dexterity, efficiency, facility, faculty, knack, power, qualification, skill, talent. ANT.-disability, inability, incapacity, incompetence, unreadiness.

arbitrary, *a.* SYN.-absolute, despotic, discretionary, inconsistent, irrational, willful.

arbitrate, *v.* SYN.-decide, decree, determine; adjudicate, condemn, judge, try, umpire; appreciate, consider, estimate, evaluate, measure, think.

arbitrator, *n.* SYN.-arbitrator, critic, judge, justice, magistrate, referee,

umpire.

archetype, *n.* SYN.-example, illustration, instance, model, pattern, prototype, sample, specimen. ANT.-concept, precept, principle, rule.

archives, *n. pl.* SYN.-file, library, museum, repository, vault.

ardent, *a.* SYN.-eager, enthusiastic, fervent, fervid, fiery, glowing, hot, impassioned, intense, keen, passionate, vehement, zealous. ANT.-apathetic, cool, indifferent, nonchalant.

ardor, *n.* SYN.-devotion, eagerness, enthusiasm, fervor, fire, passion, rapture, spirit, zeal. ANT.-apathy, disinterest, indifference, unconcern.

arduous, *a.* SYN.-complicated, demanding, hard, intricate, involved, laborious, obscure, perplexing, toilsome, trying burdensome, difficult, onerous, tough; cruel, harsh, rigorous, severe. ANT.-easy, effortless, facile, simple, gentle, lenient, tender.

area, *n.* SYN.-locale, locality, location, place, precinct, region, site, situation, spot, station, territory, township, vicinity, ward.

arena, *n.* SYN.-amphitheater, coliseum, field, grounds, gymnasium, park,

argue, *v.* SYN.-debate, discuss, dispute, plead, reason, wrangle; denote, imply, indicate, prove, show. ANT.-ignore, overlook, reject, spurn.

argument, *n.* SYN.-contention, controversy, debate, disagreement, dispute, quarrel, squabble. ANT.-agreement, concord, decision, harmony.

arid, *a.* SYN.-dehydrated, desiccated, drained, dry, parched, thirsty; barren, dull, insipid, plain, tedious,

tiresome, uninteresting, vapid.
ANT.-damp, moist; fresh, interesting, lively.
aristocracy, n. SYN.-elite, gentry, nobility, noblemen, patricians, privileged, rulers. ANT.-commoners, peasants, peons.
armed, a. SYN.-equipped, fortified, loaded, outfitted, protected. ANT.-unprotected, vulnerable.
armistice, n. SYN.-compromise, concession, reconciliation, settlement, truce.
aroma, n. SYN.-fragrance, fume, incense, odor, perfume, redolence, scent, smell, stench, stink.
arouse, v. SYN.-awaken, excite, incite, provoke, rouse, spur, stimulate.
arrange, v. SYN.-adjust, assort, classify, dispose, organize, place, regulate; devise, plan, prepare. ANT.-confuse, disorder, disturb, jumble, scatter.
arrangement, n. SYN.-method, mode, order, organization, plan, process, regularity, rule, scheme, system. ANT.-chance, chaos, confusion, disarrangement, disorder, irregularity.
array, n. SYN.-apparel, attire, clothes, clothing, drapery, dress, garb, garments, raiment, vestments, vesture. ANT.-nakedness, nudity.
arrest, v. SYN.-apprehend, check, detain, hinder, interrupt, obstruct, restrain, seize, slow, stop, withhold. ANT.-activate, discharge, free, liberate, release.
arrive, v. SYN.-appear, attain, come, emerge, land, reach, visit. ANT.-depart, exit, leave.
arrogant, a. SYN.-disdainful, haughty, overbearing, proud, state-

ly, supercilious, vain, vainglorious.
ANT.-ashamed, humble, lowly, meek.
art, n. SYN.-adroitness, aptitude, cunning, knack, skill, tact; artifice, duplicity, guile, shrewdness, subtlety. ANT.-clumsiness, unskillfulness; forthrightness, honesty, innocence.
artery, n. SYN.-conduit, highway, thoroughfare, vein.
artful, a. SYN.-conniving, cunning, deceitful, deceptive, sly, tricky.
article, n. SYN.-object, particular, thing.
articulate, v. SYN.-enunciate, lecture, pronounce, speak, talk, verbalize, vocalize.
artifice, n. SYN.-craftiness, deception, device, duplicity, ingenuity, intrigue, machination, ruse, stratagem, trickery, wile,
artificial, a. SYN.-affected, assumed, bogus, counterfeit, ersatz, fake, feigned, fictitious, phony, sham, spurious, synthetic, unreal. ANT.-genuine, natural, real, true.
artist, n. SYN.-actor, composer, creator, dancer, dramatist, impresario, musician, painter, performer, poet, sculptor, writer.
artistic, a. SYN.-creative, cultured, imaginative, inventive, sensitive, talented.
ascend, v. SYN.-climb, mount, rise, scale, soar, tower. ANT.-descend, fall, sink.
ascertain, v. SYN.-detect, devise, discover, expose, find, find out, invent, learn, originate, reveal. ANT.-cover, hide, lose, mask, screen.
ashamed, a. SYN.-abashed, debased, embarrassed, mortified, shamefaced.
asinine, a. SYN.-absurd, brainless,

crazy, foolish, idiotic, irrational, nonsensical, preposterous, ridiculous, senseless, silly, simple. ANT.-judicious, prudent, sagacious, sane, wise.

ask, v. SYN.-beg, claim, demand, entreat, invite, request, solicit; inquire, interrogate, query, question. ANT.-command, dictate, insist, order, reply.

asperse, v. SYN.-abuse, defame, disparage, ill-use, malign, revile, scandalize, traduce, vilify; misapply, misemploy, misuse. ANT.-cherish, honor, praise, protect, respect.

aspiration, n. SYN.-aim, ambition, craving, desire, goal, hope, longing, objective, passion.

aspire, v. SYN.-attempt, endeavor, strive, struggle, undertake, aim, design, intend, mean, try. ANT.-abandon, decline, ignore, neglect, omit.

assail, v. SYN.-assault, attack, besiege, charge, encounter, invade, abuse, censure, impugn. ANT.-aid, defend, protect, repel, resist.

assassinate, v. SYN.-butcher, execute, kill, massacre, murder, put to death, slaughter, slay. ANT.-animate, protect, resuscitate, save, vivify.

assault, v. SYN.-assail, attack, bombard, charge, invade, pound, storm, strike. ANT.-defend, oppose, protect.

assembly, n. SYN.-aggregation, band, brood, bunch, class, cluster, collection, crowd, flock, group, herd, horde, lot, mob, pack, party, set, swarm, throng, troupe.

assent, v. SYN.-accede, acquiesce, agree, comply, consent; coincide, concur, conform, tally. ANT.-contradict, differ, disagree, dissent, protest.

assert, v. SYN.-affirm, allege, aver, claim, declare, express, maintain, state; defend, support, uphold, vindicate. ANT.-contradict, deny, refute.

assess, v. SYN.-appraise, assign, calculate, compute, estimate, evaluate, fix, levy, reckon, tax.

assessment, n. SYN.-assessment, custom, duty, exaction, excise, impost, levy, rate, tax, toll, tribute. ANT.-gift, remuneration, reward, wages.

assign, v. SYN.-allot, apportion, appropriate, ascribe, attribute, cast, designate, distribute, specify. ANT.-discharge, release, relieve, unburden.

assimilate, v. SYN.-absorb, consume, engulf, imbibe, swallow up; engage, engross, occupy. ANT.-discharge, dispense, emit, expel, exude.

assist, v. SYN.-abet, aid, back, further, help, promote, serve, support, sustain. ANT.-hamper, hinder, impede, prevent.

assistance, n. SYN.-aid, alms, backing, furtherance, help, patronage, relief, succor, support. ANT.-antagonism, counteraction, defiance, hostility, resistance.

assistant, n. SYN.-aide, auxiliary, bodyguard, colleague, deputy, helper, henchman, lieutenant, secretary.

associate, n. SYN.-attendant, colleague, comrade, consort, crony, friend, mate, partner. ANT.-adversary, enemy, stranger.

associate, v. SYN.-affiliate, ally, combine, companion, conjoin, connect, join, link, mingle, mix. ANT.-disrupt, divide, estrange, separate.

association, *n.* SYN.-affinity, alliance, bond, conjunction, connection, link, relationship, tie, union. ANT.-disunion, isolation, separation.

assorted, *a.* SYN.-diverse, heterogeneous, indiscriminate, miscellaneous, mixed, motley, sundry, varied. ANT.-alike, classified, homogeneous, ordered, selected.

assortment, *n.* SYN.-change, difference, dissimilarity, diversity, heterogeneity, medley, miscellany, mixture, multifariousness, variety, variousness. ANT.-homogeneity, likeness, monotony, sameness, uniformity.

assuage, *v.* SYN.-abate, decrease, diminish, lessen, lower, moderate, reduce, suppress. ANT.-amplify, enlarge, increase, intensify, revive.

assume, *v.* SYN.-appropriate, arrogate, conjecture, take, usurp, adopt, affect, pretend, simulate, wear, postulate, presume, suppose, theorize. ANT.-concede, grant, surrender, doff, demonstrate, prove.

assurance, *n.* SYN.-assuredness, certainty, confidence, conviction, courage, firmness, security, self-reliance, surety, pledge, promise, word; assertion, declaration, statement. ANT.-bashfulness, humility, modesty, shyness, suspicion.

assure, *v.* SYN.-corroborate, substantiate, verify; acknowledge, establish, settle; approve, fix, ratify, sanction; strengthen.

astonishment, *n.* SYN.-admiration, amazement, astonishment, awe, bewilderment, curiosity, marvel, surprise, wonder, wonderment. ANT.-familiarity, triviality; apathy, expectation, indifference.

astound, *v.* SYN.-amaze, astonish, disconcert, dumbfound, flabbergast, shock, startle, stun, surprise, take aback. ANT.-admonish, caution, forewarn, prepare.

atrocity, *n.* SYN.-barbarity, brutality, cruelty, inhumanity, outrage, wickedness.

attach, *v.* SYN.-adjoin, affix, annex, append, connect, join, stick, unite; assign, associate, attribute. ANT.-detach, disengage, separate, unfasten, untie.

attachment, *n.* SYN.-adherence, affection, affinity, devotion, friendship, liking, regard. ANT.-alienation, aversion, estrangement, opposition, separation.

attack, *n.* SYN.-aggression, assault, criticism, denunciation, invasion, offense, onslaught; convulsion, fit, paroxysm. ANT.-defense, opposition, resistance, surrender, vindication.

attack, *v.* SYN.-assail, assault, besiege, charge, encounter, invade, abuse, censure, impugn. ANT.-aid, defend, protect, repel, resist.

attain, *v.* SYN.-accomplish, achieve, acquire, arrive, effect, gain, get, obtain, procure, reach, secure, win. ANT.-abandon, desert, discard, relinquish.

attempt, *n.* SYN.-effort, endeavor, essay, experiment, trial, undertaking. ANT.-inaction, laziness, neglect.

attend, *v.* SYN.-accompany, escort, follow, guard, lackey, protect, serve, tend, watch; be present, frequent.

attention, *n.* SYN.-alertness, care, circumspection, consideration, heed, mindfulness, notice, observance, watchfulness; application, contemplation, reflection, study.

ANT.-disregard, indifference, negligence, omission, oversight.

attentive, *a.* SYN.-alert, alive, awake, aware, careful, considerate, heedful, mindful, observant, thoughtful, wary, watchful; assiduous, diligent, studious. ANT.-apathetic, indifferent, oblivious, unaware.

attire, *n.* SYN.-apparel, array, clothes, clothing, drapery, dress, garb, garments, raiment, vestments, vesture. ANT.-nakedness, nudity.

attitude, *n.* SYN.-air, demeanor, disposition, emotion, inclination, mood, propensity, reaction, standpoint, temper, temperament, viewpoint; aspect, pose, position, posture, stand.

attract, *v.* SYN.-allure, captivate, charm, enchant, entice, fascinate, lure. ANT.-alienate, deter, repel, repulse.

attractive, *a.* SYN.-alluring, charming, enchanting, engaging, inviting, magnetic, pleasant, pleasing, seductive, winning. ANT.-forbidding, obnoxious, repellent, repulsive.

attribute, *n.* SYN.-characteristic, distinction, feature, peculiarity, property, quality, trait.

audacious, *a.* SYN.-adventurous, bold, brave, courageous, daring, dauntless, fearless, intrepid; brazen, forward, impudent, insolent, pushy, rude; abrupt, conspicuous, prominent, striking. ANT.-cowardly, flinching, timid; bashful, retiring.

audacity, *n.* SYN.-boldness, effrontery, fearlessness, hardihood, temerity. ANT.-circumspection, fearfulness, humility, meekness.

audible, *a.* SYN.-clear, discernible, emphatic, heard, loud, plain, re-

sounding.

audience, *n.* SYN.-assemblage, band, company, crew, group, horde, party, spectators, throng, troop, witnesses.

audit, *n.* SYN.-check, inspection, report, review, scrutiny.

augment, *v.* SYN.-accrue, amplify, enhance, enlarge, expand, extend, grow, heighten, increase, intensify, magnify, multiply, raise, wax. ANT.-atrophy, contract, decrease, diminish, reduce.

august, *a.* SYN.-dignified, grand, grandiose, high, imposing, lofty, magnificent, majestic, noble, pompous, stately, sublime. ANT.-common, humble, lowly, ordinary, undignified.

austere, *a.* SYN.-harsh, rigid, rigorous, severe, stern, strict, stringent, unyielding. ANT.-elastic, flexible, resilient, supple, yielding.

authentic, *a.* SYN.-genuine, pure, real, true, verifiable, accurate, authoritative, correct, reliable, trustworthy. ANT.-counterfeit, erroneous, false, spurious.

author, *n.* SYN.-columnist, composer, creator, father, inventor, journalist, maker, originator, writer.

authoritarian, *a.* SYN.-arrogant, dictatorial, doctrinaire, dogmatic, domineering, magisterial, opinionated, overbearing, positive; authoritative, doctrinal, formal. ANT.-fluctuating, indecisive, openminded, questioning, skeptical.

authority, *n.* SYN.-control, domination, dominion, force, justification, power, supremacy, authorization, license, permission, sanction, ground, importance, influence, prestige, weight. ANT.-impotence, incapacity, weakness, denial, prohibition.

autobiography, *n.* SYN.-adventures, biography, experiences, history, journal, letters, life, memoirs.

automated, *a.* SYN.-automatic, computerized, electronic, mechanical, mechanized, motorized, programmed. ANT.-manual.

autonomous, *a.* SYN.-emancipated, exempt, free, independent, liberated, unconfined, uncontrolled, unrestricted, unobstructed. ANT.-confined, restrained, restricted; blocked, clogged, contingent, dependent, impeded; subject.

auxiliary, *a.* SYN.-ancillary, assisting, conducive, furthering, helping, instrumental, subsidiary. ANT.-cumbersome, obstructive, opposing, retarding.

available, *a.* SYN.-accessible, convenient, handy, obtainable, prepared, ready, usable. ANT.-inaccessible, unavoidable.

avaricious, *a.* SYN.-covetous, grasping, greedy, rapacious, selfish; devouring, gluttonous, insatiable, ravenous, voracious. ANT.-generous, munificent; full, satisfied.

avenge, *v.* SYN.-requite, retaliate, revenge, vindicate. ANT.-forgive, pardon, pity, reconcile.

aver, *v.* SYN.-affirm, assert, declare, maintain, protest, state, swear. ANT.-contradict, demur, deny, dispute, oppose.

average, *a.* SYN.-fair, intermediate, mean, median, mediocre, medium, middling, moderate, ordinary. ANT.-exceptional, extraordinary, outstanding.

averse, *a.* SYN.-disinclined, hesitant, loath, reluctant, slow, unwilling. ANT.-disposed, eager, inclined,

ready, willing.

aversion, *n.* SYN.-abhorrence, antipathy, disgust, disinclination, dislike, distaste, dread, hatred, loathing, repugnance, repulsion, reluctance. ANT.-affection, attachment, devotion, enthusiasm.

avert, *v.* See **avoid.**

avoid, *v.* SYN.-avert, dodge, escape, eschew, elude, forbear, forestall, free, shun, ward. ANT.-confront, encounter, face, meet, oppose.

awake, *a.* SYN.-alert, alive, aware, conscious, stirring, up. ANT.-asleep, dozing, napping, unconscious.

aware, *a.* SYN.-apprised, cognizant, conscious, informed, mindful, observant, perceptive, sensible. ANT.-ignorant, insensible, oblivious, unaware.

away, *a.* SYN.-abroad, absent, departed, inattentive, preoccupied. ANT.-attending, present; attentive, watchful.

awful, *a.* SYN.-appalling, dire, dreadful, frightful, horrible, terrible, awe-inspiring, imposing, majestic, solemn. ANT.-commonplace, humble, lowly, vulgar.

awkward, *a.* SYN.-clumsy, gauche, gawky, inept, rough, unpolished, untoward. ANT.-adroit, graceful, neat, polished, skillful.

axis, *n.* SYN.-axle, divider, pole, shaft, spindle.

axiom, *n.* SYN.-adage, aphorism, apothegm, byword, fundamental, maxim, postulate, principle, proverb, saw, saying, theorem, truism.

B

babble, *v.* SYN.-chatter, gabble, gush, jabber, prattle, rant, rave.

back, *a.* SYN.-aft, after, astern, behind, following, hind, hindmost, rear. ANT.-ahead, fore, forward, front, head, leading.

backed, *a.* SYN.-abetted, aided, assisted, boosted, championed, encouraged, established, furthered, propelled, pushed.

backward, *a.* SYN.-regressive, retrograde, revisionary, dull, sluggish, stupid, disinclined, hesitating, indisposed, loath, reluctant, unwilling, wavering. ANT.-advanced, civilized, progressive.

bad, *a.* SYN.-baleful, base, deleterious, evil, immoral, iniquitous, noxious, pernicious, sinful, unsound, unwholesome, villainous, wicked. ANT.-excellent, good, honorable, moral, reputable.

badger, *v.* SYN.-aggravate, annoy, bother, disturb, harass, harry, irritate, molest, nag, pester, plague, provoke, tantalize, taunt, tease, torment, vex, worry. ANT.-comfort, delight, gratify, please, soothe.

baffle, *v.* SYN.-balk, circumvent, defeat, disappoint, foil, frustrate, hinder, outwit, prevent, thwart. ANT.-accomplish, fulfill, further, promote.

bag, *n.* SYN.-attaché case, backpack, briefcase, pack, pocketbook, purse, satchel, suitcase, tote.

balance, *n.* SYN.-composure, equilibrium, poise, stability, steadiness, proportion, symmetry, excess, remainder, remains, residue, rest. ANT.-fall, imbalance, instability, unsteadiness.

balance, *v.* SYN.-dangle, hang, poise, suspend, swing. ANT.-continue, maintain, persist, proceed, prolong.

bald, *a.* bare, exposed, naked, nude, stripped, unclad, uncovered, bar-

ren, plain, simple, defenseless, open, unprotected. ANT.-clothed, covered, dressed; concealed; protected.

ban, *v.* SYN.-debar, forbid, hinder, inhibit, interdict, prevent, prohibit. ANT.-allow, permit, sanction, tolerate.

banal, *a.* SYN.-commonplace, hackneyed, inane, insipid, trite, vapid. ANT.-fresh, novel, original, stimulating, striking.

band, *n.* SYN.-circle, circumference, latitude, meridian, orbit, zone; bandage, belt, obi, ring, sash, scarf.

banish, *v.* SYN.-deport, dismiss, dispel, eject, exclude, exile, expatriate, expel, ostracize, oust. ANT.-accept, admit, harbor, receive, shelter.

banquet, *n.* SYN.-celebration, dinner, entertainment, feast, festival, regalement.

barbaric, *a.* See **barbarous.**

barbarous, *a.* SYN.-barbarian, barbaric, brutal, crude, cruel, inhuman, merciless, remorseless, rude, ruthless, savage, uncivilized, uncultured, unrelenting. ANT.-civilized, humane, kind, polite, refined.

bargain, *n.* SYN.-agreement, compact, contract, covenant, pact, promise, stipulation, treaty.

barren, *a.* SYN.-devoid, empty hollow, unfilled, unfurnished, unoccupied, vacant, vacuous, void, worthless. ANT.-full, inhabited, occupied, replete, supplied.

barrier, *n.* SYN.-barricade, blockade, fence, hindrance, hurdle, impediment, obstacle, obstruction, restriction, wall.

base, *a.* SYN.-abject, contemptible,

despicable, dishonorable, groveling, ignoble, ignominious, low, lowly, mean, menial, servile, sordid, vile, vulgar. ANT.-teemed, exalted, honored, lofty, noble, righteous.

base, *n.* SYN.-basis, bottom, foundation, ground, groundwork, root, substructure, support, underpinning. ANT.-building, cover, superstructure, top.

bashful, *a.* SYN.-abashed, coy, diffident, embarrassed, humble, modest, recoiling, retiring, shamefaced, sheepish, shy, timid, timorous. ANT.-adventurous, daring, fearless, gregarious, outgoing.

basic, *a.* SYN.-elementary, fundamental, primary, rudimentary, simple. ANT.-abstract, abstruse, complex, elaborate, intricate.

basis, *n.* SYN.-base, bottom, foundation, ground, groundwork, support, underpinning, assumption, postulate, premise, presumption, presupposition, principle. ANT.-derivative, implication, superstructure, trimming.

bath, *n.* SYN.-bathroom, lavatory, sauna, shower, toilet, tub, washroom.

bathe, *v.* SYN.-clean, cleanse, launder, rinse, scrub, wash, wet. ANT.-dirty, foul, soil, stain.

battle, *n.* SYN.-combat, conflict, contest, fight, fray, skirmish, strife, struggle. ANT.-agreement, concord, peace, truce.

battle, *v.* SYN.-brawl, combat, conflict, contend, dispute, encounter, fight, quarrel scuffle, skirmish, squabble, struggle, wrangle.

bay, *n.* SYN.-bayou, cove, gulf, harbor, inlet, lagoon, mouth, sound.

beacon, *n.* SYN.-beam, flare, guide, lamp, lantern, radar, signal, sonar.

bear, *v.* SYN.-support, sustain, uphold, allow, brook, endure, permit, stand, suffer, tolerate, undergo; carry, convey, take, transport; produce, spawn, yield. ANT.-avoid, dodge, evade, refuse, shun.

beast, *n.* SYN.-animal, barbarian, brute, creature, fiend, lout, monster, pervert, savage.

beastly, *a.* SYN.-abominable, base, brutal, coarse, degraded, depraved, disgusting, low, obscene, repulsive, savage, vulgar. ANT.-kind, nice, pleasant, refined, suave.

beat, *v.* SYN.-belabor, buffet, dash, hit, knock, pound, pummel, punch, smite, strike, thrash, thump; conquer, defeat, overpower, overthrow, rout, subdue, vanquish, palpitate, pulsate, pulse, throb. ANT.-defend, shield, stroke, fail, surrender.

beautiful, *a.* SYN.-beauteous, charming, comely, elegant, fair, fine, gorgeous, handsome, lovely, pretty. ANT.-foul, hideous, homely, repulsive, unsightly.

beauty, *n.* SYN.-attractiveness, charm, comeliness, elegance, fairness, grace, handsomeness, loveliness, pulchritude. ANT.-deformity, disfigurement, eyesore, homeliness, ugliness.

because, *conj.* SYN.-as, for, inasmuch as, since.

beckon, *v.* SYN.-call, signal, summon, wave.

bed, *n.* SYN.-berth, bunk, cot, couch, cradle, hammock, mattress; accumulation, deposit, layer, stratum, vein.

bedlam, *n.* SYN.-chaos, clamor, commotion, confusion, disorder, tumult, turmoil, uproar. ANT.-order, quiet, serenity.

befoul, v. SYN.-corrupt, contaminate, defile, infect, poison, pollute, sully, taint. ANT.-disinfect, purify.

beg, v. SYN.-adjure, ask, beseech, crave, entreat, implore, importune, petition, pray, request, solicit, supplicate. ANT.-bestow, cede, favor, give, grant.

beget, v. SYN.-breed, create, engender, father, generate, originate, procreate, produce, propagate, sire. ANT.-abort, destroy, extinguish, kill, murder.

beggar, n. SYN.-mendicant, pauper, ragamuffin, scrub, starveling, tatterdemalion, vagabond, wretch.

begin, v. SYN.-arise, commence, enter, inaugurate, initiate, institute, open, originate, start. ANT.-close, complete, end, finish, terminate.

beginner, n. SYN.-apprentice, amateur, dabbler, dilettante, learner, neophyte, novice. ANT.-adept, authority, expert, master, professional.

beginning, n. SYN.-commencement, inception, genesis, opening, origin, outset, source, start. ANT.-close, completion, consummation, end, termination.

behalf, n. SYN.-account, advantage, avail, benefit, favor, gain, good, interest, profit, service. ANT.-calamity, distress, handicap, trouble.

behave, v. SYN.-act, bear, carry, comport, conduct, demean, deport, interact, manage, operate.

behavior, n. SYN.-action, bearing, carriage, conduct, deed, demeanor, deportment, disposition, manner.

behind, a. SYN.-after, back, delayed, following, trailing; backward, retarded, slow. ANT.-ahead, forward, leading; clever, quick, smart.

behold, v. SYN.-contemplate, descry, discern, distinguish, espy, glimpse, inspect, look at, notice, observe, perceive, scan, scrutinize, see, view, watch, witness.

belief, n. SYN.-certitude, confidence, conviction, credence, faith, feeling, notion, opinion, persuasion, reliance, trust. ANT.-denial, doubt, heresy, incredulity.

believe, v. SYN.-accept, apprehend, conceive, credit, fancy, hold, imagine, support, suppose. ANT.-distrust, doubt, question, reject.

belittle, v. SYN.-decry, depreciate, disparage, derogate, discredit, lower, undervalue minimize, underrate. ANT.-admire, appreciate, esteem, aggrandize, commend, exalt, magnify, praise.

belongings, n. SYN.-commodities, effects, estate, goods, possessions, property, stock, wealth.

beloved, a. SYN.-adored, dear, esteemed, precious, prized, valued; valuable. ANT.-despised, unwanted.

below, prep. SYN.-beneath, lower, under, underneath. ANT.-above, aloft, over, overhead.

bend, v. SYN.-bow, crook, curve, deflect, incline, lean, stoop, turn, twist, influence, mold, submit, yield. ANT.-break, resist, stiffen, straighten.

beneath, prep. SYN.-below, under, underneath. ANT.-above, over.

beneficial, a. SYN.-advantageous, good, helpful, profitable, salutary, serviceable, useful, wholesome. ANT.-deleterious, destructive, detrimental, harmful, injurious.

benefit, n. SYN.-account, advantage, avail, behalf, favor, gain, good, interest, profit, service. ANT.-calamity, distress, handicap, trouble.

benefit, v. SYN.-aid, assist, attend, help, oblige, succor; advance, forward, promote.

benevolence, n. SYN.-altruism, beneficence, charity, generosity, humanity, kindness, liberality, magnanimity, philanthropy, tenderness. ANT.-cruelty, inhumanity, malevolence, selfishness, unkindness.

benevolent, a. SYN.-altruistic, benign, charitable, friendly, generous, humane, kind, liberal, merciful, obliging, philanthropic, tender, unselfish. ANT.-greedy, harsh, malevolent, wicked.

bent, n. SYN.-bending, inclination, leaning, affection, attachment, bent, bias, desire, disposition, penchant, predilection, preference. ANT.-apathy, aversion, distaste, nonchalance, repugnance.

bequeath, v. SYN.-donate, endow, give, will.

bequest, n. SYN.-appropriation, benefaction, boon, bounty, concession, donation, endowment, gift, grant, subsidy.

berate, v. SYN.-admonish, blame, censure, lecture, rebuke, reprehend, reprimand, scold, upbraid, vituperate. ANT.-approve, commend, praise.

besides, prep. SYN.-also, furthermore, in addition, likewise, moreover, similarly, too.

best, a. SYN.-finest, greatest, incomparable, top, unequaled. ANT.-common, ordinary, worst.

bestial, a. SYN.-barbarous, brutal, brutish, carnal, coarse, cruel, ferocious, gross, inhuman, merciless, remorseless, rough, rude, ruthless, savage, sensual. ANT.-civilized, courteous, gentle, humane, kind.

bestow, v. SYN.-confer, contribute, deliver, donate, furnish, give, grant, impart, present, provide, supply, ANT.-keep, retain, seize, withdraw.

bet, v. SYN.-gamble, hazard, risk, speculate, venture, wager.

better, v. SYN.-ameliorate, amend, help, improve, rectify, reform. ANT.-corrupt, damage, debase, impair, vitiate.

bevy, n. SYN.-crowd, crush, horde, host, masses, mob, multitude, populace, press, rabble, swarm, throng.

bewilder, v. SYN.-confound, confuse, dumfound, mystify, nonplus, perplex, puzzle. ANT.-clarify, explain, illumine, instruct, solve.

bewildered, a. SYN.-deranged, disconcerted, disordered, disorganized, indistinct, mixed, muddled, perplexed. ANT.-clear, lucid, obvious, organized, plain.

bias, n. SYN.-bent, disposition, inclination, leaning, partiality, penchant, predilection, predisposition, prejudice, proclivity, proneness, propensity, slant, tendency, turn. ANT.-equity, fairness, impartiality, justice.

bicker, v. SYN.-altercate, argue, contend, contest, debate, discuss, dispute, quarrel, squabble, wrangle. ANT.-agree, allow, assent, concede.

big, a. SYN.-august, bulky, colossal, enormous, grand, great,. huge, hulking, immense, large, majestic, massive, monstrous. ANT.-little, petite, small, tiny.

bigoted, a. SYN.-dogmatic, fanatical, illiberal, intolerant, narrow-minded, prejudiced. ANT.-liberal, progressive, radical, tolerant.

bind, v. SYN.-attach, connect, engage, fasten, fetter, join, link, oblige, restrain, restrict, tie. ANT.-free, loose, unfasten, untie.

binding, a. SYN.-cogent, conclusive, convincing, effective, efficacious, legal, logical, powerful, sound, strong, telling, valid, weighty. ANT.-counterfeit, null, spurious, void, weak.

biography, n. SYN.-adventures, biography, experiences, history, journal, letters, life, memoirs.

bit, n. SYN.-amount, fraction, fragment, morsel, part, piece, portion, scrap. ANT.-all, entirety, sum, total, whole.

bite, v. SYN.-champ, chew, crunch, gnash, gnaw, nibble, nip, pierce, rend, tear.

bitter, a. SYN.-acrid, biting, distasteful, pungent, sour, tart; galling, grievous, painful, poignant; cruel, fierce, relentless, ruthless; acrimonious, caustic, harsh, sardonic, severe. ANT.-delicious, mellow, pleasant, sweet.

bizarre, a. SYN.-abnormal, curious, eccentric, extraordinary, grotesque, irregular, odd, peculiar, quaint, queer, singular, strange, uncommon, unique, unusual. ANT.-common, conventional, familiar, normal, ordinary, regular, typical.

blab, v. SYN.-chatter, confess, divulge, squeal, talk, tell.

black, a. SYN.-dark, dim, gloomy, murky, obscure, shadowy, unilluminated; dusky, opaque, sable, swarthy; dismal, gloomy, mournful, somber, sorrowful; evil, sinister, sullen, wicked; hidden, mystic, occult, secret. ANT.-light; bright, clear; pleasant; lucid.

blackball, v. SYN.-bar, except, exclude, expel, hinder, omit, ostracize, prevent, prohibit, restrain, shut out. ANT.-accept, admit, include, welcome.

blame, v. SYN.-accuse, censure, charge, condemn, implicate, involve, prosecute, rebuke, reproach, slander, upbraid. ANT.-absolve, acquit, exonerate.

blameless, a. SYN.-faultless, holy, immaculate, perfect, pure, sinless. ANT.-blemished, defective, faulty, imperfect.

bland, a. SYN.-boring, dull, flat, insipid, lifeless, tasteless; gentle, mild soothing. ANT.-exciting, interesting, spicy; irritating, stimulating.

blank, a. SYN.-clear, empty, new, open, untouched, vacant, white.

blaze, n. SYN.-burning, combustion, conflagration, fire, flame, glow, heat, warmth.

bleak, a. SYN.-cheerless, dark, dismal, doleful, dreary, dull, funereal, gloomy, lonesome, melancholy, sad, somber. ANT.-cheerful, gay, joyous, lively.

bleakness, n. SYN.-blackness, darkness, gloom, obscurity, shadow; dejection, depression, despondency, melancholy, misery, sadness, woe. ANT.-exultation, frivolity, joy, light, mirth.

blemish, n. SYN.-blot, speck, stain; defect, disgrace, fault, flaw, imperfection, tarnish. ANT.-adornment, embellishment, perfection, purity.

blend, v. SYN.-amalgamate, coalesce, combine, commingle, conjoin, consolidate, fuse, mingle, mix, merge, unify, unite. ANT.-analyze, decompose, disintegrate, separate.

bless, v. SYN.-adore, baptize, celebrate, consecrate, delight, exalt, extol, gladden, glorify. ANT.-blaspheme, curse, denounce, slander.

blessing, *n.* SYN.-absolution, consecration, miracle, unction; asset, boon, benefit, help, luck, windfall.

blind, *a.* SYN.-ignorant, oblivious, sightless, undiscerning, unmindful, unseeing; headlong, heedless, rash. ANT.-aware, calculated, discerning, perceiving, sensible.

bliss, *n.* SYN.-blessedness, blissfulness, ecstasy, felicity, happiness, joy, rapture. ANT.-grief, misery, sorrow, woe, wretchedness.

blithe, *a.* SYN.-effervescent, light, resilient; animated, buoyant, cheerful, elated, hopeful, jocund, lively, spirited, sprightly, vivacious. ANT.-dejected, depressed, despondent, hopeless, sullen.

block, *v.* SYN.-bar, barricade, clog, close, obstruct, stop, delay, impede; hinder. ANT.-clear, open; aid, further, promote.

blockade, *v.* SYN.-barricade, besiege, encircle, isolate.

blossom, *v.* SYN.-bloom, burgeon, flourish, succeed

blond, *a.* SYN.-attractive, comely, fair, light, pale.

blot, *n.* SYN.-blemish, speck, stain; defect, disgrace, fault, flaw, imperfection. ANT.-adornment, embellishment, perfection, purity.

blow, *n.* SYN.-bang, box, clout, cuff, hit, jab, punch, slam, slap, strike, swat, whack.

bluff, *v.* SYN.-con, deceive, delude, fool, mislead, threaten, trick.

blunder, *n.* SYN.-error, indiscretion, lapse, mistake, oversight.

blunt, *a.* SYN.-dull, edgeless, obtuse, pointless, stolid, thick-witted, unsharpened; abrupt, bluff, brusque, impolite, outspoken, plain, rough,

rude, unceremonious. ANT.-polished, polite, suave, subtle, tactful.

blustery, *a.* SYN.-gusty, inclement, roaring, rough, stormy, tempestuous, turbulent, windy. ANT.-calm, clear, peaceful, quiet, tranquil.

boast, *v.* SYN.-brag, crow, flaunt, glory, vaunt. ANT.-apologize, deprecate, humble, minimize.

bodily, *a.* SYN.-animal, base, carnal, corporeal, fleshly, gross, lustful, sensual, voluptuous, worldly, ANT.-exalted, intellectual, refined, spiritual, temperate.

body, *n.* SYN.-carcass, corpse, remains; form, frame, physique, torso; bulk, corpus, mass; aggregate, association, company, society. ANT.-intellect, mind, soul, spirit.

boisterous, *a.* SYN.-disruptive, loud, noisy, rude, unruly.

bold, *a.* SYN.-adventurous, audacious, brave, courageous, daring, dauntless, fearless, intrepid; brazen, forward, impudent, insolent, pushy, rude; abrupt, conspicuous, prominent, striking. ANT.-cowardly, flinching, timid; bashful, retiring.

boldness, *n.* SYN.-effrontery, audacity, fearlessness, hardihood, temerity. ANT.-circumspection, fearfulness, humility, meekness.

bolt, *v.* SYN.-bar, clasp, fastening, hook, latch, lock, padlock.

bombast, *n.* harangue, lecture, sermon.

bond, *n.* SYN.-connection, connective, coupler, juncture, link, tie, union. ANT.-break, gap, interval, opening, split.

bondage, *n.* SYN.-captivity, confinement, imprisonment, serfdom, servitude, slavery, thralldom, vassalage. ANT.-freedom, liberation.

bonus, *n.* SYN.-award, bounty, compensation, premium, prize, recompense, remuneration, reward. ANT.-assessment, charge, earnings, punishment, wages.

book, *n.* SYN.-booklet, brochure, compendium, edition, handbook, manual, monograph, pamphlet, publication, textbook, tract, treatise, volume, work.

bookkeeper, *n.* SYN.-accountant, auditor, clerk, comptroller, controller; treasurer.

boor, *n.* SYN.-boob, bumpkin, lout, peasant, rustic, yokel.

boost, *v.* SYN.-advance, assist, abet, encourage, help, promote, support.

border, *n.* SYN.-boundary, brim, brink, edge, fringe, frontier, limit, margin, outskirts, rim, termination, verge. ANT.-center, core, interior, mainland.

boredom, *n.* SYN.-apathy, doldrums, dullness, ennui, indifference, monotony, tedium, weariness. ANT.-activity, excitement, motive, stimulus.

boring, *a.* SYN.-dense, slow, stupid; blunt, obtuse; commonplace, dull, dismal, dreary, monotonous, sad, tedious. ANT.-animated, lively, sharp; clear, interesting.

borrowed, *a.* SYN.-acquired, adopted, appropriated, copied, imitated, plagiarized, taken.

botch, *v.* SYN.-blunder, bungle, mishandle, mismanage, muddle, ruin, spoil, wreck.

bother, *v.* SYN.-annoy, disturb, harass, haunt, inconvenience, molest, perplex, pester, plague, tease, trouble, upset, worry. ANT.-gratify, please, relieve, soothe.

bottle, *n.* SYN.-canteen, carafe, cruet, decanter, flagon, flask, jar, vial.

bottom, *n.* SYN.-base, basis, foot, foundation, fundament, groundwork. ANT.-apex, peak, summit, top.

bought, *a.* SYN.-acquired, contracted, ordered, procured, purchased, requisitioned.

boulder, *n.* SYN.-rock, slab, stone.

bounce, *v.* SYN.-bolt, bound, hop, jump, leap, ricochet, spring, vault.

bound, *v.* SYN.-circumscribe, confine, enclose, encompass, envelop, fence, limit, surround. ANT.-develop, distend, enlarge, expand, expose, open.

boundary, *n.* SYN.-brim, brink, edge, fringe, frontier, limit, margin, outskirts, rim, termination, verge, border, extremity, hem, periphery. ANT.-center, core, interior, mainland.

bountiful, *a.* SYN.-ample, abundant, copious, overflowing, plenteous, plentiful, profuse, rich, teeming. ANT.-deficient, insufficient, scant, scarce.

bow, *v.* SYN.-bend, crook, curve, deflect, incline, lean, stoop, turn, twist, influence, mold, submit, yield. ANT.-break, resist, stiffen, straighten.

boycott, *v.* SYN.-disapprove, oppose, picket, protest, quit, resist.

brag, *v.* SYN.-bluster, boast, crow, flaunt, flourish, vaunt. ANT.-debase, degrade, demean, denigrate.

brand, *n.* SYN.-mark, scar, stain, stigma, trace, vestige; badge, label, sign; characteristic, feature, indication, property, trait.

brave, *a.* SYN.-adventurous, audacious, bold, chivalrous, courageous, daring, dauntless, fearless, gallant, heroic, intrepid, magnanimous, valiant, valorous. ANT.-cowardly, cringing, fearful, timid, weak.

bravery, n. SYN.-boldness, chivalry, courage, fearlessness, fortitude, intrepidity, mettle, prowess, resolution. ANT.-cowardice, fear, pusillanimity, timidity.

brazen, a. SYN.-adventurous, audacious, bold, brave, courageous, daring, dauntless, fearless, intrepid; forward, impudent, insolent, pushy, rude; abrupt, conspicuous, prominent, striking. ANT.-cowardly, flinching, timid; bashful, retiring.

break, v. SYN.-burst, crack, crush, demolish, destroy, fracture, infringe, pound, rack, rend, rupture, shatter, smash, squeeze; disobey, transgress, violate. ANT.-join, mend, renovate, repair, restore.

breakthrough, n. SYN.-creation, discovery, finding, innovation, invention.

breed, n. SYN.-kind, sort, stock, strain, subspecies, variety. ANT.-homogeneity, likeness, monotony, sameness, uniformity.

breed, v. SYN.-bear, beget, conceive, engender, generate, procreate, propagate; foster, nurture, raise, rear, train.

breeding, n. SYN.-civilization, culture, cultivation, education, enlightenment, refinement. ANT.-boorishness, ignorance, illiteracy, vulgarity.

breeze, n. SYN.-draft, gust, wind, zephyr.

bribe, n. SYN.-blackmail, compensation, fee, graft, gratuity, present, protection, reward.

bridge, n. SYN.-bond, connection, link, span.

brief, a. SYN.-compendious, concise, curt, laconic, pithy, short, succinct, terse; fleeting, momentary, passing, transient. ANT.-extended, lengthy, long, prolonged, protracted.

bright, a. SYN.-brilliant, clear, gleaming, lucid, luminous, lustrous, radiant, shining, translucent, transparent; clever, intelligent, witty. ANT.-dark, dull, gloomy, murky, sullen.

brightness, n. SYN.-brilliance, brilliancy, effulgence, luster, radiance, splendor. ANT.-darkness, dullness, gloom, obscurity.

brilliant, a. See **bright.**

brim, n. SYN.-border, edge, lip, margin, rim, top.

bring, v. SYN.-carry, convey, transmit, transport; bear, support, sustain. ANT.-abandon, drop.

brisk, a. SYN.-cool, fresh, refreshing. ANT.-hackneyed, musty, stagnant.

brittle, a. SYN.-breakable, crisp, crumbling, delicate, fragile, frail, splintery. ANT.-enduring, thick, tough, unbreakable.

broad, a. SYN.-expanded, extensive, immense, large, sweeping, vast, wide; liberal, tolerant. ANT.-confined, narrow, restricted.

broadcast, v. SYN.-air, announce, disseminate, notify, scatter, transmit.

broke, a. SYN.-bankrupt, indebted, owing, penniless, poverty-stricken, ruined. ANT.-rich, wealthy.

broken, a. SYN.-crushed, destroyed, flattened, fractured, interrupted, reduced, rent, ruptured, separated, shattered, smashed, wrecked. ANT.-integral, repaired, united, whole.

brood, v. SYN.-care, fret, grieve, mope, muse, ponder, sulk, think, worry.

brook, *n.* SYN.-rill, rivulet, stream.

broth, *n.* SYN.-brew, concoction, consommé, purée, soup, stock.

brotherhood, *n.* SYN.-brotherliness, fellowship, kindness, solidarity; association, clan, fraternity, society. ANT.-acrimony, discord, opposition, strife.

browbeat, *v.* SYN.-berate, bully, frighten, intimidate, scold, threaten.

browse, *v.* SYN.-examine, glance, peruse, scan, skim.

brusque, *a.* SYN.-abrupt, blunt, curt, discourteous, gruff, short.

brutal, *a.* SYN.-barbarous, bestial, brute, brutish, carnal, coarse, cruel, ferocious, gross, inhuman, merciless, remorseless, rough, rude, ruthless, savage, sensual. ANT-civilized, courteous, gentle, humane, kind.

budget, *v.* SYN.-allocate, allow, estimate, forecast, plan, provide.

build, *n.* SYN.-appearance, configuration, contour, cut, figure, form, frame, guise, image, mold, outline, pattern, shape. ANT.-contortion, deformity, distortion, mutilation.

build, *v.* SYN.-construct, erect, establish, found, raise, rear. ANT.-demolish, destroy, overthrow, raze, undermine.

bulletin, *n.* SYN.-advertisement, announcement, declaration, notification, promulgation. ANT.-hush, muteness, silence, speechlessness.

bulge, *n.* SYN.-appendage, excess, lump, projection, prominence, promontory.

bulk, *n.* SYN.-best, biggest, greater, majority, most. ANT.-least, lesser, fraction, remnant.

bulky, *a.* SYN.-big, cumbersome, large, huge, massive, unwieldy.

bum, *n.* SYN.-beggar, hobo, rover, tramp, vagabond, vagrant, wanderer. ANT.-gentleman, laborer, worker.

bump, *n.* SYN.-bang, clash, crash, hit, jar, jolt, knock, pat, push, shove.

bunch, *n.* SYN.-aggregation, assembly, band, brood, class, cluster, collection, crowd, flock, group, herd, horde, lot, mob, pack, party, set, swarm, throng, troupe.

bungle, *v.* SYN.-blunder, botch, mishandle, mismanage, muddle, ruin, spoil, wreck.

buoyant, *a.* SYN.-effervescent, light, resilient; animated, blithe, cheerful, elated, hopeful, jocund, lively, spirited, sprightly, vivacious. ANT.-dejected, depressed, despondent, hopeless, sullen.

burden, *v.* SYN.-afflict, encumber, load, oppress, overload, tax, trouble, weigh. ANT.-alleviate, console, ease, lighten, mitigate.

burdensome, *a.* SYN.-boring, dilatory, dreary, dull, humdrum, irksome, monotonous, slow, sluggish, tardy, tedious, tire-some, uninteresting, wearisome. ANT.-amusing, entertaining, exciting, interesting, quick.

burglarize, *v.* SYN.-loot, pilfer, pillage, plunder, purloin, rob, snatch, steal, swipe. ANT.-buy, refund, repay, restore, return.

burglary, *n.* SYN.-break in, depredation, larceny, pillage, plunder, robbery, theft.

burn, *v.* SYN.-blaze, char, consume, cremate, incinerate, scald, scorch, sear, singe. ANT.-extinguish, put out, quench.

burst, *v.* SYN.-break, crack, erupt,

explode, fracture, rupture, split.

bury, *v.* SYN.-conceal, cover, entomb, hide, immure, inhume, inter, secrete, stash, stow. ANT.-display, expose, open, reveal.

business, *n.* SYN.-art, commerce, employment, engagement, enterprise, job, occupation, profession, trade, trading, vocation, work. ANT.-avocation, hobby, pastime.

bustle, *n.* SYN.-ado, bother, commotion, confusion, flutter, flurry, haste, hurry, rush, speed.

busy, *a.* SYN.-working; industrious, alert, brisk, lively, nimble, quick, sprightly, supple, active, assiduous, hard-working, industrious, diligent, persevering. ANT.-dormant, inactive; indolent, lazy, passive, apathetic, indifferent, lethargic, unconcerned.

butchery, *n.* SYN.-carnage, massacre, pogrom, slaughter.

buy, *v.* SYN.-acquire, bargain, get, market, obtain, procure, purchase, secure. ANT.-dispose of, sell, vend.

by, *prep.* SYN.-beside, near, next to; by means of, through, with; according to; from.

C

cabal, *n.* SYN.-collusion, combination, conspiracy, intrigue, machination, plot, treachery, treason.

cabinet, *n.* SYN.-administrators, advisors, assistants, council, committee, ministry.

calamity, *n.* SYN.-adversity, accident, casualty, catastrophe, disaster, misfortune, mishap, ruin. ANT.-advantage, fortune, welfare calculation, design, intention, purpose.

calculate, *v.* SYN.-compute, consider, count, estimate, figure,

reckon. ANT.-conjecture, guess, miscalculate.

caliber, *n.* SYN.-attribute, characteristic, distinction, feature, peculiarity, property, quality, trait, caliber, grade, value. ANT.-being, essence, nature, substance.

çall, *v.* SYN.-cry, exclaim, hail, shout, signal, yell; convene, invite, muster, request, summon.

callous, *a.* SYN.-hard, impenitent, indurate, insensible, insensitive, obdurate, tough, unfeeling. ANT.-compassionate, sensitive, soft, tender.

calm, *a.* SYN.-appease, composed, dispassionate, imperturbable, pacific, peaceful, placid, quiet, serene, still, tranquil, undisturbed, unruffled. ANT.-excited, frantic, stormy, turbulent, wild.

calm, *n.* SYN.-calmness, hush, peace, quiescence, quiet, quietude, repose, rest, serenity, silence, stillness, tranquility. ANT.-agitation, disturbance, excitement, noise, tumult.

calm, *v.* SYN.-allay, alleviate, assuage, compose, lull, pacify, placate, quell, quiet, relieve, satisfy, soothe, still, tranquilize. ANT.-arouse, excite, incense, inflame.

calumny, *n.* SYN.-aspersion, backbiting, defamation, libel, scandal, slander, vilification. ANT.-applause, commendation, defense, flattery, praise.

camouflage, *n.* SYN.-cloak, cover, disguise, hide, mask, shroud, veil; deceit, misdirection.

cancel, *v.* SYN.-cross out, delete, eliminate, erase, expunge, obliterate; abolish, abrogate, annul, invalidate, nullify, quash, repeal, rescind, revoke. ANT.-confirm, enact, enforce, perpetuate

candid, *a.* SYN.-frank, free, honest, ingenuous, open, plain, sincere, straightforward, truthful; fair, impartial, just, unbiased. ANT.-contrived, scheming, sly, wily.

candidate, *n.* SYN.-aspirant, competitor, contestant, nominee.

candor, *n.* SYN.-fairness, frankness, honesty, integrity, justice, openness, rectitude, responsibility, sincerity, trustworthiness, uprightness. ANT.-cheating, deceit, dishonesty, fraud, trickery.

canny, *a.* SYN.-careful, cautious, discreet, prudent, shrewd, wary.

capability, *n.* See **capacity.**

capable, *a.* SYN.-able, clever, competent, efficient, fitted, qualified, skillful. ANT.-inadequate, incapable, incompetent, unfitted.

capacity, *n.* SYN.-ability, capability, faculty, power, skill, talent; magnitude, room, size, volume. ANT.-impotence, inability, incapacity, stupidity.

caper, *n.* SYN.-act, activity, escapade, prank, trick.

capital, *n.* SYN.-assets, cash, equipment, property, wealth.

capitulate, *v.* SYN.-abandon, acquiesce, cede, relinquish, renounce, resign, sacrifice, submit, surrender, yield. ANT.-conquer, overcome, resist, rout.

caprice, *n.* SYN.-fancy, humor, inclination, notion, quirk, vagary, whim, whimsy.

capricious, *a.* SYN.-changeable, fickle, fitful, inconstant, restless, unstable, variable. ANT.-constant, reliable, stable, steady, trustworthy.

captivity, *n.* SYN.-bondage, confinement, imprisonment, serfdom, servitude, slavery, thralldom, vassalage. ANT.-freedom, liberation.

capture, *v.* SYN.-apprehend, arrest, catch, clutch, grasp, grip, lay hold of, seize, snare, trap. ANT.-liberate, lose, release, throw.

carcass, *n.* SYN.-body, corpse, remains; form, frame, torso; bulk, corpus, mass. ANT.-intellect, mind, soul, spirit.

care, *n.* SYN.-anxiety, concern, solicitude, worry; attention, caution, circumspection, regard, vigilance, wariness; charge, custody, guardianship, ward. ANT.-disregard, indifference, neglect, negligence.

careen, *a.* SYN.-incline, list, tip.

careful, *a.* SYN.-attentive, exact, finicky, fussy, heedful, meticulous, painstaking, prudent, scrupulous, thorough, thoughtful; cautious, circumspect, discreet, guarded, suspicious, vigilant, wary. ANT.-forgetful, improvident, indifferent, lax.

careless, *a.* SYN.-heedless, imprudent, inattentive, inconsiderate, indiscreet, reckless, thoughtless, unconcerned; desultory, inaccurate, lax, neglectful, negligent, remiss. ANT.-accurate, careful, meticulous, nice.

carelessness, *n.* SYN.-default, disregard, failure, heedlessness, neglect, negligence, omission, oversight, slight, thoughtlessness. ANT.-attention, care, diligence, watchfulness.

caress, *v.* SYN.-coddle, cuddle, embrace, fondle, hug, kiss, pet, stroke. ANT.-annoy, buffet, spurn, tease, vex.

carnal, *a.* SYN.-animal, base, bodily, corporeal, fleshly, gross, lustful, sensual, voluptuous, worldly. ANT.-exalted, intellectual, refined, spiritual, temperate.

carouse, v. SYN.- celebrate, frolic, indulge, party, play, revel.

carping, a. SYN.-caviling, censorious, critical, faultfinding, hypercritical. ANT.-cursory, shallow, superficial, uncritical; appreciative, approving, commendatory, encouraging.

carriage, n. SYN.-air, attitude, bearing, cast, demeanor, look, poise, pose, posture, presence.

carry, v. SYN.-bring, convey, fetch, move, take, transmit, transport; bear, support, sustain. ANT.-abandon, drop.

carve, v. SYN.-chisel, create, fashion, form, model, mold, pattern, shape.

case, n. SYN.-bag, box, carton, container, crate, grip, holder, sheath.

cast, v. SYN.-fling, hurl, pitch, sling, throw, toss.

caste, n. SYN.-category, class, denomination, genre, kind; grade, order, rank, set.

casual, a. SYN.-accidental, chance, fortuitous, unexpected; incidental, informal, nonchalant, offhand, relaxed, unconcerned, unpremeditated. ANT. expected, intended; formal, planned, pretentious.

casualty, n. SYN.-accident, calamity, contingency, disaster, fortuity, misfortune, mishap. ANT.-calculation, design, intention, purpose.

catalogue, n. SYN.-bulletin, classification, directory, file, listing, record, register.

catastrophe, n. SYN.-accident, adversity, affliction, calamity, casualty, devastation, disaster, distress, misfortune, mishap, ruin. ANT.-advantage, blessing, fortune, welfare.

catch, v. SYN.-apprehend, arrest, capture, clutch, grasp, grip, lay

hold of, seize, snare, trap. ANT.-liberate, lose, release, throw.

catching, a. SYN.-communicable, contagious, infectious, pestilential, virulent. ANT.-healthful, hygienic, non-communicable.

categorical, a. SYN.-absolute, certain, definite, indubitable, undeniable.

category, n. SYN.-caste, class, denomination, genre, kind; grade, order, rank, set.

cause, n. SYN.-agent, determinant, incentive, inducement, motive, origin, principle, reason, source. ANT.-consequence, effect, end, result.

cause, v. SYN.-create, effect, evoke, incite, induce, make, occasion, originate, prompt.

caustic, a. SYN.-acrimonious, biting, cutting, derisive, ironic, sarcastic, sardonic, satirical, sneering, taunting. ANT.-affable, agreeable, amiable, pleasant.

caution, n. SYN.-care, heed, prudence, vigilance, wariness, watchfulness; admonition, counsel, injunction, warning. ANT.-abandon, carelessness, recklessness.

cautious, a. SYN.-attentive, heedful, prudent, scrupulous, thoughtful; careful, circumspect, discreet, guarded, vigilant, wary. ANT.-forgetful, improvident, indifferent, lax.

cease, v. SYN.-abandon, abstain, arrest, check, desist, discontinue, end, halt, quit, stop; give up, relinquish, resign, stop, surrender, terminate; abandon, depart, leave, withdraw. ANT.-continue, endure, occupy, persist, stay.

celebrate, v. SYN.-commemorate, keep, observe, solemnize; commend, extol, glorify, honor, laud,

praise. ANT.-disregard, overlook;
decry, disgrace, dishonor, profane.

celebration, n. SYN.-anniversary,
carnival, commemoration, ceremony, feast, festival, festivity, holiday, jubilee, observance, revelry,
spree.

celebrity, n. SYN.-dignitary, hero,
leader, luminary, notable, person-
age, star.

celestial, a. SYN.-divine, godlike,
heavenly, holy, superhuman, supernatural, transcendent. ANT.-
blasphemous, diabolical, mundane, profane, wicked.

cell, n. SYN.-cage, compartment,
coop, keep, lockup, pen, vault.

censor, v. SYN.-abridge, ban, control, edit, forbid, inspect, restrict,
suppress, void.

censure, v. SYN.-blame, condemn,
denounce, reprehend, reproach,
reprobate, reprove, upbraid; convict, sentence. ANT.-approve, commend, condone, forgive, praise; absolve, acquit, exonerate, pardon.

center, n. SYN.-core, heart, middle,
midpoint, midst, nucleus. ANT.-bor-
der, boundary, outskirts, periphery, rim.

ceremonious, a. SYN.-affected, correct, decorous, exact, formal, methodical, precise, proper, regular,
solemn, stiff. ANT.-easy, natural,
unconstrained, unconventional.

ceremony, n. SYN.-formality, observance, parade, pomp, protocol,
rite, ritual, solemnity.

certain, a. SYN.-assured, convinced,
definite, fixed, indubitable, inevitable, positive, satisfied, secure,
sure, undeniable, unquestionable.
ANT.-doubtful, probable, questionable, uncertain.

certainty, n. SYN.-assurance, as-

suredness, confidence, conviction,
courage, firmness, security, self-
reliance, surety, pledge, promise,
word, assertion, declaration,
statement. ANT.-bashfulness, humility, modesty, shyness, suspicion.

certificate, n. SYN.-credential, declaration, endorsement, guarantee,
license, testimonial, ticket, warrantee.

certify, v. SYN.-aver, attest, declare,
state, swear, testify.

challenge, v. SYN.-object to, question; brave, dare, defy; call, invite,
summon; demand, require.

chance, a. SYN.-accidental, casual,
contingent, fortuitous, incidental,
undesigned, unintended. ANT.-cal-
culated, decreed, intended,
planned, willed.

chance, n. SYN.-accident, contingency, fortuity, fortune, happening,
misfortune, mishap, occasion, occurrence, opening, opportunity,
possibility. ANT.-calculation, design, intention, purpose.

chance, v. SYN.-accidentally,
bechance, befall, betide, coincidence, happen, occur, unexpect-
edly, risk, take place, transpire.

change, n. SYN.-alteration, alternation, modification, mutation, substitution, variation, variety, vicissitude. ANT.-monotony, stability, uniformity.

change, v. SYN.-exchange, substitute; alter, convert, modify, remodel, shift, transfigure, transform, vary, veer. ANT.-retain; continue, establish, preserve, settle,
stabilize.

changeable, a. SYN.-fickle, fitful, inconstant, shifting, unstable, vacillating, variable, wavering. ANT.-con-

stant, stable, steady, unchanging, uniform.

channel, n. SYN.-artery, canal, conduit, course, ditch, duct, furrow, gutter, tube, vein.

chaos, n. SYN.-anarchy, confusion, disorder, disorganization, jumble, muddle. ANT.-order, organization, system.

chaperone, v. SYN.-accompany, attend, escort, go with. ANT.-abandon, avoid.

character, n. SYN.-class, description, disposition, individuality, kind, nature, reputation, repute, temperament, sort, standing, style; figure, mark, sign, symbol, representation.

characteristic, n SYN.-attribute, feature, mark, peculiarity, property, quality, trait.

charade, n. SYN.-deception, dodge, fake, fraud, hoax, pretense, pretext, sham, swindle, trick

charge, n. SYN.-accusation, arraignment, imputation, incrimination, indictment. ANT.-exculpation, exoneration, pardon.

charge, v. SYN.-accuse, arraign, censure, incriminate, indict. ANT.-absolve, acquit, exonerate, release, vindicate.

charisma, n.SYN.-allure, appeal, attraction, charm, seductiveness.

charitable, a. SYN.-altruistic, benevolent, benign, friendly, generous, humane, kind, liberal, merciful, obliging, philanthropic, tender, unselfish. ANT.-greedy, harsh, malevolent, wicked.

charity, n. SYN.-altruism, beneficence, benevolence, generosity, humanity, kindness, liberality, magnanimity, philanthropy, tenderness. ANT.-cruelty, inhumanity,

malevolence, selfishness, unkindness.

charlatan, n. SYN.-cheat, cheater, fraud, imposter, phoney, swindler.

charm, v. SYN.-beguile, bewitch, delight, enrapture, entice, entrance, mesmerize, please.

charming, a. SYN.-alluring, attractive, bewitching, captivating, enchanting, engaging, fascinating, winning. ANT.-repugnant, repulsive, revolting.

chart, n. SYN.-diagram, graph, map, outline, plan, poster, presentation.

chary, a. SYN.-careful, cautious, circumspect, shy, timid, wary.

chase, v. SYN.-follow, hunt, persist, pursue, trace, track, trail, seek; drive, scatter. ANT.-abandon, elude, escape, evade, flee.

chaste, a. SYN.-decent, demure, guiltless, innocent, modest, moral, proper, pure, sincere, strong, uncorrupted, undefiled, virginal. ANT.-brash, corruptible, foul, polluted, sullied, tainted, tarnished, weak.

chasten, v. See **chastise.**

chastise, v. SYN.-berate, castigate, correct, discipline, pummel, punish, scold, strike, upbraid. ANT.-acquit, exonerate, free, pardon, release.

chat, n. SYN.-chatter, colloquy, conference, conspiracy, conversation, dialogue, interview, intrigue, parley, plan, plot, scheme, talk.

chat, v. SYN.-converse, gossip, jabber, speak, talk, tattle; confer, consult, deliberate, discuss, reason.

chattel, n. SYN.-assets, belongings, goods, property, wealth.

chatter, n. SYN.-conversation, dialogue, discussion, gossip, rumor, talk. ANT.-correspondence, meditation, silence, writing.

chatty, *a.* SYN.-amiable, amicable, friendly, spontaneous, talkative, effusive, garrulous,

cheap, *a.* SYN.-budget, inexpensive, low-priced, moderate, poor, reasonable, thrifty; beggarly, common, inferior, mean, shabby. ANT.-costly, dear, expensive; dignified, honorable, noble.

cheat, *n.* SYN.-chicanery, con, deception, duplicity, fraud, guile, imposture, swindle, trick; charlatan, cheater, chiseler, conniver, crook, fake, fraud, rogue, swindler, trickster. ANT.-fairness, honesty, integrity, sincerity.

cheat, *v.* SYN.-bilk, circumvent, deceive, defraud, dupe, fool, gull, hoax, hoodwink, outwit, swindle, trick, victimize.

check, *v.* SYN.-analyze, assess, audit, contemplate, dissect, examine, inquire, interrogate, notice, question, quiz, review, scan, scrutinize, survey, view, watch; block, hamper, hinder, impede, obstruct, prevent, resist, restrain, retard, stop, thwart. ANT.-disregard, neglect, omit, overlook; assist, expedite, facilitate, further, promote.

cheeky, *a.* SYN.-audacious, bold, brazen, impertinent, impudent.

cheer, *v.* SYN.-comfort, consolation, contentment, ease, enjoyment, relief, solace, succor. ANT.-affliction, discomfort, misery, suffering, torment, torture.

cheerful, *a.* SYN.-gay, glad, happy, jolly, joyful, lighthearted, merry, sprightly. ANT.-depressed, glum, mournful, sad, sullen.

cherish, *v.* SYN.-appreciate, hold dear, prize, treasure, value; foster, nurture, sustain. ANT.-dislike, disregard, neglect; abandon, reject.

chief, *a.* SYN.-cardinal, essential, first, foremost, highest, leading, main, paramount, predominant, supreme. ANT.-auxiliary, minor, subordinate, subsidiary, supplemental.

chief, *n.* SYN.-captain, chieftain, commander, head, leader, master, principal, ringleader, ruler, sovereign. ANT.-attendant, follower, servant, subordinate.

childish, *a.* SYN.-adolescent, childlike, foolish, immature, infantile, juvenile, youthful.

chilly, *a.* SYN.-arctic, brisk, cold, cool, crisp, freezing, frigid, frozen, icy, wintry; passionless, phlegmatic, stoical, unfeeling. ANT.-burning, fiery, heated, hot, torrid; ardent, passionate.

chivalrous, *a.* SYN.-brave, courteous, dauntless, gallant, generous, heroic, noble, polite, valiant. ANT.-base, crass, cowardly, crass, ignoble.

choice, *n.* SYN.-alternative, election, favorite, option, preference, selection.

choose, *v.* SYN.-adopt, cull, decide, discriminate, elect, embrace, espouse, favor, judge, opt, pick, prefer, select, take. ANT.-deline, discard, dismiss, refuse, reject.

chronic, *a.* SYN.-continual, continuing, lasting, lingering, perennial, persisting, recurring.

chronicle, *n.* SYN.-account, accounting, annals, history, narrative, record, report.

chronicle, *v.* SYN.-account, elucidate, explain, expound, narrate, record, recount, report, tell.

chronological, *a.* SYN.-classified, consecutive, dated, historical, sequential.

cinema, *n.* SYN.-film, movie, picture.

circle, *n.* SYN.-belt, circuit, circumference, cycle, disk, loop, meridian, orbit, ring, sphere, wheel.

circuitous, *a.* SYN.-crooked, devious, distorted, erratic, indirect, roundabout, swerving, tortuous, wandering, winding; crooked, cunning, tricky. ANT.-direct, straight; honest, straightforward.

circular, *a.* SYN.-complete, curved, cylindrical, entire, globular, round, spherical.

circumspection, *n.* SYN.-anxiety, care, concern, solicitude, worry; attention, caution, regard, vigilance, wariness. ANT.-disregard, indifference, neglect, negligence.

circumstance, *n.* SYN.-cause, condition, contingency, event, fact, factor, happening, incident, occurrence, position, situation.

citation, *n.* SYN.-charge, summons, ticket; award, certificate, commendation.

cite, *v.* SYN.-adduce, advance, affirm, allege, assign, claim, declare, extract, maintain, paraphrase, quote, recite, refer, repeat. ANT.-contradict, deny, disprove, gainsay, refute.

citizen, *n.* SYN.-civilian, commoner, householder, inhabitant, national, native, occupant, resident, subject, taxpayer, voter. ANT.-alien, foreigner, outsider.

city, *n.* SYN.-metropolis, municipality, town, township, village. ANT.-country, suburb.

civil, *a.* SYN.-considerate, courteous, cultivated, genteel, polite, refined, urbane, well-bred, well-mannered. ANT.-boorish, impertinent, rude, uncivil, uncouth.

civilization, *n.* SYN.-cultivation, cul-

ture, education, enlightenment, refinement. ANT.-boorishness, ignorance, illiteracy, vulgarity.

claim, *n.* SYN.-application, declaration, deed, interest, petition, right, suit, title.

claim, *v.* SYN.-affirm, allege, assert, aver, avow, declare, express, maintain, recite, recount, say, tell, state, utter; defend, support, uphold, vindicate. ANT.-contradict, deny, imply, refute.

clamor, *n.* SYN.-babel, cry, din, noise, outcry, racket, row, sound, tumult, uproar. ANT.-hush, quiet, silence, stillness.

clan, *n.* SYN.-brotherhood, fellowship, solidarity; association, clan, fraternity, society. ANT.-acrimony, discord, individual, opposition, strife.

clandestine, *a.* SYN.-concealed, covert, hidden, latent, private, secret, surreptitious, unknown. ANT.-conspicuous, disclosed, exposed, known, obvious, overt.

clarify, *v.* SYN.-decipher, elucidate, explain, expound, illustrate, interpret, resolve, unfold, unravel. ANT.-baffle, confuse, darken, muddy, obscure.

clarity, *n.* SYN.-clearness, directness, distinctness, exactness, explicitness, precision, prominence, purity, transparency.

clash, *v.* SYN.-argue, collide, conflict, differ, disagree, encounter, oppose.

clasp, *v.* SYN.-cling, clutch, grasp, grip; have, hold, keep, maintain, possess, retain. ANT.-relinquish, vacate.

class, *n.* SYN.-breed, category, degree, denomination, distinction, genre, family, kind; caste, grade, order, rank, standing, set; elegance, excellence.

classify, v. SYN.-arrange, catalogue, categorize, correlate, grade, group, index, label, order, organize, rank, rate. ANT.-combine, disorganize, mix.

clean, v. SYN.-cleanse, mop, purify, scrub, sweep, wash. ANT.-dirty, pollute, soil, stain, sully.

cleanse, v. SYN.-bathe, clean, launder, mop, purify, sanitize, scald, scrub, sterilize, wash. ANT.-dirty, foul, pollute, soil, stain, sully.

clear, a. SYN.-cloudless, fair, sunny; limpid, transparent; apparent, distinct, evident, intelligible, lucid, manifest, obvious, plain, unmistakable, visible; open, unobstructed. ANT.-cloudy, foul, overcast; ambiguous, obscure, unclear, vague.

clemency, n. SYN.-charity, compassion, forgiveness, grace, leniency, mercy, mildness, pity. ANT.-cruelty, punishment, retribution, vengeance.

clerical, a. SYN.-apostolic, cleric, ecclesiastical, holy, monastic, monkish, ministerial, pontifical, priestly, sacred.

clerk, n. SYN.-assistant, bookkeeper, cashier, recorder, registrar, salesperson, stenographer, teller, timekeeper.

clever, a. SYN.-adroit, apt, dexterous, quick, quick-witted, skillful, talented, witty; bright, ingenious, sharp, smart. ANT.-awkward, bungling, clumsy, slow, unskilled; dull, foolish, stupid.

cleverness, n. SYN.-comprehension, intellect, intelligence, mind, perspicacity, reason, sagacity, sense, understanding; banter, cleverness, fun, humor, irony, pleasantry,

raillery, sarcasm, satire, wit, witticism. ANT.-commonplace, frivolity, inanity, platitude, silliness, sobriety, solemnity, stupidity.

cliché, n. SYN.-platitude, proverb, saw, saying, slogan.

client, n. SYN.-buyer, customer, patron, user.

climax, n. SYN.-acme, apex, consummation, crown, culmination, end, extremity, height, peak, pinnacle, summit, zenith. ANT.-anticlimax, base, depth, floor.

climb, v. SYN.-ascend, clamber, escalate, mount, rise, scale, soar, tower. ANT.-descend, fall, sink.

cling, v. SYN.-adhere, clasp, clutch, grab, grasp, grip, hold, keep, maintain, retain. ANT.-abandon, loose, relinquish.

clip, v. SYN.-crop, curtail, cut, prune, shorten, snip, trim.

clique, n. SYN.-clan, club, faction, group.

cloak, v. SYN.-clothe, conceal, cover, disguise, envelop, guard, hide, mask, protect, screen, shield, shroud, veil. ANT.-bare, divulge, expose, reveal, unveil.

cloister, n. SYN.-abbey, convent, hermitage, monastery, nunnery, priory.

close, a. SYN.-abutting, adjacent, adjoining, immediate, impending, near, nearby, neighboring; confidential, dear, devoted, intimate. ANT.-afar, distant, faraway, removed.

close, n. SYN.-completion, conclusion, end, finale, settlement, termination; ANT.-beginning, commencement, inception, prelude, start.

close, v. SYN.-occlude, seal, shut; clog, obstruct, stop; cease, complete, conclude, end, finish, terminate. ANT.-open, unbar, unlock; begin, commence, inaugurate, start.

clothes, *n.* SYN.-apparel, array, attire, clothing, drapery, dress, garb, garments, raiment, vestments, vesture. ANT.-nakedness, nudity.

cloudy, *a.* SYN.-dark, dim, indistinct, hazy, murky, mysterious, obscure, overcast, shadowy. ANT.-bright, clear, distinct, limpid, sunny.

clue, *n.* SYN.-evidence, hint, information, mark, sign, spoor, trace, track.

clumsy, *a.* SYN.-awkward, gauche, inept, rough, unpolished, untoward. ANT.-adroit, graceful, neat, polished, skillful.

clutch, *v.* SYN.-clasp, cling, grasp, grip; have, hold, keep, maintain, possess, retain. ANT.-relinquish, vacate.

coach, *n.* SYN.-drill, instill, instruct, prompt, teach, train, tutor.

coalition, *n.* SYN.-alliance, association, combination, confederacy, entente, federation, league, partnership, union; compact, covenant, marriage, treaty. ANT.-divorce, schism, separation.

coarse, *a.* SYN.-crude, impure, rough, rugged, unrefined; gross, gruff, immodest, indelicate, rude, unpolished, vulgar. ANT.-fine, polished, refined, smooth; cultivated, cultured, delicate.

coax, *v.* SYN.-cajole, inveigle, persuade, wheedle.

coerce, *v.* SYN.-coerce, constrain, drive, enforce, force, impel, oblige. ANT.-allure, convince, induce, persuade, prevent.

coercion, *n.* SYN.-compulsion, con-

straint, force, restraint, violence. ANT.-persuasion.

cognizant, *a.* SYN.-apprised, aware, conscious, informed, mindful, observant, perceptive, sensible. ANT.-ignorant, insensible, oblivious, unaware.

coherent, *a.* SYN.-articulate, comprehensible, consistent, logical, reasonable, sound, understandable.

coincide, *v.* SYN.-accede, acquiesce, agree, assent, comply, consent; agree, concur, conform, harmonize, match, tally. ANT.-contradict, differ, disagree, dissent, protest; casual, random.

cold, *a.* SYN.-arctic, chilly, cool, freezing, frigid, frozen, icy, wintry; apathetic, indifferent, passionless, phlegmatic, reserved, stoical, unconcerned, unfeeling. ANT.-burning, fiery, heated, hot, torrid; ardent, passionate.

collapse, *v.* SYN.-decline, decrease, deflate, diminish, drop, fall, sink, subside; implode, topple, tumble. ANT.-arise, ascend, climb, mount, soar.

colleague, *n.* SYN.-associate, attendant, collaborator, companion, comrade, consort, crony, friend, mate, partner. ANT.-adversary, enemy, stranger.

collect, *v.* SYN.-accumulate, amass, assemble, concentrate, congregate, consolidate, gather, heap, hoard, mass, pile. ANT.-assort, disperse, distribute, divide, dole.

collected, *a.* SYN.-calm, composed, cool, imperturbable, peaceful, placid, quiet, sedate, tranquil, unmoved. ANT.-agitated, aroused, excited, perturbed, violent.

collection, *n.* SYN.-aggregate,

amount, conglomeration, entirety, sum, total, whole. ANT.-element, ingredient, part, particular, unit.

collision, n. SYN.-battle, combat, conflict, duel, encounter, fight, struggle; contention, controversy, discord, inconsistency, interference, opposition, variance. ANT.-amity, concord, consonance, harmony.

collusion, n. SYN.-cabal, combination, conspiracy, intrigue, machination, plot, treachery, treason.

color, n. SYN.-complexion, dye, hue, paint, pigment, shade, stain, taint, tincture, tinge, tint. ANT.-achromatism, paleness, transparency.

colossal, a. SYN.-elephantine, enormous, gargantuan, gigantic, huge, immense, large, prodigious, vast. ANT.-diminutive, little, minute, small, tiny.

combat, n. SYN.-battle, collision, conflict, duel, encounter, fight, struggle; contention. ANT.-amity, concord, consonance, harmony.

combat, v. SYN.-battle, brawl, conflict, contend, dispute, encounter, fight, quarrel skirmish, struggle.

combination, n. SYN.-alliance, association, coalition, confederacy, entente, federation, league, partnership, union, unification; compact, covenant, marriage, treaty. ANT.-divorce, schism, separation.

combine, v. SYN.-adjoin, amalgamate, associate, attach, blend, conjoin, connect, consolidate, couple, go with, join, link, merge, unite, unify. ANT.-detach, disconnect, disjoin, separate.

comedy, n. SYN.-burlesque, farce, humor, mimicry, satire, slapstick.

comfort, n. SYN.-cheer, consolation, contentment, ease, enjoyment,

luxury, plenty, relaxation, relief, rest, restfulness, solace, succor, warmth. ANT.-affliction, discomfort, misery, suffering, torment, torture.

comfort, v. SYN.-aid, alleviate, calm, cheer, console, encourage, gladden, help, solace, soothe, support, sympathize. ANT.-antagonize, aggravate, depress, dishearten.

comfortable, a. SYN.-acceptable, agreeable, contented, gratifying, pleasing, pleasurable, relaxed, restful, soothed, untroubled; cozy, luxurious, protected, rich, roomy, satisfying, sheltered, snug, spacious, warm, wealthy. ANT.-distressing, miserable, troubled, uncomfortable, wretched; mean, poor, wanting.

comical, a. SYN.-amusing, droll, farcical, funny, humorous, laughable, ludicrous ridiculous, slapstick, witty. ANT.-melancholy, sad, serious, sober, solemn.

coming, a. SYN.-advancing, approaching, anticipated, arriving, close, due, expected, foreseen, imminent, impending, near, nearing, predicted. ANT.-departing, going, leaving.

command, n. SYN.-bidding, decree, dictate, injunction, instruction, law, mandate, order, proclamation, requirement. ANT.-consent, license, permission.

command, v. SYN.-conduct, govern, guide, manage, regulate, rule; bid, charge, direct, instruct, order, tell. ANT.-deceive, distract, misdirect, misguide.

commemorate, v. SYN.-celebrate, honor, remember, solemnize.

commence, v. SYN.-arise, begin, enter, inaugurate, initiate, institute, open, originate, start. ANT.-

close, complete, end, finish, terminate.

commencement, *n.* SYN.-beginning, birth, inception, opening, origin, origination, outset, source, start. ANT.-close, completion, consummation, end, termination.

commend, *v.* SYN.-acclaim, applaud, appreciate, approve, compliment, extol, flatter, laud, like, praise; authorize, confirm, endorse, ratify, sanction. ANT.-criticize, disparage; condemn, nullify.

commensurate, *a.* SYN.-adequate, alike, equal, equitable, equivalent, even, fair, judicious, like, proportional, same, similar, uniform. ANT-different, disparate, dissimilar, diverse.

comment, *n.* SYN.-annotation, assertion, conversation, criticism, declaration, notation, observation, remark, statement, talk, utterance.

comment, *v.* SYN.-affirm, assert, aver, criticize, interject, mention, note, observe, remark, speak.

commerce, *n.* SYN.-business, employment, engagement, enterprise, job, occupation, profession, trade, trading, vocation, work. ANT.-avocation, hobby, pastime.

commission, *v.* SYN.-appoint, authorize, charge, command, delegate, deputize, employ, empower, engage, entrust, hire, ordain, select.

commit, *v.* SYN.-do, perform, perpetrate; commend, consign, entrust, relegate, trust; bind, obligate, pledge. ANT.-fail, miscarry, neglect; mistrust, release, renounce; free, loose.

commodious, *a.* SYN.-accessible, appropriate, convenient, fitting, handy, suitable. ANT.-awkward, inconvenient, inopportune, troublesome.

common, *a.* SYN.-familiar, frequent, general, ordinary, popular, prevalent, universal, usual; low, mean, vulgar. ANT.-exceptional, extraordinary, odd, scarce; noble, refined.

commotion, *n.* SYN.-agitation, chaos, confusion, disarrangement, disarray, disorder, ferment, jumble, stir, tumult, turmoil. ANT.-certainty, order, peace, tranquility.

communicable, *a.* SYN.-catching, contagious, infectious, pestilential, virulent. ANT.-healthful, hygienic, non-communicable.

communicate, *v.* SYN.-advise, confer, contact, convey, disclose, divulge, impart, inform, notify, relate, reveal, tell, transmit. ANT.-conceal, hide, withhold.

communion, *n.* SYN.-association, fellowship, intercourse, participation, sacrament, union. ANT.-alienation, non participation.

compact, *a.* SYN.-constricted, contracted, firm, small, snug, tight; mash, tamp. ANT.-lax, loose, open, relaxed, slack.

compact, *n.* SYN.-agreement, bargain, compact, contract, covenant, pact, stipulation. ANT.-disagreement, discord, dissension, variance.

companion, *n.* SYN.-associate, attendant, colleague, comrade, consort, crony, friend, guide, mate, partner, protector. ANT.-adversary, enemy, stranger.

company, *n.* SYN.-assemblage, band, crew, group, horde, party, throng, troop; association, fellowship, society; corporation, firm. ANT.-dispersion, individual, seclusion, solitude.

comparable, *a.* SYN.-akin, alike, allied, analogous, correlative, correspondent, corresponding, equivalent, like, parallel, similar. ANT.-different, dissimilar, divergent, incongruous, opposed.

compare, *v.* SYN.-associate, connect, contrast, critique, describe, differentiate, discriminate, distinguish, equate, examine, link, match, measure, oppose, rate, relate, sample.

comparison, *n.* SYN.-analogy, association, contrast, correspondence, example, metaphor, parable, relation, resemblance.

compassion, *n.* SYN.-commiseration, concern, condolence, consideration, empathy, mercy, pity, sensitivity, sympathy, tenderness, warmth. ANT.-brutality, cruelty, hardness, inhumanity, ruthlessness.

compassionate, *a.* SYN.-affable, benevolent, benign, forbearing, forgiving, gentle, good, humane, indulgent, kind, kindly, merciful, sympathetic, tender, thoughtful. ANT.-cruel, inhuman, merciless, severe, unkind.

compatible, *a.* SYN.-accordant, agreeing, conforming, congruous, consistent, consonant, constant, correspondent. ANT.-contradictory, discrepant, incongruous, inconsistent, paradoxical.

compel, *v.* SYN.-coerce, constrain, drive, enforce, force, impel, oblige. ANT.-allure, convince, induce, persuade, prevent.

compensation, *n.* SYN.-allowance, bonus, commission, consideration, earnings, fee, indemnity, pay, payment, recompense, reimbursement, remuneration, repayment,

salary, stipend, wages. ANT.-gift, gratuity, present.

compete, *v.* SYN.-battle, clash, contest, encounter, engage, face, oppose, rival, spar, strive, struggle, vie.

competent, *a.* SYN.-able, capable, clever, efficient, fitted, qualified, skillful. ANT.-inadequate, incapable, incompetent, unfitted.

competitor, *n.* SYN.-adversary, antagonist, enemy, foe, opponent, rival. ANT.-accomplice, ally, comrade, confederate, friend, teammate.

compile, *v.* SYN.-accumulate, amass, arrange, assemble, catalogue, collect, correlate, gather, group, index, label, order, organize, rank, rate.

complacent, *a.* SYN.-contented, happy, pleased, self-satisfied, smug; accommodating, complaisant, compliant, yielding.

complain, *v.* SYN.-criticize, denounce, deplore, deprecate, disapprove, fuss, grouch, grumble, lament, murmur, object, oppose, protest, regret, remonstrate, repine, whine. ANT.-applaud, approve, praise, rejoice.

complete, *a.* SYN.-concluded, consummated, detailed, ended, entire, finished, full, perfect, thorough, total, unbroken, undivided. ANT.-imperfect, lacking, unfinished.

complete, *v.* SYN.-accomplish, achieve, close, conclude, consummate, do, end, execute, finish, fulfill, get done, perfect, perform, terminate.

complex, *a.* SYN.-complicated, compound, intricate, involved, manifold, perplexing. ANT.-plain, simple, uncompounded.

complexion, *n.* SYN.-color, coloration, hue, pigment, pigmentation, shade, texture, tone.

complicated, *a.* SYN.-complex, compound, intricate, involved, perplexing. ANT.-plain, simple, uncompounded.

compliment, *n.* SYN.-adulation, appreciation, approval, commendation, endorsement, eulogy, flattery, honor, praise, regards, respects, salute, tribute. ANT.-affront, criticism, insult, taunt.

comply, *v.* SYN.-accede, acquiesce, agree, assent, consent; coincide, concur, conform, tally. ANT.-contradict, differ, disagree, dissent, protest.

component, *n.* SYN.-division, fragment, moiety, piece, portion, scrap, section, segment, share; element, ingredient, member, organ, part. ANT.-entirety, whole.

compose, *v.* SYN.-construct, create, fashion, forge, make, mold, produce, shape; constitute, form, make up; arrange, combine, organize; devise, frame, invent. ANT.-destroy, disfigure, dismantle, misshape, wreck.

composed, *a.* SYN.-calm, collected, cool, imperturbable, peaceful, placid, quiet, sedate, self-controlled, tranquil, unmoved. ANT.-agitated, aroused, excited, perturbed, violent.

composer, *n.* SYN.-author, creator, father, inventor, maker, originator, writer.

composure, *n.* SYN.-balance, calmness, carriage, complacence, contentment, control, equanimity, equilibrium, poise, self-control, serenity, tranquility. ANT.-agitation, anger, excitement, rage, turbulence.

compound, *v.* SYN.-alloy, amalgamate blend, combine, composite, concoct,, fuse, jumble, mingle, mix. ANT.-dissociate, divide, segregate, separate, sort.

comprehend, *v.* SYN.-appreciate, apprehend, conceive, discern, grasp, know, learn, perceive, realize, see, understand. ANT.-ignore, misapprehend, mistake, misunderstand.

comprehension, *n.* SYN.-apprehension, cognizance, conception, discernment, insight, perception, understanding. ANT.-ignorance, insensibility, misapprehension, misconception.

compress, *v.* SYN.-abbreviate, abridge, compact, condense, consolidate, pack, reduce, shorten, shrink.

comprise, *v.* SYN.-contain, embody, embrace, encompass, hold, include. ANT.-discharge, emit, exclude; encourage, yield.

compulsion, *n.* SYN.-dint, energy, force, intensity, might, potency, power, strength, vigor; coercion. ANT.-feebleness, frailty, impotence, weakness; persuasion.

compute, *v.* SYN.-add, ascertain, calculate, consider, count, derive, divide, divine, estimate, figure, multiply, reckon, subtract. ANT.-conjecture, guess, miscalculate.

comrade, *n.* SYN.-associate, attendant, colleague, companion, consort, crony, friend, mate, partner. ANT.-adversary, enemy, stranger.

conceal, *v.* SYN.-cloak, cover, curtain, disguise, envelop, guard, hide, mask, protect, screen, secrete, shield, shroud, suppress, veil, withhold. ANT.-bare, disclose, divulge, expose, reveal, show, uncover, unveil.

concede, *v.* SYN.-let, permit, suffer, tolerate; authorize, give, grant, yield; acknowledge, admit, allow, ANT.-forbid, object, protest, refuse, resist.

conceit, *n.* SYN.-complacency, egotism, pride, self-esteem, vanity; caprice, conception, fancy, idea, imagination, notion, whim. ANT.-diffidence, humility, meekness, modesty.

conceited, *a.* SYN.-proud, vain, vainglorious. ANT.-effective, potent, profitable; meek, modest.

conceive, *v.* SYN.-begin, comprehend, concoct, contrive, create, design, devise, fabricate, frame, grasp, invent, understand. ANT.-copy, imitate, reproduce.

concentrated, *a.* SYN.-close, compact, compressed, crowded, dense, thick, undiluted. ANT.-dispersed, dissipated, sparse.

concept, *n.* SYN.-abstraction, conception, fancy, idea, image, impression, notion, opinion, sentiment, thought. ANT.-entity, matter, object, substance, thing.

conception, *n.* SYN.-apprehension, cogitation, cognition, comprehension, consideration, fancy, idea, imagination, impression, judgment, memory, notion, opinion, recollection, reflection, sentiment, thought, understanding, view.

concern, *n.* SYN.-affair, business, matter, transaction; anxiety, care, solicitude, worry. ANT.-apathy, indifference, negligence, unconcern.

concise, *a.* SYN.-brief, compact, condensed, compendious, curt, incisive, laconic, neat, pithy, short, succinct, summary, terse. ANT.-extended, lengthy, long, prolonged,

protracted, verbose, wordy.

conclude, *v.* SYN.-close, complete, conclusion, consummate, end, finale, finish, fulfill, get done, perfect, settlement, terminate, termination. ANT.-beginning, commencement, inception, prelude, start.

conclusion, *n.* SYN.-close, completion, end, finale, issue, settlement, termination; decision, deduction, inference, judgment. ANT.-beginning, commencement, inception, prelude, start.

conclusive, *a.* SYN.-concluding, decisive, ending, eventual, final, last, latest, terminal, ultimate. ANT.-first, inaugural, incipient, original, rudimentary.

concord, *n.* SYN.-accordance, agreement, coincidence, concurrence, harmony, understanding, unison, bargain, compact, contract, covenant, pact, stipulation. ANT.-difference, disagreement, discord, dissension, variance.

concrete, *a.* SYN.-definite, firm, positive, precise, real, solid, specific.

concur, *v.* SYN.-accede, acquiesce, agree, assent, comply, consent; coincide, conform, tally. ANT.-contradict, differ, disagree, dissent, protest.

condemn, *v.* SYN.-blame, censure, denounce, reprehend, reproach, reprobate, reprove, upbraid; convict, sentence. ANT.-approve, commend, condone, forgive, praise; absolve, acquit, exonerate, pardon.

condense, *v.* SYN.-abbreviate, abridge, compress, consolidate, compact, dehydrate, reduce, shorten, summarize.

condescend, *v.* SYN.-accommodate,

comply, concede, deign, oblige, patronize.

condition, *n.* SYN.-case, circumstance, plight, predicament, situation, state; prohibition, provision, requirement, restraint, restriction, stipulation, term.

condition, *v.* SYN.-adapt, equip, fit, furnish, get ready, make ready, modify, predispose, prepare, provide, qualify, ready.

conditional, *a.* SYN.-contingent, dependent, depending, relying, subject, subordinate. ANT.-absolute, autonomous, casual, independent, original.

condolence, *n.* SYN.-commiseration, compassion, empathy, pity, sympathy, tenderness, warmth. ANT.-antipathy, harshness, indifference, malevolence, unconcern.

condone, *v.* SYN.-accept, allow, excuse, overlook, pardon.

conduct, *n.* SYN.-action, bearing, behavior, carriage, deed, demeanor, deportment, disposition, manner.

conduct, *v.* SYN.-direct, escort, guide, lead, steer; control, manage, regulate, supervise.

confederate, *n.* SYN.-abettor, accessory, accomplice, ally, assistant, associate. ANT.-adversary, enemy, opponent, rival.

confederation, *n.* SYN.-alliance, association, coalition, combination, confederacy, entente, federation, league, partnership, union; compact, covenant, marriage, treaty. ANT.-schism, separation.

confer, *v.* SYN.-chat, converse, speak; consult, counsel, deliberate, discuss, negotiate, reason, talk.

conference, *n.* SYN.-conversation, discussion, gathering, interchange, meeting.

confess, *v.* SYN.-acknowledge, admit, allow, avow, concede, divulge, grant, own, reveal. ANT.-conceal, deny, disclaim, disown, renounce.

confession, *n.* SYN.-apology, defense, excuse, explanation, justification. ANT.-accusation, complaint, denial, dissimulation.

confidence, *n.* SYN.-assurance, assuredness, certainty, conviction, courage, firmness, security, self-reliance, surety, pledge, promise, word, assertion, declaration, statement. ANT.-bashfulness, humility, modesty, shyness, suspicion.

confine, *v.* SYN.-bound, circumscribe, enclose, encompass, envelop, fence, limit, surround. ANT.-develop, distend, enlarge, expand, expose, open.

confirm, *v.* SYN.-authenticate, corroborate, substantiate, validate, verify; acknowledge, assure, establish, settle; approve, fix, ratify, sanction; strengthen.

confirmation, *n.* SYN.-corroboration, demonstration, evidence, proof, test, testimony, trial, validation, verification. ANT.-failure, fallacy, invalidity.

confiscate, *v.* SYN.-appropriate, capture, catch, purloin, remove, steal, take; grasp, grip, seize; get, obtain; claim, demand; adopt, choose, espouse, select.

conflagration, *n.* SYN.-blaze, burning, combustion, fire, flame, heat.

conflict, *n.* SYN.-battle, collision, combat, duel, encounter, fight, struggle; contention, controversy, discord, inconsistency, interference, opposition, variance. ANT.-amity, concord, consonance, harmony.

conform, v. SYN.-acclimate, accommodate, adjust, comply, follow, obey, reconcile, suit.

confounded, a. SYN.-abashed, amazed, bewildered, confused, disconcerted, perplexed, puzzled.

confront, v. SYN.-contradict, counteract, defy, face, hinder, obstruct, oppose, resist, thwart, withstand. ANT.-agree, cooperate, submit, succumb, support.

confuse, v. SYN.-bewilder, confound, disorient, disconcert, dumfound, fluster, mislead, misinform, muddle, mystify, nonplus, obscure, perplex, puzzle. ANT.-clarify, explain, illumine, instruct, solve.

confused, a. SYN.-bewildered, chaotic, confounded, deranged, disconcerted, disordered, disorganized, indistinct, jumbled, mistaken, misunderstood, mixed, muddled, perplexed. ANT.-clear, lucid, obvious, organized, plain.

confusion, n. SYN.-agitation, chaos, commotion, disarrangement, disarray, disorder, ferment, jumble, stir, tumult, turmoil. ANT.-certainty, order, peace, tranquility.

congratulate, v. SYN.-commend, compliment, praise, salute, toast.

congruous, a. SYN.-accordant, agreeing, compatible, conforming, consistent, consonant, constant, correspondent. ANT.-contradictory, discrepant, incongruous, inconsistent, paradoxical.

conjecture, n. SYN.-hypothesis, supposition, theory. ANT.-certainty, fact, proof.

conjecture, v. SYN.-chance, guess, hazard, infer. ANT.-determine, guard, insure, know.

connect, v. SYN.-adjoin, affix, an-
nex, append, associate, attach, couple, join, link, stick, unite; assign, associate. ANT.-detach, disengage, separate, unfasten, untie.

connection, n. SYN.-affinity, alliance, association, bond, conjunction, link, relationship, tie, union. ANT.-disunion, isolation, separation.

conquer, v. SYN.-beat, crush, defeat, humble, master, overcome, quell, rout, subdue, subjugate, surmount, vanquish. ANT.-capitulate, cede, lose, retreat, surrender.

conquest, n. achievement, triumph, victory. ANT.-defeat, failure.

conscientious, a. SYN.-attentive, careful, exact, fastidious, heedful, meticulous, painstaking, prudent, scrupulous, thorough, thoughtful. ANT.-forgetful, improvident, indifferent, lax.

conscious, a. SYN.-alert, alive, apprised, aware, cognizant, discerning, informed, keen, knowing, mindful, observant, perceptive, sensible, understanding, wary. ANT.-ignorant, impassive, indifferent, insensible, oblivious, unaware, unconscious, unfeeling.

consecrate, v. SYN.-adore, dignify, enshrine, enthrone, exalt, extol, glorify, hallow, honor, revere, sanctify, venerate. ANT.-abuse, debase, degrade, dishonor, mock.

consecrated, a. SYN.-blessed, devout, divine, hallowed, holy, pious, religious, sacred, saintly, spiritual. ANT.-evil, profane, sacrilegious, secular, worldly.

consecutive, a. SYN.-chronological, connected, continuous, progressive, sequential, successive.

consensus, n. SYN.-accord, agreement, opinion.

consent, *n.* SYN.-approval, authority, authorization, leave, liberty, license, permission, permit. ANT.-denial, opposition, prohibition, refusal.

consent, *v.* SYN.-accede, acquiesce, agree, assent, comply, coincide, concur, conform, tally. ANT.-contradict, differ, disagree, dissent, protest.

consequence, *n.* SYN.-conclusion, effect, importance, outcome, result.

consequently, adv. SYN.-accordingly, hence, so, then, thence, therefore.

conservation, *n.* SYN.-conserving, guarding, keeping, maintenance, preservation, preserving, protecting, protection, safekeeping, saving.

conservative, *a.* SYN.-careful, constant, conventional, cautious, guarded, inflexible, prudent, sober, steady, traditional, unchanging, unimaginative, wary.

consider, *v.* SYN.-contemplate, deliberate, examine, heed, meditate, ponder, reflect, study, weigh; esteem, regard, respect. ANT.-ignore, neglect, overlook.

considerate, *a.* SYN.-attentive, careful, cautious, charitable, concerned, heedful, kind, provident, prudent, thoughtful; contemplative, introspective, meditative, pensive, reflective. ANT.-heedless, inconsiderate, precipitous, rash, thoughtless.

consideration, *n.* SYN.-alertness, attention, care, circumspection, heed, kindliness, mindfulness, notice, observance, watchfulness; application, contemplation, reflection, study. ANT.-disregard, indifference, negligence, omission, over-

sight.

considered, *a.* SYN.-careful, contemplated, examined, investigated, thoughtful, weighed.

consistent, *a.* SYN.-accordant, agreeing, compatible, conforming, congruous, consonant, constant, correspondent. ANT.-contradictory, discrepant, incongruous, inconsistent, paradoxical.

consolation, *n.* SYN.-comfort, contentment, ease, enjoyment, relief, solace, succor. ANT.-affliction, discomfort, misery, suffering, torment, torture.

console, *v.* SYN.-allay, assuage, cheer, comfort, encourage, solace, soothe. ANT.-annoy, distress, worry.

consolidate, *v.* SYN.-blend, join, merge, mix, solidify, strengthen, unify, unite.

consort, *n.* SYN.-associate, colleague, companion, comrade, friend, mate, partner. ANT.-adversary, enemy, stranger.

conspicuous, *a.* SYN.-clear, distinguished, eminent, illustrious, manifest, noted, noticeable, obvious, outstanding, prominent, salient, striking, visible. ANT.-common, hidden, inconspicuous, obscure.

conspiracy, *n.* SYN.-cabal, collusion, combination, intrigue, machination, plot, treachery, treason.

constant, *a.* SYN.-abiding, ceaseless, continual, enduring, faithful, fixed, immutable, invariant, permanent, perpetual, persistent, unalterable, unchanging, uninterrupted, unwavering. ANT.-fickle, mutable, vacillating, wavering.

constantly, *adv.* SYN.-always, continually, eternally, ever, evermore, forever, invariably, incessantly, perpetually, unceasingly. ANT.-fitfully, never, occasionally, rarely, sometimes.

constituent, *n.* SYN.-component, element, ingredient, part.

constrain, *v.* coerce, compel, confine, force, restrain.

constraint, *n.* SYN.-coercion, compulsion, constriction, destiny, fate, forced, requirement, requisite; awkwardness, embarrassment, shyness. ANT.-choice, freedom, option, uncertainty; confidence.

constrict, *v.* SYN.-block, check, choke, clog, contract, hamper, restrict, retard, slow, tighten.

construct, *v.* SYN.-build, erect, fabricate, form, frame, make, raise. ANT.-demolish, destroy, raze.

construe, *v.* SYN.-analyze, decipher, decode, deduce, elucidate, explain, explicate, interpret, render, solve, translate, unravel. ANT.-confuse, distort, falsify, misconstrue, misinterpret.

consult, *v.* SYN.-chat, converse, speak; comment, discourse; argue, confer, conspire, deliberate, discuss, reason, talk.

consummate, *a.* SYN.-achieve, complete, concluded, ended, entire, finished, full, perfect, thorough, total, unbroken, undivided. ANT.-imperfect, lacking, unfinished.

consummation, *n.* SYN.-acme, apex, climax, culmination, height, peak, summit, zenith. ANT.-anticlimax, base, depth, floor.

contagious, *a.* SYN.-catching, communicable, infectious, pestilential, virulent. ANT.-healthful, hygienic, non-communicable.

contain, *v.* SYN.-accommodate, comprise, embody, embrace, hold, include; repress, restrain. ANT.-discharge, emit, exclude; encourage, yield.

contaminate, *v.* SYN.-befoul, corrupt, defile, infect, poison, pollute, sully, taint. ANT.-disinfect, purify.

contaminated, *a.* SYN.-corrupted, crooked, debased, depraved, impure, profligate, putrid, spoiled, tainted, venal, vitiated.

contamination, *n.* SYN.-ailment, contamination, disease, infection, poison, pollution, taint.

contemplate, *v.* SYN.-conceive, imagine, picture, recall, recollect, remember; cogitate, deliberate, meditate, muse, ponder, reason, reflect, speculate, think; consider, deem, esteem, judge, opine, reckon, regard, suppose. ANT.-conjecture, forget, guess.

contemplative, *a.* SYN.-dreamy, introspective, meditative, pensive, reflective, thoughtful. ANT.-heedless, inconsiderate, precipitous, rash, thoughtless.

contemporary, *a.* SYN.-current, modern, new, novel, present, recent. ANT.-ancient, antiquated, bygone, old, past.

contempt, *n.* SYN.-contumely, derision, detestation, disdain, hatred, scorn. ANT.-awe, esteem, regard, respect, reverence.

contemptible, *a.* SYN.-base, despicable, low, mean, sordid, vile, vulgar; malicious, nasty, offensive, selfish. ANT.-admirable, dignified, exalted, generous, noble.

contend, *v.* SYN.-argue, battle, compete, contest, debate, dispute, fight, rival, struggle, vie; accuse, affirm, assert, aver, claim, testify.

contented, a, SYN.-blessed, cheerful, delighted, fortunate, happy, gay, glad, joyful, joyous, lucky, merry, opportune, pleased, propitious, satisfied. ANT.-blue, depressed, gloomy, morose.

contention, n. SYN.-battle, collision, conflict, duel, encounter, fight, struggle; controversy, discord, inconsistency, opposition, variance. ANT.-amity, concord, consonance, harmony.

contentment, n. SYN.-beatitude, blessedness, bliss, delight, felicity, gladness, happiness, pleasure, satisfaction, well-being. ANT.-despair, grief, misery, sadness, sorrow.

contents, n. SYN.-essence, gist, meaning, significance, substance.

contest, v. SYN.-battle, challenge, contention, debate, dispute, duel, encounter, quarrel, squabble, test, trial. ANT.-agreement, concord, decision, harmony.

contestant, n. SYN.-adversary, challenger, combatant, competitor, opponent, player, rival.

continence, n. SYN.-abstention, abstinence, fasting, forbearance, moderation, self-denial, sobriety, temperance. ANT.-excess, gluttony, greed, intoxication, self-indulgence.

contingent, a. SYN.-conditional, dependent, depending, relying, subject, subordinate. ANT.-absolute, autonomous, casual, independent, original.

continual, a. SYN.-ceaseless, constant, continuous, endless, everlasting, incessant, perennial, perpetual, unceasing, uninterrupted, unremitting. ANT.-interrupted, occasional, periodic, rare.

continue, n. SYN.-advance, extend, proceed; endure, last, remain; persevere, persist, prolong, pursue. ANT.-arrest, check, interrupt; cease, defer, halt, stop, suspend.

contract, n. SYN.-agreement, bargain, compact, covenant, pact, pledge, promise, stipulation, treaty.

contract, v. SYN.-abbreviate, abridge, condense, curtail, diminish, lessen, limit, reduce, recede, restrict, shorten, shrink, shrivel. ANT.-elongate, extend, lengthen.

contradict, v. SYN.-confront, confute, controvert, counter, dispute, gainsay, oppose. ANT.-agree, confirm, support, verify.

contradictory, a. SYN.-contrary, discrepant, illogical, incompatible, incongruous, inconsistent, irreconcilable, paradoxical, unsteady, vacillating, wavering. ANT.-compatible, congruous, consistent, correspondent.

contrary, a. SYN.-adverse, antagonistic, hostile, opposed, opposite; counteractive, disastrous, unfavorable, unlucky. ANT.-benign, favorable, fortunate, lucky, propitious.

contrast, n. SYN.-difference, distinction, divergence, diversity, incompatibility, opposition, variance, variation. ANT.-likeness, similarity, uniformity.

contrast, v. SYN.-compare, differentiate, discriminate, distinguish, oppose.

contribute, v. SYN.-bequeath, bestow, confer, dispense, donate, endow, give, grant, present, proffer, share.

contrite, a. SYN.-penitent, regretful, remorseful, repentant, sorrowful, sorry. ANT.-obdurate, remorseless.

contrition, n. SYN.-compunction, grief, penitence, qualm, regret, remorse, repentance, self-reproach, sorrow. ANT.-complacency, impenitence, obduracy, self-satisfaction.

contrive, v. SYN.-delineate, design, devise, intend, manipulate, outline, plan, plot, prepare, project, scheme.

control, *n.* SYN.-discipline, order, regulation, restraint, supervision. ANT.-chaos, confusion, turbulence.

control, *v.* SYN.-administer, check, command, direct, dominate, drive, influence, govern, manage, master, regulate, rule, superintend, supervise; bridle, check, curb, repress, restrain. ANT.-abandon, follow, forsake, ignore, submit.

controversy, *n.* SYN.-argument, contention, debate, disagreement, discord, dispute, dissonance, quarrel, squabble. ANT.-agreement, concord, decision, harmony.

convene, *v.* SYN.-assemble, congregate, convoke, gather, meet, sit.

convenient, *a.* SYN.-accessible, accommodating, adapted, advantageous, appropriate, comfortable, commodious, favorable, fitting, handy, helpful, suitable, timely. ANT.-awkward, inconvenient, inopportune, troublesome.

conventional, *a.* SYN.-accepted, accustomed, common, customary, established, familiar, normal, ordinary, prevailing, regular, standard, typical, usual. ANT.-alien, strange, unusual.

conversation, *n.* SYN.-chat, colloquy, conference, dialogue, discussion, gossip, interview, parley, talk.

converse, *v.* SYN.-blab, chat, discuss, gossip, jabber, mutter, prattle, speak, talk, tattle; confer, consult, deliberate, discuss, reason.

convert, *v.* SYN.-exchange, substitute; alter, change, modify, shift, transfigure, transform, vary. ANT.-retain; continue, establish, preserve, settle, stabilize.

convey, *v.* SYN.-bring, carry, transmit, transport; bear. ANT.-abandon, drop.

convict, *n.* SYN.-criminal, delinquent, felon, malefactor, offender, transgressor.

convict, *v.* SYN.-blame, censure, condemn, denounce, reprehend, reproach, reprobate, reprove, upbraid; condemn, sentence. ANT.-approve, commend, condone, forgive, praise; absolve, acquit, exonerate, pardon.

conviction, *n.* SYN.-belief, certitude, confidence, credence, faith, feeling, opinion, persuasion, reliance, trust. ANT.-denial, doubt, heresy, incredulity.

convince, *v.* SYN.-allure, coax, entice, exhort, incite, induce, influence, persuade, prevail upon, satisfy, urge, win over. ANT.-coerce, compel, deter, dissuade, restrain.

cool, *a.* SYN.-brisk, chilly, cold, frigid, frosty, nippy, wintry; apathetic, composed, indifferent, passionless, phlegmatic, reserved, stoical, unconcerned, unfeeling. ANT.-burning, fiery, heated, hot, torrid; ardent, passionate.

cooperation, *n.* SYN.-alliance, coalition, collaboration, concert, confederation, federation, participation.

copious, *a.* SYN.-abundant, ample, bountiful, overflowing, plenteous, plentiful, profuse, rich, teeming. ANT.-deficient, insufficient, scant, scarce.

copy, *n.* SYN.-duplicate, exemplar, facsimile, imitation, replica, reproduction, transcript. ANT.-original, prototype.

copy, *v.* SYN.-ape, counterfeit, duplicate, imitate, impersonate, mimic, mock, simulate. ANT.-alter, distort, diverge, invent.

cordial, *a.* SYN.-ardent, earnest, friendly, gracious, hearty, sincere, sociable, warm. ANT.-aloof cool, reserved, taciturn.

core, *n.* SYN.-center, heart, middle. midpoint, midst, nucleus. ANT.-border, boundary, outskirts, periphery, rim.

corporal, *a.* SYN.-bodily, carnal, corporeal, somatic; material, natural, physical. ANT.-mental, spiritual.

corporation, *n.* SYN.-company, firm. ANT.-individual.

corpse, *n.* SYN.-body, carcass, remains; form, frame, torso; corpus. ANT.-intellect, mind, soul, spirit.

correct, *a.* SYN.-accurate, exact, faultless, impeccable, precise, proper, right, strict. ANT.-erroneous, false, faulty, untrue, wrong.

correct, *v.* SYN.-aid, amend, help, improve, mend, rectify, reform, remedy, right; admonish, discipline, punish, reprimand. ANT.-aggravate, ignore, ruin, spoil; condone, indulge.

correction, *n.* SYN.-adjustment, alteration, amendment, improvement, instruction, discipline, punishment.

correlative, *a.* SYN.-akin, alike, allied, analogous, comparable, correspondent, corresponding, like, parallel, similar. ANT.-different, dissimilar, divergent, incongruous, opposed.

correlate, *v.* SYN.-associate, compare, connect, correspond, interact, relate.

correspondent, *a.* SYN.-akin, alike, allied, analogous, comparable, correlative, corresponding, like, parallel, similar. ANT.-different, dissimilar, divergent, incongruous, op-

posed.

corroborate, *v.* SYN.-attest, authenticate, confirm, prove, substantiate, validate, verify.

corrupt, *a.* SYN.-contaminated, corrupted, crooked, debased, depraved, dishonest, fraudulent, impure, profligate, putrid, spoiled, tainted, unsound, venal, vitiated.

corrupt, *v.* SYN.-abase, adulterate, alloy, contaminate, debase, defile, degrade, deprave, disgrace, dishonor, impair, infect, lower, pervert, spoil, taint, undermine, vitiate. ANT.-enhance, improve, raise, restore, vitalize.

cosmopolitan, *a.* SYN.-cultured, polished, refined, sophisticated, suave, urbane.

cost, *n.* SYN.-charge, expense, payment, price, value, worth.

council, *n.* SYN.-admonition, advice, caution, counsel, exhortation, instruction, recommendation, suggestion, warning; information, intelligence, notification.

counsel, *n.* SYN.-advice, consultation, elucidation, guidance, information, instruction, opinion; lawyer.

counsel, *v.* SYN.-advise, allude, offer, propose, recommend, refer, suggest. ANT.-declare, demand, dictate, insist.

count, *v.* SYN.-calculate, compute, consider, enumerate, estimate, figure, inventory, reckon. ANT.-conjecture, guess, miscalculate.

countenance, *n.* SYN.-appearance, aspect, bearing, demeanor, expression, look.

counterfeit, *a.* SYN.-artificial, assumed, bogus, ersatz, fake, feigned, fictitious, phony, sham, spurious, synthetic, unreal. ANT.-

genuine, natural, real, true.

courage, n. SYN.-audacity, boldness, bravery, chivalry, daring, fearlessness, fortitude, intrepidity, mettle, prowess, resolution. ANT.-cowardice, fear, pusillanimity, timidity.

courageous, a. SYN.-adventurous, audacious, bold, brave, chivalrous, daring, dauntless, fearless, gallant, heroic, intrepid, valiant, valorous. ANT.-cowardly, cringing, fearful, timid, weak.

course, n. SYN.-avenue, channel, passage, path, road, route, street, thoroughfare, track, trail, walk, way; fashion, form, habit, manner, method, mode, plan, practice, procedure, process, style, system.

courteous, a. SYN.-civil, considerate, courtly, cultivated, genteel, polite, refined, urbane, well-bred, well-mannered. ANT.-boorish, impertinent, rude, uncivil, uncouth.

courtesy, n. SYN.-affability, consideration, cordiality, courteousness, deference, friendliness, gallantry, geniality, graciousness, kindness, manners, polish, politeness, refinement, respect, tact.

covenant, n. SYN.-accordance, understanding, agreement, bargain, compact, contract, pact, stipulation. ANT.-difference, disagreement, discord, dissension, variance.

cover, v. SYN.-cloak, clothe, conceal, curtain, disguise, envelop, guard, hide, mask, protect, screen, shield, shroud, veil, wrap. ANT.-bare, divulge, expose, reveal, unveil.

covert, a. SYN.-clandestine, concealed, hidden, latent, private, secret, surreptitious, unknown. ANT.-conspicuous, disclosed, exposed, known, obvious.

covetousness, n. SYN.-avarice, de-

sire, envy, greed, jealousy. ANT.-generosity, geniality, indifference.

cowardice, n. SYN.-alarm, apprehension, consternation, dismay, dread, fear, fright, horror, panic, scare, terror, timidity, trepidation. ANT.-assurance, boldness, bravery, courage, fearlessness.

cower, v. SYN.-cringe, crouch, fear, hide, quake, run, shake, shiver, shrink, snivel, tremble.

coy, a. SYN.-bashful, demure, diffident, humble, modest, recoiling, retiring, shy, timid. ANT.-daring, gregarious, outgoing.

cozy, a. SYN.-luxurious, protected, satisfying, secure, sheltered, snug, warm.

craft, n. SYN.-ability, aptitude, competence, dexterity, faculty, skill, talent; avocation, business, career, occupation, vocation, work; airplane, boat, jet, ship.

crafty, a. SYN.-artful, astute, clandestine, covert, cunning, foxy, furtive, guileful, insidious, shrewd, sly, stealthy, subtle, surreptitious, tricky, underhanded, wily. ANT.-candid, frank, ingenuous, open, sincere.

cranky, a. SYN.-critical, cross, disagreeable, disapproving, faultfinding, fussy, grouchy, hostile, hypercritical, peevish, surly, whiny.

crass, a. SYN.-coarse, crude, harsh, rough, uncouth, unpolished, unrefined. ANT.-finished, well-prepared; cultivated, refined.

craving, n. SYN.-hunger, relish, stomach, thirst, zest; appetite, desire, inclination, liking, longing, need, passion. ANT.-disgust, distaste, renunciation, repugnance, satiety.

crazy 51 **critique**

crazy, *a.* SYN.-delirious, demented, deranged, foolish, idiotic, imbecilic, insane, mad, maniacal. ANT.-rational, reasonable, sane, sensible, sound.

create, *v.* SYN.-cause, engender, fashion, form, formulate, generate, invent, make, originate, produce; appoint, constitute, ordain. ANT.-annihilate, demolish, destroy; disband, terminate.

creation, *n.* SYN.-beginning, birth, conception, origin.

creative, *a.* SYN.-clever, fanciful, fresh, imaginative, inventive, mystical, new, novel, original, poetical, visionary. ANT.-dull, literal, prosaic, unromantic.

creature, *n.* SYN.-animal, mammal, organism, reptile.

credence, *n.* SYN.-acceptance, belief, confidence, trust.

credentials, *n.* SYN.-certification, confirmation, evidence, proof.

credibility, *n.* SYN.-belief, confidence, credence, faith, persuasion, reliance, trust

credible, *a.* SYN.-creditable, honest, honorable, noble, reliable, reputable, trusty, virtuous.

credulity, *n.* SYN.-acceptance, belief, confidence, trust.

creed, *n.* SYN.-belief, doctrine, dogma, precept, teaching, tenet. ANT.-conduct, deed, performance, practice.

creeping, *a.* SYN.-crawling, inching, faltering, hobbling, limping, skulking, slinking, sneaking.

crest, *n.* SYN.-acme, apex, head, pinnacle, summit, top. ANT.-base, bottom, foot.

crew, *n.* SYN.-assistants, cast, company, gang, group, hands, helpers, seamen, squad, team, troupe, workers.

crime, *n.* SYN.-atrocity, outrage; aggression, crime, injustice, misdeed, misdemeanor, offense, sin, transgression, trespass, vice, wrong. ANT.-gentleness, innocence, morality, right.

criminal, *n.* SYN.-bandit, convict, crook, culprit, delinquent, felon, lawbreaker, malefactor, offender, transgressor.

crippled, *a.* SYN.-defective, deformed, disabled, feeble, halt, hobbling, lame, limping, maimed, weak. ANT.-agile, athletic, robust, sound, vigorous.

crisis, *n.* SYN.-acme, conjuncture, contingency, emergency, exigency, juncture, pass, pinch, predicament, strait. ANT.-calm, equilibrium, normality, stability.

crisp, *a.* SYN.-bracing; brittle, crumbling, delicate, fragile, frail, fresh, splintery. ANT.-enduring, thick, tough, unbreakable.

criterion, *n.* SYN.-gauge, law, measure, principle, proof, rule, standard, test, touchstone. ANT.-chance, fancy, guess, supposition.

critical, *a.* SYN.-accurate, discerning, discriminating, exact, fastidious, particular; captious, carping, caviling, censorious, faultfinding, hypercritical; acute, crucial, decisive, hazardous, important, momentous. ANT.-cursory, shallow, superficial, uncritical; appreciative, approving, commendatory, encouraging; insignificant, unimportant.

criticize, *v.* SYN.-analyze, appraise, evaluate, examine, inspect, scrutinize; blame, censure, reprehend. ANT.-approve, neglect, overlook.

critique, *n.* SYN.-commentary, criticism, critique, examination, inspection, reconsideration, retrospect, retrospection, review, revision, survey, synopsis.

crony, n. SYN.-associate, attendant, colleague, companion, comrade, consort, friend, mate, partner. ANT.-adversary, enemy, stranger.

crooked, a. SYN.-corrupt, corrupted, debased, depraved, dishonest, illegal, immoral, impure, profligate, unlawful.

crop, n. SYN.-fruit, harvest, proceeds, produce, product, reaping, result, store, yield.

crop, v. SYN.-clip, cut, prune, shorten, top, trim.

cross, a. SYN.-angry, annoyed, cantankerous, churlish, complaining, critical, exasperated, fault-finding, incensed, indignant, irate, irritable, maddened, provoked. ANT.-calm, happy, pleased, satisfied.

crowd, n. SYN.-bevy, crush, horde, host, masses, mob, multitude, populace, press, rabble, swarm, throng.

crown, n. SYN.-apex, chief, crest, head, pinnacle, summit, top, zenith; coronet, diadem, tiara. ANT.-base, bottom, foot, foundation.

crucial, a. SYN.-acute, critical, decisive, hazardous, imperative, important, momentous, threatening. ANT.-insignificant, unimportant.

crude, a. SYN.-coarse, green, harsh, ill-prepared, raw, rough, unfinished, unpolished, unrefined; crass, uncouth. ANT.-finished, well-prepared; cultivated, refined.

cruel, a. SYN.-barbaric, bloodthirsty, brutal, callous, debased, degenerate, depraved, evil, ferocious, heartless, inhuman, malevolent, malignant, merciless, monstrous, remorseless, ruthless, sadistic,

savage, sinful, spiteful, tyrannical, unfeeling, unmerciful, vengeful, viscious, wicked. ANT.-benevolent, compassionate, forbearing, gentle, humane, kind, merciful.

cruelty, n. SYN.-barbarity, brutality, coercion, domination, ferocity, harshness, indifference, inhumanity, injustice, malice, oppression, persecution, rancor, ruthlessness, sadism, severity, venom, wickedness.

crumb, n. SYN.-bit, grain, iota, jot, mite, ort, particle, scrap, shred, smidgen, speck, spot. ANT.-aggregate, bulk, mass, quantity.

crumble, v. SYN.-corrode, decay, degenerate, disintegrate, rot, rust.

cry, n. SYN.-bellow, call, cheer, clamor, exclamation, holler, hullabaloo, outcry, scream, shout, shriek, whoop, yell.

cry, v. SYN.-bawl, bemoan, bewail, blubber, grieve, lament, sob, sorrow, wail, weep, whimper, whine.

cuddle, v. SYN.-caress, coddle, embrace, fondle, hug, pet, snuggle. ANT.-annoy, buffet, spurn, tease, vex.

cue, n. SYN.-alert, hint, prompt, ready, sign, signal, warning.

cull, v. SYN.-choose, elect, opt, pick, select. ANT.-refuse, reject.

culmination, n. SYN.-acme, apex, climax, completion, consummation, end, finale, finish, height, peak, summit, zenith. ANT.-anticlimax, base, depth, floor.

culprit, n. SYN.-criminal, delinquent, felon, malefactor, offender, transgressor.

cultivation, n. SYN.-agriculture, agronomy, farming, gardening, horticulture, husbandry, tillage; breeding, education, enhancement, learning, nurturing, refinement.

culture, *n.* SYN.-breeding, civilization, clan, cultivation, education, enlightenment, family, folklore, folkways, instruction, knowledge, refinement, society. ANT.-boorishness, ignorance, illiteracy, vulgarity.

cultured, *a.* SYN.-accomplished, appreciative, blasé, civilized, cultivated, cultured, educated, enlightened, erudite, experienced, informed, lettered, polished, sophisticated, understanding, urbane, worldly, worldly-wise. ANT.-crude, ingenuous, naïve, simple, uncouth.

cunning, *a.* SYN.-clever, crooked, distorted, erratic, indirect, ingenious, roundabout, skillful, swerving, tortuous, wandering, winding; circuitous, crooked, devious, tricky. ANT.-direct, straight; honest, straightforward.

cunning, *n.* SYN.-aptitude, cleverness, faculty, ingeniousness, ingenuity, inventiveness, resourcefulness, skill ANT.-clumsiness, dullness, inaptitude, stupidity.

curb, *v.* SYN.-block, bridle, check, constrain, delay, halt, hinder, hold back, impede, inhibit, limit, repress, restrain, retard, stay, stem, stop, suppress. ANT.-aid, encourage, incite, loosen.

cure, *n.* SYN.-antidote, help, medicant, prescription, remedy, restorative; relief, solution.

curiosity, *n.* SYN.-marvel, miracle, phenomenon, oddity, peculiarity, prodigy, rarity, spectacle, wonder; concern, inquisitiveness, interest, meddling, prying, regard. ANT.-familiarity, triviality.

curious, *a.* SYN.-inquiring, inquisitive, interrogative, meddling, nosy, peeping, peering, prying, questioning, searching, snoopy; odd, peculiar, queer, strange, rare, unique, unusual. ANT.-incurious, indifferent, unconcerned, uninterested; common, ordinary.

current, *a.* SYN.-contemporary, fashionable, latest, modern, new, newest, novel, present, recent. ANT.-ancient, antiquated, bygone, old, past.

curse, *n.* SYN.-anathema, ban, blasphemy, cursing, cuss, damning, denunciation, expletive, fulmination, imprecation, irreverence, oath, profanity, vulgarism; affliction, annoyance, bane, calamity, evil, misfortune, plague.

curse, *v.* SYN.-abuse, blaspheme, damn, denounce, fulminate, imprecate, insult, profane, revile; afflict, annoy, doom, plague, scourge, trouble, vex.

cursory, *a.* SYN.-abbreviated, brief, external, flimsy, frivolous, imperfect, offhand, quick, shallow, short, slight, superficial. ANT.-abstruse, complete, deep, profound, thorough.

curt, *a.* SYN.-abrupt, blunt, brief, brusque, concise, impatient, quick, rude, terse. ANT.-anticipated, courteous, expected.

curtail, *v.* SYN.-abbreviate, abridge, condense, contract, curtail, diminish, lessen, limit, reduce, restrict, shorten. ANT.-elongate, extend, lengthen.

curve, *v.* SYN.-bend, bow, crook, turn, twist, ANT.-straighten.

custodian, *n.* SYN.-attendant, caretaker, cleaner, keeper, porter, superintendent, watchman.

custody, *n.* SYN.-care, charge, guardianship, keeping, supervision, ward. ANT.-neglect, negligence.

custom, n. SYN.-characteristic, convention, fashion, formality, habit, manner, mores, observance, practice, precedent, procedure, ritual, routine, rule, style, usage, use, way, wont.

customary, a. SYN.-accustomed, characteristic, common, conventional, every-day, familiar, general, habitual, normal, ordinary, procedural, usual. ANT.-abnormal, exceptional, extraordinary, irregular, rare.

customer, n. SYN.-buyer, client, consumer, patron, user.

cut, n. SYN.-divide, furrow, gash, gouge, groove, hole, incision, mark, nick, notch, opening, separation, slash, slice, slit, wound.

cut, v. SYN.-amputate, chop, cleave, dice, dissect, gash, gouge, lop, nick, notch, prune, score, separate, shear, slash, slice, slit, snip, split, trim, wound.

cute, a. SYN.-alluring, attractive, captivating, charming, dainty, delicate, elegant, engaging, fascinating, fetching, petite, pleasing, sensitive, slender, slight, winsome.

cylindrical, a. SYN.-circular, barrel-shaped, curved, round.

cynic, n. SYN.-detractor, doubter, egoist, egotist, misanthrope, mocker, pessimist, satirist, scoffer, sneerer, unbeliever.

cynical, a. SYN.-antisocial, acerbic, caustic, derisive, hostile, misanthropic, sardonic, unbelieving, unfriendly, unsociable.

D

dainty, a. SYN.-airy, beautiful, deli-

cate, elegant, exquisite, fastidious, feeble, fragile, frail, lacy, lovely, petite, precious, pretty, sensitive, slender, slight, weak; pleasant, pleasing, savory ANT.-brutal, coarse, rude, tough, vulgar.

dam, n. SYN.-bank, barrier, dike, ditch, embankment, gate, levee, wall.

dam, v. SYN.-bar, barricade, check, choke, clog, close, confine, impede, obstruct, restrict, retard, slow, stop.

damage, n. SYN.-adversity, affliction, blemish, breakage, corruption, defacement, deterioration, detriment, erosion, evil, hardship, harm, hurt, illness, infliction, injury, mischief, misfortune, mishap, reverse, suffering, wound, wrong. ANT.-benefit, boon, favor, kindness.

damage, v. SYN.-abuse, batter, break, crack, deface, disfigure, harm, hurt, impair, injure, mar, mutilate, ruin, scratch, spoil, tarnish, wreck. ANT.-ameliorate, benefit, enhance, mend, repair.

damaging, a. SYN.-deleterious, detrimental, harmful, hurtful, injurious, mischievous. ANT.-advantageous, beneficial, helpful, profitable, salutary.

damages, n. SYN.-compensation, cost, indemnification, indemnity, payment, recompense, reimbursement, reparations, repayment, restitution, SYN.-settlement.

danger, n. SYN.-hazard, jeopardy, menace, peril, risk, threat, uncertainty. ANT.-defense, immunity, protection, safety.

dangerous, a. SYN.-alarming, critical, hazardous, insecure, menacing, perilous, precarious, risky, serious, threatening, unsafe. ANT.-

firm, protected, safe, secure.

dare, v. SYN.-attempt, brave, challenge, defy, endeavor, hazard. risk, try, undertake, venture; challenge, confront, denounce, mock, oppose, resist, scorn, threaten.

daring, a. SYN.-adventurous, bold, brave, chivalrous, courageous, enterprising, fearless, foolhardy, precipitate, rash, risqué, unconventional. ANT.-cautious, hesitating, timid.

dark, a. SYN.-black, dim, dull, indistinct, gloomy, murky, obscure, overcast, shadowy, unilluminated, vague; dusky, opaque, sable, swarthy; dismal, gloomy, mournful, somber, sorrowful; evil, sinister, sullen, wicked; hidden, mystic, occult, secret. ANT.-light; bright, clear; pleasant; lucid.

dart, v. SYN.-bolt, dash, fling, flit, fly, heave, hurtle, plunge, rush, shoot, speed, spring, spurt, thrust,

dead, a. SYN.-deceased, defunct, departed, dull, gone, inanimate, insensible, lifeless, spiritless, unconscious. ANT.-alive, animate, living, stirring.

dash, n. SYN.-alacrity, charge, dispatch, hurry, hustle, plunge, run, rush, spurt; hint, little, sprinkling, scattering, touch, trace.

dash, v. SYN.-chill, dampen, dismay, discourage; bolt, dart, fly, hurry, race, speed.

data, n. SYN.-abstracts, details, evidence, facts, figures, information, reports, results, statistics.

date, n. SYN.-day, duration, epoch, era, generation, period, spell, term, year; appointment, assignation, call, engagement, rendezvous, tryst, visit.

daze, n. SYN.-astonishment, bewil-

derment, confusion, distraction, muddle, stupor.

daze, v. SYN.-amaze, confound, confuse, dazzle, perplex, puzzle, stun, stupefy.

deafening, a. SYN.-loud, noisy, resounding, sonorous, stentorian, vociferous ANT.-dulcet, inaudible, quiet, soft, subdued.

dead, a. SYN.-anesthetized, deadened, deceased, defunct, departed, gone, inanimate, inert, lifeless, numb, perished, spent, still, tired, unconscious, wearied, worn.

deaden, v. SYN.-anesthetize, benumb, desensitize, dull, impair, numb, paralyze, repress, slow.

deadly, a. SYN.-bloodthirsty, dangerous, deathly, destructive, fatal, harmful, injurious, lethal, mortal, violent. ANT.-invigorating, stimulating, vital, wholesome.

deal, n. SYN.-affair, agreement, business, compromise, contract, negotiation, pact, pledge, proceeding, transaction, understanding.

dear, a. SYN.-beloved, cherished, esteemed, precious, valued; costly, expensive, valuable. ANT.-despised, unwanted; cheap.

death, n. SYN.-decease, demise, departure, doom, expiration, extinction, mortality, passing, rest, end. ANT.-beginning, birth, life.

debase, v. SYN.-abase, adulterate, alloy, corrupt, defile, degrade, deprave, depress, humiliate, impair, lower, pervert, vitiate. ANT.-enhance, improve, raise, restore, vitalize.

debate, v. SYN.-altercate, argue, bicker, contend, contest, differ, discuss, dispute, quarrel, oppose, question, reason, squabble, wrangle; denote, imply, indicate, prove, refute, show. ANT.-agree, allow, assent, concede, ignore, overlook, reject, spurn.

debris, n. SYN.-fragments, garbage, litter, pieces, refuse, rubbish, ruins, trash, waste, wreckage.

debt, n. SYN.-arrears, bill, deficit, indebtedness, liability, obligation, mortgage, note. ANT.-asset, capital, credit, excess, grace, trust.

decadent, a. SYN.-brutal, callous, debased, degenerate, depraved, evil, heartless, immoral, inhuman, malignant, merciless, monstrous, remorseless, ruthless, sadistic, savage, sinful, spiteful, unfeeling, unmerciful, vengeful, viscious, wicked.

decay, n. SYN.-blight, collapse, consumption, corrosion, corruption, decadence, decline, decomposition, degeneration, deterioration, disintegration, downfall, failure, putrefaction, ruin, ruination.

decay, v. SYN.-blight, decline, decompose, decrease, disintegrate, dwindle, ebb, putrefy, rot, spoil, wane, waste, wither. ANT.-flourish, grow, increase, luxuriate, rise.

deceased, a, SYN.-dead, defunct, departed, gone, lifeless. ANT.-alive, animate, living, stirring.

deceit, n. SYN.-beguilement, cheat, chicanery, cunning, deceitfulness, deception, duplicity, fraud, guile, sham, trick, wiliness. ANT.-candor, honesty, openness, sincerity, truthfulness.

deceitful, a. SYN.-deceptive, delusive, delusory, dishonest, fallacious, false, illusive, misleading, specious. ANT.-authentic, genuine, honest, real, truthful.

deceive, v. SYN.-betray, defraud, delude, dupe, ensnare, entrap, fleece, fool, hoodwink, mislead, outwit, rob, swindle, victimize,

decent, a. SYN.-adequate, becoming, befitting, comely, decorous, ethical, fit, nice, proper, respectable, seemly, suitable, tolerable, trustworthy, upright, virtuous. ANT.-coarse, gross, indecent, reprehensible, vulgar.

deception, n. SYN.-beguilement, betrayal, cheat, chicanery, craftiness, cunning, deceit, deceitfulness, dishonesty, duplicity, fraud, guile, sham, treachery, treason, trickery, wiliness. ANT.-candor, honesty, openness, sincerity, truthfulness

deceptive, a. SYN.-deceitful, delusive, delusory, fallacious, false, illusive, misleading, specious. ANT.-authentic, genuine, honest, real, truthful.

decide, v. SYN.-adjudicate, choose, close, conclude, determine, end, judge, pick, resolve, select, settle, terminate. ANT.-doubt, hesitate, suspend, vacillate, waver.

decipher, v. SYN.-clarify, construe, decode, elucidate, explain, explicate, interpret, render, solve, translate, unravel. ANT.-confuse, distort, falsify, misconstrue, misinterpret.

declaration, n. SYN.-acknowledgment, affidavit, affirmation, allegation, announcement, assertion, avowal, communication, disclosure, manifesto, notice, notification, presentation, proclamation, profession, proposition, report, resolution, statement, thesis, utterance.

declare, v. SYN.-affirm, allege, announce, assert, aver, broadcast, certify, claim, contend, disclose, express, impart, indicate, maintain, make known, notify, proclaim, profess, promulgate, pronounce, protest, state, swear, tell. ANT.-conceal, hide, repress, suppress, withhold.

decline, *v.* SYN.-incline, slant, slope; descend, sink, wane; decay, decrease, degenerate, depreciate, deteriorate, diminish, dwindle, weaken; refuse, reject. ANT.-ameliorate, appreciate, ascend, increase; accept.

decorate, *v.* SYN.-adorn, beautify, brighten, deck, embellish, enhance, enrich, garnish, ornament, renovate, trim. ANT.-debase, defame, expose, strip, uncover.

decoration, *n.* SYN.-adornment, design, embellishment, garnish, improvement, ornament, ornamentation.

decorous, *a.* SYN.-becoming, chaste, decent, modest, proper, respectable, seemly.

decrease, *v.* SYN.-abate, abbreviate, abridge, check, compress, condense, crumble, curb, curtail, cut, decay, decline, deduct, deflate, degenerate, deteriorate, diminish, dwindle, fade, lessen, lower, melt, pare, prune, reduce, remove, shorten, shrink, shrivel, sink, slacken, subside, subtract, trim, wane. ANT.-amplify, augment, enlarge, expand, grow, increase, multiply.

decree, *n.* SYN.-declaration, edict, mandate, order, proclamation, pronouncement, ruling.

dedicated, *a.* SYN.-addicted, affectionate, ardent, attached, devoted, disposed, earnest, faithful, fond, given up to, inclined, loyal, prone, true, wedded. ANT.-detached, disinclined, indisposed, untrammeled.

dedication, *n.* SYN.-affection, ardor, attachment, celebration, consecration, devotion, devoutness, fidelity, love, loyalty, piety, religiousness, zeal. ANT.-alienation, apathy, aversion, indifference, unfaithfulness.

deduct, *v.* SYN.-decrease, diminish, lessen, reduce, remove, shorten, subtract. ANT.-amplify, enlarge, expand, grow, increase.

deduction, *n.* SYN.-answer, conclusion, inference, judgment, opinion, reasoning.

deed, *n.* SYN.-accomplishment, act, action, doing, execution, feat, operation, performance, transaction; agreement, certificate, charter, document, lease, record, voucher, warranty. ANT.-cessation, deliberation, inactivity, inhibition, intention.

deep, *a.* SYN.-below, beneath, bottomless, immersed, impenetrable, submerged, subterranean; absorbing, abstract, abstruse, acute, buried, difficult, incisive, grave, penetrating, rich.

deepen, *v.* SYN.-augment, develop, expand, exacerbate, extend, grow, increase, intensify.

deface, *v.* SYN.-abuse, batter, crack, disfigure, harm, hurt, mar, mutilate, ruin, scratch, spoil, tarnish, wreck. ANT.-ameliorate, benefit, enhance, mend, repair.

defame, *v.* SYN.-abuse, asperse, disparage, ill-use, libel, malign, revile, scandalize, slander, traduce, vilify. ANT.-cherish, honor, praise, protect, respect.

default, *n.* SYN.-dereliction, failure, lapse, neglect, omission, oversight, transgression; deficiency, lack, loss, want. ANT.-achievement, success, victory; sufficiency.

defeat, *n.* SYN.-annihilation, conquest, collapse, destruction, extermination, fall, loss, overthrow, rebuff, reverse, setback, subjugation. ANT.-conquest, triumph, victory.

defeat, *v.* SYN.-annihilate, beat, conquer, crush, decimate, demolish, humble, master, overcome, overrun, overwhelm, quell, repulse, rout, smash, subdue, subjugate, surmount, thrash, trounce, vanquish. ANT.-capitulate, cede, lose, retreat, surrender.

defect, *n.* SYN.-blemish, crack, error, failure, fault, flaw, imperfection, mark, mistake, omission, scratch, shortcoming, vice. ANT.-completeness, correctness, perfection.

defend, *v.* SYN.-fortify, guard, protect, safeguard, screen, shelter, shield; assert, back, espouse, justify, plead, maintain, rationalize, uphold, vindicate. ANT.-assault, attack, deny, oppose, submit.

defense, *n.* SYN.-barricade, bastille, bastion, bulwark, citadel, dike, fence, fort, fortification, fortress, rampart, refuge, shelter, shield, stockade, stronghold, trench, wall; backing, explanation, guard, justification, precaution, preservation, protection, resistance, safeguard, security, stand.

defer, *v.* SYN.-adjourn, delay, postpone, shelve, slacken, suspend, waive; accede, comply, concede, obey, submit, yield. ANT.-advance, dispatch, expedite, further, hasten, press, stimulate, urge.

deference, *n.* SYN.-acclaim, adoration, courtesy, esteem, fame, homage, renown, respect, reverence, veneration, worship.

defiant, *a.* SYN.-audacious, bold,

brazen, cheeky, forward, impudent, insolent.

deficient, *a.* SYN.-defective, inadequate, incomplete, insufficient, lacking, scanty, short. ANT.-adequate, ample, enough, satisfactory, sufficient.

define, *v.* SYN.-bound, circumscribe, delimit, establish, fix, limit, mark, outline, set; ascertain, characterize, designate, elucidate, explain, illustrate, interpret, specify. ANT.-confuse, distort; misinform, mislead.

definite, *a.* SYN.-absolute, categorical, certain, correct, decisive, determined, exact, explicit, fixed, positive, precise, prescribed, specific, unequivocal; bold, clear, crisp, distinct, obvious, plain, sharp, unmistakable, vivid. ANT.-ambiguous, confused, dubious, equivocal, indefinite, obscure; indistinct, hazy, unclear.

deformed, *a.* SYN.-askew, contorted, crooked, crushed, damaged, disfigured, distorted, irregular, malformed, mangled, warped. ANT.-regular, shapely, well-formed.

defy, *v.* SYN.-confront, face, hinder, impede, insult, obstruct, oppose, resist, thwart, withstand. ANT.-accede, allow, cooperate, relent, yield.

degenerate, *v.* SYN.-atrophy, descend, sink, wane; decay, decline, decrease, depreciate, deteriorate, diminish, dwindle, weaken; corrupt, debase, depraved, immoral. ANT.-ameliorate, appreciate, ascend, increase; accept.

degrade, *v.* SYN.-abase, abash, adulterate, alloy, corrupt, debase, defile, deprave, depress, humble, humiliate, impair, lower, mortify, pervert, shame, vitiate. ANT.-enhance, improve, raise, restore, vitalize.

degree, n. SYN.-caliber, extent, grade, intensity, order, proportion, quality, quantity, range, scope, stage, standing, station, status, step, strength.

deign, v. SYN.-condescend, patronize, stoop, submit.

delay, v. SYN.-defer, postpone, procrastinate; arrest, detain, hinder, impede, retard, stay; dawdle, linger, loiter, tarry. ANT.-expedite, hasten, precipitate, quicken.

delectable, a. SYN.-delicious, delightful, luscious, palatable, savory, sweet, tasty. ANT.-acrid, distasteful, nauseous, unpalatable, unsavory.

delegate, n. SYN.-agent, alternate, appointee, deputy, emissary, legate, minister, proxy, representative.

delegate, v. SYN.-appoint, assign, authorize, choose, commission, deputize, elect, empower, name, nominate, ordain, select.

deliberate, a. SYN.-calculated, conscious, considered, contemplated, designed, intended, intentional, meant, planned, premeditated, purposeful, studied, voluntary, willful. ANT.-accidental, fortuitous.

deliberate, v. SYN.-consider, contemplate, examine, heed, meditate, ponder, reflect, study, weigh. ANT.-ignore, neglect, overlook.

delicacy, n. SYN.-airiness, daintiness, flimsiness, lightness, smoothness, subtlety, tenderness, transparency; luxury, rarity, tidbit.

delicate, a. SYN.-dainty, elegant, exquisite, fastidious, feeble, frail, sensitive, slender, slight, weak; pleasant, pleasing, savory ANT.-

brutal, coarse, rude, tough, vulgar.

delicious, a. SYN.-appetizing, dainty, delectable, delightful, luscious, palatable, rich, savory, sweet, tasty, tempting. ANT.-acrid, distasteful, nauseous, unpalatable, unsavory.

delight, n. SYN.-bliss, ecstasy, enjoyment, gladness, happiness, joy, pleasure, rapture, transport. ANT.-annoyance, dejection, melancholy, misery, sorrow.

delighted, a. SYN.-amused, blessed, cheerful, contented, fascinated, fortunate, happy, gay, glad, joyful, joyous, merry, pleased, satisfied. ANT.-blue, depressed, gloomy, morose.

delineate, v. SYN.-circumscribe, define, demarcate, depict, draw, outline, restrict.

deliver, v. SYN.-commit, give, impart, transfer, yield; announce, communicate, impart, proclaim,. publish; emancipate, free, liberate, release, rescue, save. ANT.-confine, withhold; capture, imprison, restrict.

delusion, n. SYN.-deception, dream, fallacy, fancy, fantasy, hallucination, illusion, mirage, phantom, vision. ANT.-actuality, reality, substance.

demand, v. SYN.-charge, command, direct, order; ask, ask for, challenge, claim, exact, require; inquire, necessitate. ANT.-give, offer, present, tender.

demented, a. SYN.-bemused, crazy, deranged, distracted, insane, mad, maniacal, psychotic, troubled, unbalanced, unsound.

demolish, v. SYN.-annihilate, destroy, devastate, eradicate, exterminate, extinguish, obliterate, ravage, raze, ruin, wreck. ANT.-construct, establish, make, preserve, save.

demonstrate, *v.* SYN.-confirm, display, establish, evince, exhibit, explain, illustrate, manifest, present, prove, show, teach; march, parade, picket, protest. ANT.-conceal, hide.

denial, *n.* SYN.-disapproval, disavowal, disclaimer, dismissal, dissent, negation, rejection, repudiation.

denounce, *v.* SYN.-accuse, blame, castigate, censure, charge, condemn, implicate, incriminate, indict, prosecute, rebuke, reprehend, reprimand, reproach, reprobate, reprove, revile, scold, upbraid. ANT.-approve, commend, condone, forgive, praise.

dense, *a.* SYN.-close, compact, compressed, concentrated, crowded, solid, thick; dull, obtuse, slow, stupid. ANT.-dispersed, dissipated, sparse; clever, quick.

deny, *v.* SYN.-contradict, contravene, controvert, disagree, gainsay, refute; abjure, disallow, disavow, disown, forbid, refuse, repudiate, withhold. ANT.-affirm, assert, concede, confirm.

depart, *v.* SYN.-abandon, desert, exit, flee, forsake, give up, go, leave, quit, retire, withdraw. ANT.-abide, arrive, enter, remain, stay, tarry.

departure, *n.* SYN.-departing, embarkation, evacuation, exit, exodus, getaway, going, leaving, parting, starting. ANT.-arrival, landing.

dependable, *a.* SYN.-certain, reliable, safe, secure, sure, tried, trustworthy, trusty. ANT.-dubious, fallible, questionable, uncertain, unreliable.

dependent, *a.* SYN.-conditional, contingent, depending, relying, subject, subordinate. ANT.-absolute, autonomous, casual, independent, original.

depict, *v.* SYN.-characterize, describe, draw, explain, narrate, paint, picture, portray, recount, relate, represent, sketch. ANT.-caricature, misrepresent, suggest.

depleted, *a.* SYN.-consumed, destroyed, dissipated, emptied, exhausted, spent, squandered, wasted.

deposit, *v.* SYN.-accumulate, bank, entrust, hoard, invest, keep, save, secure, store. ANT.-pay, spend, withdraw.

depraved, *a.* SYN.-base, corrupted, crooked, debased, dishonest, fraudulent, impure, low, mean, profligate, putrid, spoiled, tainted, unsound, venal.

depreciate, *v.* SYN.-cheapen, decay, decline, decrease, degenerate, denigrate, descend, deteriorate, devalue, diminish, discredit, disparage, downgrade, dwindle, lessen, sink, wane; weaken, refuse, reject. ANT.-accept, ameliorate, appreciate, approve, ascend, exalt, extol, increase, magnify, praise, raise, recommend.

depress, *v.* SYN.-dampen, darken, degrade, discourage, dishearten, dismay, dull, mock, mortify, sadden; lower, reduce, squash.

depression, *n.* SYN.-blues, dejection, despair, desperation, despondency, discouragement, doldrums, gloom, hopelessness, melancholy, misery, oppression, pessimism, sorrow, trouble, unhappiness, worry. ANT.-confidence, elation, hope, optimism.

deputy, *n.* SYN.-aide, agent, alternate, appointee, assistant, delegate, emissary, legate, lieutenant, minister, proxy, representative.

derision, *n.* SYN.-banter, disdain, gibe, irony, jeering, mockery, raillery, ridicule, sarcasm, satire, scorn, sneering.

derivation, *n.* SYN.-beginning, birth, commencement, cradle, foundation, inception, origin, root, source, spring, start. ANT.-end, harvest, issue, outcome, product.

descend, *v.* SYN.-decline, degenerate, dip, drop, plunge, settle, sink, slip, tumble, wane. ANT.-ascend, increase.

describe, *v.* SYN.-characterize, depict, explain, narrate, portray, recount, relate.

describe, *v.* SYN.-characterize, depict, elucidate, illuminate, illustrate, narrate, picture, portray, relate, summarize.

description, *n.* SYN.-account, characterization, chronicle, depiction, detail, history, narration, narrative, portrayal, recital, relation, report. ANT.-caricature, confusion, distortion, misrepresentation.

desert, *v.* SYN.-abandon, defect, forsake, leave, quit. ANT.-defend, maintain, uphold; stay, support.

deserter, *n.* SYN.-betrayer, defector, delinquent, fugitive, runaway, traitor, truant.

desertion, *n.* SYN.-abandonment, defection, departure, escape, flight, renunciation, treason.

design, *n.* SYN.-blueprint, concept, delineation, diagram, draft, drawing, outline, pattern, plan, sketch, treatment; artfulness, contrivance, cunning, plotting, scheming; intent, intention, objective, purpose.

ANT.-result; candor, sincerity; accident, chance.

design, *v.* SYN.-contrive, create, devise, invent, plan, scheme; intend, mean, purpose; draw, outline, sketch.

designate, *v.* SYN.-appoint, choose, denote, disclose, indicate, intimate, manifest, reveal, select, show, signify, specify, verify. ANT.-conceal, distract, divert, falsify, mislead.

desire, *n.* SYN.-ambition, appetite, aspiration, attraction, craving, hungering, inclination, longing, lust, propensity, urge, wish, yearning, yen. ANT.-abomination, aversion, distaste, hate, loathing.

desire, *v.* SYN.-choose, covet, crave, long for, want, wish; ask, seek, solicit.

desist, *v.* SYN.-abstain, arrest, bar, cease, check, close, cork, discontinue, end, halt, hinder, impede, interrupt, obstruct, plug, seal, stop, terminate. ANT.-begin, proceed, promote, speed, start.

desolate, *a.* SYN.-abandoned, bare, bleak, deserted, forlorn, forsaken, lonely, solitary, uninhabited, waste, wild. ANT.-attended, cultivated, fertile.

despair, *n.* SYN.-depression, desperation, despondency, discouragement, gloom, hopelessness, pessimism ANT.-confidence, elation, hope, optimism.

desperate, *a.* SYN.-audacious, daring, despairing, despondent, determined, hopeless, reckless, wild. ANT.-assured, composed, confident, hopeful, optimistic.

desperation, *n.* SYN.-anxiety, depression, despair, despondency, discouragement, distress, gloom, hopelessness, pessimism. ANT.-

confidence, elation, hope, optimism.

despicable, a. SYN.-base, contemptible, low, malicious, mean, miserable, nasty, offensive, selfish, sordid, vile, vulgar, worthless, wretched. ANT.-admirable, dignified, exalted, generous, noble.

despise, v. SYN.-abhor, abominate, detest, dislike, hate, loathe. ANT.-admire, approve, cherish, like, love.

despondent, a. SYN.-dejected, depressed, disconsolate, dismal, dispirited, doleful, gloomy, glum, grave, melancholy, moody, pensive, sad, somber, sorrowful. ANT.-buOyant, cheerful, happy, joyous, lively, merry, mirthful, sparkling, spirited.

despotic, a. SYN.-absolute, arbitrary, authoritative, brutal, cruel, odious, oppressive, repressive, severe, tyrannical. ANT.-accountable, conditional, contingent, dependent, qualified.

destined, a. SYN.-compelled, fated, foreordained, forthcoming, inevitable, inexorable, predetermined,

destiny, n. SYN.-consequence, doom, fortune, lot, portion; fate, issue, necessity, outcome, result.

destitute, a. SYN.-impecunious, indigent, needy, penniless, poor, poverty-stricken; scanty, shabby. ANT.-affluent, opulent, rich, wealthy.

destroy, v. SYN.-annihilate, demolish, devastate, eradicate, exterminate, extinguish, liquidate, obliterate, ravage, raze, ruin, wreck. ANT.-construct, establish, make, preserve, save.

destroyed, a. SYN.-broken, crushed, eradicated, flattened, fractured, re-

duced, rent, ruptured, shattered, smashed, wrecked. ANT.-integral, repaired, united, whole.

destructive, a. SYN.-baneful, deadly, deleterious, detrimental, devastating, fatal, injurious, noxious, pernicious, ruinous. ANT.-beneficial, constructive, creative, profitable, salutary.

detail, n. SYN.-article, aspect, circumstance, item, minutia, part, particular, trait; detachment, force, party, squad, team, unit. ANT.-generality, haziness, vagueness.

detail, v. SYN.-analyze, catalogue, enumerate, itemize, narrate, recapitulate, recite, recount, relate, report, summarize.

detain, v. SYN.-arrest, delay, hinder, hold, impede, inhibit, keep, restrain, retard, stay. ANT.-expedite, hasten, precipitate, quicken.

detect, v SYN.-ascertain, devise, discover, expose, find, find out, invent, learn, originate, reveal. ANT.-cover, hide, lose, mask, screen.

detention, n. SYN.-apprehension, arrest, bonds, custody, confinement, constraint, imprisonment, incarceration, restraint, seizure.

determinant, n. SYN.-agent, cause, incentive, inducement, motive, origin, principle, reason, source. ANT.-consequence, effect, end, result.

determination, n. SYN.-conviction, courage, decision, firmness, fortitude, obstinacy, perseverance, persistence, resolution, resolve, steadfastness, tenacity, will. ANT.-inconstancy, indecision, vacillation.

determine, v SYN.-conclude, decide, end, fix, resolve, settle; ascertain, learn, verify; incline, induce, influence; condition, define, limit; compel, necessitate.

detest, *v.* SYN.-abhor, abominate, despise, dislike, hate, loathe. ANT.-admire, approve, cherish, like, love.

detestable, *a.* SYN.-abominable, disgusting, execrable, foul, hateful, loathsome, odious, revolting, vile. ANT.-agreeable, commendable, delightful, pleasant.

detriment, *n.* SYN.-damage, evil, harm, hurt, ill, infliction, injury, mischief, misfortune, mishap, wrong. ANT.-benefit, boon, favor, kindness.

detrimental, *a.* SYN.-damaging, deleterious, harmful, hurtful, injurious, mischievous. ANT.-advantageous, beneficial, helpful, profitable, salutary.

develop, *v* SYN.-advance, amplify, create, cultivate, elaborate, enlarge, evolve, expand, extend, mature, perfect, promote, unfold. ANT.-compress, contract, restrict, stunt, wither.

development, *n.* SYN.-elaboration, expansion, unfolding, unraveling; evolution, growth, maturing, progress. ANT.-abbreviation, compression, curtailment.

deviate, *v.* SYN.-bend, crook, deflect, digress, diverge, divert, sidetrack, stray, wander. ANT.-continue, follow, persist, preserve, remain.

device, *n.* SYN.-apparatus, appliance, channel, contraption, contrivance, instrument, means, medium, tool, utensil, vehicle; artifice, craft, design, plan, plot, scheme, trick, wile. ANT.-hindrance, impediment, obstruction, preventive.

devious, *a.* SYN.-circuitous, crooked, distorted, erratic, indirect, roundabout, swerving, tortuous, wandering, winding; crooked, cunning,

foxy, insidious, shrewd, tricky. ANT.-direct, straight; honest, straightforward.

devoted, *a.* SYN.-addicted, affectionate, ardent, attached, constant, dedicated, disposed, dutiful, earnest, faithful, fond, given up to, inclined, loyal, prone, true, wedded. ANT.-detached, disinclined, indisposed, untrammeled.

devotion, *n.* SYN.-affection, ardor, attachment, consecration, dedication, devoutness, fidelity, love, loyalty, piety, religiousness, zeal. ANT.-alienation, apathy, aversion, indifference, unfaithfulness.

devout, *a.* SYN.-devoted, godly, holy, pietistic, pious, religious, reverent, sanctimonious, spiritual, theological. ANT.-atheistic, impious, profane, secular, skeptical.

dexterity, *n.* SYN.-ability, adroitness, aptitude, aptness, capability, capacity, cleverness, deftness, facility, efficiency, faculty, power, qualification, skill, skillfulness, talent. ANT.-awkwardness, clumsiness, disability, inability, incapacity, incompetence, ineptitude, unreadiness.

dialect, *n.* SYN.-cant, diction, idiom, jargon, lingo, language, phraseology, slang, speech, tongue, vernacular. ANT.-babble, drivel, gibberish, nonsense.

dialogue, *n.* SYN.-chat, colloquy, conference, conversation, exchange, interview, meeting, negotiation, parley, remarks, talk, tête-à-tête.

dictator, *n.* SYN.-autocrat, despot, leader, lord, master, mogul, oppressor, overlord, persecutor, taskmaster, totalitarian, tyrant.

diction, *n.* SYN.-articulation, eloquence, enunciation, fluency, language, locution, style, vocabulary.

die, *v.* SYN.-cease, decay, decease, decline, depart, expire, fade, languish, perish, sink, succumb, wane, wither. ANT.-begin, flourish, grow, live, survive.

differ, *v.* SYN.-alter, change, conflict, contrast, deviate, diverge, diversify, modify, qualify, vary; argue, contradict, disagree, dispute, dissent, object, oppose, quarrel.

difference, *n.* SYN.-disparity, dissimilarity, distinction, divergence, separation, variety, variance; disagreement, discord, dissension, estrangement. ANT.-identity, resemblance, similarity; agreement, harmony.

different, *a.* SYN.-contrary, dissimilar, distinct, divergent, diverse, incongruous, opposite, unlike, variant; divers, miscellaneous, sundry, various. ANT.-alike, congruous, identical, same, similar.

differentiate, *v.* SYN.-descry, detect, discern, discriminate, distinguish, observe, perceive, recognize, see, separate. ANT.-confound, confuse, mingle, omit, overlook.

difficult, *a.* SYN.-arduous, challenging, complicated, demanding, formidable, hard, intricate, involved, laborious, obscure, perplexing, strenuous, thorny, toilsome, troublesome, trying. ANT.-easy, effortless, facile, simple.

difficulty, *n.* SYN.-adversity, annoyance, complication, crisis, distress, embarrassment, frustration, hardship, hindrance, impasse, impediment, irritation, knot, misfortune, obstacle, obstruction, predicament, scrape, setback, snag, struggle, trouble.

dig, *v.* SYN.-burrow, delve, dredge, excavate, exhume, mine, scoop, shovel, uncover, undermine, unearth.

dignified, *a.* SYN.-aristocratic, august, courtly, distinguished, elegant, formal, noble, proud, regal, reserved, solemn, somber, stately, sublime. ANT.-base, crass, rude, undignified.

dignity, *n.* SYN.-air, bearing, culture, elegance, nobility, pride, quality, refinement, restraint, stateliness, style.

digress, *v.* SYN.-deviate, diverge, divert, shift, sidetrack, stray, wander. ANT.-continue, follow, persist, preserve, remain.

dilate, *v.* SYN.-amplify, augment, broaden, distend, enlarge, expand, increase, magnify, widen. ANT.-abridge, contract, diminish, restrict, shrink.

dilemma, *n.* SYN.-complication, difficulty, fix, impasse, predicament, plight, scrape, situation, strait. ANT.-calmness, comfort, ease, satisfaction.

diligent, *a.* SYN.-active, alert, assiduous, busy, careful, earnest, hard-working, industrious, patient, persevering, quick. ANT.-apathetic, careless, indifferent, lethargic, unconcerned.

dim, *a.* SYN.-faded, faint, indistinct, pale, shadowy; feeble, languid, wearied; irresolute, weak. ANT.-conspicuous, glaring; strong, vigorous; forceful.

diminish, *v.* SYN.-abate, assuage, curtail, decline, decrease, dwindle, lessen, lower, moderate, reduce, shorten, suppress, wane. ANT.-amplify, enlarge, expand, grow, increase, intensify, revive.

din, *n.* SYN.-babel, clamor, cry, noise, outcry, racket, row, sound, tumult, uproar. ANT.-hush, quiet, silence, stillness.

dip, *v.* SYN.-bathe, baptize, douse, duck, dunk, lower, plunge, steep, submerge; ladle, scoop, spoon; decline, incline, recede, sink, slant, slide, slope, tilt.

diplomacy, *n.* SYN.-adroitness, dexterity, discretion, finesse, knack, poise, polish, refinement, savoir faire, skill, subtlety, tact. ANT.-awkwardness, blunder, incompetence, rancor, rudeness, sarcasm, vulgarity.

diplomatic, *a.* SYN.-adroit, discreet, discriminating, judicious, politic, tactful. ANT.-boorish, churlish, coarse, gruff, rude.

dire, *a.* SYN.-appalling, calamitous, catastrophic, deadly, dreadful, frightful, ghastly, grim, grisly, gruesome, hideous, horrible, terrible, threatening.

direct, *a.* SYN.-straight, undeviating, unswerving; erect, unbent, upright; fair, honest, honorable, just, square. ANT.-circuitous, winding; bent, crooked; dishonest.

direct, *v.* SYN.-aim, level, point, train; advise, conduct, govern, guide, influence, manage, oversee, regulate, rule, show; bid, command, inform, instruct, order. ANT.-deceive, distract, misdirect, misguide.

direction, *n.* SYN.-bearing, course, inclination, tendency, trend, way; administration, management, superintendence; guidance, instruction, order.

dirty, *a.* SYN.-filthy, foul, grimy, muddy, soiled, squalid; indecent, nasty, obscene; base, contempt-ible, despicable, low, mean, pitiful, shabby. ANT.-clean, neat, presentable; pure, wholesome.

disabled, *a.* SYN.-crippled, defective, deformed, feeble, halt, hobbling, lame, limping, maimed, unconvincing, unsatisfactory, weak. ANT.-agile, athletic, robust, sound, vigorous.

disagreement, *n.* SYN.-altercation, argument, bickering, challenge, conflict, contention, controversy, difference, discord, dispute, dissent, dissentience, feud, objection, protest, quarrel, spat, squabble, variance, wrangle. ANT.-acceptance, agreement, assent, compliance, harmony, peace, reconciliation.

disappear, *v.* SYN.-depart, desert, disintegrate, dissipate, dissolve, escape, evaporate, fade, flee, vanish.

disappoint, *v.* SYN.-anger, annoy, disillusion, dismay, displease, dissatisfy, fail, frustrate, mislead, nettle, offend, vex.

disappointed, *a.* SYN.-annoyed, despondent, discontented, disillusioned, dissatisfied, disturbed, irritated, unsatisfied.

disappointing, *a.* SYN.-discouraging, inadequate, ineffective, inferior, insufficient, failing, lame, mediocre, ordinary, second-rate, uninteresting, unsatisfactory.

disapprove, *v.* SYN.-condemn, criticize, denounce, disparage, object, oppose, resist.

disaster, *n.* SYN.-accident, adversity, calamity, casualty, catastrophe, defeat, emergency, failure, misadventure, mishap, ruin, setback, tragedy. ANT.-advantage, fortune, welfare.

disavow, *v.* SYN.-abandon, forego,

forsake, quit, relinquish, resign;
deny, disclaim, disown, reject, renounce, retract, revoke. ANT.-de-
fend, maintain, uphold; acknowledge, assert, recognize.
discard, v. SYN.-abandon, discharge,
dismiss, eject, expel, reject, renounce, repudiate.
discern, v. SYN.-descry, detect, determine, differentiate, discriminate,
distinguish, observe, perceive,
recognize, see, separate. ANT.-con-
found, confuse, mingle, omit, overlook.
discerning, a. SYN.-accurate, critical, discriminating, exact, fastidious, particular, perceptive. ANT.-
cursory, shallow, superficial, uncritical.
discernment, n. SYN.-acumen, cultivation, discrimination, insight, intuition, judgment, penetration, perception, perspicuity, refinement,
taste. ANT.-obtuseness.
discharge, v. SYN.-banish, belch,
discard, dismiss, eject, emanate,
emit, exile, expel, fire, liberate,
oust, release, remove, send off,
shed, shoot, spurt, terminate, vent.
ANT.-accept, detain, recall, retain.
disciple, n. SYN.-adherent, believer,
devotee, follower, supporter, votary; learner, pupil, scholar, student.
discipline, n. SYN.-control, limitation, order, regulation, restraint,
self-control; cultivation, exercise,
instruction, practice, training; correction, chastisement, punishment.
ANT.-chaos, confusion, turbulence.
disclaim, v. SYN.-abandon, forego,
forsake, quit, relinquish, resign;
deny, disavow, disown, reject, renounce, retract, revoke. ANT.-de-
fend, maintain, uphold; acknowl-

edge, assert, recognize.
disclose, v. SYN.-betray, communicate, confess, divulge, expose,
identify, impart, mention, reveal,
show, testify, uncover, unveil. ANT.-
cloak, conceal, cover, disguise,
hide, mask, obscure, secrete, withhold.
disconsolate, a. SYN.-cheerless, dejected, depressed, despondent, dismal, distressed, doleful, downcast,
forlorn, gloomy, heartbroken, lugubrious, melancholy, mournful, sad,
somber, sorrowful. ANT.-cheerful,
content, ecstatic, glad, happy, joyous, merry, spirited.
discontinue, v. SYN.-adjourn, interrupt, postpone, stay, suspend.
ANT.-continue, maintain, persist,
proceed, prolong.
discourage, v. SYN.-abash, appall,
chill, dampen, daunt, demoralize,
deter, dishearten, dissuade, dull,
forbid, hinder, inhibit, prevent, repress, warn. ANT.-advance, advocate, bolster, embolden, encourage,
nourish.
discourteous, a. SYN.-blunt, boorish, gruff, impolite, impudent,
insolent, rough, rude, saucy, surly,
uncivil, vulgar; coarse, crude, ignorant, rough, savage, unpolished,
fierce, harsh, inclement, tumultuous, violent. ANT.-civil, genteel,
polished; courtly, dignified, noble,
stately; calm, mild, peaceful.
discover, v. SYN.-ascertain, catch,
create, detect, determine, devise,
discern, expose, find, find out,
glimpse, identify, invent, learn, observe, originate, perceive, recognize, reveal, uncover, unearth.
ANT.-cover, hide, lose, mask,
screen.
discreet, a. SYN.-cautious, circum-

spect, considerate, diplomatic, discerning, discriminating, guarded, judicious, politic, prudent, reserved, sensible, strategic, tactful, wary, watchful. ANT.-boorish, churlish, coarse, gruff, rude.

discrepant, *a.* SYN.-contradictory, contrary, illogical, incompatible, incongruous, inconsistent, irreconcilable, paradoxical. ANT.-compatible, congruous, consistent, correspondent.

discretion, *n.* SYN.-calculation, care, caution, concern, consideration, deliberation, diplomacy, discrimination, foresight, forethought, heed, prudence, responsibility, tact.

discriminate, *v.* SYN.-differentiate, distinguish, favor, incline, know, notice, segregate, separate. ANT.-group, mingle, overlook, unite.

discriminating, a, SYN.-accurate, aesthetic, artistic, critical, cultered, discerning, exact, fastidious, particular, polished, refined. ANT.-cursory, indiscriminate, shallow, superficial, uncritical, uninformed, unselective.

discrimination, *n.* SYN.-discernment, intelligence, judgment, perception, perspicacity, sagacity, taste, understanding, wisdom; bigotry, isolation, persecution. ANT.-arbitrariness, senselessness, stupidity, thoughtlessness.

discuss, *v.* SYN.-chat, converse, speak, tattle; argue, comment, contest, declaim, debate, discourse, dispute; confer, consult, deliberate, explain, reason, talk.

discussion, *n.* SYN.-chat, conference, consultation, conversation, debate, dialogue, discourse, exchange, gossip, lecture, report, symposium,

talk. ANT.-correspondence, meditation, silence, writing.

disdain, *n.* SYN.-contempt, contumely, derision, detestation, hatred, scorn. ANT.-awe, esteem, regard, respect, reverence.

disease, *n.* SYN.-ailment, complaint, disorder, illness, infirmity, malady, sickness. ANT.-health, healthiness, soundness, vigor.

diseased, *a.* SYN.-ill, indisposed, infirm, morbid, sick, unhealthy, unwell. ANT.-healthy, robust, sound, strong, well.

disgrace, *n.* SYN.-abashment, chagrin, humiliation, mortification; dishonor, disrepute, ignominy, odium, opprobrium, scandal, shame. ANT.-dignity, glory, honor, praise, renown.

disgraceful, *a.* SYN.-discreditable, dishonorable, disreputable, ignominious, scandalous, shameful. ANT. teemed, honorable, renowned, respectable.

disguise, *n.* SYN.-affectation, cloak, deception, garb, mask, pretense, pretension, pretext, semblance, simulation, subterfuge. ANT.-actuality, fact, reality, sincerity, truth.

disguise, *v.* SYN.-cloak, conceal, cover, hide, mask, screen, secrete, suppress, veil, withhold. ANT.-disclose, divulge, expose, reveal, show, uncover.

dishonest, *a.* SYN.-corrupt, corrupted, crooked, crafty, cunning, debased, deceitful, deceiving, deceptive, depraved, fraudulent, immoral, lying, profligate, treacherous, underhanded.

dishonor, *n.* SYN.-humiliation, mortification; disgrace, disrepute, ignominy, odium, opprobrium, scandal, shame. ANT.-dignity, glory, honor, praise, renown.

disintegrate, v. SYN.-decay, decompose, decrease, diffuse, dispell, disseminate, dissipate, dwindle, putrefy, rot, spoil, waste. ANT.-flourish, grow, increase, luxuriate.

dislike, n. SYN.-abhorrence, animosity, antipathy, aversion, detestation, disgust, dislike, disinclination, distaste, dread, enmity, hatred, hostility, loathing, malevolence, rancor, repugnance, repulsion, reluctance. ANT.-affection, attachment, attraction, devotion, enthusiasm, friendship, love.

dislike, v. SYN.-abhor, abominate, deplore, despise, detest, disapprove, hate, loathe, revulse. ANT.-admire, approve, cherish, like, love.

disloyal, a. SYN.-apostate, faithless, false, inconstant, perfidious, recreant, traitorous, treacherous, treasonable. ANT.-constant, devoted, loyal, true.

dismal, a. SYN.-bleak, cheerless, dark, depressing, discouraging, doleful, dreary, dull, funereal, gloomy, lonesome, melancholy, sad, somber. ANT.-cheerful, gay, joyous, lively.

dismiss, v. SYN.-banish, discard, discharge, eject, exile, expel, fire, oust, reject, release, remove, send off, terminate. ANT.-accept, detain, recall, retain.

disobedient, a. SYN. defiant, forward, insubordinate, rebellious, refractory, undutiful, unruly. ANT.-compliant, dutiful, obedient, submissive.

disobey, v. SYN.-balk, decline, defy, differ, disagree, disregard, ignore, rebel, refuse, resist, revolt, transgress, violate. ANT.-follow, fulfill,

obey.

disorder, n. SYN.-agitation, anarchy, chaos, commotion, confusion, disarrangement, disarray, disorganization, ferment, jumble, muddle, stir, tumult, turmoil. ANT.-certainty, order, organization, peace, system, tranquility.

disorganization, n. SYN.-anarchy, chaos, confusion, disorder, jumble, muddle. ANT.-order, organization, system.

disorganized, a. SYN.-bewildered, confused, deranged, disconcerted, disordered, indistinct, mixed, muddled, perplexed. ANT.-clear, lucid, obvious, organized, plain.

disparage, v. SYN.-belittle, decry, defame, depreciate, derogate, discredit, disparage, libel, lower, malign, minimize, slander, undervalue, vility. ANT.-aggrandize, commend, exalt, magnify, praise.

dispatch, v. SYN.-cast, discharge, dispatch, emit, impel, propel, send, throw, transmit. ANT.-bring, get, hold, receive, retain.

dispel, v. SYN.-diffuse, disperse, disseminate, dissipate, scatter, separate. ANT.-accumulate, amass, assemble, collect, gather.

dispense, v. SYN.-allot, apportion, deal, distribute, divide, mete; allocate, appropriate, assign, give, grant, measure. ANT.-confiscate, keep, refuse, retain, withhold.

disperse, v. SYN.-diffuse, dispel, disseminate, dissipate, scatter, separate. ANT.-accumulate, amass, assemble, collect, gather.

displace, v. SYN.-dislodge, move, remove, shift, transfer, transport; discharge, dismiss, eject, oust, vacate. ANT.-leave, remain, stay; retain.

display, v. SYN.-arrange, demonstrate, disclose, exhibit, expose, flaunt, open, parade, present, reveal, show, spread out, uncover, unveil. ANT.-cloak, conceal, cover, disguise, hide, secrete, withhold.

disposition, n. SYN.-action, bearing, behavior, bent, bias, carriage, conduct, demeanor, deportment, inclination, leaning, manner, partiality, penchant, predilection, predisposition, prejudice, proclivity, proneness, propensity, slant, tendency, turn. ANT.-equity, fairness, impartiality, justice.

dispute, n. SYN.-altercation, argument, conflict, contention, controversy, debate, disagreement, discussion, misunderstanding, quarrel, squabble. ANT.-agreement, concord, decision, harmony.

dispute, v. SYN.-altercate, argue, bicker, contend, contest, debate, disagree, discuss, quarrel, squabble, wrangle. ANT.-agree, allow, assent, concede.

disregard, v. SYN.-disdain, disobey, ignore, neglect, omit, overlook, scorn, skip, slight, snub. ANT.-include, notice, regard.

disreputable, a. SYN.-discreditable, disgraceful, dishonorable, ignominious, scandalous, shameful. ANT. teemed, honorable, renowned, respectable.

dissent, n. SYN.-challenge, difference, disagreement, dissentience, noncompliance, nonconformity, objection, protest, rejection, remonstrance, variance. ANT.-acceptance, agreement, assent, compliance.

dissimilar, a. SYN.-different, distinct, divergent, diverse, incongruous, opposite, unlike, variant; divers, miscellaneous, sundry, vari-

ous. ANT.-alike, congruous, identical, same, similar.

dissipate, v. SYN.-despoil, destroy, devastate, strip; consume, corrode, dispel, lavish, misuse, scatter, spend, squander, waste, wear out; decay, diminish, dwindle, pine, conserve, wither. ANT.-accumulate, concentrte, conserve, economize, integrate, preserve, save, unite.

distant, a. SYN.-far, faraway, remote, removed; aloof, cold, reserved, stiff, unfriendly. ANT.-close, near, nigh; cordial, friendly.

distinct, a. SYN.-apparent, clear, evident, intelligible, lucid, manifest, obvious, plain, unmistakable, visible; open, unobstructed. ANT.-ambiguous, obscure, unclear, vague.

distinction, n. SYN.-attribute, characteristic, feature, peculiarity, property, quality, trait; eminence, fame, honor, luster, notability, reputation. ANT.-being, essence, nature, substance; disgrace, disrepute, obscurity.

distinctive, v. SYN. eccentric, exceptional, extraordinary, odd, rare, singular, strange, striking, unusual; characteristic, individual, particular, peculiar, special, unique. ANT.-common, general, normal, ordinary.

distinguish, v. SYN.-descry, detect, differentiate, discern, discriminate, observe, perceive, recognize, see, separate. ANT.-confound, confuse, mingle, omit, overlook.

distinguished, a. SYN.-branded, characterized, conspicuous, differentiated, distinct, identified, marked, separate, unique; elevated, eminent, famed, famous, glorious, illustrious, noted, notori-

ous, outstanding, prominent, renowned, singular. ANT.-common,
obscure, ordinary, unimportant,
unknown.

distort, v. SYN.-alter, deceive, embellish, falsify, fib, lie, misconstrue, misinterpret, mislead, pervert, prevaricate, rig; bend, buckle,
contort, crush, deform, twist, warp,
wrench.

distress, n. SYN.-adversity, affliction,
agony, anguish, anxiety, depriva-
tion, destitution, discomfort. grief,
indigence, misery, pain, poverty,
sorrow, suffering, torment, torture,
tribulation, worry. ANT.-comfort,
joy, relief, solace.

distribute, v. SYN.-allot, apportion,
bestow, deal, dispense, disperse,
divide, dole, issue, mete, scatter,
share, spread; arrange, catalogue,
categorize, classify, group, sort.
ANT.-accmmulate, amass, conserve,
hoard, keep, safeguard, save;
blend, combine, consolidate, unify,
unite.

district, n. SYN.-area, community,
division, domain, neighborhood,
place, province, quarter, region,
section, territory.

distrust, n. SYN.-ambiguity, doubt,
hesitation, incredulity, scruple,
skepticism, suspense, suspicion,
unbelief, uncertainty. ANT.-belief,
certainty, conviction, determination. faith.

disturb, v. SYN.-agitate, alarm, annoy, confuse, decompose, derange,
interrupt, perplex, perturb, rattle,
rouse, trouble, unsettle, vex, worry.
ANT.-order, pacify, quiet, settle,
soothe.

disturbance, n. SYN.-agitation,
bother, clamor, disruption, erup-
tion, racket, riot, stir, turbulence,

turmoil, uproar.

disturbing, a. SYN.-alarming, annoying, bothersome, disquieting, distressing, foreboding, frightening,
ominous, perturbing, startling,
threatening, troublesome, trying,
upsetting.

diverse, a. SYN.-different, dissimilar,
divergent, incongruous, opposite,
unlike, variant; assorted, divers,
miscellaneous, sundry, various.
ANT.-alike, congruous, identical,
same, similar.

diversity, n. SYN.-assortment,
change, difference, dissimilarity,
heterogeneity, medley, miscellany,
mixture, multifariousness, variety,
variousness. ANT.-homogeneity,
likeness, monotony, sameness,
uniformity.

divert, v. SYN.-avert, deflect, deviate,
swerve, turn; alter, change, redi-
rect, transmute. ANT.-arrest, fix,
stand, stop; continue, proceed; endure, perpetuate.

divide, v. SYN.-carve, chop, cleave,
cut, detach, part, rend, separate,
sever, splinter, split, sunder, tear;
allocate, allot, apportion, deal out,
dispense, distribute, share. ANT.-
combine, convene, gather, join
unite.

divine, a. SYN.-celestial, godlike,
hallowed, heavenly, holy, sacred,
superhuman, supernatural, transcendent. ANT.-blasphemous, diabolical, mundane, profane, wicked.

divulge, v. SYN.-betray, disclose, expose, impart, inform, reveal, show,
uncover. ANT.-cloak, conceal, cover,
hide, obscure.

do, v. SYN.-accomplish, achieve, act,
create, complete, conclude, consummate, effect, execute, finish,
fulfill, perform, settle, terminate;

carry on, conduct, discharge, labor, transact, work; observe, perform, practice; make, produce, work; answer, serve, suffice.

docile, *a.* SYN.-adaptable, compliant, obedient, pliant, submissive, tame, teachable, tractable, yielding. ANT.-mulish, obstinate, stubborn, ungovernable, unruly.

doctrinaire, *a.* SYN.-opinionated, overbearing, positive; authoritative, theoretical, visionary. ANT.-fluctuating, indecisive, open-minded, questioning, skeptical.

doctrine, *n.* SYN.-belief, concept, convention, creed, dogma, precept, principle, teaching, tenet, tradition. ANT.-conduct, deed, performance, practice.

document, *n.* SYN.-account, archive, chronicle, letter, memorandum, minutes, note, paper, permit, record, report, register; testimonial, trace, verification, vestige.

dogma, *n.* SYN.-creed, doctrine, precept, tenet. ANT.-conduct, deed, performance, practice.

dogmatic, *a.* SYN.-arbitrary, arrogant, authoritarian, bigoted, confident, determined, dictatorial, doctrinaire, domineering, emphatic, fanatical, intolerant, magisterial, narrow-minded, obstinate, opinionated, overbearing, positive; authoritative, doctrinal, formal. ANT.-fluctuating, indecisive, open-minded, questioning, skeptical.

dole, *v.* SYN.-allot, apportion, deal, dispense, distribute, divide, measure, mete, parcel, scatter, share, spread.

doleful, *a.* SYN.-bleak, cheerless, dark, dismal, dreary, dull, funereal, gloomy, lonesome, melancholy, sad, somber. ANT.-cheerful,

gay, joyous, lively.

domain, *n.* SYN.-country, district, division, dominion, land, place, province, quarter, region, section, territory.

dominate, *v.* SYN.-command, control, dictate, direct, domineer, govern, influence, manage, regulate, rule, subjugate, superintend, tyrannize. ANT.-abandon, follow, forsake, ignore, submit.

domination, *n.* SYN.-ascendancy, control, mastery, predominance, rule, sovereignty, supremacy, sway, transcendence. ANT.-inferiority.

donation, *n.* SYN.-appropriation, benefaction, bequest, boon, charity, endowment, favor, gift, grant, gratuity, largess, offering, present, subsidy. ANT.-deprivation, earnings, loss, purchase.

done, *a.* SYN.-accomplished, completed, executed, over, perfected, performed, realized, through, settled. ANT.-failed, incomplete, unfinished.

donor, *n.* SYN.-benefactor, contributor, giver, patron, sponsor, subscriber.

doomed, *a.* SYN.-condemned, cursed, fated, foreordained, predestined, sentenced.

dormant, *a.* SYN.-idle, inactive indolent, inert, lazy, quiescent, quiet, slothful, still, unemployed, unoccupied. ANT.-active, employed, industrious, occupied, working.

doubt, *n.* SYN.-ambiguity, apprehension, disbelief, distrust, hesitation, incredulity, misgiving, mistrust, scruple, skepticism, suspense, suspicion, unbelief, uncertainty. ANT.-belief, certainty, conviction, determination, faith.

doubt, v. SYN.-hesitate, question, uncertain, waver; distrust, mistrust, puzzled, suspect, wonder. ANT.-believe, confide, decide, rely on, trust.

dour, a. SYN.-crabby, fretful, gloomy, glum, moody, morose, sulky, surly. ANT.-amiable, gay, joyous, merry, pleasant.

drab, a. SYN.-colorless, dingy, dreary, dull, homely, monotonous, plain.

draw, v. SYN.-drag, haul, pull, tow, tug; extract, remove, take out, unsheathe; allure, attract, entice, induce, lure, persuade; delineate, depict, sketch, trace; compose, draft, formulate, write; deduce, derive, get, infer, obtain; extend, lengthen, prolong, protract, stretch. ANT.-alienate, contract, drive, propel, shorten.

drawing, n. SYN.-cartoon, engraving, etching, illustration, image, likeness, picture, portrait, portrayal, rendering, representation, resemblance, scene, schematic, sketch, view.

dread, n. SYN.-alarm, apprehension, awe, fear, foreboding, horror, reverence, terror. ANT.-assurance, boldness, confidence, courage.

dreadful, a. SYN.-appalling, awful, dire, fearful, frightening, frightful, ghastly, hideous, horrible, horrid, repulsive, terrible. ANT.-beautiful, enchanting, enjoyable, fascinating, lovely.

dream, n. SYN.-apparition, hallucination, idea, image, nightmare, trance.

dream, v. SYN.-conceive, conjure, fancy, hallucinate, idealize, imagine, picture, visualize.

dreary, a. SYN.-bleak, cheerless, dark, dismal, doleful, dull, funereal, gloomy, lonesome, melancholy, sad, somber. ANT.-cheerful, gay, joyous, lively.

dress, n. SYN.-apparel, array, attire, clothes, clothing, drapery, ensemble, garb, garments, habit, raiment, trappings, vestments, vesture. ANT.-nakedness, nudity.

drift, n. SYN.-bent, bias, digression, inclination, leaning, tendency, tenor, trend.

drill, n. SYN.-activity, application, conditioning, employment, exercise, exertion, lesson, operation, performance, practice, preparation, repetition, task, training, use. ANT.-idleness, indolence, relaxation, repose, rest.

drive, v. SYN.-coerce, compel, constrain, encourage, enforce, force, hasten, impel, incite, induce, instigate, oblige, press, stimulate, urge. ANT.-allure, convince, persuade, prevent.

droll, a. SYN.-amusing, comical, farcical, funny, humorous, laughable, ludicrous ridiculous, witty; curious, odd, queer. ANT.-melancholy, sad, serious, sober, solemn.

drop, v. SYN.-collapse, decline, decrease, descend, diminish, fall, sink, subside; stumble, topple, tumble; droop, extend downward, hang. ANT.-arise, ascend, climb, mount, soar; steady.

drunk, a. SYN.-drunken, high, inebriated, intoxicated, tight, tipsy. ANT.-clearheaded, sober, temperate.

dry, a. SYN.-arid, dehydrated, desiccated, drained, parched, thirsty; barren, dull, insipid, plain, tedious, tiresome, uninteresting, vapid. ANT.-damp, moist; fresh, interesting, lively.

dull, *a.* SYN.-dense, obtuse, retarded, slow, stupid; blunt, blunted, toothless, unsharpened; commonplace, dingy, dismal, drab, dreary, gloomy, insipid, plain, sad, sober, somber; banal, boring, common, dry, flat, hackneyed, heavy, monotonous, ordinary, pointless, prosaic, repetitious, routine, senseless, tedious, tiresome, trite, uninspiring, uninteresting, vapid. ANT.-animated, lively, sharp; clear, interesting.

dumb, *a.* SYN.-brainless, crass, dense, dull, foolish, inarticulate, obtuse, senseless, stupid, witless. ANT.-alert, bright, clever, discerning, intelligent.

dunk, *v..* SYN.-dip, douse, immerse, plunge, sink, submerge.

duplicate, *n.* SYN.-carbon, copy, exemplar, facsimile, imitation, likeness, replica, reproduction, transcript. ANT.-original, prototype.

duplicate, *v.* SYN.-copy, counterfeit, iterate, recapitulate, reiterate, repeat, replicate, reproduce.

durability, *n.* SYN.-endurance, fortitude, intensity, might, potency, power, stamina, stoutness, strength, sturdiness, toughness. ANT.-feebleness, frailty, infirmity, weakness.

durable, *a.* SYN.-abiding, changeless, constant, enduring, fixed, indestructible, lasting, permanent, stable, strong, unchangeable. ANT.-ephemeral, temporary, transient, transitory, unstable.

duration, *n.* SYN.-continuance, interval, length, limit, period, season, span, term, time.

duty, *n.* SYN.-accountability, burden, charge, compulsion, contract, obligation, responsibility; assessment, custom, exaction, excise, impost, levy, rate, revenue, tax, toll, tribute. ANT.-choice, exemption, freedom; gift, remuneration, reward, wages.

dwelling, *n.* SYN.-abode, apartment, domicile, flat, habitat, hearth, home, house, hovel, manor, mansion, quarters, residence, seat.

dying, *a.* SYN.-expiring, fading, failing, going, perishing, sinking.

dynamic, *a.* SYN.-active, changing, charismatic, compelling, effective, energetic, forceful, influential, live, potent, productive, progressive, vigorous, vital, vivid.

E

each, *a.* SYN.-all, any, individual, particular, specific; apiece, every, individually, proportionately, respectively, singly.

eager, *a.* SYN.-anxious, ardent, avid, enthusiastic, fervent, hot, impassioned, impatient, keen, yearning. ANT.-apathetic, indifferent, unconcerned, uninterested.

eagerly, *a.* SYN.-actively, anxiously, earnestly, fervently, gladly, heartily, intently, willingly, zealously.

early, *a.* SYN.-ahead, beforehand, preceding, premature, prompt, punctual, quick, speedy, unexpected. ANT.-belated, late, over-due, tardy.

earn, *v.* SYN.-achieve, acquire, attain, derive, deserve, gain, get, merit, obtain, realize, win. ANT.-consume, forfeit, lose, spend, waste.

earned, *a.* SYN.-deserved, merited, proper, suitable. ANT.-improper, undeserved, unmerited.

earnest, *a.* SYN.-candid, frank,

genuine, heartfelt, honest, open, sincere, straightforward, true, truthful, unfeigned, upright. ANT.-affected, dishonest, hypocritical, insincere, untruthful.

earth, n. SYN.-continent, country, domain, field, island, land, plain, region, tract; earth, orb, planet, sphere; dirt, ground, humus, loam, soil.

ease, v. SYN.-allay, alleviate, assuage, calm, comfort, facilitate, lighten, mitigate, pacify, peace, rest, relieve, soften, soothe, unburden. ANT.-confound, distress, disturb, trouble, worry.

easily, a. SYN.-efficiently, effortlessly, freely, readily, simply, smoothly; doubtless, unquestionably.

easy, a. SYN.-facile, light, manageable, paltry, pleasant, relaxed, simple, slight, uncomplicated. ANT.-arduous, demanding, difficult, hard.

eat, v. SYN.-bite, chew, consume, devour, dine, gorge, nibble, swallow; corrode, decay, rust, squander, waste.

ebb, n. SYN.-abatement, decline, decrease, lessening, reduction, regression, shrinkage, wane.

ebb, v. SYN.-abate, decline, decrease, recede, retreat, subside, wane.

eccentric, a. SYN.-bizarre, curious, distinctive, odd, peculiar, quaint, queer, singular, strange, unique, unusual. ANT.-common, familiar, normal, regular, typical.

economical, a. SYN.-careful, close, frugal, mean, miserly, niggardly, provident, prudent, saving, sparing, thrifty; cheap, inexpensive, moderate, reasonable. ANT.-extravagant, improvident, lavish, prod-

igal, wasteful; expensive, overpriced.

economize, v. SYN.-conserve, husband, manage, pinch, save, scrimp, skimp, stint.

ecstasy, n. SYN.-delight, exaltation, gladness, rapture, transport; frenzy, madness, trance. ANT.-depression, melancholy.

edge, n. SYN.-border, boundary, brim, brink, extremity, hem, margin, periphery, rim, verge; intensity, keenness, sharpness, sting. ANT.-center, interior; bluntness, dullness.

edgy, a. SYN.-cross, grouchy, irritable, nervous, peevish, touchy. ANT.-calm, serene.

edict, n. SYN.-act, decree, demand, law, ordinance, statute.

edit, v. SYN.-alter, arrange, compile, correct, polish, rearrange, revise, rewrite, select; condense, cut, delete, trim; distribute, issue, publish, regulate.

editorial, n. SYN.-article, column, essay, feature; opinion, viewpoint.

educate, v. SYN.-discipline, inculcate, inform, instill, instruct, school, train, teach, tutor. ANT.-misguide, misinform.

educated, a. SYN.-accomplished, civilized, cultured, enlightened, informed, instructed, intelligent, lettered, literate, polished, prepared, scholarly, taught, trained.

education, n. SYN.-cultivation, development, instruction, knowledge, learning, schooling, study, training, tutoring.

effect, n. SYN.-aftermath, consequence, outcome, results.

effect, v. SYN.-accomplish, achieve, attain, cause, complete, consummate, do, execute, finish, fulfill,

perfect, perform. ANT.-block, defeat,
fail, frustrate, spoil.

effective, a. SYN.-capable, competent, efficient, potent, practical,
productive, serviceable, telling,
useful.

effects, n. SYN.-assets, belongings,
estate, holdings, possessions,
property.

efficiency, n. SYN.-ability, capability, competency, effectiveness, efficacy, potency, skillfulness, ANT.-in-
ability, ineptitude, wastefulness.

efficient, a. SYN.-adept, capable,
competent, dynamic, effective, ef-
fectual, efficacious, expedient,
practiced, productive, proficient,
skillful, streamlined. ANT.-incompe-
tent, ineffectual, inefficient, unskilled.

effort, n. SYN.-attempt, endeavor,
essay, exertion, trial; labor, pains,
strain, strife, struggle, toil, trouble,
undertaking.

effortless, a. SYN.-easy, offhand,
simple, smooth, unconstrained.

effrontery, n. SYN.-assurance,
audacity, boldness, impertinence,
impudence, insolence, presumption, rudeness, sauciness. ANT.-dif-
fidence, politeness, subserviency,
truckling.

egotism, n. SYN.-arrogance, conceit,
overconfidence, pride, self-confidence, self-esteem, vanity. ANT.-
diffidence, humility, meekness,
modesty.

egotistic, a. SYN.-arrogant, boastful,
conceited, overbearing, pretentious, proud, self-centered, selfish,
self-satisfied, vain.

elaborate, a. SYN.-decorated, elegant, embellished, flashy, gaudy,
luxurious, showy; complex, complicated, extensive, intricate.

elaborate, n. SYN.-comment, develop, embellish, explain, expound,
particularize.

elastic, a. SYN.-compliant, flexible,
lithe, pliable, pliant, resilient,
supple, tractable. ANT.-brittle,
hard, rigid, stiff, unbending.

elder, n. SYN.-ancestor, counselor,
dignitary, patriarch, senior, superior, veteran.

elderly, a. SYN.-aged, declining, old,
patriarchal, venerable

elect, v. SYN.-choose, name, opt,
pick, select. ANT.-refuse, reject.

elegance, n. SYN.-beauty, charm,
comeliness, courtliness, culture,
fairness, grace, handsomeness,
loveliness, polish, politeness, pulchritude, splendor, sophistication.
ANT.-deformity, disfigurement, eyesore, homeliness, ugliness.

elegant, a. SYN.-beauteous, beautiful, charming, comely, fair, fine,
handsome, lovely, ornate, pretty.
ANT.-foul, hideous, homely, repulsive, unsightly.

elementary, a. SYN.-basic, fundamental, introductory, primary, rudimentary, simple. ANT.-abstract,
abstruse, complex, elaborate, intricate.

elevate, v. SYN.-exalt, heighten,
hoist, lift, raise, uplift; promote.
ANT.-abase, depreciate, depress,
destroy, lower.

elevated, a. SYN.-high, lofty, tall,
towering; eminent, exalted, proud.
ANT.-small, stunted, tiny; base, low,
mean.

eligible, a. SYN.-acceptable, authorized, available, fit, qualified, satisfactory, suitable, suited. ANT.-ineli-
gible, unfit, unsuitable.

eliminate, v. SYN.-abolish, discard,
dislodge, disqualify, eject, eradi-

cate, erase, exclude, expel, exterminate, extirpate, oust, remove. ANT.-accept, admit, include, involve.

elongate, v. SYN.-distend, distort, expand, extend, lengthen, protract, spread, strain, stretch. ANT.-contract, loosen, shrink, slacken, tighten.

elite, n. SYN.-aristocracy, chosen, nobility, privileged, royalty, selected, society, wealthy.

eloquence, n. SYN.-appeal, articulation, delivery, diction, expressiveness, fluency, poise, power, wit.

elude, v. SYN.-abscond, avert, avoid, dodge, escape, eschew, evade, flee, forbear, forestall, free, shun, ward. ANT.-confront, encounter, face, meet, oppose.

emanate, v. SYN.-belch, breathe, discharge, eject, emit, expel, exude, hurl, radiate, shed, shoot, spurt, vent.

emancipate, v. SYN.-deliver, discharge, free, let go, liberate, release, set free. ANT.-confine, imprison, oppress, restrict, subjugate.

embargo, n. SYN.-ban, injunction, penalty, prohibition, punishment, restriction, sanction.

embarrass, v. SYN.-abash, chagrin, discomfit, distress, entangle, fluster, hamper, hinder, mortify, perplex, rattle, shame, trouble. ANT.-cheer, encourage, help, relieve.

embarrassing, a. SYN.-annoying, awkward, delicate, distressing, flustering, inauspicious, mortifying, shameful, touchy, uncomfortable, unpleasant.

embarrassment, n. SYN.-abashment, chagrin, clumsiness, confusion, discomfiture, distress, humiliation,

mortification, unease; indebtedness, poverty. ANT.-composure, self-confidence.

embellish, v. SYN.-adorn, beautify, deck, decorate, enhance, enrich, garnish, ornament, trim. ANT.-debase, defame, expose, strip, uncover.

embezzle, v. SYN.-forge, misappropriate, pilfer, steal.

emblem, n. SYN.-badge, crest, design, flag, image, insignia, mark, seal, sign, symbol.

embody, v. SYN.-accommodate, combine, comprise, contain, embrace, hold, include, incorporate, integrate, unitize. ANT.-discharge, emit, exclude.

embrace, v. SYN.-clasp, hug; accept, adopt, espouse, receive, welcome; comprehend, comprise, contain, embody, include, incorporate, subsume. ANT.-reject, renounce, repudiate, scorn, spurn.

emerge, v. SYN.-appear, arise, arrive, emanate, issue. ANT.-be, exist; disappear, vanish, withdraw.

emergency, n. SYN.-contingency, crisis, exigency, jam, juncture, pass, pinch, predicament, scrape, strait, urgency.

emigrant, n. SYN.-alien, colonist, émigré, exile, expatriot, foreigner, migrant, refugee.

emigration, n. SYN.-crossing, departure, displacement, exodus, expatriation, flight, journey, migration, shift, trek, voyage, wandering.

eminent, a. SYN.-celebrated, conspicuous, distinguished, elevated, famous, glorious, illustrious, noted, prominent, renowned. ANT.-common, obscure, ordinary, unimportant, unknown.

emissary, n. SYN.-agent, ambassador, consul, delegate, deputy, envoy, intermediary, proxy, representative.

emit, v. SYN.-belch, breathe, discharge, eject, emanate, erupt, expel, hurl, ooze, shed, shoot, spew, spurt, squirt, vent.

emotion, n. SYN.-affection, agitation, feeling, passion, perturbation, sentiment, trepidation, turmoil. ANT.-calm, dispassion, indifference, restraint, tranquility.

emotional, a. SYN.-demonstrative, excitable, fervent, hysterical, highstrung, impetuous, irrational, maudlin, neurotic, overwrought, passionate, sensitive, sentimental, temperamental. ANT.- calm, rational, tranquil, unruffled.

empathy, n. SYN.-feeling, insight, pity, understanding.

emphasize, v. SYN.-accent, accentuate, articulate, dramatize, highlight, stress, underscore.

emphatic, a. SYN.-definitive, dogmatic, earnest, energetic, forceful, pointed, positive, powerful, stressed, strong.

employ, v. SYN.-adopt, apply, avail, busy, devote, engage, manipulate, occupy, operate, use, utilize. ANT.-banish, discard, discharge, reject.

employed, a. SYN.-active, busy, engaged, hired, laboring, occupied, operating, performing, used, utilized, working.

employee, n. SYN.-agent, assistant, flunky, hireling, laborer, lackey, servant, worker.

employer, n. SYN.-boss, business, company, corporation, executive, manager, owner, proprietor; operator, user.

employment, n. SYN.-business, engagement, function, occupation,

service, vocation, work. ANT.-idleness, leisure, slothfulness.

empty, a. SYN.-bare, barren, devoid, hollow, senseless, unfilled, unfurnished, unoccupied, vacant, vacuous, vain, void, worthless. ANT.-full, inhabited, occupied, replete, supplied.

empty, v. SYN.-deplete, drain, dump, evacuate, exhaust, leak, pour, spill.

enact, v. SYN.-constitute, decree, institute, legislate, ordain, order, pass, ratify.

enchant, v. SYN.-allure, bewitch, captivate, charm, enrapture, enthrall, entice, entrance, fascinate.

enclose, v. SYN.-bound, circumscribe, confine, encompass, envelop, fence, limit, surround. ANT.-develop, distend, enlarge, expand, expose, open.

encounter, n. SYN.-battle, collision, combat, conflict, duel, fight, meeting, struggle. ANT.-amity, concord, consonance, harmony.

encounter, v. SYN.-collide, confront, engage, greet, intersect, meet. ANT.-cleave, disperse, part, scatter, separate.

encourage, v. SYN.-animate, cheer, countenance, embolden, exhilarate, favor, foster, hearten, impel, incite, promote, sanction, stimulate, support, urge. ANT.-reject, deter, discourage, dispirit, dissuade.

encouraged, a. SYN.-cheered, confident, enlivened, enthusiastic, heartened, inspired, revived, roused.

encouragement, n. SYN.-assistance, backing, comfort, help, reassurance, support.

encroach, v. SYN.-infringe, intrude, invade, penetrate, trespass, violate.

ANT.-abandon, evacuate, relinquish, vacate.

end, n. SYN.-aim, cessation, close, completion, conclusion, culmination, expiration, extremity, finish, fulfillment, intention, object, purpose, realization, result, termination, terminus, tip. ANT.-beginning, commencement, inception, introduction.

end, v. SYN.-close, complete, conclude, consummate, execute, finish, fulfill, get done, perfect, terminate.

endanger, v. SYN.-expose, hazard, imperil, jeopardize, peril; risk. ANT.-insure, protect, secure.

endeavor, n. SYN.-attempt, effort, enterprise, exertion, trial; labor, strain, strife, struggle, toil.

endless, a. SYN.-boundless, eternal, illimitable, immeasurable, immense, incalculable, infinite, interminable, unbounded, unlimited, vast. ANT.-bounded, circumscribed, confined, finite, limited.

endorse, v. SYN.-affirm, approve, praise, recommend, sanction, sign, support, underwrite.

endorsement, n. SYN.-approbation, approval, assent, commendation, consent, praise, sanction, support. ANT.-censure, reprimand, reproach, stricture.

endow, v. SYN.-bequeath, bestow, contribute, donate, give, grant, subsidize.

endurance, n. SYN.-forbearance, fortitude, long-suffering, patience, perseverance, resignation, tolerance. ANT.-impatience, nervousness, restlessness, unquiet.

endure, v. SYN.-bear, brook, experience, suffer, sustain, tolerate, undergo; abide, continue, last, persist, remain, survive. ANT.-fail, falter, succumb; disperse, wane.

enduring, a. SYN.-abiding, ceaseless, constant, continual, durable, eternal, faithful, firm, fixed, immutable, invariant, lasting, permanent, perpetual, persistent, stable, steadfast, unalterable, unchanging, unwavering. ANT.-changeable, fickle, irresolute, mutable, vacillating, wavering.

enemy, n. SYN.-adversary, antagonist, competitor, foe, opponent, rival. ANT.-accomplice, ally, comrade, confederate, friend.

energetic, a. SYN.-active, animated, blithe, brisk, frolicsome, lively, spirited, sprightly, supple, vigorous, vivacious. ANT.-dull, insipid, listless, stale, vapid.

enforce, v. SYN.-administer, compel, demand, dictate, impel, oblige, require.

energy, n. SYN.-dint, force, might, potency, power, strength, vigor. ANT.-feebleness, frailty, impotence, weakness; persuasion.

engage, v. SYN.-commission, contract, employ, hire, retain, secure; absorb, bewitch, captivate, charm, engross, fascinate.

engaged, a. SYN.-absorbed, busy, employed, occupied, working.

engender, n. SYN.-cause, create, fashion, form, formulate, generate, invent, make, originate, produce. ANT.-annihilate, demolish, destroy; disband, terminate.

engross, v. SYN.-assimilate, consume, engulf, swallow up; absorb, engage, occupy. ANT.-discharge, dispense, emit, expel, exude.

enhance, v. SYN.-amplify, embellish, heighten, improve, increase, inflate, magnify.

enigma, *n.* SYN.-ambiguity, conundrum, mystery, problem, puzzle, riddle. ANT.-answer, clue, key, resolution, solution.

enjoyment, *n.* SYN.-amusement, comfort, delight, ecstasy, entertainment, gladness, gratification, happiness, joy, pleasure, rapture, satisfaction. ANT.-affliction, annoyance, dejection, melancholy, misery, pain, sorrow, suffering, trouble, vexation.

enlarge, *v.* SYN.-amplify, augment, broaden, dilate, distend, expand, increase, magnify, spread, swell, widen. ANT.-abridge, contract, diminish, restrict, shrink.

enlighten, *v.* SYN.-brighten, clarify, educate, elucidate, illuminate, illumine, illustrate, inform, irradiate, show, teach. ANT.-complicate, confuse, darken, obfuscate, obscure.

enlist, *v.* SYN.-enroll, induce, join, obtain, procure, volunteer; employ, engage, hire, recruit, retain.

enmity, *n.* SYN.-animosity, antagonism, antipathy, hatred, hostility, ill-will, invidiousness, malice, malignity. ANT.-affection, cordiality, friendliness, good will, love.

ennoble, *v.* SYN.-aggrandize, consecrate, dignify, elevate, exalt, extol, glorify, hallow, raise. ANT.-debase, degrade, dishonor, humble, humiliate.

enormous, *a.* SYN.-colossal, elephantine, gargantuan, gigantic, huge, immense, large, prodigious, vast. ANT.-diminutive, little, minute, small, tiny.

enough, *a.* SYN.-abundant, adequate, ample, commensurate, fitting, plenty, satisfactory, sufficient, suitable. ANT.-deficient, lacking, scant.

enrage, *v.* SYN.-affront, agitate, anger, annoy, arouse, bait, chafe, goad, inflame, incense, infuriate, madden, provoke, vex.

enrich, *v.* SYN.-adorn, embellish, improve.

ensue, *v.* SYN.-succeed, come next; trail; follow, result. ANT.-precede; guide, lead; avoid, elude, flee; cause.

entangle, *v.* SYN. embroil, entwine, envelop, implicate, include, incriminate, involve, ravel, snare. ANT.-disconnect, disengage, extricate, separate.

entente, *n.* SYN.-alliance, association, coalition, combination, confederacy, federation, league, partnership, union; compact, covenant, marriage, treaty. ANT.-divorce, schism, separation.

enterprise, *n.* SYN.-art, business, commerce, employment, engagement, job, occupation, profession, trade, trading, vocation, work. ANT.-avocation, hobby, pastime.

enterprising, *a.* SYN.-adventurous, bold, chivalrous, clever, daring, precipitate, rash. ANT.-cautious, hesitating, timid.

entertain, *v.* SYN.-consider, contemplate, harbor, hold; amuse, beguile, cheer, delight, divert, gladden, please, regale. ANT. -annoy, bore, disgust, disturb, repulse.

entertainment, *n.* SYN.-amusement, diversion, fun, game, pastime, play, recreation, sport. ANT.-boredom, labor, toil, work.

enthusiasm, *n.* SYN.-ardor, devotion, earnestness, excitement, fanaticism, fervency, fervor, inspiration, intensity, vehemence, warmth, zeal. ANT.-apathy, detachment, ennui, indifference, unconcern.

enthusiastic, *a.* SYN.-absorbed, anxious, ardent, avid, delighted, eager, ecstatic, enraptured, excited, exhilarated, fascinated, fervent, fevered, hot, impassioned, impatient, keen, thrilled, yearning. ANT.-apathetic, indifferent, unconcerned, uninterested.

entice, *v.* SYN.-allure, attract, captivate, charm, enchant, fascinate, lure. ANT.-alienate, deter, repel, repulse.

entire, *a.* SYN.-all, complete, intact, integral, perfect, total, undivided, unimpaired, whole. ANT.-deficient, imperfect, in complete, partial.

entrance, *n.* SYN.-access, doorway, entry, inlet, opening, portal; admission, arrival, debut, entry, induction, penetration. ANT.-departure, exit.

entreaty, *n.* SYN.-appeal, invocation, petition, plea, prayer, request, suit, supplication.

entrust, *v.* SYN.-commend, commit, consign, relegate, trust; bind, obligate, pledge. ANT.-fail, miscarry, neglect; mistrust, release, renounce; free, loose.

envious, *a.* SYN.-begrudging, covetous, desirous, greedy, jealous, resentful.

environment, *n.* SYN.-background, conditions, habitat, scene, setting, surroundings.

envoy, *n.* SYN.-agent, ambassador, consul, delegate, deputy, emissary, intermediary, proxy, representative.

envy, *n.* SYN.-covetousness, jealousy, malevolence, malice, rivalry, spitefulness. ANT.-generosity, geniality, indifference.

episode, *n.* SYN.-circumstance, event, happening, incident, issue; occurrence, outcome.

epoch, *n.* SYN.-age, antiquity, date, epoch, era, generation, period, time.

equal, *a.* SYN.-alike, commensurate, equitable, equivalent, even, identical, impartial, like, proportionate, regular, same, uniform, unvarying. ANT-different, disparate, dissimilar, diverse.

equal, *n.* SYN.-complement, counterpart, double, likeness, match, parallel, peer, twin.

equality, *n.* SYN.-balance, equilibrium, evenness, fairness, impartiality, parity, symmetry, uniformity.

equalize, *v.* SYN.-balance, even, level, match.

equilibrium, *n.* SYN.-balance, composure, poise, stability, steadiness, proportion, symmetry. ANT.-fall, imbalance, instability, unsteadiness.

equip, *v.* SYN.-fit out, furnish, provide. supply; afford, give. ANT.-denude, despoil, divest, strip.

equipment, *n.* SYN.-apparatus, gear, implements, machinery, material, paraphernalia, supplies, tools, trappings, utensils.

equitable, *a.* SYN.-fair, honest, impartial, just, reasonable, unbiased. ANT.-dishonorable, fraudulent, partial.

equity, *n.* SYN.-fairness, impartiality, justice, justness, law, rectitude, right; investment, money, property. ANT.-inequity, partiality, unfairness, wrong.

equivalent, *a.* SYN.-coincident, equal, identical, indistinguishable, like, same. ANT.-contrary, disparate, dissimilar, distinct, opposed.

equivocal, *a.* SYN.-ambiguous, dubious, enigmatical, obscure, uncertain, vague. ANT.-clear, explicit, obvious, plain, unequivocal.

equivocate, v. SYN.-conceal, dissemble, dodge, evade, prevaricate, sidestep.

era, n. SYN.-age, antiquity, date, epoch, generation, period, time.

eradicate, v. SYN.-abolish, delete, demolish, destroy, erase, eliminate, expel, expunge, exterminate, extirpate, level, obliterate, oust, raze, remove, terminate. ANT.-accept, admit, include, involve.

erase, v. SYN.-cancel, cross out, delete, eliminate, expunge, obliterate; abolish, abrogate, annul, invalidate, nullify, quash, repeal, rescind, revoke. ANT.-confirm, enact, enforce, perpetuate

erect, a. SYN.-straight, unbent, upright, vertical. ANT.-bent, crooked.

erect, v. SYN.-build, construct, establish, fabricate, found, raise. ANT.-demolish, destroy, overthrow, raze, undermine.

err, v. SYN.-blunder, bungle, confound, mistake, overlook, slip, stumble, trip

erratic, a. SYN.-eccentric, inconsistent, irregular, random, unpredictable.

erroneous, a. SYN.-amiss, askew, awry, fallacious, false, faulty, inaccurate, incorrect, mistaken, unprecise, untrue; improper, inappropriate, unsuitable, wrong. ANT.-correct, right, true; suitable; proper.

error, n. SYN.-blunder, erratum, fallacy, fault, inaccuracy, misconception, misinterpretation, misprint, mistake, oversight, slip. ANT.-accuracy, precision, truth.

erudite, a. SYN.-academic, bookish, educated, enlightened, knowledgeable, learned, pedantic, scholarly,

scholastic, theoretical. ANT.-common-sense, ignorant, practical, simple.

erudition, n. SYN.-discretion, education, enlightenment, foresight, information, insight, intelligence, judgment, knowledge, learning, prudence, reason, refinement, sagacity, sageness, sense, wisdom. ANT.-foolishness, ignorance, imprudence, nonsense, stupidity.

escalate, v. SYN.-complicate, compound, enlarge, extend, increase, intensify, grow, heighten, multiply. ANT.-lessen, reduce.

escape, n. SYN.-avoidance, breakout, departure, evasion, flight, release.

escape, v. SYN.-abscond, decamp, flee, fly; avert, avoid, elude, evade, shun. ANT.-catch, confront, face, invite, meet.

eschew, v. SYN.-abstain, avert, avoid, dodge, escape, elude, forbear, forestall, free, shun, ward. ANT.-confront, encounter, meet, oppose.

escort, v. SYN.-accompany, associate with, attend, chaperone, conduct, consort with, convoy, go with, guard, guide, protect, squire. ANT.-abandon, avoid, desert, leave, quit.

especially, a. SYN.-abnormally, extraordinarily, notably, particularly, remarkably, unusually; chiefly, mainly, primarily.

essay, n. SYN.-composition, subject, text, theme, thesis, topic.

essence, n. SYN.-basis, core, fundamentals, gist, heart, pith, root, substance.

essential, a. SYN.-basic, fundamental, imperative, important, indispensable, intrinsic, necessary, requisite, vital. ANT.-expendable, extrinsic, optional, peripheral.

establish, v. SYN.-form, found, institute, organize, raise; confirm, fix, ordain, sanction, settle, strengthen; prove, substantiate, verify. ANT.-abolish, demolish, overthrow, unsettle, upset; disprove, refute.

estate, n. SYN.-belongings, bequest, commodities, effects, goods, lands, manor, merchandise, possessions, property, stock, wealth; inheritance. ANT.-deprivation, destitution, poverty, privation, want.

esteem, v. SYN.-admire, appreciate, honor, prize, regard, respect, revere, reverence, value, venerate; consider, deem, hold, regard, think. ANT.-abhor, depreciate, dislike, scorn.

esteemed, a. SYN.-dear, distinguished, honored, precious, respectable, respected, valued, venerable. ANT.-despised, unwanted; cheap.

esthetic, a. SYN.-artistic, beautiful, creative, emotional, natural, pleasant.

estimate, v. SYN.-appraise, assess, calculate, compute, consider, count, evaluate, figure, fix, guess, levy, reckon.

eternal, a. SYN.-ceaseless, deathless, endless, everlasting, immortal, infinite, perpetual, timeless, undying. ANT. ephemeral, finite, mortal, temporal, transient.

eternally, adv. SYN.-always, constantly, continually, eternally, ever, evermore, forever, incessantly, perpetually, unceasingly. ANT.-fitfully, never, occasionally, rarely, sometimes.

ethereal, a. SYN.-celestial, divine, ghostly, holy, immaterial, incorporeal, religious, sacred, spiritual, supernatural, unearthly, unworldly. ANT.-carnal, corporeal, material, mundane, physical.

ethical, a. SYN.-decent, good, honorable, just, moral, pure, right, righteous, scrupulous, virtuous. ANT.-amoral, libertine, licentious, sinful, unethical.

evacuate, v. SYN.-abandon, desert, empty, leave, vacate.

evade, v. SYN.-avert, avoid, deceive, dodge, elude, escape, lie, shun. ANT.-catch, confront, face, invite, meet.

evaluate, v. SYN.-analyze, appraise, assess, assign, calculate, compute, criticize, estimate, evaluate, examine, inspect, rate, scrutinize.

evaporate, v. SYN.-disappear, dissipate, dissolve, fade, vanish.

even, a. SYN.-balance, flat, level, smooth, uniform.

evenly, a. SYN.-equally, equitably, fairly, impartially, justly, proportionately, symmetrically.

event, n. SYN.-circumstance, episode, happening, incident, issue, occasion, occurrence, phenomenon; consequence, end, outcome, result.

ever, adv. SYN.-always, constantly, continually, eternally, evermore, forever, incessantly, perpetually, unceasingly. ANT.-fitfully, never, occasionally, rarely, sometimes.

everlasting, a. SYN.-ceaseless, deathless, endless, eternal, immortal, infinite, perpetual, timeless, undying. ANT. ephemeral, finite, mortal, temporal, transient.

every, a. SYN.-all, each.

evidence, n. SYN.-confirmation, corroboration, demonstration, proof, testimony, verification. ANT.-fallacy, invalidity.

evident, *a.* SYN.-apparent, clear, conspicuous, indubitable, manifest, obvious, open, overt, patent, unmistakable. ANT.-concealed, covert, hidden, obscure.

evil, *a.* SYN.-bad, baleful, base, deleterious, immoral, iniquitous, noxious, pernicious, sinful, unsound, unwholesome, villainous, wicked. ANT.-excellent, good, honorable, moral, reputable.

evil, *n.* SYN.-crime, iniquity, offense, sin, transgression, ungodliness, vice, wickedness, wrong. ANT.-goodness, innocence, purity, righteousness, virtue.

evolve, *v.* SYN.-create, develop, elaborate, enlarge, expand, mature, unfold. ANT.-compress, contract, restrict, stunt, wither.

exact, *a.* SYN.-accurate, correct, definite, distinct, precise, strict, unequivocal; ceremonious, formal, prim, rigid, stiff. ANT. erroneous, loose, rough, vague; careless, easy, informal.

exaggerate, *v.* SYN.-amplify, caricature, embroider, enlarge, expand, heighten, magnify, misrepresent, overstate, stretch. ANT.-belittle, depreciate, minimize, understate.

exalt, *v.* SYN.-aggrandize, consecrate, dignify, elevate, ennoble, erect, extol, glorify, hallow, raise. ANT.-debase, degrade, dishonor, humble, humiliate.

exalted, *a.* SYN.-dignified, elevated, eminent, grand, illustrious, lofty, majestic, noble, stately. ANT.-base, low, mean, plebeian, vile.

examination, *n.* SYN.-audit, exploration, inquiry, interrogation, investigation, observation, query, quest, question, research, scrutiny, test, trial. ANT.-disregard, inactivity, inattention, negligence.

examine, *v.* SYN.-analyze, assess, audit, check, contemplate, dissect, inquire, interrogate, notice, probe, question, quiz, review, scan, scrutinize, survey, view, watch. ANT.-disregard, neglect, omit, overlook.

example, *n.* SYN.-archetype, illustration, instance. model, pattern, prototype, sample, specimen. ANT.-concept, precept, principle, rule.

exasperate, *v.* SYN.-aggravate, annoy, chafe, embitter, inflame, irritate, nettle, provoke, vex. ANT.-appease, mitigate, palliate soften, soothe.

exasperation, *n.* SYN.-annoyance, chagrin, irritation, mortification, pique, vexation. ANT.-appeasement, comfort, gratification, pleasure.

exceed, *v.* SYN.-beat, excel, outdo, pass, surpass, transcend.

excellent, *a.* SYN.-conscientious, exemplary, honest, moral, pure, reliable, virtuous, worthy; admirable, commendable, genuine, good, precious, safe, sound, valid; benevolent, gracious, humane, kind; agreeable, cheerful, friendly, genial, pleasant; fair, honorable, immaculate; auspicious, beneficial, favorable, profitable, useful; able, capable, efficient, expert, proficient, skillful.

exception, *n.* SYN.-exclusion, omission, preclusion; anomaly, deviation, unusual case; affront, objection, offense. ANT.-inclusion, rule, standard.

exceptional, *a.* SYN.-choice, incomparable, precious, rare, scarce, singular, uncommon, unique. ANT.-customary, ordinary, usual; abundant, commonplace, numerous, worthless.

excess, n. SYN.-abundance, extravagance, immoderation, intemperance, profusion, superabundance, superfluity, surplus. ANT.-dearth, deficiency, lack, paucity, want.

excessive, a. SYN.-abundant, copious, extravagant, exuberant, immoderate, improvident, lavish, luxuriant, overflowing, plentiful, prodigal, profuse, wasteful. ANT.-economical, meager, poor, skimpy, sparse.

exchange, v. SYN.-barter, change, substitute, swap, trade, transpose; alter, convert, transfigure, transform. ANT.-retain; continue, establish, preserve, settle, stabilize.

excite, v. SYN.-agitate, arouse, awaken, disquiet, disturb, incite, irritate, provoke, rouse, stimulate, stir up. ANT.-allay, calm, pacify, quell, quiet.

exclaim, v. SYN.-call out, cry, cry out, ejaculate, shout, vociferate. ANT.-intimate, whisper, write.

exclude, v. SYN.-bar, blackball, except, expel, hinder, omit, ostracize, prevent, prohibit, reject, restrain, shut out. ANT.-accept, admit, include, welcome.

exclusive, a. SYN.-aristocratic, choice, clannish, excluding, fashionable, only, particular, private, privileged, prohibitive, restricted, segregated, select, sole, special.

excusable, a. SYN.-allowable, defensible, forgivable, justifiable, pardonable, permissible, plausible, reasonable, trivial, understandable.

excuse, n. SYN.-alibi, apology, defense, explanation, justification, reason. ANT.-accusation, complaint, denial, dissimulation.

excuse, v. SYN.-absolve, acquit, condone, exculpate, exempt, forgive, free, justify, overlook, pardon, remit. ANT.-convict, prosecute, punish, retaliate, revenge.

execrable, a. SYN.-abominable, detestable, foul, hateful, loathsome, odious, revolting, vile. ANT.-agreeable, commendable, delightful, pleasant.

execution, n. SYN.-accomplishment, act, action, deed, doing, feat, operation, performance, transaction. ANT.-cessation, deliberation, inactivity, inhibition, intention.

exemplar, n. SYN.-copy, duplicate, example, facsimile, imitation, model, replica, reproduction, specimen. ANT.-original, prototype.

exemplary, a. SYN.-faultless, excellent, honest, honorable, ideal, immaculate, moral, perfect, pure, reliable, supreme, virtuous. ANT.-faulty, imperfect.

exercise, n. SYN.-activity, application, drill, employment, exertion, lesson, operation, performance, practice, task, training, use. ANT.-idleness, indolence, relaxation, repose, rest.

exhaust, v. SYN.-bore, fatigue, jade, tire, tucker, wear out, weary. ANT.-amuse, invigorate, refresh, restore, revive.

exhausted, a. SYN.-fatigued, spent, tired, wearied, weary, worn; consumed, depleted, expended, used. ANT.-fresh, hearty, invigorated, rested.

exhaustion, n. SYN.-enervation, fatigue, languor, lassitude, tiredness, weariness. ANT.-freshness, rejuvenation, restoration, vigor, vivacity.

exhibit, v. SYN.-display, expose, flaunt, parade, present, reveal, show, spread out; demonstrate, evidence, prove, verify. ANT.-conceal, cover, disguise, hide.

exhibition, n. SYN.-array, display, exposition; demonstration, flourish, ostentation, parade, show, spectacle, splurge.

exile, n. SYN.-banishment, deportation, expatriation, expulsion, extradition, ostracism, proscription. ANT.-admittance, recall, reinstatement, retrieval, welcome.

existence, n. SYN.-being, life, liveliness, spirit, vitality, vivacity. ANT.-death, demise.

exorbitant, a. SYN.-excessive, extravagant, immoderate, unreasonable.

exotic, a. SYN.-alien, different, extrinsic, foreign, outstanding, strange, unusual.

expand, v. SYN.-augment, develop, distend, enlarge, extend, grow, increase, swell. ANT.-contract, diminish, shrink, wane.

expanse, n. SYN.-area, extent, magnitude, measure, range, reach, scope, size.

expansion, n. SYN.-development, elaboration, unfolding, unraveling; evolution, growth, maturing, progress. ANT.-abbreviation, compression, curtailment.

expatriation, n. SYN.-banishment, deportation, exile, expulsion, extradition, ostracism, proscription. ANT.-admittance, recall, reinstatement, retrieval, welcome.

expect, v. SYN.-anticipate, await, contemplate, demand, hope for, suppose; demand, exact, require. ANT.-get, obtain, realize, receive.

expectation, n. SYN.-anticipation, contemplation, expectancy, foresight, forethought, hope, optimism, preconception, prescience, presen-

timent. ANT.-doubt, dread, fear, worry.

expedient, a. SYN.-advantageous, appropriate, convenient, desirable, discreet, fit, judicious, opportune, practical, proper, prudent, suitable, useful.

expedite, v. SYN.-accelerate, dispatch, facilitate, forward, hasten, hurry, push, quicken, rush, speed. ANT.-block, hinder, impede, retard, slow.

expedition, n. SYN.-cruise, incursion, jaunt, journey, passage, pilgrimage, safari, tour, travel, trip, voyage.

expel, v. SYN.-banish, discharge, dismiss, disown, excommunicate, exile, expatriate, ostracize, oust, proscribe; dislodge, eject, eliminate, void. ANT.-admit, favor, include, recall.

expend, v. SYN.-consume, disburse, employ, exhaust, pay, spend, use.

expense, n. SYN.-budget, charge, cost, debt, expenditure, liability, price.

expensive, a. SYN.-costly, high-priced, precious; dear, prized, valuable. ANT.-cheap, mean, poor; trashy, worthless.

experience, n. SYN.-background, judgment, knowledge, maturity, practice, seasoning, training, wisdom.

experiment, v. SYN.-analyze, assay, examine, explore, inspect, investigate, probe, research, sample, test, try.

expert, a. SYN.-able, accomplished, adept, clever, competent, cunning, ingenious, practiced, proficient, skilled, skillful, versed. ANT.-awkward, bungling, clumsy, inexpert, untrained.

expire, *v.* SYN.-cease, conclude, decease, die, end, finish, perish, stop, terminate. ANT.-begin, live, survive.

explain, *v.* SYN.-clarify, decipher, elucidate, expound, illustrate, interpret, resolve, unfold, unravel. ANT.-baffle, confuse, darken, obscure.

explanation, *n.* SYN.-alibi, apology, clarification, confession, defense, elucidation, excuse, justification, recapitulation, report. ANT.-accusation, complaint, denial, dissimulation.

explicit, *a.* SYN.-categorical, clear, definite, definitive, express, lucid, manifest, outspoken, plain, specific. ANT.-ambiguous, diplomatic, equivocal, implicit, obscure, vague.

exploit, *n.* SYN.-accomplishment, achievement, attainment, deed, escapade, feat, performance, realization, venture. ANT.-neglect, omission; defeat, failure.

exploit, *v.* SYN.-apply, avail, employ, manipulate, operate, use, utilize; consume, exhaust, expend; handle, manage, treat. ANT.-ignore, neglect, overlook, waste.

explore, *v.* SYN.-examine, hunt, inspect, seek, test.

explorer, *n.* SYN.-adventurer, forerunner, searcher, trailblazer, pioneer, voyager.

explosive, *a.* SYN.-fiery, forceful, frenzied, hysterical, raging, savage, uncontrollable, violent.

expose, *v.* SYN.-air, bare, betray, debunk, disclose, display, open, reveal, show, unmask.

exposed, *a.* SYN.-disclosed, discovered, revealed, unclosed, uncovered; accessible, open, public, unrestricted; candid, frank, honest,

overt, plain.

expound, *v.* SYN.-clarify, comment, decipher, elucidate, explain, explicate, illustrate, interpret, resolve, unfold, unravel. ANT.-baffle, confuse, darken, obscure.

express, *a.* SYN.-clear, definitive, explicit, lucid, manifest, specific. ANT.-ambiguous, equivocal, implicit, obscure, vague.

express, *v.* SYN.-affirm, assert, avow, claim, declare, explain, propound, recite, recount, say, specify, state, tell, utter. ANT.-conceal, deny, imply, retract.

expressive, *a.* SYN.-bright, brilliant, dramatic, intense, spirited, stirring, striking; animated, clear, demonstrative, eloquent, fresh, graphic, lively, lucid, vivid. ANT.-dull, vague; dim, dreary, dusky.

extend, *v.* SYN.-distend, distort, elongate, expand, lengthen, protract, spread, stretch. ANT.-contract, loosen, shrink, slacken, tighten.

extended, *a.* SYN.-drawn out, elongated, lasting, lengthy, lingering, long, prolix, prolonged, protracted, tedious, wordy. ANT.-abridged, brief, concise, short, terse.

extensive, *a.* SYN.-broad, expanded, large, sweeping, vast, wide; liberal. ANT.-confined, narrow, restricted.

extending, *a.* SYN.-continuing, perpetual, ranging, reaching, spreading, stretching.

extent, *n.* SYN.-amount, area, compass, degree, expanse, limit, length, magnitude, measure, range, reach, scope, size, stretch.

exterior, *n.* SYN.-cover, facade, face, front, outer, surface, veneer. ANT.-back, interior, rear.

extol, *v.* SYN.-aggrandize, celebrate,

elevate, ennoble, observe; commend, exalt, glorify, hallow, honor, laud, praise, raise. ANT.-disregard, overlook; decry, disgrace, dishonor, profane.

extra, *a.* SYN.-added, additional, another, auxiliary, other, reserve, spare, supplementary.

extract, *v.* SYN.-dislodge, eject, extricate, oust, remove, vacate; derive, distill, withdraw. ANT.-leave, remain, stay; retain.

extradition, *n.* SYN.-banishment, deportation, exile, expatriation, expulsion, ostracism, proscription. ANT.-admittance, recall, reinstatement, retrieval, welcome.

extraneous, *a.* SYN.-alien, contrasted, extraneous, foreign, irrelevant, remote, strange, unconnected. ANT.-akin, germane, kindred, relevant.

extraordinary, *a.* SYN.-exceptional, marvelous, peculiar, rare, remarkable, singular, uncommon, unusual, wonderful. ANT.-common, frequent, ordinary, usual.

extravagance, *n.* SYN.-excess, immoderation, intemperance, profusion, superabundance, superfluity, surplus. ANT.-dearth, deficiency, lack, paucity, want.

extravagant, *a.* SYN.-abundant, copious, excessive, exuberant, immoderate, improvident, lavish, luxuriant, overflowing, plentiful, prodigal, profuse, wasteful. ANT.-economical, meager, poor, skimpy, sparse.

extreme, *a.* SYN.-acute, exacting, excessive, harsh, inordinate, intense, radical, relentless, rigorous, severe, unmitigated, unreasonable, unyielding. ANT.-genial, indulgent, yielding.

F

fable, *n.* SYN.-allegory, chronicle, fiction, legend, myth, parable, saga, tale. ANT.-fad, history.

fabricate, *v.* SYN.-build, construct, erect, form, frame, make, manufacture, raise; contrive, devise, fake, lie, prevaricate. ANT.-demolish, destroy, raze.

facade, *n.* SYN.-appearance, deceit, face, front, look, mask.

face, *n.* SYN.-countenance, mug, visage; assurance, audacity; cover, exterior, front, surface. ANT.-timidity; back, interior, rear.

facilitate, *v.* SYN.-aid, allay, alleviate, assuage, calm, comfort, ease, lighten, mitigate, pacify, relieve, soothe. ANT.-confound, distress, disturb, trouble, worry.

facility, *n.* SYN.-ability, adroitness, cleverness, cunning, deftness, dexterity, ingenuity, knack, readiness, skill, skillfullness; building, company, plant, tools. ANT.-awkwardness, clumsiness, inability, ineptitude.

facsimile, *n.* SYN.-copy, duplicate, facsimile, imitation, replica, reproduction, transcript. ANT.-original, prototype.

fact, *n.* SYN.-actuality, certainty, reality, truth; act, circumstance, deed, event, incident, occurrence. ANT.-fiction, supposition, theory; delusion, falsehood.

faction, *n.* SYN.-division, fragment, moiety, piece, portion, section, segment; component, element, ingredient, member, organ; concern, interest, part, party, side. ANT.-entirety, whole.

factual, *a.* SYN.-accurate, authentic, exact, genuine, specific, true.

faculty, *n.* SYN.-ability, aptitude, aptness, capability, capacity, dexterity, efficiency, power, qualification, skill, talent. ANT.-disability, incapacity, incompetence, unreadiness.

fad, *n.* SYN.-craze, curiosity, fashion, gimmick, innovation, novel, oddity, style, vogue,

faded, *a.* SYN.-dim, faint, indistinct, pale; feeble, languid, wearied; irresolute, timid, weak. ANT.-conspicuous, glaring; strong, vigorous; brave, forceful.

fail, *v.* SYN.-blunder, cease, crash, decline, default, deteriorate, disappoint, falter, fizzle, flag, flop, founder, miss.

failure, *n.* SYN.-fiasco, miscarriage; default, dereliction, omission; decay, decline; deficiency, lack, loss, want. ANT.-achievement, success, victory; sufficiency.

faint, *a.* SYN.-dim, faded, indistinct, pale; feeble, languid, wearied; irresolute, timid, weak. ANT.-conspicuous, glaring; strong, vigorous; brave, forceful.

fair, *a.* SYN.-bright, clear, light; attractive, blond, comely, lovely; equitable, honest, impartial, just, reasonable, unbiased; average, mediocre, passable. ANT.-foul, ugly; dishonorable, fraudulent, partial; excellent, first-rate, worst.

fairness, *n.* SYN.-decency, equity, honesty, impartiality, integrity, justice, justness, law, truth, rectitude, right. ANT.-inequity, partiality, unfairness, wrong.

faith, *n.* SYN.-confidence, credence, dependence, reliance, trust; belief, creed, doctrine, dogma, persuasion, religion, tenet; constancy, fidelity, loyalty. ANT.-doubt, incredulity, mistrust, skepticism; infidelity.

faithful, *a.* SYN.-conscientious, constant, dependable, devoted, honest, incorruptible, loyal, staunch, steadfast, true; accurate, genuine, reliable, trusty. ANT.-disloyal, false, fickle, treacherous, untrustworthy.

faithless, *a.* SYN.-apostate, disloyal, false, perfidious, recreant, traitorous, treacherous, treasonable. ANT.-constant, devoted, loyal, true.

fake, *a.* SYN.-affected, artificial, assumed, bogus, counterfeit, ersatz, fabrication, feigned, fictitious, imitation, phony, sham, spurious, synthetic, unreal. ANT.-genuine, natural, real, true.

fall, *v.* SYN.-collapse, decline, decrease, descend, diminish, drop, sink, subside; stumble, topple, tumble; droop, extend downward, hang. ANT.-arise, ascend, climb, mount, soar; steady.

fallacy, *n.* SYN.-ambiguity, error, fault, inaccuracy, inconsistency, mistake, paradox, slip. ANT.-accuracy, precision, truth.

falling, *a.* SYN.-declining, decreasing, descending, diminishing, dropping, ebbing, plunging, sinking, tumbling.

false, *a.* SYN.-amiss, deceitful, dishonest, disloyal, erroneous, fallacious, faulty, inaccurate, incorrect, lying, mistaken, treacherous, underhanded, untrue, wrong; bogus, copied, counterfeit, fabricated, faked, forged, pseudo, spurious, synthetic. ANT.-authentic, correct, factual, genuine, right, true.

falsehood, *n.* SYN.-deception, delusion, equivocation, exaggeration, fib, fiction, illusion, lie, prevarication, untruth. ANT.-axiom, canon, fact, truism.

falsify, *v.* SYN.-alter, counterfeit, deceive, equivocate, fib, lie, misrepresent, prevaricate. ANT.-confirm, establish, prove.

falter, *v.* SYN.-delay, demur, doubt, hesitate, pause, scruple, stammer, stutter, vacillate, waver. ANT.-continue, decide, persevere, proceed, resolve.

fame, *n.* SYN.-acclaim, credit, distinction, eminence, glory, honor, notoriety, renown, reputation. ANT.-disrepute, ignominy, infamy, obscurity.

familiar, *a.* SYN.-acquainted, aware, cognizant, conversant, intimate, knowing, versed; affable, amicable, close, courteous, friendly, informal, sociable, unreserved; accustomed, common, commonplace, customary, everyday, homespun, prosaic, simple, unsophisticated, well-known. ANT.-affected, cold, distant, reserved, unfamiliar.

familiarity, *n.* SYN.-acquaintance, fellowship, friendship, sociability; frankness, informality, intimacy, liberty, unreserve. ANT.-constraint, distance, haughtiness, presumption, reserve.

family, *n.* SYN.-ancestry, clan, descendants, extraction, forbears, genealogy, genre, group, heirs, house, kin, kindred, kinsfolk, lineage, pedigree, progeny, relations, relationship, relatives, tribe, type. ANT.-disconnection, foreigners, strangers.

famished, *a.* SYN.-craving, hungry, ravenous, starved, thirsting, voracious. ANT.-full, gorged, sated, satiated; satisfied.

famous, *a.* SYN.-acclaimed, celebrated, distinguished, eminent, glorious, illustrious, influential, noted, notorious, prominent, recognized, renowned, well-known. ANT.-hidden, ignominious, infamous, obscure, unknown.

fanatical, *a.* SYN.-arbitrary, dogmatic, excessive, extravagant, extreme, fanatic, frenzied, intemperate, intolerant, narrow-minded, obsessed, obstinate, passionate, stubborn, zealous.

fanciful, *a.* SYN.-dreamy, fantastic, fictitious, ideal, idealistic, imaginative, maudlin, mawkish, picturesque, poetic, romantic, sentimental. ANT.-factual, literal, matter-of-fact, practical, prosaic.

fancy, *a.* SYN.-adorned, capricious, distinctive, elaborate, elegant, embellished, fanciful, gaudy, lavish, ornate, ostentatious, resplendent, showy, whimsical.

fancy, *n.* SYN.-caprice, conception, creation, dream, fantasy, hallucination, idea, imagination, impression, invention, notion, thought, whimsy; fondness, inclination, liking, preference, taste, whim.

fantastic, *a.* SYN.-capricious, extravagant, farfetched, freakish, outlandish, preposterous, ridiculous, whimsical, wonderful. ANT.-conventional, ordinary, routine.

fantasy, *n.* SYN.-caprice, dream, fancy, hallucination, illusion, imagination, vision, whim.

far, *a.* SYN.-away, distant, faraway, remote, removed. ANT.-close, near, nigh; cordial, friendly.

farewell, *n.* SYN.-departure, good-by, leave-taking, valediction. ANT.-greeting, salutation, welcome.

farming, *n.* SYN.-agriculture, agronomy, cultivation, gardening, horticulture, husbandry, tillage.

fascinate, *v.* SYN.-attract, beguile,

bewitch, captivate, charm, delight, enamor, enchant, enrapture, enthrall, entice, intoxicate, lure, overpower, overwhelm, stimulate, titillate. ANT.-alienate, deter, disgust, displease, repel, repulse, tire.

fascinating, *a.* SYN.-alluring, appealing, attractive, bewitching, captivating, charming, delightful, enchanting, engaging, seductive, winning. ANT.-repugnant, repulsive, revolting.

fashion, *n.* SYN.-approach, conformity, convention, custom, formality, manner, method, mode, practice, tendency, usage, way; craze, fad, rage, style, vogue.

fashion, *v.* SYN.-construct, create, forge, form, make, mold, produce, shape; compose, constitute, make up; arrange, combine, organize; devise, frame, invent. ANT.-destroy, disfigure, dismantle, misshape, wreck.

fast, *a.* SYN.-expeditious, fleet, quick, rapid, speedy, swift; constant, firm, inflexible, secure, solid, stable, steadfast, steady, unswerving, unyielding. ANT.-slow, sluggish; insecure, loose, unstable, unsteady.

fasten, *v.* SYN.-affix, anchor, attach, bind, fix, link, place, secure, set, stick, tie. ANT.-displace, remove, unfasten.

fastidious, *a.* SYN.-accurate, choosy, critical, delicate, discerning, discriminating, exact, finicky, fussy, particular, precise. ANT.-cursory, shallow, superficial, uncritical.

fat, *a.* SYN.-chubby, corpulent, heavy, husky, obese, paunchy, plump, portly, pudgy, rotund, stocky, stout, thickset. ANT.-gaunt, lean, slender, slim, thin.

fatal, *a.* SYN.-deadly, destructive, disastrous, final, lethal, mortal, predestined. ANT.-life-giving; divine, immortal.

fate, *n.* SYN.-consequence, doom, fortune, lot, portion; circumstance, destiny, issue, karma, necessity, outcome, result.

father, *v.* SYN.-beget, create, engender, father, generate, originate, procreate, produce, propagate, sire. ANT.-abort, destroy, extinguish, kill, murder.

fatigue, *n.* SYN.-enervation, exhaustion, languor, lassitude, tiredness, weariness. ANT.-freshness, rejuvenation, restoration, vigor, vivacity.

fatigued, *a.* SYN.-bored, exhausted, faint, jaded, spent, tired, wearied, weary, worn. ANT.-fresh, hearty, invigorated, rested.

fault, *n.* SYN.-blemish, defect, error, failure, flaw, imperfection, mistake, omission, shortcoming, vice, weakness. ANT.-completeness, correctness, perfection.

faultless, *a.* SYN.-complete, entire, finished, full, utter, whole; blameless, holy, immaculate, perfect, pure, sinless; consummate, excellent, ideal, superlative, supreme; absolute, downright, unqualified, utter. ANT.-deficient, incomplete, lacking; blemished, defective, faulty, imperfect.

faulty, *a.* SYN.-blemished, damaged, defective, deficient, flawed, imperfect, tainted, unsound; inadequate, incomplete, insufficient, substandard, unfit, unsatisfactory. ANT.-complete, perfect, whole.

favor, *n.* SYN.-advantage, bias, exemption, immunity, liberty, license, partiality, preference, prerogative, privilege, right, sanction; accommodation, boon, courtesy, kindness. ANT.-disallowance, inhibition, prohibition, restriction.

favor, *v.* SYN.-animate, cheer, countenance, embolden, encourage, exhilarate, hearten, impel, incite, inspirit, urge; esteem, foster, like, prefer, prize, promote, sanction, stimulate, support ANT.-reject, deter, discourage, dispirit, dissuade.

favorite, *a.* SYN.-adored, beloved, cherished, pet, popular, precious, preferred, prevailing, prevalent. ANT.-ignored, unimportant, unpopular.

fealty, *n.* SYN.-allegiance, constancy, devotion, faithfulness, fidelity, homage, loyalty. ANT.-disloyalty, faithlessness, perfidy, treachery.

fear, *n.* SYN.-alarm, apprehension, consternation, cowardice, dismay, dread, fright, horror, panic, scare, terror, timidity, trepidation. ANT.-assurance, boldness, bravery, courage, fearlessness.

fearful, *a.* SYN.-afraid, apprehensive, fainthearted, frightened, scared, timid, timorous. ANT.-assured, bold, composed, courageous, sanguine.

fearless, *a.* SYN.-adventurous, audacious, bold, brave, courageous, daring, dauntless, intrepid; brazen, forward. ANT.-cowardly, flinching, timid; bashful, retiring.

feasible, *a.* SYN.-achievable, attainable, credible, expedient, likely, plausible, possible, practicable, practical, probable, usable, workable, worthwhile. ANT.-impossible, impracticable, visionary.

feast, *n.* SYN.-banquet, celebration, dinner, entertainment, festival, regalement.

feature, *n.* SYN.-attribute, characteristic, mark, peculiarity, property, quality, trait; highlight, innovation, specialty.

fecund, *a.* SYN.-bountiful, fertile, fruitful, luxuriant, plenteous, productive, prolific, rich, teeming. ANT.-barren, impotent, sterile, unproductive.

feeble, *a.* SYN.-decrepit, delicate, enervated, exhausted, faint, forceless, impaired, infirm, languid, powerless, puny, weak. ANT.-forceful, lusty, stout, strong, vigorous.

feed, *v.* SYN.-cater, cram, dine, encourage, fatten, feast, nourish, nurture, provide, stock, stuff, supply, support, sustain.

feel, *v.* SYN.-accept, acknowledge, believe, consider, deem, observe, perceive, savor, sense, think; caress, clutch, fondle, grip, grope, handle, paw, press, squeeze.

feeling, *n.* SYN.-awareness, consciousness, perception, reaction, sensation, sensibility; affection, emotion, intuition, judgment, passion, sensibility, sentiment, sympathy, tenderness; impression, opinion. ANT.-anesthesia; coldness, imperturbability, insensibility; fact.

feign, *v.* SYN.-act, affect, assume, fabricate, pretend, profess, sham, simulate. ANT.-display, exhibit, expose, reveal.

felicity, *n.* SYN.-beatitude, blessedness, bliss, contentment, delight, gladness, happiness, pleasure, satisfaction, well-being. ANT.-despair, grief, misery, sadness, sorrow.

fellowship, *n.* SYN.-amity, brotherhood, brotherliness, camaraderie, communion, friendliness, intimacy, solidarity, togetherness; alliance, association, brotherhood, clan, club, fraternity, society. ANT.-acrimony, discord, opposition, strife.

felon, n. SYN.-convict, criminal, culprit, delinquent, malefactor, offender, transgressor.

feminine, a. SYN.-delicate, fair, female, gentle, girlish, ladylike, maidenly, sensitive, tender, womanish, womanly. ANT.-male, manly, mannish, masculine, virile.

ferment, n. SYN.-agitation, chaos, commotion, confusion, disorder, disturbance, excitement, hubbub, insurrection, stir, revolt, tempest, tumult, turbulence, turmoil, uprising. ANT.-certainty, order, peace, tranquility.

ferocious, a. SYN.-barbarous, bestial, brutal, brute, brutish, carnal, coarse, cruel, fierce, gross, inhuman, merciless, remorseless, rough, rude, ruthless, savage, sensual. ANT-civilized, courteous, gentle, humane, kind.

fertile, a. SYN.-bountiful, fecund, fruitful, luxuriant, plenteous, productive, prolific, rich, teeming. ANT.-barren, impotent, sterile, unproductive.

fervent, a. SYN.-ardent, eager, enthusiastic, fervid, fiery, glowing, hot, impassioned, intense, keen, passionate, vehement, zealous. ANT.-apathetic, cool, indifferent, nonchalant.

fervor, n. SYN.-ardor, devotion, earnestness, enthusiasm, excitement, fanaticism, fervency, inspiration, intensity, vehemence, warmth, zeal. ANT.-apathy, detachment, ennui, indifference, unconcern.

festive, a. SYN.-blithe, cheerful, gay, gleeful, hilarious, jolly, jovial, joyous, lively, merry, mirthful, sprightly. ANT.-gloomy, melancholy, morose, sad, sorrowful.

fetish, n. SYN.-compulsion, craze, fixation, mania, obsession, passion; amulet, charm, talisman.

fetter, v. SYN.-attach, bind, connect, fasten, join, link, restrain, restrict, tie. ANT.-free, loose, unfasten, untie.

feud, n. SYN.-affray, altercation, argument, bickering, contention, disagreement, dispute, quarrel, spat, squabble, wrangle. ANT.-agreement, friendliness, harmony, peace, reconciliation.

few, a. SYN.-any, inconsiderable, meager, negligible, rare, scant, scanty, scattering, some, sparse, thin, trifling.

fickle, a. SYN.-capricious, changeable, erratic, fitful, flighty, frivolous, inconstant, restless, unstable, variable. ANT.-constant, reliable, stable, steady, trustworthy.

fiction, n. SYN.-allegory, fable, fabrication, falsehood, invention, narrative, novel, romance, story, tale. ANT.-fact, history, reality, truth, verity.

fictitious, a. SYN.-affected, artificial, assumed, bogus, counterfeit, ersatz, fake, feigned, phony, sham, spurious, synthetic, unreal, untrue. ANT.-genuine, natural, real, true.

fidelity, n. SYN.-allegiance, constancy, devotion, faithfulness, fealty, loyalty; accuracy, exactness, precision. ANT.-disloyalty, faithlessness, perfidy, treachery

field, n. SYN.-acreage, ground, land, meadow, pasture, patch, plain, plot, range, region, soil, tract; domain, estate, farm, realm.

fiend, n. SYN.-barbarian, beast, brute, demon, devil, maniac, monster; addict, aficionado, fan, fanatic, junkie.

fierce, *a.* SYN.-angry, boisterous, enraged, forceful, frenzied, frightening, furious, impetuous, monstrous, passionate, powerful, raging, raving, savage, turbulent, untamed, vehement, violent, wild; acute, awful, extreme, intense, severe, violent. ANT.-calm, feeble, gentle, quiet, soft.

fiery, *a.* SYN.-burning, hot, scalding, scorching, torrid, warm; ardent, fervent, fiery, hot-blooded, impetuous, intense, passionate; peppery, pungent. ANT.-cold, cool, freezing, frigid; apathetic, impassive, indifferent, passionless, phlegmatic; bland.

fight, *n.* SYN.-altercation, battle, brawl, clash, combat, conflict, confrontation, contention, dispute, encounter, feud, fracas, quarrel, scuffle, skirmish, strife,

fight, *v.* SYN.-argue, attack, battle, brawl, combat, conflict, contend, debate, dispute, encounter, grapple, oppose, quarrel, scuffle, skirmish, squabble, struggle, tussle, wrangle.

fighter, *n.* SYN.-aggressor, antagonist, assailant, bully, competitor, contender, opponent, rival.

figurative, *a.* SYN.-allegorical, emblematic, illustrative, metaphorical, symbolic.

figure, *n.* SYN.-appearance, build, cast, configuration, contour, cut, form, frame, guise, image, mold, outline, pattern, shape. ANT.-contortion, deformity, distortion, mutilation.

figure, *v.* SYN.-calculate, compute, consider, count, estimate, number, reckon. ANT.-conjecture, guess, miscalculate.

fill, *v.* SYN.-fill up, occupy, pervade; furnish, replenish, stock, store, supply; content, glut, gorge, pack, sate, satiate, satisfy, stuff. ANT.-deplete, drain, empty, exhaust, void.

filling, *n.* SYN.-contents, dressing, filler, insides, lining, padding, stuffing, wadding.

film, *n.* SYN.-celluloid, cinema, filmstrip, image, movie, negative, photograph, picture, portrayal, print, representation, slide, transparency; coating, covering, fabric, gauze, membrane, skin.

filter, *v.* SYN.-clarify, clean, distill, filtrate, purify, refine, separate, sift, strain; seep, trickle.

filth, *n.* SYN.-contamination, dirt, garbage, grime, impurity, muck, pollution, sewage, slop, trash.

filthy, *a.* SYN.-dirty, foul, grimy, muddy, soiled, squalid. ANT.-clean, neat, presentable.

final, *a.* SYN.-concluding, conclusive, decisive, ending, eventual, last, latest, terminal, ultimate. ANT.-embryonic, first, inaugural, incipient, original, rudimentary.

finally, *a.* SYN.-at last, conclusively, decisively, definitely, irrevocably, permanently, ultimately.

find, *v.* SYN.-ascertain, detect, devise, discern, discover, encounter, expose, find out, learn, locate, notice, reveal, uncover. ANT.-cover, hide, lose, mask, screen.

fine, *a.* SYN.-choice, dainty, delicate, elegant, exquisite, nice, pure, refined, splendid, subtle; beautiful, handsome, pretty; minute, powdered, pulverized, sharp, slender, small, thin. ANT.-blunt, coarse, large, rough, thick.

finish, *v.* SYN.-accomplish, achieve, close, complete, conclude, consummate, do, end, execute, fulfill, get done, perfect, perform, terminate.

finished, *a.* SYN.-accomplished, ceased, complete, concluded, consummated, done, ended, executed, finalized, full, perfect, settled, stopped, thorough, total, unbroken, undivided. ANT.-imperfect, lacking, unfinished.

fire, *n.* SYN.-blaze, burning, combustion, conflagration, embers, flame, glow, heat, sparks, warmth. ANT.-cold; apathy, quiescence.

firm, *a.* SYN.-constant, durable, enduring, established, fixed, hardy, immovable, immutable, lasting, permanent, secure, stable, staunch, steadfast, steady, strong, sturdy, tough, unwavering; callous, incorruptible, obdurate, stubborn. ANT.-changeable, erratic, irresolute, vacillating, variable.

firm, *n.* SYN.-association, business, company, concern, corporation, partnership. ANT.-dispersion, individual.

first, *a.* SYN.-beginning, earliest, initial, original, primary, prime, primeval, primitive, pristine; chief, foremost. ANT.-hindmost, last, latest; least, subordinate.

fit, *a.* SYN.-applicable, appropriate, becoming, befitting, beneficial, comely, competent, decent, decorous, desirable, equitable, fitting, likely, proper, qualified, respectable, rightful, seemly, suitable, suited, tolerable; healthy, robust, trim. ANT.-awkward, brash, gross, ill-timed, improper, inappropriate, unqualified.

fit, *v.* SYN.-accommodate, adapt, adjust, agree, belong, conform, harmonize, match, relate, suit. ANT.-clash, disturb, misapply, misfit.

fitting, *a.* SYN.-applicable, appropriate, apt, becoming, particular, proper, suitable. ANT.-contrary, improper, inappropriate.

fix, *v.* SYN.-affix, attach, bind, fasten, link, place, plant, secure, set, stick, tie; define, determine, establish, limit, set, settle; adjust, correct, mend, patch, rectify, regulate, rejuvenate, repair. ANT.-displace, remove, unfasten; alter, change, disturb, modify; damage, mistreat.

fixed, *a.* SYN.-abiding, ceaseless, constant, continual, enduring, faithful, immutable, invariant, permanent, perpetual, persistent, unalterable, unchanging, unwavering; adjusted, corrected, improved, mended, restored. ANT.-fickle, mutable, vacillating, wavering.

flagrant, *a.* SYN.-conspicuous, disgraceful, glaring, gross, heinous, obvious, outrageous, overt, prominent, shameful.

flamboyant, *a.* SYN.-adorned, bombastic, decorated, elaborate, flashy, lavish, ornate, ostentatious, resplendent, showy, superficial

flame, *n.* SYN.-brightness, fire, flare, illumination, light, radiance. ANT.-darkness, gloom, obscurity, shadow.

flash, *n.* SYN.-burst, flicker, glimmer, glitter, illumination, impulse, moment, reflection, spark, sparkle, vision, wink.

flashy, *a.* SYN.-adorned, decorated, elaborate, embellished, flamboyant, garnished, gaudy, lavish, ornate, ostentatious, pretentious, showy, superficial, tawdry.

flat, *a.* SYN.-even, horizontal, level, low, plane, smooth; boring, pointless, prosaic, tedious, unanimated; dull, flavorless, insipid, stale, tasteless, unsavory, vapid; absolute, downright, positive, unqualified. ANT.-broken, hilly, irregular, sloping; exciting, racy; savory, tasty.

flattery, n. SYN.-acclamation, adulation, applause, approval, commendation, compliment, eulogy, fawning, homage, praise, tribute. ANT.-affront, criticism, insult, taunt.

flaunt, v. SYN.-boast, brag, crow, display, glory, flourish, parade, show, vaunt. ANT.-apologize, deprecate, humble, minimize.

flavor, n. SYN.-characteristic, essence, quality, relish, savor, seasoning, style, tang, taste.

flaw, n. SYN.-blemish, blot, scar, speck, stain; defect, error, fault, imperfection, mistake, omission, shortcoming, vice. ANT.-adornment, embellishment, perfection, purity.

flee, n. SYN.-abscond, decamp, escape, fly, hasten, run away. ANT.-appear, arrive, remain, stay.

fleet, a. SYN.-expeditious, fast, quick, rapid, speedy, swift. ANT.-slow, sluggish.

fleeting, a. SYN.-brief, ephemeral, evanescent, momentary, short-lived, temporary, transient. ANT.-abiding, immortal, lasting, permanent, timeless.

flexible, a. SYN.-compliant, ductile, elastic, formative, impressionable, limber, lithe, pliable, pliant, resilient, supple, tractable, yielding. ANT.-brittle, hard, rigid, stiff, unbending.

flighty, a. SYN.-capricious, erratic, fickle, frivolous, inconstant, unstable, volatile, whimsical. ANT.-disciplined, reliable, restrained.

flimsy, a. SYN.-decrepit, fragile, frail, inadequate, weak; ineffectual,

poor, superficial.

flippant, a. SYN.-disrespectful, facetious, frivolent, impertinent, impudent, offhand, rude, saucy, smart.

flop, v. SYN.-blunder, bomb, fail, falter, flunk, founder, miscarry; flap, flounder, flounce, jerk, quiver, squirm, wiggle, wriggle.

flourish, v. SYN.-burgeon, flower, grow, increase, luxuriate, prosper, thrive; brandish, display, flaunt, gesture, parade, vaunt, wave; adorn, decorate, embellish.

flow, v. SYN.-gush, run, spout, spurt, stream; come, emanate, issue, originate, proceed, result; abound, be copious.

flowing, a, SYN.-ample, complete, copious, extensive, plentiful, sweeping; full, loose, voluminous. ANT.-depleted, devoid, empty, vacant; insufficient, lacking, partial.

fluctuate, v. SYN.-change, hesitate, oscillate, undulate, vacillate, vary, waver. ANT.-adhere, decide, persist, resolve, stick.

fluent, a. SYN.-articulate, eloquent, garrulous, glib, mellifluent, persuasive, smooth, talkative, vocal, wordy; copious, flowing.

fluid, a. SYN.-flowing, fluent, juicy, liquid, running, watery. ANT.-congealed, frozen, solid, stiff.

fluster, v. SYN.-abash, chagrin, discomfit, distress, embarrass, entangle, hamper, hinder, mortify, perplex, rattle, trouble. ANT.-cheer, encourage, help, relieve

fly, v. SYN.-flit, float, flutter, glide, hover, mount, sail, soar; dart, rush, shoot, spring; abscond, decamp, escape, flee, run away. ANT.-descend, fall, plummet, sink.

foil, v. SYN.-baffle, balk, circumvent, defeat, disappoint, frustrate, hin-

der, outwit, prevent, thwart. ANT.-
accomplish, fulfill, further, promote.

folk, *n.* SYN.-clan, community, culture, family, kindred, lineage, nation, relations, society, tribe.

follow, *v.* SYN.-succeed, come next;
comply, heed, obey, observe;
adopt, copy, imitate; accompany,
attend; chase, pursue, trail; ensue,
result. ANT.-precede; guide, lead;
avoid, elude, flee; cause.

follower, *n.* SYN.-adherent, admirer,
advocate, attendant, backer, believer, companion, devotee, disciple, helper, henchman, member,
partisan, participant, pupil, successor, supporter, votary, witness.
ANT.-chief, head, leader, master.

folly, *n.* SYN.-foolishness, imbecility,
silliness; absurdity, extravagance,
imprudence, indiscretion. ANT.-
sense, wisdom; judgment, prudence, reasonableness.

fond, *a.* SYN.-affectionate, attached,
dedicated, devoted, disposed, given
up to, inclined, prone, wedded.
ANT.-detached, disinclined, indisposed, untrammeled.

fondle, *v.* SYN.-caress, coddle, cuddle, embrace, hug, kiss, pet. ANT.-
annoy, buffet, spurn, tease, vex.

fondness, *n.* SYN.-affection, attachment, endearment, kindness, love,
tenderness; disposition, emotion,
feeling, inclination. ANT.-aversion,
hatred, indifference, repugnance,
repulsion.

food, *n.* SYN.-diet, edibles, fare, feed,
meal, nutriment, provisions, ra-
tions, repast, sustenance, viands,
victuals. ANT.-drink, hunger, starvation, want.

fool, *n.* SYN.-buffoon, clown, harlequin, jester; blockhead, dolt,

dunce, idiot, imbecile, nincompoop, numbskull, oaf, simpleton.
ANT.-genius, philosopher, sage,
scholar.

foolish, *a.* SYN.-absurd, asinine,
brainless, crazy, idiotic, irrational,
nonsensical, preposterous, ridiculous, senseless, silly, simple. ANT.-
judicious, prudent, sagacious,
sane, wise.

forbear, *v.* SYN.-abstain, cease, desist, omit, refrain, spare, stop,
withhold. ANT.-continue, indulge,
persist.

forbid, *v.* SYN.-ban, bar, block, deny,
debar, disallow, embargo, hinder,
inhibit, interdict, prevent, prohibit,
restrain. ANT.-allow, authorize,
permit, recommend, sanction, tolerate.

force, *n.* SYN.-dint, emphasis, energy, intensity, might, potency,
power, strength, vigor; coercion,
compulsion, constraint, domi-
nance, violence. ANT.-feebleness,
frailty, impotence, weakness; persuasion.

force, *v.* SYN.-coerce, command,
compel, constrain, demand, drive,
enforce, impel, impose, insist,
make, oblige, order, require. ANT.-
allure, convince, induce, persuade,
prevent.

forceful, *a.* SYN.-cogent, commend-
ing, dominant, firm, forcible, fortified, hale, hardy, impregnable,
mighty, potent, powerful, robust,
sinewy, strong, sturdy, tough. ANT.-
brittle, delicate, feeble, fragile, insipid.

foreboding, *n.* SYN.-anticipation,
apprehension, dread, expectation,
fear, feeling, premonition, prescience, presentiment.

forecast, *n.* SYN.-anticipation,

augury, conjecture, divination, estimate, guess, prediction, prognosis, prognostication, projection, prophecy.

foreign, *a.* SYN.-alien, contrasted, exotic, extraneous, imported, irrelevant, outlandish, remote, strange, unconnected, unknown. ANT.-akin, germane, kindred, relevant.

foreigner, *n.* SYN.-alien, immigrant, newcomer, outsider, stranger. ANT.-acquaintance, associate, countryman, friend, neighbor.

foresight, *n.* SYN.-anticipation, carefulness, contemplation, expectation, forethought, hope, preconception, prescience, presentiment, prudence. ANT.-doubt, dread, fear, worry.

foretell, *v.* SYN.-augur, divine, forecast, foresee, portend, predict, prophesy.

forever, adv. SYN.-always, constantly, continually, eternally, ever, evermore, forever, incessantly, perpetually, unceasingly. ANT.-fitfully, never, occasionally, rarely, sometimes.

forge, *v.* SYN.-coin, copy, counterfeit, duplicate, fabricate, falsify, imitate, reproduce; create, fabricate, fashion, make, produce.

forgery, *n.* SYN.-bogus, copy, counterfeit, fabrication, fake, hoax, phony.

forgive, *v.* SYN.-absolve, acquit, condone, excuse, exonerate, forget, overlook, pardon, release, remit. ANT.-accuse, chastise, condemn, convict, punish.

forgiveness, *n.* SYN.-absolution, acquittal, amnesty, clemency, leniency, mercy, pardon, remission. ANT.-conviction, penalty, punishment, sentence.

forlorn, *a.* SYN.-abandoned, alone, comfortless, deserted, desolate, disconsolate, destitute, distressed, forgotten, forsaken, heartbroken, miserable, pitiable, sad, wretched. ANT.-contented, fortunate, happy.

form, *n.* SYN.-approach, ceremony, conformity, custom, formality, manner, method, practice, procedure, ritual, system; appearance, arrangement, configuration, design, fashion, formation, structure,

form, *v.* SYN.-construct, create, fashion, forge, make, mold, produce, shape; compose, constitute, make up; arrange, combine, organize; devise, frame, invent. ANT.-destroy, disfigure, dismantle, misshape, wreck.

formal, *a.* SYN.-affected, ceremonious, correct, decorous, exact, methodical, precise, proper, regular, solemn, stiff; external, outward, perfunctory. ANT.-easy, natural, unconstrained, unconventional; heartfelt.

formed, *a.* SYN.-built, carved, created, cultivated, developed, established, modeled, molded, patterned, shaped.

former, *a.* SYN.-aforesaid, antecedent, earlier, erstwhile, late, once, onetime, preceding, previous, prior. ANT.-consequent, following, later, subsequent, succeeding.

formulate, *v.* SYN.-compose, create, draw, engender, fashion, form, frame, generate, invent, make, originate, prepare, produce. ANT.-annihilate, demolish, destroy; disband, terminate.

fornication, *n.* SYN.-adultery, carnality, debauchery, lechery, lewdness, licentiousness, promiscuity.

forsake, v. SYN.-abandon, abdicate, abjure, abstain, relinquish, renounce, resign, surrender, vacate, waive; desert, leave, quit. ANT.-defend, maintain, uphold; stay, support.

forthcoming, a. SYN.-anticipated, approaching, coming, destined, expected, fated, imminent, impending, inevitable, near, prospective.

fortified, a. SYN.-armed, armored, defended, enclosed, guarded, protected, secured, walled; heartened, invigorated, reinforced, strengthened.

fortitude, n. SYN.-boldness, bravery, chivalry, courage, durability, fearlessness, intrepidity, mettle, might, potency, power, prowess, stamina, stoutness, strength, sturdiness, resolution, toughness. ANT.-cowardice, fear, pusillanimity, timidity.

fortuity, n. SYN.-accident, chance, contingency, exigency, incidence, luck, mishap, predicament. ANT.-calculation, design, intention, purpose.

fortunate, a. SYN.-advantageous, auspicious, benign, blessed, favored, felicitous, flourishing, fortuitous, happy, lucky, propitious, prosperous, successful. ANT.-cheerless, condemned, ill-fated, persecuted, unlucky.

fortune, n. SYN.-accident, break, chance, fate, fluke, lot, luck, windfall; assets, bundle, estate, inheritance, mint, money, possessions, property, riches, treasure, wealth.

forward, n. SYN.-beginning, introduction, overture, preamble, preface, prelude, prologue, start. ANT.-completion, conclusion, end, epilogue, finale.

forward, v. SYN.-advance, further, promote; improve, proceed, progress, rise, thrive. ANT.-hinder, oppose, retard, retreat, withhold.

fossil, a. SYN.-ancient, antique, archaic, out-of-date, prehistoric, venerable.

foster, v. SYN.-advance, cherish, cultivate, encourage, favor, further, help, nourish, nurture, raise, retain, support, sustain. ANT.-abandon, dislike, disregard, neglect, reject.

foul, a. SYN.-dirty, filthy, grimy, muddy, soiled, squalid; indecent, nasty, obscene; base, contemptible, despicable, low, mean, pitiful, shabby. ANT.-clean, neat, presentable; pure, wholesome.

found, v. SYN.-begin, create, endow, erect, establish, form, institute, organize, raise. ANT.-abolish, demolish, overthrow, unsettle, upset.

foundation, n. SYN.-base, basis, bedrock, bottom, footing, ground, groundwork, root, substructure, support, underpinning; authority, data, facts, justification, observation, reason; association, charity, company, endowment, establishment, institute, institution, organization, society. ANT.-building, cover, superstructure, top.

fracture, v. SYN.-break, burst, cleave, crack, crush, demolish, destroy, rend, rupture, separate, sever, shatter, shear, smash, split. ANT.-join, mend, renovate, repair, restore.

fragile, a. SYN.-breakable, brittle, delicate, exquisite, feeble, fine, frail, infirm, weak. ANT.-durable, hardy, strong, sturdy, tough.

fragment, n. SYN.-division, moiety, part, piece, portion, remnant, scrap, section, segment, share; component, element, faction, fraction, ingredient. ANT.-entirety, whole.

fragrance, *n.* SYN.-aroma, bouquet, essence, incense, odor, perfume, scent, smell.

frail, *a.* SYN.-breakable, brittle, dainty, delicate, feeble, fragile, infirm, weak. ANT.-durable, hardy, strong, sturdy, tough.

frame, *v.* SYN.-build, conceive, construct, contrive, devise, erect, fabricate, form, make, outline, sketch. ANT.-demolish, destroy, raze.

frank, *a.* SYN.-artless, blunt, bold, candid, direct, familiar, free, forthright, honest, ingenious, open, outspoken, plain, sincere, straightforward, truthful, undisguised; fair, impartial, just, unbiased, uninhibited. ANT.-contrived, scheming, sly, wily.

frantic, *a.* SYN.-crazy, delirious, deranged, desperate, distracted, excited, frenzied, mad, raging, rash, reckless, raving, wild. SYN.-calm, composed, serene.

fraternity, *n.* SYN.-brotherliness, fellowship, kindness, solidarity; association, brotherhood, clan, society. ANT.-acrimony, discord, opposition, strife.

fraternize, *v.* SYN.-associate, consort, hobnob, join, mingle, mix, socialize. ANT.-dissociate, divide, segregate, separate, sort.

fraud, *n.* SYN.-artifice, cheat, chicanery, deceit, deception, duplicity, guile, imposition, imposture, misrepresentation, racket, sham, swindle, trick, trickery; charlatan, cheat, fake, impostor, pretender, quack. ANT.-fairness, honesty, integrity, sincerity.

freak, *n.* SYN.-aberration, curiosity, malformation, monstrosity, mutation, oddity, rarity; abnormal, bizarre, capricious, erratic odd, peculiar, strange, unusual.

free, *a.* SYN.-autonomous, emancipated, exempt, freed, independent, liberated, unconfined, unrestricted; clear, loose, open, unfastened, unobstructed; immune, uninfected; artless, careless, easy, familiar, frank; bounteous, bountiful, complimentary, generous, gratis, liberal, munificent. ANT.-confined, restrained, restricted; blocked, clogged, impeded; subject; illiberal, parsimonious, stingy.

free, *v.* SYN.-absolve, acquit, deliver, discharge, disentangle, dismiss, emancipate, let go, liberate, loosen, pardon, release, rid, set free, untie. ANT.-confine, imprison, oppress, restrict, subjugate.

freedom, *n.* SYN.-exemption, familiarity, immunity, impunity, independence, latitude, leeway, liberation, liberty, license, privilege, unrestraint. ANT.-bondage, compulsion, constraint, necessity, servitude.

freely, *a.* SYN.-abundantly, deliberately, easily, extravagantly, frankly, intentionally, loosely, openly, profusely, spontaneously, unhindered, voluntarily, willingly.

freezing, *a.* SYN.-arctic, chilly, cold, cool, frigid, frosty, frozen, icy, polar, wintry. ANT.-burning, fiery, heated, hot, torrid.

freight, *n.* SYN.-burden, cargo, encumbrance, goods, load, packages, shipment.

frenzied, *a.* SYN.-frantic, impetuous, irregular, mad, turbulent, wanton, wayward, wild; boisterous, stormy, tempestuous; extravagant, foolish, giddy, rash, reckless. ANT.-civilized, gentle; calm, placid, quiet.

frequent, *a.* SYN.-common, continual, general, habitual, incessant, often, periodic, persistent, repeated, usual. ANT.-exceptional, rare, recurrent, regular, scanty, solitary, unique.

frequent, *v.* SYN.-attend, hang out, haunt, visit.

frequently, *adv.* SYN.-commonly, generally, often, recurrently, regularly, repeatedly. ANT.-infrequently, occasionally, rarely, seldom, sporadically.

fresh, *a.* SYN.-modern, new, novel, original, recent; additional, further; bracing brisk, cool, invigorating, refreshing, stimulating; artless, green, inexperienced, natural, raw, unskilled, untrained. ANT.-decayed, faded, hackneyed, musty, stagnant.

fretful, *a.* SYN.-fractious, ill-natured, ill-tempered, irritable, peevish, petulant, snappish, testy, touchy, waspish. ANT.-affable, genial, good-natured, good-tempered, pleasant.

friend, *n.* SYN.-acquaintance, ally, associate, chum, colleague, companion, compatriot, comrade, confidant, crony, intimate; accomplice, advocate, backer, defender, patron, supporter, well-wisher. ANT.-adversary, enemy, stranger.

friendly, *a.* SYN.-affable, affectionate, amiable, amicable, attentive, civil, close, companionable, congenial, cordial, devoted, familiar, gracious, helpful, intimate, kind, kindly, neighborly, pleasant, sociable, social, sympathetic, warmhearted. ANT.-aloof, antagonistic, cool, distant, hostile, reserved.

friendship, *n.* SYN.-acquaintance, affection, association, brotherhood, camaraderie, cognizance, companionship, congeniality, devotion, esteem, familiarity, fellowship, friendship, harmony, intimacy, kindliness, kindness, sympathy. ANT.-ignorance, inexperience, unfamiliarity.

fright, *n.* SYN.-affright, alarm, apprehension, consternation, dread, fear, horror, panic, scare, terror, trepidation. ANT.-assurance, boldness, calm, composure, bravery, courage, fearlessness, quiet, security, tranquillity.

frighten, *v.* SYN.-affright, alarm, appall, astound, badger, daunt, dismay, disturb, horrify, intimidate, panic, petrify, scare, startle, terrify, terrorize, threaten. ANT.-allay, compose, embolden, reassure, soothe.

frightened, *a.* SYN.-afraid, apprehensive, disturbed, fainthearted, fearful, horrified, intimidated, scared, terrified, timorous. ANT.-assured, bold, composed, courageous, sanguine.

frigid, *a.* SYN.-arctic, chilly, cold, cool, freezing, frosty, frozen, icy, wintry; indifferent, passionless, phlegmatic, stoical, unfeeling. ANT.-burning, fiery, heated, hot, torrid; ardent, passionate.

frisky, *a.* SYN.-active, alive, animated, boisterous, dapper, dashing, gleeful, jaunty, lively, playful, spirited.

frivolous, *a.* SYN.-childish, cursory, dizzy, exterior, flighty, flimsy, foolish, imperfect, paltry, petty, shallow, slight, superficial, trifling, trivial, unimportant. ANT.-abstruse, complete, deep, profound, thorough.

frolic, n. SYN.-fun, lark, merriment, play, prank, sport.

frolic, v. SYN.-caper, cavort, gamble, gambol, play, revel, rollick, romp, sport.

front, n. SYN.-anterior, bow, exterior, facade, face, foreground, frontage, nose, prow, vanguard; appearance, aspect, carriage, countenance, demeanor, expression, mask, mien, presence. ANT.-back, posterior, rear.

frontier, n. SYN.-border, boundary, brim, brink, edge, fringe, hinterland, limit, outskirts, rim, termination, verge. ANT.-center, core, interior, mainland.

frozen, a. SYN.-arctic, chilled, cold, freezing, frigid, frosted, frosty, iced, icy, wintry. ANT.-burning, fiery, heated, hot, torrid.

frugal, a. SYN.-careful, economical, niggardly, parsimonious, provident, prudent, saving, spare, sparing, stingy, temperate, thrifty. ANT.-extravagant, intemperate, self-indulgent, wasteful.

frustrate, v. SYN.-baffle, balk, bewilder, circumvent, confuse, defeat, disappoint, foil, hinder, mystify, nonplus, outwit, perplex, prevent, thwart. ANT.-accomplish, fulfill, further, promote.

fulfill, v. SYN.-accomplish, achieve, complete, comply, conclude, consummate, discharge, effect, execute, finish, perform, terminate.

full, a. SYN.-abundant, ample, complete, copious, crammed, entire, extensive, filled, gorged, lavish, packed, perfect, plentiful, replete, satiated, satisfied, saturated, soaked, sufficient; baggy, flowing, loose, voluminous; broad, detailed, exhaustive, ranging, unlimited. ANT.-depleted, devoid, empty, va-

cant; insufficient, lacking, partial.

fully, a. SYN.-abundantly, adequately, amply, completely, entirely, perfectly, sufficiently, thoroughly, well, wholly.

fun, n. SYN.-amusement, antic, caper, comedy, diversion, enjoyment, entertainment, festivity, foolery, frolic, game, glee, jest, lark, laughter, mirth, pastime, play, pleasure, prank, recreation, relaxation, romp, sport, trifling.

function, n. SYN.-business, capacity, duty, employment, faculty, office, province, purpose, service, utility; banquet, celebration, meeting, party, reception, social.

function, n. SYN.-business, capacity, duty, office, purpose, service.

function, v. SYN.-act, do, go, move, officiate, operate, perform, run, work.

fund, n. SYN.-accumulation, donation, endowment, hoard, provision, reserve, stock, store, supply.

fundamental, a. SYN.-absolute, basic, cardinal, central, crucial, elemental, elementary, essential, first, important, intrinsic, key, precise, primary, rudimentary, simple, specific. ANT.-abstract, abstruse, auxiliary, common, complex, dispensable, elaborate, intricate, secondary, subordinate, unimportant.

funds, n. SYN.-assets, capital, cash, collateral, currency, money, reserves, resources, revenue, savings, wealth, wherewithal

funny, a. SYN.-amusing, comic, comical, droll, entertaining, facetious, farcical, hilarious, humorous, jocular, laughable, ludicrous, ridiculous, whimsical, witty; curious, odd, peculiar, queer, strange, suspicious, unusual. ANT.-melancholy, sad, serious, sober, solemn.

furious, *a.* SYN.-agitated, angry, enraged, exasperated, incensed, indignant, irate, maddened, provoked, raging, tumultuous, wrathful, wroth; extreme, frantic, frenetic, frenzied, intense. ANT.-calm, happy, pleased, satisfied.

furnish, *v.* SYN.-appoint, endow, equip, fit, fit out provide, purvey, stock, supply; afford, cater, give, produce, yield. ANT.-denude, despoil, divest, strip.

further, *v.* SYN.-advance, aggrandize, elevate, forward, promote, bring forward, offer, propose, propound, proceed, progress, rise, thrive, augment, enlarge, increase. ANT.-hinder, oppose, retard, retreat, withhold.

furor, *n.* SYN.-agitation, bedlam, clamor, commotion, disturbance, excitement, rumpus, shouting, stir, tumult.

fury, *n.* SYN.-anger, choler, fierceness, indignation, ire, irritation, passion, petulance, rage, resentment, temper, turbulence, vehemence, violence, wrath. ANT.-conciliation, forbearance, patience, peace, self-control.

fusion, *n.* SYN.-combination, concurrence, incorporation, joining, solidarity, unification, union; alliance, amalgamation, coalition, concert, confederacy, league, marriage. ANT.-division, schism, separation; disagreement, discord.

fussy, *a.* SYN.-careful, conscientious, demanding, exact, exacting, fastidious, meticulous, particular, precise.

futile, *a.* SYN.-abortive, bootless, empty, fruitless, idle, ineffective, ineffectual, pointless, unavailing, unproductive, unsatisfactory, useless, valueless, vain, vapid, worthless. ANT.-effective, potent, profitable.

G

gab, *v.* SYN.-babble, chatter, discuss, gossip, jabber, prate, prattle, ramble, speak, talk.

gaily, *a.* SYN.-brightly, brilliantly, colorfully, extravagantly, jovially, joyfully, joyously, gaudily, showily, spiritedly.

gain, *n.* SYN.-accrual, accumulation, addition, advantage, benefit, favor, goods, increase, interest, profit, profits. ANT.-calamity, distress, handicap, trouble.

gain, *v.* SYN.-achieve, acquire, advance, approach, attain, augment, benefit, earn, get, improve, net, obtain, procure, profit, progress, reach, secure, win. ANT.-forfeit, lose, surrender.

gale, *n.* SYN.-blow, gust, hurricane, squall, storm, typhoon, wind.

gallant, *a.* SYN.-bold, brave, chivalrous, courageous, courtly, daring, dauntless, fine, intrepid, magnificent, noble, polite, splendid, valiant.

gallery, *n.* SYN.-arcade, balcony, grandstand, mezzanine, veranda; audience, onlookers, public, spectators; exhibit, hall, museum, salon, showroom, wing.

game, *n.* SYN.-amusement, contest, diversion, fun, match, merriment, pastime, play, recreation, sport. ANT.-business drudgery, hardship, labor, work.

gap, *n.* SYN.-aperture, breach, break, cavity, fissure, gulf, hole, opening, orifice, pore, rift, void; arroyo, canyon, chasm, gulch, gully, hollow, ravine; hiatus, interim, intermission, lag, lull, pause, recess.

garb, n. SYN.-appearance, fashion, form, guise, mode, style, uniform; attire, clothes, garments, vestments.

garish, a. SYN.-colorful, flashy, gaudy, loud, ornate, ostentatious, showy, spirited, tawdry.

garment, garments, n. SYN.-apparel, array, attire, clothes, clothing, drapery, dress, garb, raiment, vestments, vesture. ANT.-nakedness, nudity.

garnish, v. SYN.-adorn, beautify, bedeck, decorate, embellish, enhance, enrich, ornament, trim. ANT.-debase, defame, expose, strip, uncover.

garrulous, a. SYN.-articulate, chattering, chatty, communicative, effusive, glib, loquacious, talkative, verbose, voluble. ANT.-laconic, reticent, silent, taciturn, uncommunicative.

gash, n. SYN.-cut, slash, slit, wound.

gate, n. SYN.-barrier, entrance, entry, inlet, opening, passage, portal.

gather, v. SYN.-accumulate, amass, associate, assemble, collect, congregate, convene, hoard, muster, rally, reunite, swarm; cull, garner, glean, harvest, pick, pluck, reap, select, sort; assume, conclude, deduce, infer, judge, learn. ANT.-disband, disperse, distribute, scatter, separate.

gathered, a. SYN.-assembled, collected, congregated, convened, convoked, grouped, joined, massed, met, rallied, thronged, united.

gathering, n. SYN.-assembly, association, caucus, committee, com-

pany, conclave, conference, congregation, convention, convocation, council, crowd, flock, herd, legislature, meet, reunion, society, throng, turnout.

gaudy, a. SYN.-colorful, decorated, elaborate, embellished, flamboyant, flashy, garish, loud, meretricious, ornamented, ornate, ostentatious, showy, spirited, superficial, tasteless, tawdry, vulgar.

gaunt, a. SYN.-emaciated, haggard, lank, lean, scrawny, skinny, slender, slight, slim, spare, tenuous, thin. ANT.-broad, bulky, fat, thick, wide.

gay, a. SYN.-cheerful, frolicsome, glad, happy, jolly, jovial, joyful, joyous, lighthearted, merry, sprightly, vivacious. ANT.-depressed, glum, mournful, sad, sullen.

gear, n. SYN.-accouterments, equipment, material, outfit, rigging, tackle, things.

gem, n. SYN.-bauble, jewel, ornament, stone; cherished, prized, treasured.

general, n. SYN.-broad, common, comprehensive, customary, ecumenical, extensive, inclusive, ordinary, popular, prevalent, regular, ubiquitous, universal, usual, widespread; imprecise, indefinite, inexact, vague. ANT.-exceptional, rare, singular; definite, particular, specific.

generate, v. SYN.-afford, bear, bestow, breed, cause, create, engender, form, impart, induce, make, originate, pay, produce, provoke, sire, spawn, supply, yield.

generation, n. SYN.-age, antiquity, date, epoch, era, period, span, time; creation, formation, inven-

tion, procreation, production. ANT.-
childhood, infancy, youth; breeding, creation, procreation, reproduction.

generous, *a.* SYN.-altruistic, benefi-
cent, charitable, giving, lavish, liberal, magnanimous, munificent,
noble, openhanded, philanthropic,
unselfish; abundant, ample, bountiful, copious, flowing, overflowing,
plentiful. ANT.-covetous, greedy,
miserly, selfish, stingy.

genial, *a.* SYN.-affable, agreeable,
amicable, companionable, cordial,
friendly, hearty, kindly, neighborly,
pleasant, sociable, social. ANT.-an-
tagonistic, cool, distant, hostile, reserved.

genius, *n.* SYN.-ability, aptitude,
brains, capability, creativity, faculty, gift, inspiration, intellect, intelligence, originality, sagacity, talent, wisdom; adept, gifted, intellectual, prodigy, proficient. ANT.-in-
eptitude, obtuseness, shallowness,
stupidity; dolt, dullard, moron.

genre, *n.* SYN.-category, class, grade,
kind, order, rank, set, sort, variety.

gentle, *a.* SYN.-amiable, benign,
calm, considerate, cultivated, disciplined, docile, kind, mild, peaceful, placid, pliant, polite, refined,
relaxed, respectable, sensitive, serene, soft, soothing, tame, temperate, tender, tractable, well-bred.
ANT.-fierce, harsh, rough, savage,
violent.

gently, *a.* SYN.-benevolently, care-
fully, cautiously, considerately,
delicately, kindly, mildly, sensi-
tively, tenderly.

genuine, *a.* SYN.-accurate, actual,
authentic, bona fide, certain, certified, legitimate, natural, original,
precise, positive, proven, real, sin-

cere, tested, true, unadulterated,
unaffected, valid, veritable. ANT.-
artificial, bogus, counterfeit, false,
sham.

germ, *n.* SYN.-antibody, bacteria,
contagion, infection, microbe, pest,
virus; ailment, contamination, disease, poison, pollution, taint; beginning, genesis, inception, origin,
seed, source.

gesture, *n.* SYN. indication, motion,
portent, sign, signal, symbol, token; appearance, attitude, concession, display, formality, posture.

get, *v.* SYN.-achieve, acquire, attain,
earn, gain, get, obtain, procure,
purchase, reach, realize, receive,
secure, seize, take, win; apprehend, comprehend, grasp, learn,
perceive, understand. ANT.-forfeit,
leave, lose, renounce, surrender.

ghastly, *a.* SYN.-abhorrent, cadaver-
ous, deathlike, disgusting, dreadful, frightful, grisly, gruesome,
hideous, horrible, repulsive,
shocking.

ghost, *n.* SYN.-apparition, demon,
phantom, shade, specter, spirit,
spook, vision; hint, shadow, suggestion.

giant, *a.* SYN.-colossal, enormous,
gigantic, huge, immense, large,
monstrous, tremendous.

gift, *n.* SYN.-award, benefaction, bequest, boon, bounty, charity, donation, endowment, favor, grant,
gratuity, handout, largess, legacy,
offering, present, token; ability,
aptitude, capability, capacity,
faculty, forte, genius, power, talent.
ANT.-deprivation, earnings, loss,
purchase; incapacity, ineptitude,
stupidity.

gigantic, *a.* SYN.-broad, colossal,
elephantine, enormous, gargan-

tuan, huge, immense, large, prodigious, tremendous, vast. ANT.-diminutive, little, minute, small, tiny.

giggle, n. SYN.-cackle, chortle, chuckle, laugh, snicker, snigger, titter.

gimmick, n. SYN.-apparatus, artifice, contraption, contrivance, device, gadget, mechanism, ruse, scheme, trick, trickery.

gingerly, SYN.-carefully, cautiously, daintily, easily, fastidiously, gently. ANT.-boisterous, brusk, roughly.

girl, n. SYN.-child, coed, damsel, lassie, maid, maiden, miss, young lady, young woman.

gist, n. SYN.-basis, connotation, core, drift, essence, explanation, heart, implication, import, intent, interpretation, meaning, meat, point, purport, purpose, sense, significance, signification, substance.

give, v. SYN.-assign, award, bequeath, bestow, confer, contribute, deliver, donate, endow, furnish, grant, impart, issue, offer, present, provide, render, supply. ANT.-keep, retain, seize, withdraw.

glad, a. SYN.-cheerful, contented, delighted, exhilarated, exulting, gratified, happy, jovial, joyous, lighthearted, merry, pleased. ANT.-dejected, depressed, despondent, melancholy, sad.

gladly, a. SYN.-blissfully, cheerfully, cordially, delightfully, enthusiastically, gaily, gleefully, happily, heartily, joyfully, joyously, lovingly, passionately, readily, sweetly, warmly, willingly.

gladness, n. SYN.-beatitude, blessedness, bliss, contentment, cheer, delight, felicity, gaiety, glee, happi-

ness, merriment, pleasure, satisfaction, well-being. ANT.-despair, grief, misery, sadness, sorrow.

glance, n. SYN.-behold, eye, gaze, glimpse, look, observe, regard, scan, see, survey, view. ANT.-avert, miss, overlook, stare.

glare, v. SYN.-blind, dazzle, gleam, radiate, shine; frown, glower, scowl, stare.

gleam, v. SYN.-beam, flash, flicker, glare, glimmer, glisten, glitter, glow, shimmer, shine, sparkle, twinkle.

glib, a. SYN.-artful, articulate, diplomatic, facile, fluent, polished, sleek, slick, smooth, suave, superficial, urbane. ANT.-bluff, blunt, harsh, rough, rugged.

glide, v. SYN.-coast, descend, drift, float, flow, fly, slide, slip, slither, soar, waft,

gloom, n. SYN.-blackness, bleakness, darkness, dimness, obscurity, shadow; apprehension, dejection, depression, despair, despondency, foreboding, grief, malaise, melancholy, misery, misgiving, mourning, pessimism, sadness, sorrow, woe. ANT.-exultation, frivolity, joy, light, mirth.

gloomy, a. SYN.-bleak, cheerless, dark, dejected, depressed, despondent, disconsolate, dismal, dispirited, doleful, dreary, dull, funereal, glum, lonesome, melancholy, moody, sad, somber, sorrowful. ANT.-cheerful, gay, happy, joyous, lively, merry.

glorify, v. SYN.-acclaim, adore, aggrandize, bless, commend, consecrate, dignify, enshrine, enthrone, exalt, extol, hallow, honor, laud, revere, venerate. ANT.-abuse, debase, degrade, dishonor, mock.

glorious, *a.* SYN.-admirable, celebrated, distinguished, elevated, esteemed, exalted, excellent, grand, gratifying, high, honorable, honored, illustrious, lofty, magnificent, majestic, memorable, noble, notable, praiseworthy, raised, splendid, sublime, supreme. ANT.-base, ignoble, low, ordinary, ridiculous.

glory, *n.* SYN.-admiration, adoration, deference, dignity, esteem, fame, homage, honor, praise, renown, respect, reverence, worship; beauty, brilliance, grandeur, magnificence, majesty, pomp, radiance, resplendence, richness; exult, rejoice, triumph. ANT.-contempt, derision, disgrace, dishonor, reproach.

glow, *v.* SYN.-blaze, flicker, glare, gleam, glimmer, glisten, glitter, radiate, scintillate, shimmer, shine, sparkle, twinkle.

glum, *a.* SYN.-dejected, depressed, despondent, disconsolate, dismal, dispirited, doleful, dour, fretful, gloomy, melancholy, moody, morose, plaintive, sad, somber, sorrowful, sulky, sullen, surly. ANT.-amiable, cheerful, happy, joyous, merry, pleasant.

glut, *v.* SYN.-clog, congest, fill up, inundate, occupy, overstock, pervade; cram, devour, feast, fill, gorge, overeat, sate, satiate, satisfy, stuff. ANT.-deplete, drain, empty, exhaust, void.

go, *v.* SYN.-depart, exit, fade, flee, leave, move, proceed, quit, retire, run, vacate, vanish, walk, withdraw; advance, continue, endeavor, journey, operate, perform, persevere, persist, proceed, progress, travel ANT.-arrive, come, enter, stand, stay.

goad, *v.* SYN.-coerce, drive, encourage, force, impel, induce, press, prod, prompt, push, stimulate, spur, urge, whip; bully, instigate, needle, provoke, tease.

goal, *n.* SYN.-aim, ambition, aspiration, craving, design, desire, hope, intent, intention, longing, object, objective, plan, passion.

godlike, *a.* SYN.-almighty, boundless, celestial, divine, eternal, excellent, heavenly, holy, invincible, omnipotent, spiritual, superhuman, supernatural, transcendent, universal. ANT.-blasphemous, diabolical, mundane, profane, wicked.

godly, *a.* SYN.-angelic, divine, devout, holy, pious, righteous, spiritual.

going, *v.* SYN.-auspicious, flourishing, growing, operating, profitable, running, successful, thriving; bound, destined, directed.

gone, *a.* SYN.-abandoned, departed, disappeared, disintegrated, dissipated, dissolved, extinct, left, moved, removed, retired, vanished, withdrawn.

good, *a.* SYN.-able, admirable, agreeable, benevolent, capable, cheerful, commendable, conscientious, efficient, exemplary, expert, fair, friendly, genial, gracious, honest, honorable, humane, kind, moral, pleasant, proficient, pure, reliable, skillful, virtuous, worthy; excellent, genuine, immaculate, precious, safe, sound, valid; auspicious, beneficial, favorable, profitable, useful; adequate, ample, sufficient.

gossip, *n.* SYN.-babble, chatter, hearsay, meddling, news, rumor, scandal, slander; backbiter, blabbermouth, chatterbox, meddler, muckraker, snoop, tattler.

gouge, *v.* SYN.-channel, chisel, cut, dig, scoop; cheat, defraud, extort, overcharge.

govern, *v.* SYN.-administer, command, conduct, control, dictate, direct, handle, legislate, manage, oversee, regulate, reign, rule, superintend, supervise, sway, tyrannize. ANT.-acquiesce, assent, obey, submit, yield.

graceful, *a.* SYN.-adroit, agile, controlled, dexterous, elegant, flowing, fluid, lithe, natural, nimble, pliant, poised, skilled, smooth, sprightly, supple, willowy; artistic, balanced, beautiful, comely, dainty, delicate, elegant, exquisite, harmonious, neat, pretty, slender, trim. ANT.-awkward, clumsy, deformed, gawky, ungainly.

gracious, *a.* SYN.-agreeable, amiable, condescending, cordial, courteous, courtly, earnest, engaging, elegant, friendly, good-natured, hearty, hospitable, kind, patronizing, pleasing, polite, sincere, warm. ANT.-churlish, disagreeable, hateful, ill-natured, surly.

grade, *n.* SYN.-caliber, category, class, denomination, genre, kind, order, rank, set; attribute, characteristic, distinction, feature, peculiarity, property, quality, trait, value. ANT.-being, essence, nature, substance.

gradual, *a.* SYN.-continuous, creeping, dawdling, delaying, deliberate, leisurely, slow, sluggish, unhurried. ANT.-fast, quick, rapid, speedy, swift.

grandeur, *n.* SYN.-amplitude, beauty, brilliance, ceremony, dignity, greatness, immensity, impressiveness, luxury, magnificence, pomp, resplendence, richness, splendor, stateliness, vastness.

grandiose, *a.* SYN.-august, dignified, grand, high, imposing, lofty, magnificent, majestic, noble, ostentatious, pretentious, pompous, showy, stately, sublime. ANT.-common, humble, lowly, ordinary, undignified.

grant, *n.* SYN.-allowance, appropriation, benefaction, bequest, boon, bounty, concession, donation, endowment, gift, gratuity, present, reward, subsidy.

grant, *v.* SYN.-allocate, allot, apportion, appropriate, assign, award, bestow, bequeath, confer, dispense, distribute, divide, give, measure, mete; accord, allow, concede, grant, permit, yield. ANT.-confiscate, keep, refuse, retain, withhold.

graph, *n.* SYN.-chart, design, diagram, picture, plan, plot, sketch.

graphic, *a.* SYN.-clear, colorful, comprehensive, depicted, descriptive, detailed, distinct, drawn, eloquent, explicit, forcible, illustrated, moving, outlined, pictured, picturesque, portrayed, sketched, striking, strong, telling, visual.

grasp, *v.* SYN.-capture, catch, clutch, grip, lay hold of, seize; assimilate, comprehend, conceive, follow, perceive, realize, understand. ANT.-liberate, lose, release.

grateful, *a.* SYN.-appreciative, beholden, gracious, indebted, obliged, pleased, thankful. ANT.-heedless, rude, thankless, unappreciative, unmindful.

gratifying, *a.* SYN.-acceptable, agreeable, amusing, comfortable, convenient, cozy, delightful, enjoyable, pleasant, pleasing, pleasurable, relaxed, restful, welcome.

ANT.-distressing, miserable, troubling, uncomfortable, wretched.

grave, *a.* SYN.-consequential, critical, dangerous, important, momentous, ominous, serious, weighty; dignified, sedate, serious, sober, solemn, staid, thoughtful. ANT.-insignificant, trifling, trivial; flighty, frivolous, light, merry.

grave, *n.* SYN.-barrow, catacomb, crypt, mausoleum, mound, pit, sepulcher, tomb, vault.

great, *a.* SYN.-big, enormous, gigantic, huge, immense, large, vast; countless, numerous; celebrated, eminent, famed, illustrious, prominent, renowned; critical, important, momentous, serious, vital, weighty; august, dignified, elevated, grand, majestic, noble; excellent, fine, magnificent. ANT.-diminutive, little, minute, small; common, obscure, ordinary, unknown; menial, paltry.

greedy, *a.* SYN.-avaricious, covetous, grasping, mercenary, miserly, niggardly, parsimonious, rapacious, selfish, stingy, tight; devouring, gluttonous, insatiable, intemperate, ravenous, voracious. ANT.-generous, munificent; full, satisfied.

green, *a.* SYN.-artless, callow, fresh, immature, ignorant, inexperienced, innocent, naive, natural, new, novice, raw, unsophisticated, untrained, young, youthful. ANT.-decayed, faded, hackneyed, musty, stagnant.

greet, *v.* SYN.-accost, acknowledge, address, approach, bow, hail, nod, receive, recognize, salute, speak to, welcome. ANT.-avoid, pass by.

gregarious, *a.* SYN.-affable, civil, communicative, congenial, convivial, friendly, gay, genial, hospitable, jovial, merry, outgoing, socia-

ble, social. ANT.-antisocial, disagreeable, hermitic, inhospitable.

grief, *n.* SYN.-affliction, anguish, desolation, distress, gloom, heartache, lamentation, malaise, melancholy, misery, mourning, pain, regret, remorse, sadness, sorrow, trial, tribulation, unhappiness, woe. ANT.-comfort, consolation, happiness, joy, solace.

grievance, *n.* SYN.-affliction, burden, complaint, damage, detriment, encumbrance, hardship, harm, injury, mischief, injustice, ordeal, prejudice, trial, wrong. ANT.-benefit, improvement, repair.

grieve, *v.* SYN.-agonize, bemoan, bewail, deplore, depress, distress, lament, mourn, sadden, sorrow, suffer, weep. ANT.-carouse, celebrate, rejoice, revel.

grieved, *a.* SYN.-afflicted, aggrieved, depressed, distressed, hurt, pained, sad, sorrowful, sorry, vexed. ANT.-cheerful, delighted, splendid.

grim, *a.* SYN.-appalling, austere, bleak, crusty, dire, forbidding, frightful, gloomy, glowering, glum, grouchy, grumpy, harsh, morose, scowling, severe, sour, stern, sullen, sulky.

grip, *v.* SYN.-capture, catch, clasp, clench, clutch, embrace, grab, grasp, hold, seize, snare, squeeze, trap. ANT.-liberate, loose, release, throw.

groceries, *n.* SYN.-comestibles, edibles, food, foodstuffs, perishables, produce, staples.

gross, *a.* SYN.-aggregate, entire, total, whole; brutal, enormous, glaring, grievous, manifest, plain; coarse, crass, earthy, indelicate, lewd, obscene; rough, rude, vulgar;

big, bulky, corpulent, fat, great,
large, obese. ANT.-proper, refined;
appealing, comely, delicate.

grotesque, *a.* SYN.-abnormal, deformed, distorted, hideous, malformed, repulsive, ugly; absurd,
fantastic, ludicrous, outrageous,
ridiculous, scary.

grouch, *n.* SYN.-bear, complainer,
crank, growler, grumbler, sour-
puss.

grouch, *v.* SYN.-complain, grouse,
grumble, lament, murmur, mutter,
protest, remonstrate, repine,
whine. ANT.-applaud, approve,
praise, rejoice.

group, *n.* SYN.-aggregation, assembly, band, brood, bunch, class,
cluster, collection, crowd, flock,
herd, horde, lot, mob, pack, party,
set, swarm, throng, troupe.

grovel, *v.* SYN.-abase, beg, cower,
crawl, flatter, kneel, kowtow, obey,
prostrate, snivel, stoop, surrender,
wheedle, yield.

grow, *v.* SYN.-advance, alter, build,
develop, distend, enlarge, evolve,
expand, extend, flourish, gain,
germinate, increase, mature,
mount, multiply, progress, spread,
sprout, swell, thrive. ANT.-atrophy,
contract, decay, diminish, shrink,
wane.

growth, *n.* SYN.-augmentation, development, elaboration, evolution,
expansion, increase, maturing,
progress, unfolding, unraveling.
ANT.-abbreviation, compression,
curtailment.

gruff, *a.* SYN.-abrupt, blunt,
brusque, churlish, coarse, crude,
curt, discourteous, harsh, rough,
rude, severe, short, uncivil, unpolished. ANT.-calm, placid, tranquil,
unruffled; civil, courteous, gentle,

mild.

guarantee, *n.* SYN.-assurance, bail,
bond, earnest, guaranty, pawn,
pledge, promise, security, surety,
token, warrant, warrantee.

guarantee, *v.* SYN.-affirm, assure,
attest, confirm, endorse, insure,
pledge, reassure, secure, stake,
support, vouch, wager, warrant.

guard, *n.* SYN.-bulwark, defense,
protection, safeguard, safety, security, shelter, shield; defender,
guardian, protector, sentinel, sentry, watchman..

guard, *v.* SYN.-cloak, conceal, cover,
curtain, defend, envelop, hide,
protect, safeguard, screen, shelter,
shield, shroud, veil; attend, check,
observe, oversee, patrol, picket,
superintend, supervise, tend,
watch. ANT.-bare, divulge, expose,
reveal, unveil; desert, disregard,
forsake, ignore, leave, neglect.

guardian, *n.* SYN.-baby-sitter, cura-
tor, custodian, defender, guard,
keeper, nursemaid, overseer, par-
ent, preserver, protector, regent,
sentinel, sentry, trustee.

guess, *n.* SYN.-assumption, conjecture, estimate, hypothesis, notion,
opinion, presumption, speculation,
supposition, suspicion, theory.

guess, *v.* SYN.-assume, believe, conjecture, estimate, hypothesize,
imagine, predicate, presume,
reckon, speculate, suppose, surmise, suspect, theorize, think.

guidance, *n.* SYN.-administration,
care, conduct, control, direction,
execution, instruction, leadership,
management, supervision.

guide, *n.* SYN.-conductor, director,
escort, guru, helmsman, lead,
leader, pathfinder, pilot, scout;
beacon, mark, sign, signal.

guide, *v.* SYN.-conduct, direct, escort, instruct, lead, manage, pilot, point, teach, train, steer.

guile, *n.* SYN.-beguilement, chicanery, cunning, deceit, deceitfulness, deception, duplicity, fraud, trick, wiliness. ANT.-candor, honesty, openness, sincerity, truthfulness.

guilt, *n.* SYN.-blame, culpability, fault, liability; compunction, contrition, remorse, shame.

guilty, *a.* SYN.-censured, charged, condemned, damned, derelict, impeached, incriminated, indicted, judged, liable, sentenced; ashamed, contrite, sorrowful, remorseful.

gullible, *a.* SYN.-artless, believing, credulous, guileless, innocent, naive, simple, trustful, trusting, unsophisticated.

gypsy, *n.* SYN.-bohemian, itinerant, maverick, nomad, nonconformist, outcast, rover, traveler, vagabond, wanderer.

H

habit, *n.* SYN.-addiction, bent, characteristic, convention, custom, disposition, fashion, fixation, manner, mode, observance, penchant, practice, routine, tradition, turn, usage, use, way, wont; clothes, costume, dress, garb.

habitual, *a.* SYN.-accustomed, automatic, common, continual, established, fixed, frequent, general, ingrained, often, periodic, perpetual, persistent, recurrent, regular, repeated, repetitious, routine, usual. ANT.-exceptional, rare, scanty, solitary, unique.

hackneyed, *a.* SYN.-banal, common, ordinary, overused, pedestrian, prosaic, stale, stereotyped, trite. ANT.-fresh, modern, momentous, novel, stimulating.

hag, *n.* SYN.-crone, fishwife, harridan, shrew, virago, witch.

hairy, *a.* SYN.-bearded, bewhiskered, bristly, downy, fluffy, furry, fuzzy, hirsute, shaggy, unshorn, whiskered.

hall, *n.* SYN.-anteroom, armory, assembly, auditorium, ballroom, chamber, church, clubroom, corridor, dormitory, entry, foyer, gallery, gym, gymnasium, hallway, lobby, lounge, room, salon, theater.

hallow, *v.* SYN.-aggrandize, bless, consecrate, dedicate, dignify, elevate, ennoble, erect, exalt, extol, glorify, worship, raise. ANT.-debase, degrade, dishonor, humble, humiliate.

hallowed, *a.* SYN.-blessed, consecrated, devotional, divine, holy, religious, reverential, sacred, sacrosanct.

hallucination, *n.* SYN.-aberration, allusion, apparition, chimera, fantasy, ghost, illusion, phantasm, specter, vision.

halt, *v.* SYN.-abstain, arrest, bar, block, cease, check, contravene, curb, desist, discontinue, end, hinder, impede, interrupt, obstruct, quell, stall, stem, stop, suspend, terminate. ANT.-begin, proceed, promote, speed, start.

hamlet, *n.* SYN.-community, settlement, village.

hamper, *v.* SYN.-block, check, constrain, delay, encumber, fetter, hinder, impede, obstruct, restrain, restrict, retard. ANT.-encourage, facilitate, promote.

handicap, *n.* SYN.-affliction, block, disability, disadvantage, hindrance, impairment, impediment, inability, incapacity, limitation, obstacle, penalty, weakness. ANT.-ability, capability, power, strength.

handle, v. SYN.-advise, check, control, examine, feel, finger, manage, manipulate, operate, supervise, touch, wield, work.

handsome, a. SYN.-aristocratic, athletic, attractive, beautiful, charming, clean-cut, comely, dapper, elegant, fair, fine, gracious, jaunty, noble, personable, princely, robust, stately, well-dressed; ample, considerable, generous, magnanimous. ANT.-foul, hideous, homely, repulsive, unsightly.

handy, a. SYN.-accessible, advantageous, appropriate, convenient, fitting, helpful, near, suitable, timely, usable, valuable; able, adept, dexterous, ingenious, resourceful, skillful. ANT.-awkward, inconvenient, inopportune, troublesome; clumsy, inept, unskilled.

hanging, a. SYN.-attached, dangling, drooping, flapping, hovering, projecting, swaying, swinging, waving; deadlocked, iffy, pending, tentative, uncertain, unresolved.

haphazard, a. SYN.-capricious, careless, casual, erratic, infrequent, incidental, irregular, loose, offhand, random, slipshod, uncoordinated, unplanned.

happen, v. SYN.-bechance, befall, betide, chance, ensue, occur, take place, transpire.

happening, n. SYN.-accident, affair, circumstance, event, incident, instance, moment, occasion.

happily, a. SYN.-agreeably, brightly, cheerfully, contentedly, delightedly, freely, gaily, gladly, graciously, joyfully, pleasantly,

happiness, n. SYN.-beatitude, blessedness, bliss, contentment, delight, felicity, gaiety, gladness, glee, joy, pleasure, satisfaction, well-being. ANT.-despair, grief, misery, sadness, sorrow.

happy, a. SYN.-blissful, carefree, cheerful, congenial, contented, delighted, ecstatic, elated, exuberant, gay, glad, intoxicated, jesting, joyful, joyous, jubilant, laughing, merry, smiling, sparkling; apt, befitting, blessed, favored, fortunate, lucky, opportune, propitious, prosperous. ANT.-blue, depressed, gloomy, morose.

harass, v. SYN.-aggravate, annoy, badger, bother, disturb, harry, irritate, molest, nag, pester, plague, provoke, tantalize, taunt, tease, torment, vex, worry. ANT.-comfort, delight, gratify, please, soothe.

hard, a. SYN.-compact, firm, impenetrable, rigid, solid, strong, tempered, unyielding; arduous, burdensome, complex, difficult, formidable, intricate, laborious, onerous, perplexing, puzzling, strenuous, tough, trying; callous, cruel, exacting, harsh, oppressive, rigorous, severe, stern, strict, unfeeling, unmerciful. ANT.-brittle, elastic, flabby, fluid, plastic, soft; easy, effortless, facile; simple; gentle, lenient, tender.

harden, v. SYN.-clot, coagulate, compact, crystallize, fossilize, freeze, petrify, solidify, stiffen; acclimate, accustom, discipline, fortify, toughen.

hardship, n. SYN.-affliction, burden, calamity, difficulty, distress, grief, misery, misfortune, ordeal, pain, problem, sorrow, suffering, test, trial, tribulation, trouble, woe.

ANT.-alleviation, consolation, ease, pleasure.

harm, *n.* SYN.-damage, detriment, evil, hurt, ill, infliction, injury, mischief, misfortune, mishap, wrong. ANT.-benefit, boon, favor, kindness.

hardy, *a.* SYN.-acclimatized, bold, conditioned, courageous, dauntless, firm, fit, hale, hardened, healthy, hearty, robust, rugged, solid, sound, sturdy, tough. ANT.-delicate, feeble, fragile, weak.

harm, *v.* SYN.-damage, disfigure, hurt, impair, injure, maltreat, mar, spoil, wound; abuse, affront, dishonor, insult, wrong. ANT.-ameliorate, benefit, help, preserve; compliment, praise.

harmful, *a.* SYN.-corrupting, damaging, deleterious, detrimental, destructive, evil, hurtful, injurious, malignant, menacing, painful, ruinous, sinister, subversive, toxic, unhealthy, virulent. ANT.-advantageous, beneficial, helpful, profitable, salutary.

harmless, *a.* SYN.-disarmed, docile, friendly, impotent, innocent, innocuous, passive, powerless, pure, reliable, safe, secure, sterile, trustworthy. ANT.-dangerous, hazardous, insecure, perilous, unsafe.

harmony, *n.* SYN.-accordance, agreement, coincidence, compatibility, concord, concurrence, congruence, congruity, equanimity, peace, rapport, understanding, unison. ANT.-difference, disagreement, discord, dissension, strife, variance.

harsh, *a.* SYN.-cacophonous, clashing, discordant, dissonant, grating, jangling, jarring, rasping, shrill; austere, acrimonious, blunt, brusque, coarse, gruff, rigorous,

rough, rugged, severe, strict, stringent. ANT.-melodious, tuneful; gentle, mild, smooth, soft.

harvest, *n.* SYN.-crop, fruit, gathering, proceeds, produce, product, reaping, result, store, yield.

harvest, *v.* SYN.-acquire, amass, collect, cull, gain, garner, gather, glean, pick, reap. ANT.-lose, plant, sow, squander.

haste, *n.* SYN.-abruptness, alacrity, bustle, carelessness, dispatch, excitement, flurry, hurry, hustle, impatience, impetuosity, rashness, recklessness.

hasten, *v.* SYN.-accelerate, expedite, goad, hurry, hustle, precipitate, press, push, quicken, rush, scoot, scramble, scurry, speed, stimulate, urge. ANT.-delay, detain, hinder, retard, tarry.

hasty, *a.* SYN.-abrupt, brisk, careless, fast, fleet, foolhardy, hurried, impetuous, indiscreet, lively, precipitate, quick, rapid, rash, reckless, speedy, sudden, swift, thoughtless, unannounced, unexpected. ANT.-anticipated, expected; courteous, gradual, smooth.

hate, *v.* SYN.-abhor, abominate, despise, detest, dislike, loathe, resent, scorn, spurn. ANT.-admire, approve, cherish, like, love.

hateful, *a.* SYN.-abominable, abusive, detestable, execrable, foul, insulting, loathsome, nasty, odious, offensive, repugnant, revolting, vile. ANT.-agreeable, commendable, delightful, pleasant.

hatred, *n.* SYN.-abhorrence, abomination, alienation, animosity, antagonism, antipathy, bitterness, contempt, detestation, disgust, dislike, enmity, grudge, hostility, ill will, loathing, malevolence, prejudice, rancor, repugnance, venom. ANT.-affection, attraction, friendship, love.

haughty, *a.* SYN.-arrogant, disdainful, egotistical, lofty, overbearing, proud, stately, supercilious, vain, vainglorious. ANT.-ashamed, humble, lowly, meek.

haunt, *v.* SYN.-annoy, bedevil, beset, bother, frighten, harass, hound, obsess, pester, plague, possess, terrify, terrorize, trouble, worry, vex,

have, *v.* SYN.-contain, control, hold, occupy, own, possess, retain. ANT.-abandon, lose, renounce, surrender.

haven, *n.* SYN.-asylum, harbor, hermitage, hideaway, port, refuge, retreat, sanctuary, shelter.

hazard, *n.* SYN.-chance, danger, jeopardy, peril, risk, uncertainty, venture. ANT.-defense, immunity, protection, safety.

hazard, *v.* SYN.-chance, conjecture, dare, endanger, gamble, imperil, jeopardize, peril, risk, speculate, try, venture. ANT.-determine, guard, insure, know.

hazardous, *a.* SYN.-chancy, dangerous, menacing, perilous, precarious, risky, speculative, threatening, uncertain, unsafe. ANT.-firm, protected, safe, secure.

hazy, *a.* SYN.-ambiguous, blurred, cloudy, dim, dull, foggy, indefinite, indistinct, misty, murky, obscure, smoky, uncertain, unclear, undetermined, unsettled, vague, veiled. ANT.-clear, explicit, lucid, precise, specific.

head, *n.* SYN.-authority, chief, commander, director, leader, master, principal, ruler; acme, crest, peak, pinnacle, summit, top; climax, cri-

sis, conclusion, culmination, ending, finale. ANT.-follower, subordinate, underling; base, bottom, foot.

head, *v.* SYN.-command, direct, govern, lead, manage, oversee, precede, supervise.

heading, *n.* SYN.-banner, caption, headline, legend, preface, streamer, title.

heal, *v.* SYN.-attend, cure, medicate, purify, regenerate, rehabilitate, remedy, renew, restore, salve, soothe, treat. ANT.-damage, harm, infect, injure.

healthful, *a.* SYN.-beneficial, bracing, clean, fresh, healing, hygienic, invigorating, nourishing, nutritious, preventive, pure, regenerative, salubrious, sanitary, stimulating, sustaining, unpolluted, untainted, wholesome.

healthy, *a.* SYN.-able-bodied, blooming, fit, hale, hardy, hearty, hygienic, invigorating, normal, nourishing, robust, salubrious, salutary, sound, strong, vigorous, virile, well, wholesome. ANT.-delicate, diseased, frail, infirm; injurious, noxious.

hear, *v.* SYN.-apprehend, attend, detect, eavesdrop, hearken, heed, listen, overhear, perceive, regard.

hearing, *n.* SYN.-audience, audit, audition, conference, consultation, interview, meeting, review, test, trial, tryout.

heart, *n.* SYN.-center, core, crux, essence, middle. midpoint, midst, nucleus; bravery, courage, fortitude, gallantry, mettle, nerve, valor. ANT.-border, boundary, outskirts, periphery, rim.

heartache, *n.* SYN.-affliction, anguish, despair, distress, grief, lamentation, misery, mourning, sadness, sorrow, trial, tribulation, woe. ANT.-comfort, consolation, happiness, joy, solace.

heartbroken, *a.* SYN.-comfortless, disconsolate, distressed, doleful, forlorn, melancholy, miserable, pitiable, sorrowful, wretched. ANT.-contented, fortunate, happy.

hearten, *v.* SYN.-assure, cheer, embolden, encourage, enthuse, exhilarate, favor, foster, impel, incite, inspire, promote, reassure, stimulate, support, urge. ANT.-deter, discourage, dispirit, dissuade, reject.

hearty, *a.* SYN.-ardent, authentic, cheery, cordial, eager, earnest, enthusiastic, genial, gracious, hale, healthy, jovial, profuse, robust, sincere, sociable, sound, strong, unrestrained, warm, well, wholehearted, wholesome, zealous. ANT.-aloof cool, reserved, taciturn.

heat, *v.* SYN.-boil, char, cook, fry, roast, scald, scorch, sear, singe, warm.

heathen, *a.* SYN.-amoral, barbarous, uncivilized.

heathen, *n.* SYN.-atheist, barbarian, infidel, nonbeliever, pagan.

heavenly, *a.* SYN.-celestial, divine, godlike, holy, superhuman, supernatural, transcendent. ANT.-blasphemous, diabolical, mundane, profane, wicked.

heavy, *a.* SYN.-bulky, hefty, huge, massive, ponderous, portly, stout, weighty; burdensome, cumbersome, depressing, distressing, gloomy, grave, grievous, harsh, oppressive, serious, troublesome, trying; boring, clumsy, dull, listless, ponderous, slow, sluggish, tedious, tiresome; complicated, complex, concentrated, difficult, important, intense, momentous,

obscure, pithy, serious, trying. ANT.-animated, brisk, light.

heckle, *v.* SYN.-badger, bait, bother, harass, pester, ridicule, tease, torment.

heed, *n.* SYN.-alertness, attention, care, consideration, mindfulness, notice, observance, watchfulness. ANT.-disregard, indifference, negligence, omission, oversight.

heed, *v.* SYN.-attend, consider, contemplate, deliberate, examine, listen, mark, mind, notice, obey, ponder, reflect, study, weigh. ANT.-ignore, neglect, overlook.

heedless, *a.* SYN.-blind, careless, hasty, headlong, ignorant, impetuous, impulsive, oblivious, rash, unaware, undiscerning, unmindful, unseeing. ANT.-aware, calculated, discerning, perceiving, sensible.

height, *n.* SYN.-apex, climax, culmination, elevation, extent, peak, prominence, stature, summit, zenith. ANT.-anticlimax, base, depth, floor.

heighten, *v.* SYN.-aggravate, amplify, augment, elevate, emphasize, enhance, exalt, increase, intensify, lift, magnify, raise, uplift. ANT.-appease, lessen, lower, mitigate, palliate soften, soothe.

help, *n.* SYN.-advice, aid, assistance, backing, comfort, encouragement, furtherance, guidance, patronage, relief, succor, support. ANT.-antagonism, counteraction, defiance, hostility, resistance.

help, *v.* SYN.-abet, accommodate, advise, advocate, aid, assist, back, bolster, encouragement, facilitate, foster, further, mitigate, promote, relieve, remedy, succor, support, uphold. ANT.-afflict, hinder, impede, oppose, resist, thwart.

helpful, *a.* SYN.-accommodating, advantageous, beneficial, essential, good, invaluable, kind, obliging, practical, profitable, salutary, serviceable, useful, valuable, wholesome. ANT.-deleterious, destructive, detrimental, harmful, ineffective, injurious, useless.

hence, adv. SYN.-accordingly, consequently, so, then, thence, therefore.

heretic, *n.* SYN.-apostate, cynic, dissenter, dissident, nonconformist, schismatic, sectarian, sectary, skeptic, unbeliever.

heritage, *n.* SYN.-ancestry, birthright, estate, inheritance, legacy, lot; convention, culture, custom, endowment, fashion, tradition.

hero, *n.* SYN.-champion, conqueror, master, model, protagonist, protector, star.

heroic, *a.* SYN.-adventurous, audacious, bold, brave, chivalrous, courageous, daring, dauntless, desperate, drastic, excessive, extreme, fearless, gallant, great, intrepid, magnanimous, noble, valiant, valorous. ANT.-cowardly, cringing, fearful, timid, weak.

hesitant, *a.* SYN.-averse, diffident, disinclined, doubtful, irresolute, loath, reluctant, skeptical, slow, uncertain, unwilling. ANT.-disposed, eager, inclined, ready, willing.

hesitate, *v.* SYN.-consider, defer, delay, deliberate, demur, doubt, falter, pause, ponder, scruple, stammer, stop, stutter, vacillate, wait, waver, weigh. ANT.-continue, decide, persevere, proceed, resolve.

hesitation, *n.* SYN.-ambiguity, dawdling, delaying, distrust, doubt, faltering, halting, incredulity, indecision, irresolution, pause, procrastination, scruple, skepticism, stammering, suspicion, unbelief, uncertainty. ANT.-belief, certainty, conviction, determination, faith.

hidden, *a.* SYN.-clandestine, clouded, concealed, covert, disguised, eclipsed, latent, obscured, potential, private, quiescent, secluded, secret, shadow, shrouded, suppressed, surreptitious, undeveloped, unseen. ANT.-conspicuous, evident, explicit, manifest, visible.

hide, *v.* SYN.-cloak, conceal, cover, curtain, disguise, mask, screen, secrete, shelter, shroud, suppress, veil, withhold. ANT.-disclose, divulge, expose, reveal, show, uncover.

high, *a.* SYN.-elevated, lofty, tall, towering; distinguished, eminent, exalted, important, preeminent, prominent, proud. ANT.-small, stunted, tiny; base, low, mean.

hinder, *v.* SYN.-arrest, bar, block, bottleneck, burden, check, delay, encumber, foil, frustrate, hamper, handicap, impede, inhibit, interrupt, neutralize, obstruct, prevent, resist, restrain, retard, stall, stop, thwart. ANT.-assist, expedite, facilitate, further, promote.

hint, *n.* SYN.-allusion, clue, cue, implication, inference, inkling, innuendo, insinuation, intimation, reference, reminder, taste, tip, trace. ANT.-affirmation, declaration, statement.

hint, *v.* SYN.-advert, allude, foreshadow, imply, infer, insinuate, intimate, mention, prompt, refer, suggest. ANT.-declare, demonstrate, specify, state.

hire, *v.* SYN.-appoint, charter, commission, delegate, employ, engage, enlist, lease, retain, use, utilize. ANT.-banish, discard, discharge, reject.

history, *n.* SYN.-account, annals, antiquity, archives, chronicle, evidence, memoir, records, writings.

hit, *v.* SYN.-bash, beat, buffet, bump, collide, cuff, hurt, jab, knock, pelt, pound, pummel, punch, rap, slap, smack, smite, sock, strike, thump, whack.

hoard, *n.* SYN.-accumulation, cache, riches, stockpile, store, treasure, wealth.

hoard, *v.* SYN.-accumulate, acquire, keep, save, stash, store, stow.

hoarse, *a.* SYN.-harsh, husky, grating, gruff, guttural, rasping, raucous, rough, scratchy, thick, throaty.

hoax, *n.* SYN.-antic, artifice, deceit, deception, fabrication, fraud, joke, ploy, prank, ruse, stratagem, stunt, swindle, subterfuge, trick, wile. ANT.-candor, exposure, honesty, openness, sincerity.

hobby, *n.* SYN.-activity, amusement, avocation, craft, diversion, fancy, pastime, relaxation, sideline, whimsy.

hold, *v.* SYN.-adhere, attach, clasp, cling, clutch, continue, endure, fasten, grasp, grip, have, keep, last, maintain, occupy, own, persist, possess, remain, retain, stick, support, sustain; check, confine, contain, curb, detain, hinder, restrain; believe, consider, deem, embrace, entertain, espouse, esteem, think. ANT.-abandon, relinquish, surrender, vacate.

hole, *n.* SYN.-abyss, aperture, breach, break, burrow, cavity, chasm, cleft, crack, cranny, crater,

fissure, fracture, gap, gash, gorge, gulf, incision, opening, orifice, perforation, pit, pore, puncture, ravine, rent, rupture, shaft, slit, split, tear, tunnel, void.

hollow, *a.* SYN.-depressed, empty, unfilled, vacant, vacuous, void; false, hypocritical, insincere, vain. ANT.-full, solid, sound; genuine, sincere.

holy, *a.* SYN.-angelic, blessed, consecrated, dedicated, devout, divine, godly, good, hallowed, humble, just, moral, pious, religious, reverent, righteous, sacred, saintly, sanctified, spiritual, venerable. ANT.-evil, profane, sacrilegious, secular, worldly.

home, *n.* SYN.-abode, apartment, base, chalet, domicile, dwelling, flat, habitat, hearth, homestead, house, household, hovel, lodging, mansion, quarters, residence, seat, shelter.

homely, *a.* SYN.-coarse, ill-favored, inelegant, plain, repellent, simple, ugly, unattractive, uncomely, unrefined; cozy, crude, modest, simple, snug, unpretentious. ANT.-attractive, beautiful, fair, handsome, pretty.

honest, *a.* SYN.-above-board, candid, conscientious, decent, factual, fair, genuine, honorable, just, legitimate, moral, open, realistic, scrupulous, sincere, sound, straightforward, true, trustworthy, truthful, unreserved, upright, virtuous. ANT.-deceitful, dishonest, fraudulent, lying, tricky.

honesty, *n.* SYN.-candor, character, conscience, fairness, fidelity, frankness, goodness, integrity, justice, morality, openness, rectitude, reliability, responsibility, sin-

cerity, trustworthiness, uprightness, virtue. ANT.-cheating, deceit,
dishonesty, fraud, trickery.

honor, *n.* SYN.-admiration, adoration, deference, dignity, distinction,
esteem, faith, fame, glory, homage,
praise, renown, recognition, reference, reputation, repute, respect,
reverence, trust, veneration, worship. ANT.-contempt, derision, disgrace, dishonor, reproach.

honor, *v.* SYN.-admire, adore, celebrate, commemorate, esteem, extol,
glorify, keep, laud, observe, praise,
regard, respect, revere, solemnize,
value, venerate, worship. ANT.-de-
cry, disgrace, dishonor, disregard,
overlook, profane.

honorable, *a.* SYN.-admirable, creditable, dignified, distinguished,
eminent, equitable, esteemed, es-
timable, ethical, fair, honest, illustrious, just, noble, proper, reputable, respectable, true, trusty, upright, virtuous. ANT.-disgraceful,
ignominious, infamous, shameful.

hope, *n.* SYN.-anticipation, assurance, belief, confidence, desire,
dream, expectancy, expectation,
faith, goal, longing, optimism, reliance, trust, wish. ANT.-despair, despondency, pessimism.

hopeless, *a.* SYN.-desperate, disastrous, fatal, foreboding, impossible,
incurable, irreversible, lost, pointless, trágic, vain, worthless.

hopelessness, *n.* SYN.-depression,
despair, desperation, despondency,
discouragement, gloom, grief,
heartache, pessimism, sorrow,
torture. ANT.-confidence, elation,
hope, optimism.

horde, *n.* SYN.-band, bevy, crowd,
crush, gathering, group, host,
masses, mob, multitude, pack,

populace, press, rabble, swarm,
throng.

horrible, *a.* SYN.-abominable, ap-
palling, awful, deplorable, dire,
disgusting, dreadful, fearful, frightful, ghastly, hideous, horrid, odious, offensive, repulsive, shameful,
shocking, terrible. ANT.-beautiful,
enchanting, enjoyable, fascinating,
lovely.

horror, *n.* SYN.-abomination, alarm,
antipathy, apprehension, aversion,
awe, dread, fear, foreboding, fright,
hatred, loathing, panic, repugnance, terror. ANT.-assurance,
boldness, confidence, courage.

hostile, *a.* SYN.-adverse, antagonistic, conflicting, hateful, inimical,
opposed, repugnant, unfriendly,
warlike. ANT.-amicable, cordial, favorable.

hostility, *n.* SYN.-abhorrence, animosity, aversion, bitterness, dislike, enmity, grudge, hatred, ill
will, malevolence, rancor, spite.
ANT.-friendliness, good will, love.

hot, *a.* SYN.-baking, blazing, blister-
ing, burning, flaming, parching,
scalding, scorching, sizzling; ardent, fervent, fiery, hot-blooded,
impetuous, intense, passionate,
torrid; acrid, biting, peppery, pi-
quant, pungent, spicy. ANT.-cold,
cool, freezing, frigid; apathetic, impassive, indifferent, passionless,
phlegmatic; bland.

however, *adv.* SYN.-but, neverthe-
less, notwithstanding, still, yet.

hue, *n.* SYN.-color, complexion, pigment, shade, stain, tincture, tinge,
tint. ANT.-achromatism, paleness,
transparency.

hug, *v.* SYN.-caress, clinch, coddle,
cuddle, embrace, squeeze. ANT.-
buffet, spurn.

huge, *a.* SYN.-ample, big, capacious, colossal, enormous, extensive, giant, great, immense, large, mammoth, tremendous, vast, wide. ANT.-little, mean, short, small, tiny.

humane, *a.* SYN.-benevolent, charitable, clement, compassionate, forbearing, forgiving, humanitarian, kind, kindhearted, kindly, lenient, merciful, softhearted, sympathetic, tender, tenderhearted, tolerant, understanding, warmhearted. ANT.-brutal, cruel, pitiless, remorseless, unfeeling.

humanity, *n.* SYN.-altruism, beneficence, benevolence, charity, compassion, generosity, kindness, liberality, love, magnanimity, philanthropy, sympathy, tenderness, understanding. ANT.-cruelty, inhumanity, malevolence, selfishness.

humble, *a.* SYN.-compliant, deferential, diffident, lowly, meek, mild, modest, ordinary, passive, plain, quiet, simple, submissive, unassuming, unpretentious. ANT.-arrogant, boastful, haughty, proud, vain.

humble, *v.* SYN.-abase, abash, break, chasten, crush, debase, degrade, demean, humiliate, mortify, shame, subdue. ANT.-elevate, exalt, honor, praise.

humiliate, *v.* See **humble**

humiliation, *n.* SYN.-abasement, chagrin, mortification, shame; disgrace, dishonor, disrepute, embarrassment, ignominy, mortification, scandal, shame. ANT.-dignity, glory, honor, praise, renown.

humor, *n.* SYN.-amusement, comedy, facetiousness, fun, irony, jocularity, joke, pleasantry, sarcasm, satire, waggery, wit; disposition, mood, temper, tendency, tempera-

ment, vagary, whim. ANT.-gravity, seriousness, sorrow.

humor, *v.* SYN.-comfort, coddle, gratify, indulge, pamper, placate, please, spoil.

humorous, *a.* SYN.-amusing, comic, comical, droll, entertaining, farcical, funny, laughable, ludicrous, ridiculous, whimsical, witty. ANT.-melancholy, serious, sober, solemn.

hunch, *n.* SYN.-clue, feeling, foreboding, idea, intuition, notion, portent, premonition, prescience; bulge, bump, hump, protuberance.

hunger, *n.* SYN.-appetite, craving, desire, inclination, liking, longing, passion, relish, thirst, yearning, zest. ANT.-disgust, distaste, renunciation, repugnance, satiety.

hungry, *a.* SYN.-craving, famished, ravenous, starved, thirsting, voracious; avid, greedy, longing. ANT.-full, gorged, sated, satiated; satisfied.

hunt, *v.* SYN.-chase, explore, follow, hound, inquire, investigate, pursue, probe, ransack, rummage, scour, scrutinize, search, seek, stalk, trail, trace, track.

hurl, *v.* SYN.-cast, fling, heave, pitch, propel, throw, thrust, toss. ANT.-draw, haul, hold, pull, retain.

hurry, *v.* SYN.-accelerate, dash, expedite, hasten, precipitate, quicken, race, rush, scoot, speed. ANT.-delay, detain, hinder, retard, tarry.

hurt, *n.* SYN.-damage, detriment, disservice, harm, injury, mischief, grievance, injustice, prejudice, wound, wrong. ANT.-benefit, improvement, repair.

hurt, *v.* SYN.-abuse, affront, damage, disfigure, dishonor, distress, harm,

impair, injure, insult, lash, mar,
smite, spoil, wound, wrong. ANT.-
ameliorate, benefit, compliment,
help, praise, preserve.

hush, n. SYN.-calm, lull, peace,
quiet, serenity, silence, stillness.

hustle, v. SYN.-hasten, hurry, race,
rush, scramble; beg, con,
panhandle, swindle.

hygienic, a. SYN.-clean, decontami-
nated, disinfected, healthy, pure,
sanitary, wholesome. ANT.-contami-
nated, diseased, infected, injurious, noxious, unsanitary.

hypocrisy, n. SYN.-bigotry, cant, deceit, dissimulation, pretense,
sanctimony. ANT.-candor, frankness, honesty, openness, truth.

hypothesis, n. SYN.-assumption,
conjecture, law, notion, postulate,
supposition, theory. ANT.-certainty,
fact, proof.

hysterical, a. SYN.-delirious, demonstrative, distraught, emotional,
excitable, fervent, frenzied, overwrought, possessed, raging, raving,
uncontrolled.

I

idea, n. SYN.-abstraction, belief, concept, conception, fancy, image, impression, notion, opinion, sentiment, theory, thought. ANT.-entity,
matter, object, substance, thing.

ideal, a. SYN.-exemplary, fancied,
faultless, imaginary, perfect, supreme, unreal, utopian, visionary.
ANT.-actual, faulty, imperfect, material, real.

idealistic, a. SYN.-dreamy, extravagant, fanciful, fantastic, fictitious,
ideal, imaginative, impractical,
maudlin, mawkish, picturesque,
poetic, quixotic, romantic, senti-

mental, utopian, visionary. ANT.-
factual, literal, matter-of-fact, practical, prosaic.

identical, a. SYN.-coincident, equal,
equivalent, indistinguishable, like,
same, twin. ANT.-contrary, disparate, dissimilar, distinct, opposed.

identify, v. SYN.-acknowledge, apprehend, avow, concede, confess,
own, perceive, recognize, recollect,
remember. ANT.-disown, renounce,
repudiate.

ideology, n. SYN.-belief, convictions,
culture, dogma, ethics, ideas, phi-
losophy, tenets.

idiot, n. SYN.-buffoon, clown, harlequin, jester; blockhead, dolt,
dunce, fool, imbecile, nincompoop,
numbskull, oaf, simpleton. ANT.-
genius, philosopher, sage, scholar.

idiotic, a. SYN.-absurd, asinine,
brainless, crazy, foolish, irrational,
nonsensical, preposterous, ridiculous, senseless, silly, simple. ANT.-
judicious, prudent, sagacious,
sane, wise.

idle, a. SYN.-dormant, inactive, indolent, inert, fallow, lazy, slothful,
unemployed, unoccupied; insignificant, trifling, trivial, unimportANT.
ANT.-active, employed, engaged, industrious, occupied, working.

idol, n. SYN.-deity, figurine, icon,
image, statue, symbol, totem; beloved, favorite, hero, model.

ignominious, a. SYN.-abject, base,
contemptible, despicable, dishonorable, groveling, ignoble, ignominious, low, lowly, mean, menial,
shameful, sordid, vile, vulgar. ANT.-
teemed, exalted, honored, lofty,
noble, righteous.

ignorant, a. SYN.-coarse, crude,
dense, dumb, illiterate, oblivious,
shallow, superficial, uncultured,

uneducated, uninformed, unlearned, unlettered, untaught, vulgar. ANT.-cultured, educated, erudite, informed, literate.

ignore, v. SYN.-disdain, disregard, neglect, omit, overlook, skip, slight. ANT.-include, notice, regard.

ill, a. SYN.-afflicted, ailing, diseased, indisposed, infirm, morbid, sick, unhealthy, unwell; bad, evil, naughty, wicked. ANT.-healthy, robust, sound, strong, well; good.

illegal, a. SYN.-criminal, dishonest, illegitimate, illicit, outlawed, prohibited, unlawful, wrongful. ANT.-honest, lawful, legal, permitted.

illicit, a. SYN.-banned, illegal, illegitimate, outlawed, prohibited, unauthorized, unlawful. ANT.-allowed, authorized, lawful, legal, permitted.

illness, n. SYN.-ailment, complaint, disease, disorder, infirmity, malady, sickness. ANT.-health, healthiness, soundness, vigor.

illogical, a. SYN.-absurd, contradictory, fallacious, groundless, implausible, inconsistent, incongruous, irrational, untenable.

illuminate, v. SYN.-brighten, clarify, edify, elucidate, enlighten, explain, illumine, illustrate, inform, irradiate. ANT.-complicate, confuse, darken, obfuscate, obscure.

illusion, n. SYN.-apparition, delusion, dream, fantasy, hallucination, mirage, phantom, vision. ANT.-actuality, reality, substance.

illusive, a. SYN.-apparent, deceptive, delusive, delusory, fallacious, false, misleading, ostensible, presumable, seeming, specious. ANT.-authentic, genuine, real, truthful.

illustration, n. SYN.-drawing, effigy, engraving, etching, image, landscape, likeness, painting, panorama, picture, portrayal, print, rendering, representation, resemblance, scene, sketch, view.

illustrious, a. SYN.-august, celebrated, dignified, distinguished, elevated, eminent, excellent, famed, famous, fine, grand, great, magnificent, majestic, noble, prominent, renowned. ANT.-common, menial, obscure, ordinary, paltry, unknown.

image, n. SYN.-concept, conception, idea, notion, perception; copy, effigy, figure, form, icon, idol, likeness, picture, representation, semblance, statue.

imagination, n. SYN.-awareness, conception, creation, daydream, fancy, fantasy, idea, insight, invention, inventiveness, notion, wit.

imaginative, a. SYN.-artistic, clever, creative, fanciful, inventive, mystical, poetical, sublime, talented, visionary. ANT.-dull, literal, prosaic, unromantic.

imagine, v. SYN.-assume, believe, conceive, conjecture, dream, envision, fancy, guess, opine, perceive, picture, pretend, suppose, surmise, think.

imbecile, n. SYN.-blockhead, dolt, dunce, fool, idiot, jerk, moron, nincompoop, numbskull, oaf, simpleton. ANT.-genius, philosopher, sage, scholar.

imbibe, v. SYN.-absorb, assimilate, consume, drink, ingest, guzzle, partake, receive, swallow. ANT.-discharge, dispense, emit, expel, exude.

imitate, v. SYN.-ape, copy, counterfeit, duplicate, echo, impersonate, mimic, mirror, mock, parallel, reflect, reproduce, simulate. ANT.-alter, distort, diverge, invent.

imitation, *n.* SYN.-copy, duplicate, exemplar, facsimile, fake, forgery, replica, reproduction, simulation, transcript. ANT.-original, novelty, prototype.

immaculate, *a.* SYN.-bright, clean, impeccable, spotless, unsullied; innocent, sinless, virginal.

immaterial, *a.* SYN.-extraneous, inapplicable, insubstantial, irrelevant.

immature, *a.* SYN.-callow, childish, childlike, green, innocent, juvenile, naive, provincial, puerile, raw, silly, unseasoned, unsophisticated, young, youthful. ANT.-aged, elderly, mature, old, senile.

immeasurable, *a.* SYN.-boundless, endless, eternal, immense, indefinite, infinite, interminable, limitless, unbounded, unlimited, vast. ANT.-bounded, circumscribed, confined, finite, limited.

immediately, adv. SYN.-directly, forthwith, instantaneously, instantly, now, presently, promptly, straight-away. ANT.-distantly, hereafter, later, shortly, sometime.

immense, *a,* SYN.-colossal, elephantine, enormous, gargantuan, gigantic, huge, large, prodigious, tremendous, vast. ANT.-diminutive, little, minute, small, tiny.

immerse, *v.* SYN.-dip, douse, dunk, plunge, sink, submerge; absorb, bury, engage, engross, involve. ANT.-elevate, recover, uplift.

immigration, *n.* SYN.-arrival, colonization, journey, migration, relocation, settlement. ANT.-displacement, emigration, exodus.

imminent, *a.* SYN.-approaching, close, coming, impending, menacing, near, nigh, overhanging, threatening. ANT.-afar, distant, im-

probable, remote, retreating.

immodest, *a.* SYN.-bold, candid, forthright, frank, indelicate, indiscreet, open, outspoken, unblushing.

immoderation, *n.* SYN.-dissipation, excess, extravagance, glut, intemperance, luxuriance, overindulgence, profusion, superabundance, superfluity, surplus. ANT.-dearth, deficiency, lack, paucity, wANT.

immoral, *a.* SYN.-anti-social, bad, corrupt, debased, debauched, dissolute, indecent, libertine, licentious, profligate, shameless, sinful, unprincipled, vicious, wicked. ANT.-chaste, high-minded, noble, pure, virtuous.

immortal, *a.* SYN.-ageless, deathless, endless, eternal, everlasting, imperishable, indestructible, infinite, permanent, perpetual, timeless, undying. ANT. ephemeral, finite, mortal, temporal, transient.

immune, *a.* SYN.-excused, exempt, free, freed, independent, liberated, unaffected, unconfined, unrestricted.

immunity, *n.* SYN.-exemption, freedom, immunization, impunity, liberty, license, prerogative, privilege, resistance, right.

immutable, *a.* SYN.-abiding, ceaseless, consistent, constant, continual, enduring, even, faithful, fixed, invariable, permanent, perpetual, persistent, steady, unalterable, unchanging, uniform, unwavering. ANT.-fickle, mutable, vacillating, wavering.

impact, *n.* SYN.-collision, crash, effect, influence.

impair, *v.* SYN.-damage, deface, diminish, harm, hurt, injure, lessen, mar, spoil. ANT.-ameliorate, benefit, enhance, mend, repair, vitiate.

impart, *v.* SYN.-bestow, cede, communicate, confer, convey, disclose, divulge, give, grant, inform, notify, relate, relinquish, reveal, tell, transmit. ANT.-conceal, hide, withhold.

impartial, *a.* SYN.-detached, dispassionate, equitable, fair, honest, just, reasonable, unbiased. ANT.-dishonorable, fraudulent, partial.

impartiality, *n.* SYN.-candor, disinterestedness, equality, fairness, indifference, insensibility, justice, neutrality, objectivity. ANT.-bias, favoritism, prejudice.

impasse, *n.* SYN.-deadlock, delay, draw, halt, stalemate, standoff, standstill; circumstance, condition, plight, predicament.

impeach, *v.* SYN.-accuse, arraign, challenge, charge, cite, criticize, denounce, discredit, incriminate, question. ANT.-absolve, acquit, clear, exonerate.

impeccable, *a.* SYN.-excellent, exquisite, faultless, flawless.

impede, *v.* SYN.-arrest, bar, block, check, clog, delay, deter, encumber, frustrate, hamper, hinder, interrupt, obstruct, restrain, retard, stop, thwart. ANT.-advance, assist, further, help, promote.

impediment, *n.* SYN.-bar, barrier, block, check, difficulty, handicap, hindrance, limitation, obstacle, obstruction, setback, snag. ANT.-aid, assistance, backing, encouragement, guidance, help, relief, support.

impel, *v.* SYN.-coerce, compel, drive, enforce, force, incite, motivate, oblige, prod, push, spur, urge. ANT.-allure, convince, induce, persuade, prevent.

impending, *a.* SYN.-approaching, close, immediate, imminent, menacing, nigh, overhanging, threatening. ANT.-distant, improbable, remote, retreating.

impertinent, *a.* SYN.-arrogant, discourteous, impolite, impudent, insolent, rude. ANT.-civil, courteous, humble, refined.

impenetrable, *a.* SYN.-compact, firm, hard, impervious, inscrutable, inviolable, rigid, solid, tough; incomprehensible, inexplicable, inscrutable, obscure, unintelligible. ANT.-flabby, plastic, soft; clear, understandable.

imperative, *a.* SYN.-cogent, compelling, critical, crucial, exigent, immediate, impelling, important, importunate, insistent, instant, necessary, pressing, serious, urgent; aggressive, autocratic, bossy commanding, domineering, imperial, masterful, powerful. ANT.-insignificant, petty, trifling, trivial, unimportant; feeble, impotent, powerless, weak, yielding.

imperceptible, *a.* SYN.-ambiguous, blurred, cryptic, dim, esoteric, inaudible, indistinct, indistinguishable, invisible, obscure, shadowy, indiscernible, unseen. ANT.-evident, perceptible, seen, visible.

imperfection, *n.* SYN.-blemish, defect, deformity, error, failure, fault, flaw, mistake, omission, shortcoming, vice. ANT.-completeness, correctness, perfection.

imperial, *a.* SYN.-majestic, princely, monarchical, regal, royal.

imperil, *v.* SYN.-hazard, jeopardize, risk, venture.

imperious, *a.* SYN.-arrogant, despotic, dictatorial, domineering, lordly, tyrannical.

impersonal, *a.* SYN.-detached, fair, impartial, objective, unbiased.

impersonate, *v.* SYN.-ape, copy, counterfeit, duplicate, imitate, mimic, mock, portray, pose, pretend, represent, simulate. ANT.-alter, distort, diverge, invent.

impertinence, *n.* SYN.-affront, audacity, boldness, disrespectfulness, effrontery, impudence, inappropriateness, injury, insolence, insult, offense, rudeness, sauciness, slight, slur. ANT.-diffidence, politeness, subserviency.

impertinent, *a.* SYN.-abusive, arrogant, brazen, contemptuous, discourteous, impolite, impudent, insolent, insulting, offensive, rude, saucy. ANT.-considerate, courteous, polite, respectful.

impetus, *n.* SYN.-cause, force, impulse, incentive, pressure, push, stimulus, thrust.

impetuous, *a.* SYN.-blind, careless, hasty, headlong, heedless, impulsive, irrational, passionate, quick, rash, uncontrolled, unreasonable. ANT.-calculating, cautious, reasoning.

implicate, *v.* SYN.-accuse, associate, blame, charge, cite, concern, condemn, hint, imply, include, involve, link, relate, suggest. ANT.-absolve, acquit, exonerate, ignore.

implicit, *a.* SYN.-absolute, accurate, assured, certain, confident, definite, doubtless, positive, satisfied, unequivocal, unquestionable; alluded, indicated, inferred, insinuated, intended, meant, suggested, tacit, understood.

implore, *v.* SYN.-adjure, appeal, ask, beg, beseech, crave, entreat, importune, petition, plead, pray, request, solicit, supplicate. ANT.-be-

stow, cede, favor, give, grANT.

imply, *v.* SYN.-connote, infer, insinuate, involve, mean, signify, suggest. ANT.-assert, express, state.

impolite, *a.* SYN.-arrogant, blunt, boorish, brazen, coarse, crude, discourteous, gruff, impudent, insolent, insulting, moody, primitive, rough, rude, saucy, surly, uncivil, unpolished, vulgar. ANT.-civil, genteel, polished; courtly, dignified, noble, stately.

importance, *n.* SYN.-emphasis, gravity, heaviness, import, influence, pressure, significance, stress, value, weight. ANT.-buoyancy, levity, lightness; insignificance, triviality.

important, *a.* SYN.-consequential, critical, decisive, grave, influential, material, meaningful, momentous, paramount, pressing, primary, prominent, relevant, significant, substantial, valuable, weighty. ANT.-commonplace, foolish, insignificant, irrelevant, little, mean, paltry, petty, trivial.

imposing, *a.* SYN.-august, dignified, exciting, grand, grandiose, high, impressive, lofty, magnificent, majestic, noble, overwhelming, pompous, stately, stirring, sublime, substantial. ANT.-common, humble, lowly, ordinary, undignified.

impossible, *a.* SYN.-fruitless, futile, hopeless, impractical, inaccessible, inconceivable, unattainable, unworkable, useless, vain.

impression, *n.* SYN.-concept, conjecture, feeling, image, notion, opinion, perception, sensation, sense, supposition, understanding; dent, indentation, mark, scar. ANT.-fact, insensibility, reality.

impressive, *a.* SYN.-absorbing, af-

fecting, arresting, august, beautiful, commanding, dazzling, dramatic, eloquent, exciting, extraordinary, forceful, gorgeous, grand,
grandiose, imposing, inspiring,
magnificent, majestic, moving, notable, overpowering, profound, remarkable, splendid, stirring,
striking, sumptuous, superb, thrilling, touching. ANT.-commonplace,
ordinary, regular, unimpressive.

improve, *v.* SYN.-ameliorate, amend,
augment, better, correct, enhance,
enrich, help, modernize, progress,
rectify, refine, reform, update. ANT.-
corrupt, damage, debase, impair,
vitiate.

improvement, *n.* SYN.-advance, advancement, alteration, amendment,
betterment, development, enhancement, enrichment, growth,
modernization, progress, progression, reformation, renovation, reor-
ganization. ANT.-decline, delay, regression, relapse, retrogression.

imprudent, *a.* SYN.-careless, excessive, heedless, immoderate, improvident, inattentive, indiscreet,
inordinate, lavish, lax, neglectful,
negligent, prodigal, reckless, remiss, thoughtless. ANT.-accurate,
careful, meticulous, nice.

impudence, *n.* SYN.-assurance,
audacity, boldness, brass, cheek,
discourtesy, effrontery, impertinence, insolence, nerve, presumption, rudeness, sauciness, temerity. ANT.-diffidence, politeness,
subserviency, truckling.

impudent, *a.* SYN.-bold, brazen, discourteous, forward, fresh, impertinent, insolent, pushy, rude. ANT.-
cowardly, flinching, timid; bashful,
retiring.

impulsive, *a.* SYN.-careless, hasty,
heedless, impetuous, offhand,
passionate, quick, rash, spontaneous, unconstrained. ANT.-calculat-
ing, cautious, reasoning.

impure, *a.* SYN.-adulterated, contaminated, corrupt, corrupted,
crooked, debased, depraved, diluted, dirty, immoral, profligate,
putrid, spoiled, tainted, unclean,
unsound, venal, vitiated.

inability, *n.* SYN.-disability, failure,
handicap, impotence, incapacity,
incompetence, weakness. ANT.-
ability, capability, power, strength.

inaccurate, *a.* SYN.-amiss, askew,
awry, distorted, erroneous, fallacious, false, faulty, imprecise, inexact, incorrect, mistaken, unprecise, untrue, wrong. ANT.-correct,
right, true.

inactive, *a.* SYN.-dead, dormant,
idle, indolent, inert, lazy, sluggish,
slothful, stagnant, still, torpid, unemployed, unoccupied. ANT.-active,
employed, industrious, occupied,
working.

inadequate, *a.* SYN.-bare, defective,
deficient, imperfect, incomplete,
ineffective, insufficient, lacking,
little, meager, scanty, scarce,
short, spare, sparse, sufficient,
wanting, weak. ANT.-adequate,
ample, enough, satisfactory, sufficient.

inadvisable, *a.* SYN.-improper, imprudent, inappropriate, injudicious, unsuitable, unwise, wrong.
ANT.-appropriate, correct, recommended, suitable.

inane, *a.* SYN.-absurd, dumb, foolish, pointless, ridiculous, silly,
stupid.

inanimate, *a.* SYN.-dead, deceased,
defunct, inert, insensible, lifeless,
senseless, spiritless, unconscious,

unfeeling. ANT.-alive, animate, living, spirited, stirring.

inattentive, *a.* SYN.-away, absent, absent-minded, abstracted, careless, distracted, forgetful, heedless, indifferent, indiscreet, neglectful, preoccupied, slack. ANT.-attending, present; attentive, watchful.

inaudible, *a.* SYN.-faint, indistinct, soft.

inaugurate, *v.* SYN.-begin, commence, induct, initiate, install, launch, originate, start.

inauspicious, *a.* SYN.-adverse, detrimental, negative, unfavorable.

incalculable, *a.* SYN.-bounless, immense, indefinite, infinite, limitless, uncertain, unpredictable, vast.

incantation, *n.* SYN.-charm, hex, spell.

incapacity, *n.* SYN.-disability, handicap, impotence; inability, incompetence, weakness. ANT.-ability, capability, power, strength.

incentive, *n.* SYN.-aim, bait, consideration, enticement, impetus, inducement, instigation, motive, rationale, reason, stimulation.

inception, *n.* SYN.-beginning, cause, commencement, derivation, opening, origin, outset, root, source, start. ANT.-close, completion, consummation, end, termination.

incessant, *a.* SYN.-ceaseless, constant, continual, continuous, endless, everlasting, nonstop, perennial, perpetual, persistent, unceasing, uninterrupted, unremitting. ANT.-interrupted, occasional, periodic, rare.

incident, *n.* SYN.-circumstance, condition, episode, event, fact, happening, occurrence, situation.

incidental, *a,* SYN.-accidental, ancillary, casual, chance, fortuitous, lucky, random, secondary, subordinate, supplemental, unplanned.

incinerate, *v.* SYN.-burn, char, consume, cremate, incinerate, scorch, sear, singe. ANT.-extinguish, put out, quench.

incisive, *a.* SYN.-acute, biting, brief, concise, condensed, crisp, cutting, neat, penetrating, pithy, succinct, summary, terse. ANT.-casual, lengthy, prolix, verbose, wordy.

incite, *v.* SYN.-arouse, cause, encourage, excite, foment, galvanize, goad, induce, inspire, instigate, prompt, provoke, rouse, spur, stimulate, urge. ANT.-bore, pacify, quiet, soothe.

inclination, *n.* SYN.-angle, bending, incline, lean, pitch, slope, tilt; affection, attachment, bent, bias, desire, disposition, leaning, liking, penchant, predilection, preference, propensity. ANT.-antipathy, apathy, aversion, coldness, dislike, distaste, indifference, nonchalance, repugnance, unconcern.

include, *v.* SYN.-accommodate, admit, combine, comprise, contain, cover, embody, embrace, entail, hold, incorporate, involve. ANT.-bar, discharge, emit, exclude, omit.

included, *a.* SYN.-admitted, combined, counted, entered, incorporated, inserted, merged, noted, numbered

incongruous, *a.* SYN.-absurd, alien, bizarre, contradictory, contrary, discrepant, inappropriate, incompatible, inharmonious, paradoxical, strange, unfitting, unsuitable. ANT.-consistent, harmonious, logical, proper, sensible.

inconsistency, *n.* SYN.-conflict, contention, controversy, deviation, difference, disagreement, discord, discrepancy, disparity, paradox, variance. ANT.-amity, concord, consonance, harmony.

inconsistent, *a.* SYN.-contradictory, changeable, contrary, discrepant, erratic, fickle, illogical, incompatible, incongruous, irreconcilable, paradoxical, unstable, unsteady, vacillating, wavering. ANT.-compatible, congruous, consistent, correspondent, harmonious, suitable.

inconspicuous, *a.* SYN.-blurred, cloudy, dim, faded, faint, indistinct, murky, obscure, quiet, sly, subtle.

inconstant, *a.* SYN.-capricious, changeable, fickle, fitful, shifting, uncertain, unreliable, unstable, vacillating, variable, wavering. ANT.-constant, stable, steady, unchanging, uniform.

inconvenient, *a.* SYN.-annoying, awkward, bothersome, difficult, disturbing, troublesome, untimely. ANT.-convenient, opportune, welcome.

incorporate, *v.* SYN.-add, blend, combine, consolidate, embody, fuse, include, join, merge, unite.

increase, *v.* SYN.-accrue, aggrandize, amplify, augment, boost, broaden, build, deepen, develop, dilate, enhance, enlarge, expand, extend, grow, heighten, intensify, lengthen, magnify, multiply, raise, supplement, thicken, wax, widen. ANT.-atrophy, contract, decrease, diminish, lessen, reduce.

incredible, *a.* SYN.-extraordinary, implausible, improbable, inconceivable, suspect, unbelievable, unimaginable, unthinkable. ANT.-believable, convincing, probable, rational.

indebted, *a.* SYN.-accountable, appreciative, beholden, grateful, gratified, obligated, obliged, responsible, thankful. ANT.-thankless, unappreciative.

indecent, *a.* SYN.-coarse, dirty, disgusting, filthy, gross, immodest, immoral, impure, indelicate, lascivious, lewd, nasty, obscene, offensive, pornographic, shameless, smutty, sordid. ANT.-decent, modest, pure, refined.

indefinite, *a.* SYN.-ambiguous, dim, equivocal, hazy, indecisive, indistinct, inexact, obscure, uncertain, unclear, vague; boundless, endless, eternal, infinite, unlimited.

indelible, *a.* SYN.-abiding, enduring, impressive, lasting, memorable, permanent, unforgettable.

independence, *n.* SYN.-autonomy, exemption, freedom, immunity, liberation, liberty, license, privilege, unrestraint. ANT.-bondage, captivity, compulsion, constraint, necessity, servitude, submission.

independent, *a.* SYN.-alone, autonomous, free, self-reliant, separate, unconstrained, uncontrolled, unrestrained, unrestricted, voluntary. ANT.-contingent, dependent, enslaved, restricted.

indestructible, *a.* SYN.-abiding, changeless, constant, durable, enduring, fixed, lasting, imperishable, permanent, stable, unchangeable. ANT.-ephemeral, temporary, transient, transitory, unstable.

indicate, *v.* SYN.-announce, attest, betoken, connote, denote, designate, disclose, hint, imply, insinuate, intimate, manifest, mark, point, reveal, say, show, signify, specify, suggest, symbolize, verify. ANT.-conceal, contradict, distract, divert, falsify, misdirect, mislead.

indication, *n.* SYN. clue, evidence, gesture, hint, implication, mark, omen, portent, proof, sign, signal, symbol, symptom, token.

indictment, *n.* SYN.-accusation, allegation, arraignment, censure, charge, complaint, imputation, incrimination, reproach. ANT.-exculpation, exoneration, pardon.

indifference, *n.* SYN.-aloofness, apathy, callousness, coldness, coolness, detachment, disdain, disinterestedness, heedlessness, impartiality, insensibility, insensitivity, neutrality, nonchalance, unconcern. ANT.-affection, ardor, attention, compassion, concern, enthusiasm, feeling, fervor, heed, importance, inclination, passion.

indifferent, *a.* SYN.-aloof, apathy, callous, cold, cool, detached, distant, heartless, impassive, mediocre, nonchalant, reserved, unemotional, unfeeling, unmoved, unsympathetic; average, common, conventional, fair, mediocre, ordinary, passable, undistinguished. ANT.-aroused, concerned, warm; exceptional, outstanding.

indigence, *n.* SYN.-destitution, distress, insolvency, necessity, need, penury, poverty, privation, wANT. ANT.-abundance, affluence, plenty, riches, wealth.

indigenous, *a.* SYN.-congenital, domestic, endemic, inborn, inherent, innate, local, native, natural.

indigent, *a.* SYN.-broke, destitute, distressed, impoverished, insolvent, needy, poor, poverty-stricken.

indignation, *n.* SYN.-anger, exasperation, ire, irritation, outrage, passion, resentment, temper, umbrage, wrath. ANT.-conciliation, for-

bearance, patience, peace, self-control.

indignity, *n.* SYN.-abuse, affront, betrayal, defilement, insolence, insult, mistreatment, offense, violation. ANT.-apology, homage, salutation

indirect, *a.* SYN.-circuitous, crooked, cunning, devious, distorted, erratic, implied, meandering, oblique, obscure, rambling, roundabout, sinister, swerving, tricky, tortuous, wandering, winding. ANT.-direct, honest, straight, straightforward.

indiscreet, *a.* SYN.-extravagant, foolish, hasty, naive, precipitate, rash, reckless, silly, tactless.

indiscretion, *a.* SYN.-absurdity, extravagance, folly, foolishness, imprudence, silliness. ANT.-judgment, prudence, reasonableness, sense, wisdom.

indispensable, *a.* SYN.-basic, essential, fundamental, imperative, important, intrinsic, necessary, needed, required, requisite, vital. ANT.-expendable, extrinsic, optional, peripheral.

indistinct, *a.* SYN.-abstruse, ambiguous, blurred, cloudy, cryptic, dark, dim, dusky, enigmatic, mysterious, obscure, unintelligible, unknown, vague. ANT.-bright, clear, distinct, lucid.

individual, *a.* SYN.-definite, distinct, distinctive, exclusive, marked, particular, personal, private, select, separate, singular, special, specific, unique. ANT.-common, general, ordinary, universal.

individuality, *n.* SYN.-character, description, disposition, distinctiveness, habit, identity, idiosyncrasy, kind, manner, nature, peculiarity, personality, reputation, repute, singularity.

indoctrinate, *v.* SYN.-convince, edify, enlighten, influence, initiate, instruct, orient, teach, train, tutor.

indomitable, *a.* SYN.-dauntless, impregnable, insurmountable, invincible, invulnerable, unassailable, unconquerable. ANT.-powerless, puny, vulnerable, weak.

induce, *v.* SYN.-begin, cause, create, effect, engender, evoke, generate, incite, influence, instigate, make, muster, occasion, originate, persuade, produce, prompt, spur, start, urge.

inducement, *n.* SYN.-cause, incentive, incitement, motive, principle, purpose, reason, spur, stimulus. ANT.-action, attempt, deed, effort, result.

indulge, *v.* SYN.-allow, cater, coddle, entertain, gratify, humor, pamper, permit, placate, please, suffer, tolerate.

indurate, *a.* SYN.-callous, cold, hard, hardened, heartless, impenitent, inured, insensible, insensitive, obdurate, tough, unfeeling. ANT.-compassionate, sensitive, soft, tender.

industrious, *a.* SYN.-active, assiduous, busy, diligent, hard-working, intent, patient, persevering. ANT.-apathetic, careless, indifferent, lethargic, unconcerned.

inebriated, *a.* SYN.-drunk, drunken, high, intoxicated, tight, tipsy. ANT.-clearheaded, sober, temperate.

ineffective, *a.* SYN.-debilitated, decrepit, delicate, feeble, impotent, infirm, illogical, inadequate, lame, poor, vague; irresolute, pliable, vacillating, wavering, weak; assailable, defenseless, exposed, vulner-

able. ANT.-potent, powerful, robust, strong, sturdy.

inept, *a.* SYN.-awkward, clumsy, dumb, foolish, graceless, inappropriate, ridiculous, unfitting, unsuited. ANT.-adroit, appropriate, apt, competent, fit, skillful, suitable.

inertia, *n.* SYN.-idleness, inactivity, indolence, laziness, listlessness, passivity, sluggishness.

inequity, *n.* SYN.-bias, favoritism, grievance, inclination, iniquity, injury, injustice, partiality, unfairness, wrong. ANT.-equity, justice, lawfulness, righteousness.

inevitable, *a.* SYN.-assured, certain, definite, destined, fated, fixed, impending, indubitable, ordained, positive, predestined, secure, sure, unavoidable, undeniable, unquestionable. ANT.-doubtful, indeterminate, possible, probable, questionable, uncertain.

inexpensive, *a.* SYN.-cheap, common, economical, fair, inferior, low-priced, mean, moderate, modest, poor, reasonable, shabby, thrifty. ANT.-costly, dear, expensive.

inexperienced, *a.* SYN.-amateur, artless, fresh, green, innocent, naive, new, raw, uncultivated, unskilled, untrained, untried, youthful.

inexplicable, *a.* SYN.-abnormal, bizarre, cryptic, dark, dim, enigmatical, extraordinary, hidden, incomprehensible, inscrutable, mysterious, mystical, obscure, occult, peculiar, recondite, secret, strange, unusual. ANT.-clear, explained, obvious, plain, simple.

infect, *v.* SYN.-adulterate, befoul, contaminate, corrupt, defile, pervert, poison, pollute, sully, taint.

ANT.-disinfect, purify.

infection, *n.* SYN.-ailment, contagion, contamination, disease, germ, pest, poison, pollution, taint, virus.

infectious, *a.* SYN.-catching, communicable, contagious, pestilential, virulent. ANT.-healthful, hygienic, non-communicable.

infer, *v.* SYN.-hint, imply, insinuate, suggest; conclude, deduce, gather,

inference, *n.* SYN.-conclusion, consequence, corollary, deduction, judgment, reason, result, supposition. ANT.-assumption, foreknowledge, preconception, presupposition.

inferior, *a.* SYN.-common, lesser, lower, mediocre, minor, poor, poorer, secondary, subordinate, substandard. ANT.-better, greater, higher, superior.

infest, *v.* SYN.-defile, fill, flood, infect, invade, jam, overrun, pack, plague, press, pollute, ravage, spread, swarm, teem.

infidel, *n.* SYN.-agnostic, atheist, heathen, unbeliever.

infidelity, *n.* SYN.-betrayal, denial, disavowal, disloyalty, faithlessness, renunciation, unfaithfulness. ANT.-fealty, loyalty.

infiltrate, *n.* SYN.-join, penetrate, permeate, pervade, saturate.

infinite, *a.* SYN.-boundless, countless, endless, eternal, illimitable, immeasurable, immense, incalculable, inexhaustible, interminable, limitless, unbounded, unlimited, vast. ANT.-bounded, circumscribed, confined, finite, limited, restricted.

infirm, *a.* SYN.-decrepit, delicate, enervated, exhausted, faint, feeble, forceless, impaired, languid, powerless, puny, weak. ANT.-forceful, lusty, stout, strong, vigorous.

infirmity, *n.* SYN.-ailment, complaint, debility, disease, disorder, frailty, illness, malady, malaise, sickness, weakness. ANT.-health, healthiness, soundness, vigor.

inflame, *v.* SYN.-aggravate, arouse, chafe, disturb, enrage, excite, gall, grate, incense, incite, provoke, rile, stimulate. ANT.-alleviate, appease, calm, mollify, pacify.

inflate, *v.* SYN.-balloon, bloat, boost, enlarge, exaggerate, exalt, expand, fill, magnify, overestimate, stretch, swell.

inflection, *n.* SYN.-accent, articulation, emphasis, enunciation, intonation, pronunciation, tone.

inflexibility, *n.* SYN.-firmness, obstinacy, rigidity, stability, stiffness, stubbornness, tenacity, toughness.

inflexible, *a.* SYN.-determined, dogged, firm, headstrong, immovable, implacable, intractable, obdurate, obstinate, pertinacious, resolute, rigid, steadfast, stubborn, taut, unbending, uncompromising, unyielding. ANT.-amenable, compliant, docile, submissive, yielding.

inflict, *v.* SYN.-coerce, compel, demand, force, require.

influence, *n.* SYN.-authority, command, control, domination, effect, esteem, importance, prestige, power, prominence, weight. ANT.-impotence, inferiority, subjection, timidity.

influence, *v.* SYN.-activate, actuate, affect, bias, control, convince, direct, impel, impress, incite, induce, influence, inspire, mold, persuade, shape, stir, sway, train.

influential, *a.* SYN.-consequential, convincing, critical, decisive, effective, forceful, grave, important, material, momentous, powerful, prominent, relevant, significant, substantial. ANT.-insignificant, irrelevant, mean, petty, trivial.

inform, v. SYN.-acquaint, advise, apprise, enlighten, familiarize, impart, instruct, notify, relate, squeal, tattle, teach, tell, testify, warn. ANT.-conceal, delude, distract, mislead.

informal, a. SYN.-congenial, easy, familiar, intimate, natural, offhand, ordinary, relaxed, simple, spontaneous, unceremonious, unofficial. ANT.-ceremonious, conventional, distant, formal, precise, proper, reserved, restrained.

informality, n. SYN.-closeness, familiarity, frankness, friendliness, intimacy, liberty, unconstrained, unreserved. ANT.-constraint, distance, haughtiness.

information, n. SYN.-data, evidence, facts, figures, knowledge, learning, material, statistics.

infraction, n. SYN.-breach, indiscretion, infringement, transgression, violation.

infrequent, a. SYN.-exceptional, limited, occasional, rare, scarce, seldom, singular, uncommon, unique, unusual. ANT.-abundant, commonplace, frequent, numerous, often, ordinary, usual.

infringe, v. SYN.-encroach, intrude, invade, offend, poach, transgress, violate.

infuriate, v. SYN.-affront, aggravate, anger, enrage, madden, provoke.

infuse, v. SYN.-fill, imbue, impregnate, indoctrinate, ingrain, permeate, saturate.

ingenious, a. SYN.-acute, adroit, apt, astute, bright, clever, dexterous, keen, original, quick, quick-witted, sharp, skillful, smart, tal-

ented, witty. ANT.-awkward, bungling, clumsy, dull, foolish, slow, stupid, unskilled.

ingenuity, n. SYN.-ability, aptitude, artifice, cleverness, cunning, faculty, imagination, ingeniousness, inventiveness, resourcefulness, skill ANT.-clumsiness, dullness, inaptitude, stupidity.

ingenuous, a. SYN.-artless, candid, frank, free, guileless, honest, innocent, instinctive, naive, open, plain, simple, sincere, spontaneous, straightforward, truthful. ANT.-contrived, scheming, sly, wily.

ingest, v. SYN.-consume, devour, eat, swallow.

ingredient, n. SYN.-additive, component, constituent, element, part.

inhabit, v. SYN.-abide, dwell, fill, live, occupy, permeate, possess, reside, stay. ANT.-abandon, release, relinquish.

inhabitant, n. SYN.-dweller, native, occupant, resident.

inherent, a. SYN.-congenital, inborn, inbred, innate, instinctive, intrinsic, native, natural, real. ANT.-acquired, external, extraneous, extrinsic, superficial.

inherit, v. SYN.-acquire, gain, get, obtain, receive, secure.

inhibit, v. SYN.-arrest, ban, bridle, check, constrain, curb, discourage, forbid, frustrate, hinder, limit, obstruct, prohibit, repress, restrain, stop, suppress. ANT.-adopt, aid, allow, authorize, consent, encourage, grant, incite, loosen.

inhuman, a. SYN.-barbarous, brutal, callous, cruel, ferocious, heartless, malignant, merciless, monstrous, pitiless, ruthless, satanic, savage. ANT.-benevolent, compassionate, forbearing, gentle, humane, kind, merciful.

inimical, *a.* SYN.-antagonistic, averse, contrary, harmful, hurtful, noxious, repugnant.

inimitable, *a.* SYN.-incomparable, matchless, peerless, rare, singular, uncommon, unequaled, unique, unsurpassed.

iniquitous, *a.* SYN.-bad, baleful, base, corrupt, deleterious, depraved, evil, immoral, noxious, pernicious, sinful, unjust, unsound, unwholesome, villainous, wicked. ANT.-excellent, good, honorable, moral, reputable.

iniquity, *n.* SYN.-corruption, depravity, evil, inequity, injury, injustice, sin, unfairness, wrong. ANT.-equity, justice, lawfulness, righteousness.

initial, *a.* SYN.-beginning, earliest, elementary, first, inaugural, introductory, original, primary, prime, primeval, primitive, pristine; chief, foremost, leading, primary. ANT.-hindmost, last, latest; least, subordinate.

initiate, *v.* SYN.-arise, begin, commence, inaugurate, induct, install, instate, institute, introduce, launch, open, originate, propose, sponsor, start. ANT.-close, complete, end, finish, terminate.

injudicious, *a.* SYN.-foolish, impolitic, imprudent, indiscreet, senseless, silly.

injure, *v.* SYN.-abuse, affront, batter, damage, disfigure, dishonor, harm, hurt, impair, insult, maltreat, mar, spoil, wound, wrong. ANT.-ameliorate, benefit, compliment, help, praise, preserve.

injurious, *a.* SYN.-abusive, damaging, defamatory, deleterious, derogatory, detrimental, destructive,

harmful, hurtful, inequitable, insulting, libelous, offensive, slanderous, unfair, unjust. ANT.-advantageous, beneficial, good, helpful, profitable, salutary, useful.

injury, *n.* SYN.-abrasion, affliction, blemish, damage, detriment, grievance, harm, hurt, impairment, injustice, laceration, mischief, outrage, prejudice, slight, wound, wrong. ANT.-aid, assistance, benefit, improvement, relief, repair, service.

injustice, *n.* SYN.-abuse, breach, crime, grievance, inequity, iniquity, injury, transgression, unfairness, villainy, wrong. ANT.-equity, fairness, honest, impartiality, integrity, just, justice, lawfulness, right, righteousness.

inkling, *n.* SYN.-clue, hint, hunch, inference, insinuation, notion, suggestion.

innate, *a.* SYN.-ancestral, congenital, hereditary, inborn, inbred, inherent, inherited, innate, intrinsic, intuitive, native, natural, real. ANT.-acquired, external, extraneous, extrinsic.

innocent, *a.* SYN.-artless, blameless, faultless, forthright, guileless, harmless, honest, innocuous, lawful, legitimate, naive, pure, simple, sinless, unblemished, undefiled, virtuous ANT.-corrupt, culpable, guilty, sinful, unrighteous.

innocuous, *a.* SYN.-harmless, innocent, safe.

innovation, *n.* SYN.-alteration, change, difference, diversity, feature, highlight, modification, specialty, variation.

innovate, *v.* SYN.-alter, change, conceive, create, ideate, modify, renew, switch, transform, vary.

innuendo, n. SYN.-affront, blot, defamation, insult, slander, slight, slur, smear, vilification.

innumerable, a. SYN.-countless, incalculable, immeasurable, indefinite, infinite, many, numerous, unlimited.

inoffensive, a. SYN.-harmless, innocent, innocuous.

inopportune, a. SYN.-awkward, embarrassing, improper, inappropriate, uncomfortable, unpleasant, untimely.

inordinate, a. SYN.-excessive, exorbitant, extravagant, imprudent, lavish, prodigal.

inquire, v. SYN.-ask, interrogate, investigate, probe, pry, query, question, search. ANT.-command, dictate, insist, order, reply.

inquiring, a. SYN.-curious, inquisitive, interrogative, meddling, nosy, peeping, peering, prying, searching, snoopy. ANT.-incurious, indifferent, unconcerned, uninterested.

inquiry, n. SYN.-examination, exploration, inquest, interrogation, investigation, probe, query, quest, question, research, scrutiny. ANT.-assumption, conjecture, disregard, guess, inactivity, inattention, intuition, negligence, supposition.

inquisitive, a. SYN.-curious, inquiring, interested, interrogative, nosy, peeping, peering, prying, questioning, searching, snoopy. ANT.-incurious, indifferent, unconcerned, uninterested.

insane, a. SYN.-crazy, daft, delirious, demented, deranged, frenzied, lunatic, mad, maniacal, psychotic, touched. ANT.-rational, reasonable, sane, sensible, sound.

insanity, n. SYN.-aberration, compulsion, craziness, delirium, dementia, derangement, frenzy, hysteria, lunacy, madness, mania, obsession, psychosis. ANT.-rationality, sanity, stability.

insatiable, a. SYN.-avaricious, gluttonous, grasping, greedy, ravenous, starved, voracious.

inscribe, v. SYN.-catalog, engrave, enter, inventory, list, record, register.

inscrutable, a. SYN.-impenetrable, incomprehensible, inexplicable, mysterious, strange.

insecurity, n. SYN.-anxiety, doubt, indecision, uncertainty, vulnerability; danger, exposure, hazard, jeopardy, liability, peril, pitfall, vulnerability.

insensitive, a. SYN.-callous, hard, impenitent, indurate, insensible, obdurate, obstinate, remorseless, tough, unfeeling. ANT.-compassionate, sensitive, soft, tender.

inseparable, a. SYN.-attached, connected, indivisible, integrated, integral, joined, united.

insert, v. SYN.-add, append, enclose, include, inject, introduce.

insidious, a. SYN.-artful, beguiling, corrupting, crafty, cunning, deceitful, evil, treacherous.

insight, n. SYN.-acumen, awareness, discernment, discretion, intuition, penetration, perception, perspicuity, recognition, sense, understanding. ANT.-obtuseness.

insignificant, a. SYN.-frivolous, irrelevant, paltry, petty, small, trifling, trivial, unimportant, worthless. ANT.-important, momentous, serious, weighty.

insincere, a. SYN.-deceitful, dishonest, hypocritical, pretentious, shifty, superficial.

insinuate, v. SYN.-allude, connote,

hint, imply, intimate, involve, mean, signify, suggest. ANT.-assert, express, state.

insipid, *a.* SYN.-banal, bland, dull, flat, prosaic, stale, tasteless, uninteresting, vapid. ANT.-exciting, racy, savory, tasty.

insist, *v.* SYN.-allege, ask, assert, charge, claim, contend, demand, expect, maintain.

insistent, *a.* SYN.-determined, obstinate, persistent, relentless, resolute, tenacious, unrelenting,

insolence, *n.* SYN.-arrogance, audacity, boldness, defiance, disdain, effrontery, haughtiness, impertinence, impudence, loftiness, presumption, pride, rudeness, sauciness. ANT.-diffidence, politeness, subserviency, truckling.

insolent, *a.* SYN.-abusive, arrogant, bold, brazen, contemptuous, defiant, disrespectful, haughty, impertinent, impudent, insulting, offensive, overbearing, proud, rude. ANT.-considerate, courteous, polite, respectful.

inspect, *v.* SYN.-ascertain, determine, examine, eye, fathom, gaze, investigate, look, observe, probe, regard, scan, see, stare, survey, view, watch, witness. ANT.-avert, hide, miss, overlook.

inspection, *n.* SYN.-critique, examination, retrospect, retrospection, review, survey, synopsis, test.

inspiration, *n.* SYN.-ability, aptitude, bent, creativity, faculty, genius, gift, hunch, impulse, inclination, intellect, motivation, notion, originality, sagacity, stimulus, talent, whim. ANT.-ineptitude, obtuseness, shallowness, stupidity.

inspire, *v.* SYN.-animate, encourage, enliven, hearten, invigorate, moti-

vate, spark, spur, stimulate.

instability, *n.* SYN.-changeability, fickleness, fluctuation, imbalance, immaturity, inconsistency, transience, vacillation.

install, *v.* SYN.-build, establish, inaugurate, induct, initiate, introduce.

instance, *n.* SYN.-case, example, illustration, occurrence, representation, sample, situation, specimen.

instantaneous, *a.* SYN.-abrupt, hasty, immediate, rapid, sudden, unexpected. ANT.-anticipated, gradual, slowly.

instantly, adv. SYN.-directly, forthwith, immediately, instantaneously, now, presently, promptly, straight-away. ANT.-distantly, hereafter, later, shortly, sometime.

instigate, *v.* SYN.-encouage, foment, foster, incite, induce, influence, persuade.

instill, *v.* SYN.-educate, imbue, impute, indoctrinate, inform, infuse, instruct.

instinctive, *a.* SYN.-automatic, extemporaneous, impulsive, inborn, inherent, innate, intuitive, offhand, spontaneous, subconscious, voluntary, willing. ANT.-compulsory, forced, planned, prepared, rehearsed.

institute, *v.* SYN.-establish, form, found, organize, raise. ANT.-abolish, demolish, overthrow, unsettle, upset.

instruct, *v.* SYN.-brief, command, direct, educate, guide, help, inculcate, inform, instill, order, school, teach, train, tutor. ANT.-misguide, misinform.

instruction, *n.* SYN.-admonition, advice, caution, counsel, exhortation, recommendation, suggestion;

information, intelligence, notification.

instrument, *n.* SYN.-agent, apparatus, device, means, medium, tool, utensil, vehicle. ANT.-hindrance, impediment, obstruction, preventive.

instrumental, *a.* SYN.-contributory, effective, helpful, useful.

insubordinate, *a.* SYN.- defiant, disobedient, mutinous, rebellious, refractory, seditious, undutiful, unruly. ANT.-compliant, dutiful, obedient, submissive.

insubstantial, *a.* SYN.-ephemeral, ethereal, flimsy, immaterial, inconsequential, insignificant, insubstantial, intangible, negligible, tenuous, trifling, trivial, unimportant.

insufferable, *a.* SYN.-disagreeable, intolerable, obnoxious, odious, offensive, onerous, painful, repulsive, taxing.

insufficient, *a.* SYN.-low, undersized; deficient, inadequate, lacking, limited, meager, short, skimpy, thin, wanting, weak. ANT.-abundant, ample, enough, extended, protracted.

insulation, *n.* SYN.-alienation, covering, isolation, loneliness, protector, quarantine, retirement, seclusion, segregation, separation, solitude, withdrawal. ANT.-association, communion, connection, fellowship, union.

insult, *n.* SYN.-abuse, affront, derision, discourtesy, indignity, insolence, invective, libel, offense, ridicule, scorn, slander, slap, slur. ANT.-apology, homage, praise, salutation

insult, *v.* SYN.-abuse, affront, belittle, dishonor, hurt, injure, libel,

mock, offend, revile, ridicule, slander, slur, taunt, wound, wrong. ANT.-compliment, praise.

insulting, *a.* SYN.-abusive, contemptuous, degrading, humiliating, impertinent, nasty, offensive, outrageous.

intact, *a.* SYN.-complete, entire, perfect, sound, unbroken, undamaged, undivided, whole

intangible, *a.* SYN.-ethereal, hypothetical, immaterial, incorporeal, vague, vaporous.

integrated, *a.* SYN.-blended, combined, mixed, synthesized, united.

integrity, *n.* SYN.-candor, fairness, frankness, goodness, honesty, honor, justice, morality, openness, perfection, principle, rectitude, responsibility, sincerity, trustworthiness, uprightness, virtue. ANT.-cheating, corruption, deceit, disgrace, dishonesty, duplicity, fraud, meanness, trickery.

intellect, *n.* SYN.-ability, acumen, brain, intelligence, mentality, mind, propensity, reason, sense, talent, understanding. ANT.-emotion, feeling, passion.

intelligence, *n.* SYN.-comprehension, discernment, information, knowledge, perspicacity, reason, sense, understanding

intelligent, *a.* SYN.-alert, astute, bright, clever, contemplative, discerning, discriminating, enlightened, intellectual, keen, knowledgeable, perceptive, profound, quick, reasonable, reasoning, smart, well-informed. ANT.-dull, foolish, insipid, obtuse, slow, stupid.

intend, *v.* SYN.-aim, aspire, contrive, delineate, design, determine, devise, expect, mean, outline, plan, plot, prepare, project, propose, resolve, scheme.

intense, *a.* SYN.-acute, animated, bright, brilliant, clear, concentrated, deep, earnest, expressive, fervent, fresh, graphic, heightened, impassioned, intensive, keen, lively, lucid, piercing, powerful, profound, severe, stinging, striking, strong, vivid. ANT.-dim, dreary, dull, dusky, vague.

intensify, *v.* SYN.-amplify, augment, compound, confound, emphasize, enhance, enlarge, exacerbate, expand, extend, grow, heighten, increase, magnify, multiply, raise, sharpen, strengthen, wax. ANT.-atrophy, contract, decrease, diminish, reduce.

intensity, *n.* SYN.-ardor, concentration, depth, emphasis, fervor, force, magnitude, passion, power, severity, stress, vehemence, vigor.

intent, *a.* SYN.-engrossed, firm, rapt, resolute, steadfast.

intent, *n.* SYN.-aim, delineation, design, focus, import, intention, meaning, objective, outline, plan, purpose, significance. ANT.-accident, chance.

intention, *n.* SYN.-aim, contrivance, delineation, design, draft, end, intention, objective, outline, plan, plotting, purpose, scheming. ANT.-accident, candor, chance, result.

intentional, *a.* SYN.-conscious, considered, contemplated, deliberate, designed, intended, premeditated, studied, voluntary, wanton, willful. ANT.-accidental, fortuitous.

intercept, *v.* SYN.-ambush, block, catch, interfere, overtake, reach.

interest, *n.* SYN.-attention, concern, curiosity, regard; advantage, benefit, claim, gain, percentage,

profit, share, stake.

interested, *a.* SYN.-absorbed, affected, attentive, attracted, biased, curious, drawn, engrossed, impressed, inquiring, inquisitive, inspired, involved, moved, prying, nosy, responsive, stimulated, stirred, touched.

interesting, *a.* SYN.-absorbing, amusing, arresting, captivating, enchanting, engaging, enticing, exciting, fascinating, impressive, pleasing, satisfying

interfere, *v.* SYN.-compete, conflict, contend, interpose, interrupt, intervene, meddle, mix in, monkey, pry, question, tamper, vie.

interior, *a.* SYN.-center, central, inmost, inner, internal, intrinsic, inward. ANT.-adjacent, exterior, external, outer.

interject, *v.* SYN.-include, inject, insert, interpose, introduce.

interjection, *n.* SYN.-cry, exclamation, utterance.

interminable, *a.* SYN.-boundless, ceaseless, dull, endless, eternal, illimitable, immeasurable, immense, infinite, monotonous, unbounded, unlimited, vast. ANT.-bounded, circumscribed, confined, finite, limited.

intermittent, *a.* SYN.-broken, disconnected, erratic, irregular, periodic, recurrent, spasmodic.

internal, *a.* SYN.-constitutional, domestic, indigenous, inherent, innate, inside, inward, organic, private.

interpose, *v.* SYN.-arbitrate, inject, insert, intercede, interfere, interject, intervene, introduce, intrude, meddle, mediate. ANT.-avoid, disregard, overlook.

interpret, *v.* SYN.-clarify, construe,

decipher, decode, define, diagnose, elucidate, explain, explicate, portray, render, solve, translate, unravel. ANT.-confuse, distort, falsify, misconstrue, misinterpret.

interpretation, *n.* SYN.-account, analysis, commentary, definition, description, diagnosis, explanation, portrayal, rendering, representation, translation, version.

interrogate, *v.* SYN.-ask, audit, check, examine, inquire, pump, query, question, quiz. ANT.-disregard, omit, overlook.

interrupt, *v.* SYN.-adjourn, break, check, defer, delay, discontinue, interfere, interject, intervene, intrude, postpone, stay, suspend. ANT.-continue, maintain, persist, proceed, prolong.

intervene, *v.* SYN.-arbitrate, intercede, interfere, interpose, meddle, mediate, negotiate. ANT.-avoid, disregard, overlook.

intimacy, *n.* SYN.-affection, closeness, familiarity, fellowship, frankness, friendship, informality, liberty, love, sociability, warmth. ANT.-constraint, distance, haughtiness, reserve.

intimate, *a.* SYN.-affectionate, chummy, close, confidential, familiar, friendly, loving, near, personal, private. ANT.-ceremonious, conventional, distant, formal.

intimation, *n.* SYN.-allusion, connotation, hint, implication, indication, inference, innuendo, insinuation, reminder, suggestion. ANT.-affirmation, declaration, statement.

intolerant, *a.* SYN.-biased, bigoted, dogmatic, fanatical, narrow, narrow-minded, opinionated, parochial, prejudiced. ANT.-liberal, progressive, radical, tolerant.

intoxicate, *v.* SYN.-befuddle, confuse, elate, excite, exhilarate, inebriate, invigorate, muddle, stimulate, thrill.

intoxicated, *a.* SYN.-drunk, drunken, high, inebriated, tight, tipsy; elated, euphoric, excited, exhilarated, infatuated, stimulated. ANT.-clearheaded, sober, temperate; calm, cool, unconcerned.

intricate, *a.* SYN.-abstract, abstruse, complex, complicated, compound, involved, perplexing, puzzling. ANT.-plain, simple, uncomplicated.

intrigue, *n.* SYN.-artifice, cabal, conspiracy, design, machination, plan, plot, scheme, stratagem.

intriguing, *a.* SYN.-appealing, attractive, charming, engaging, entertaining, fascinating, interesting, pleasing.

intrinsic, *a.* SYN.-congenital, inborn, inbred, ingrained, inherent, innate, native, natural, real. ANT.-acquired, external, extraneous, extrinsic.

introduce, *v.* SYN.-add, advance, begin, inaugurate, initiate, insert, insinuate, institute, interject, offer, present, propose,

introduction, *n.* SYN.-admittance, baptism, beginning, debut, forward, initiation, overture, preamble, preface, prelude, presentation, prologue, start. ANT.-completion, conclusion, end, epilogue, finale.

introductory, *a.* SYN.-basic, beginning, early, initial, opening, original, preparatory, primary, starting.

intrude, *v.* SYN.-encroach, impose, infringe, intervene, invade, penetrate, trespass, violate. ANT.-abandon, evacuate, relinquish, vacate.

intuition, *n.* SYN.-acumen, clue, discernment, feeling, hunch, insight, penetration, perspicuity, premonition, prescience, presentiment. ANT.-obtuseness.

intuitive, *a.* SYN.-automatic, natural, spontaneous; clairvoyant, discerning, insightful, perceptive.

invade, *v.* SYN.-assault, attack, encroach, infringe, intrude, penetrate, raid, storm, transgress, trespass, violate. ANT.-abandon, evacuate, relinquish, vacate.

invalid, *a.* SYN.-defective, erroneous, fallacious, groundless, illogical, irrational, null, void.

invalidate, *v.* SYN.-annul, belie, cancel, contradict, deny, discredit, negate, nullify, refute, reject, repeal, revoke, void.

invaluable, *a.* SYN.-expensive, inestimable, precious, priceless, valuable. ANT.-cheap, useless, worthless.

invariable, *a.* SYN.-changeless, consistent, constant, static, unchanging, uniform.

invasion, *n.* SYN.-aggression, assault, attack, incursion, offensive, onslaught, raid. ANT.-defense, opposition, resistance, surrender.

invective, *n.* SYN.-abuse, aspersion, censure, defamation, denunciation, desecration, dishonor, disparagement, insult, outrage, perversion, profanation, reproach, reviling, scorn, upbraiding, vituperation. ANT.-approval, commendation, laudation, plaudit, respect.

invent, *v.* SYN.-conceive, concoct, contrive, create, design, devise, discover, fabricate, fashion, forge, frame, originate, plan. ANT.-copy, imitate, reproduce.

inventive, *a.* SYN.-bright, clever, creative, fanciful, imaginative, resourceful, visionary. ANT.-dull, literal, prosaic, unromantic.

inventiveness, *n.* SYN.-ability, adroitness, cleverness, cunning, dexterity, expertise, faculty, imagination, ingeniousness, ingenuity, resourcefulness, skill. ANT.-clumsiness, dullness, inaptitude, stupidity.

invert, *v.* SYN.-change, overthrow, overturn, reverse, subvert, transpose, unmake, upset. ANT.-maintain, stabilize.

investigate, *v.* SYN.-analyze, examine, explore, ferret, inquire, interrogate, look, probe, question, research, scour, scrutinize, search, seek, study, test.

investigation, *n.* SYN.-examination, exploration, inquiry, interrogation, query, quest, question, research, scrutiny. ANT.-disregard, inactivity, inattention, negligence.

invincible, *a.* SYN.-impregnable, indomitable, insurmountable, invulnerable, unassailable, unconquerable. ANT.-powerless, puny, vulnerable, weak.

invigorate, *v.* SYN.-animate, energize, enliven, excite, exhilarate, rejuvenate, revive, stimulate.

invigorating, *a.* SYN.-bracing, cool, exhilarating, fresh, quickening, refreshing, stimulating.

invisible, *a.* SYN.-ethereal, imperceptible, indistinguishable, intangible, obscure, undiscernible, unseen. ANT.-evident, perceptible, seen, visible.

invitation, *n.* SYN.-attraction, encouragement, lure, offer, overture, request, summons, temptation.

invite, *v.* SYN.-ask, attract, beg, bid, draw, entice, implore, lure, persuade, petition, request, solicit, summon, tempt.

inviting, *a.* SYN.-alluring, appealing,

attractive, bewitching, captivating, encouraging, fascinating, magnetic, tempting.

involve, v. SYN.-comprise, embrace, embroil, entangle, envelop, implicate, include, incriminate. ANT.-disconnect, disengage, extricate, separate.

involved, a. SYN.-absorbed, complex, complicated, compound, elaborate, implicated, intricate, mesmerized, perplexing. ANT.-plain, simple, uncompounded.

invulnerable, a. SYN.-impenetrable, impervious, impregnable, indomitable, insurmountable, invincible, steadfast, unassailable, unconquerable. ANT.-powerless, puny, vulnerable, weak.

irate, a. SYN.-angry, enraged, furious, incensed, mad, raging.

ire, n. SYN.-anger, animosity, choler, frenzy, fury, indignation, irritation, passion, petulance, rage, raving, resentment, temper, vehemence, wrath. ANT.-conciliation, forbearance, patience, peace, self-control.

irk, v. SYN.-annoy, beset, bother, chafe, disturb, inconvenience, irritate, molest, pester, tease, torment, trouble, vex, worry. ANT.-accommodate, console, gratify, soothe.

ironic, a. SYN.-caustic, contradictory, contrary, cynical, derisive, incongruous, mocking, paradoxical, sardonic, scathing.

irrational, a. SYN.-absurd, contradictory, fallacious, foolish, illogical, inconsistent, nonsensical, preposterous, ridiculous, silly, specious, unreasonable, untenable. ANT.-consistent, rational, reasonable, sensible, sound.

irregular, a. SYN.-aberrant, abnormal, capricious, devious, divergent, eccentric, fitful, inconstant, intermittent, random, sporadic, unequal, uneven, unnatural, unusual, variable. ANT.-fixed, methodical, ordinary, regular, usual.

irrelevant, a. SYN.-alien, contrasted, extraneous, foreign, inapplicable, pointless, remote, strange, unconnected. ANT.-akin, germane, kindred, relevant.

irresistible, a. SYN.-alluring, charming compelling, enchanting, enticing, fascinating, invincible, overwhelming, tantalizing, tempting.

irresolute, a. SYN.-assailable, bending, inadequate, ineffective, insecure, pliable, pliant, undecided, unstable, unsteady, vacillating, vulnerable, wavering, weak, yielding. ANT.-potent, powerful, robust, strong, sturdy.

irresponsible, a. SYN.-capricious, fickle, flighty, immoral, loose, rash, shiftless, thoughtless, unreliable, unstable.

irritable, a. SYN.-choleric, excitable, fiery, hasty, hot, irascible, peevish, petulant, sensitive, snappish, tense, testy, touchy. ANT.-agreeable, calm, composed, tranquil.

irritant, n. SYN.-aggravation, annoyance, bother, inconvenience, nuisance, pest.

irritate, v. SYN.-annoy, bother, chafe, disturb, gall, harass, harry, haze, irk, molest, pester, provoke, tease, torment, trouble, vex. ANT.-accommodate, console, gratify, soothe.

irritation, n. SYN.-annoyance, bother, displeasure, exasperation, pique, stress, vexation. ANT.-appeasement, comfort, gratification, pleasure.

isolated, *a.* SYN.-alone, apart, deserted, desolate, lone, lonely, only, remote, secluded, segregated, separate, single, sole, solitary, withdrawn. ANT.-accompanied, attended, surrounded.

isolation, *n.* SYN.-alienation, detachment, insulation, loneliness, privacy, quarantine, retirement, seclusion, segregation, separation, solitude, withdrawal. ANT.-association, communion, connection, fellowship, union.

issue, *v.* SYN.-abound, come, discharge, emanate, emerge, emit, flow, gush, originate, release, run, spout, spurt, stream, vent.

itinerant, *a.* SYN.-drifting, nomadic, roaming, roving, wandering.

itinerant, *n.* SYN.-nomad, tramp, vagabond, vagrant, wanderer.

J

jabber, *n.* SYN.-babble, chatter, drivel, gibberish, nonsense, patter, twaddle.

jaded, *a.* SYN.-cold, impassive, indifferent, nonchalant, numbed, weary.

jam, *n.* SYN.-difficulty, predicament, problem, trouble.

jam, *v.* SYN.-compress, crowd, crush, jostle, mob, pack, press, ram, squeeze.

jammed, *a.* SYN.-blocked, caught, congested, crowded, frozen, obstructed, overflowing, swarming, wedged.

jargon, *n.* SYN.-cant, colloquialism, dialect, idiom, language, lingo, patter, phraseology, slang, speech, tongue, vernacular. ANT.-babble, drivel, gibberish, nonsense.

jaunt, *n.* SYN.-excursion, journey, junket, pilgrimage, tour, trip, voyage, walk.

jealous, *a.* SYN.-apprehensive, demanding, doubting, envious, mistrustful, possessive, resentful, suspicious, vigilant, watchful.

jealousy, *n.* SYN.-covetousness, distrust, envy, invidiousness, mistrust, possessiveness, resentfulness, resentment, suspicion. ANT.-geniality, indifference, liberality, tolerance.

jeer, *v.* SYN.-boo, deride, flout, gibe, insult, mock, ridicule, scoff, sneer, taunt. ANT.-compliment, flatter, laud, praise.

jeering, *n.* SYN.-banter, derision, gibe, insult, irony, mockery, raillery, ridicule, sarcasm, satire, sneering.

jeopardize, *v.* SYN.-endanger, expose, hazard, imperil, peril, risk, venture. ANT.-guard, insure.

jerk, *n.* SYN.-convulsion, flick, jiggle, quiver, tic, twitch; ass, fool, nincompoop, rascal, scamp, scoundrel, simpleton.

jester, *n.* SYN.-buffoon, clown, fool, harlequin. ANT.-philosopher, sage, scholar.

jewel, *n.* SYN.-adornment, bangle, bauble, gem, ornament, trinket.

job, *n.* SYN.-assignment, business, career, chore, employment, errand, function, labor, mission, obligation, occupation, pursuit, position, post, profession, situation, stint, task, toil, work, undertaking, vocation.

join, *v.* SYN.-accompany, adjoin, assemble, associate, attach, cement, clamp, combine, conjoin, connect, consolidate, contact, couple, fuse, link, marry, touch, unite, weld. ANT.-detach, disconnect, disjoin, separate.

joined, *a.* SYN.-allied, affiliated, associated, attached, banded, blended, cemented, combined, connected, coupled, fused, involved, linked, melded, mingled, unified, united, wed.

joke, *v.* SYN.-banter, fool, frolic, jest, josh, kid, laughter, play, pun, quip, tease, trick.

jolly, *a.* SYN.-cheerful, gay, glad, happy, jovial, joyful, joyous, light-hearted, merry, mirthful, sprightly. ANT.-depressed, glum, mournful, sad, sullen.

jolt, *v.* SYN.-bounce, jar, quake, rock, shake, shudder, tremble, vibrate, waver.

journey, *n.* SYN.-cruise, expedition, jaunt, passage, pilgrimage, safari, tour, travel, trip, venture, voyage.

journey, *v.* SYN.-drive, go, jaunt, ramble, ride, roam, rove, tour, travel, trek. ANT.-stay, stop.

jovial, *a.* SYN.-affable, amiable, congenial, convivial, cordial, friendly, happy, jocular, jolly, merry.

joy, *n.* SYN.-bliss, delight, ecstasy, elation, exultation, festivity, gaiety, glee, felicity, happiness, jubilation, levity, merriment, mirth, pleasure, rapture, rejoicing, transport. ANT.-affliction, depression, despair, grief, sorrow.

joyful, *a.* SYN.-blessed, cheerful, contented, delighted, fortunate, gay, glad, happy, joyous, lucky, merry, opportune, propitious. ANT.-blue, depressed, gloomy, morose.

joyous, *a.* SYN.-blithe, cheerful, festive, gay, gleeful, hilarious, jolly, jovial, lively, merry, mirthful, sprightly. ANT.-gloomy, melancholy, morose, sad, sorrowful.

judge, *n.* SYN.-adjudicator, arbitrator, critic, justice, magistrate, referee, umpire.

judge, *v.* SYN.-; adjudicate, arbitrate, condemn, try, umpire; appreciate, consider, decide, decree, deem, determine, estimate, evaluate, measure, think.

judgment, *n.* SYN.-acuity, appraisal, assessment, awareness, belief, comprehension, consideration, conviction, discernment, discrimination, finding, grasp, intelligence, knowledge, mentality, opinion, perspicacity, profundity, prudence, rationality, sagacity, taste, understanding, view, wisdom. ANT.-arbitrariness, senselessness, stupidity, thoughtlessness.

judicious, *a.* SYN.-discreet, expedient, intelligent, politic, practical, prudent, rational, sensible, sober, sound, wise. ANT.-blind, foolish, ill-advised, hasty, rash.

jumble, *n.* SYN.-agitation, chaos, clutter, commotion, confusion, disarrangement, disarray, disorder, ferment, medley, mixture, stir, tumult, turmoil. ANT.-certainty, order, peace, system, tranquility.

jumble, *v.* SYN.-amalgamate blend, combine, commingle, concoct, confound, confuse, mess, mingle, mix, muddle. ANT.-classify, dissociate, divide, file, isolate, segregate, separate, sort, straighten.

jump, *v.* SYN.-bolt, bound, caper, hop, jerk, leap, skip, spring, start, vault.

just, *a.* SYN.-appropriate, apt, fair, good, honest, honorable, equitable, honorable, impartial, legal, legitimate, proper, righteous, rightful, scrupulous, sincere, trustworthy, truthful, upright, virtuous. ANT.-deceitful, dishonest, fraudulent, lying, tricky.

justice, *n.* SYN. equity, fairness, impartiality, integrity, justness, law, rectitude, right, virtue. ANT.-inequity, partiality, unfairness, wrong.

justifiable, *a.* SYN.-admissible, allowable, defensible, fair, fit logical, permissible, probable, proper, tolerable, warranted. ANT.-inadmissible, irrelevant, unsuitable.

justify, *v.* SYN.-absolve, acquit, assert, clear, defend, excuse, exonerate, support, uphold, vindicate. ANT.-abandon, accuse, blame, convict.

K

keen, *a.* SYN.-acute, anxious, ardent, bright, clever, cunning, cutting, discerning, eager, excited, incisive, intent, interested, quick, piercing, sensitive, shrewd, wily, witty, zealous. ANT.-slow, sluggish; dull, inattentive, unaware.

keep, *v.* SYN.-celebrate, commemorate, conserve, continue, guard, honor, maintain, observe, own, possess, preserve, protect, reserve, retain, save, support, sustain, tend; confine, detain, hold, restrain, store. ANT.-abandon, discard, dismiss, forsake, ignore, neglect, reject, relinquish.

kidnap, *v.* SYN.-abduct, capture, grab, pirate, shanghai, snatch, steal, waylay.

kill, *v.* SYN.-assassinate, butcher, dispatch, execute, exterminate, liquidate, massacre, murder, sacrifice, slaughter, slay; cancel, halt, forbid, negate, nullify, prohibit, stop, veto. ANT.-animate, protect, resuscitate, save, vivify.

kin, *n.* SYN.-connection, family, kins-

man, relation, relative, sibling.

kind, *a.* SYN.-accommodating, affable, benevolent, benign, charitable, compassionate, considerate, forbearing, gentle, good, helpful, humane, indulgent, kindly, loving, merciful, obliging, solicitous, sympathetic, tender, thoughtful, understanding. ANT.-cruel, inhuman, merciless, severe, unkind.

kind, *n.* SYN.-breed, character, class, classification, denomination, designation, family, genus, race, sort, species, stock, strain, type, variety.

kindness, *n.* SYN.-altruism, benevolence, charity, compassion, consideration, courtesy, friendliness, generosity, goodness, helpfulness, humanity, mercy, philanthropy, sympathy, tact, tenderness, thoughtfulness, understanding. ANT.-cruelty, harshness, injury, malevolence, selfishness.

kindred, *a.* SYN.-alike, allied, assimilated, associated, family, germane, kin, like, related, similar

kindred, *n.* SYN.-affinity, clan, consanguinity, family, folks, house, kin, kinsfolk, relations, relationship, relatives, tribe. ANT.-disconnection, foreigners, strangers.

kingdom, *n.* SYN.-country, domain, dominion, empire, lands, nation, possessions, principality, realm, state, territory.

kinship, *n.* affiliation, affinity, alliance, cohesion, connection, familiarity, family, intimacy, kin, kindred, relationship, unity.

kiss, *v.* SYN.-caress, coddle, cuddle, embrace, greet, fondle, hug, pet. ANT.-annoy, buffet, spurn, tease, vex.

knack, *n.* SYN.-ability, adroitness, aptitude, capability, cleverness, cunning, deftness, dexterity, endowment, facility, genius, gift, ingenuity, readiness, skill, skillfulness, talent. ANT.-awkwardness, clumsiness, inability, ineptitude.

knife, *n.* SYN.-bayonet, blade, broadsword, cutter, dagger, dirk, edge, lance, machete, point, poniard, razor, saber, scalpel, scimitar, scythe, sickle, stiletto, sword.

knit, *v.* SYN.-affiliate, braid, cable, connect, crochet, intertwine, net, ossify, web

knot, *n.* SYN.-bond, bunch, clinch, cluster, conundrum, crowd, difficulty, entanglement, group, perplexity, snarl, tangle, tie, twist.

know, *v.* SYN.-acquaint, appreciate, apprehend, ascertain, befriend, cognize, comprehend, differentiate, discern, distinguish, experience, familiarize, fathom, perceive, recognize, see, understand. ANT.-dispute, doubt, ignore, suspect.

knowing, *a.* SYN.-acute, awake, aware, clever, cognizant, conscious, intelligent, sharp.

knowingly, *a.* SYN.-consciously, deliberately, intentionally, willfully.

knowledge, *n.* SYN.-apprehension, awareness, cognizance, education, enlightenment, erudition, expertise, information, intelligence, learning, lore, scholarship, science, understanding, wisdom. ANT.-ignorance, illiteracy, misunderstanding, stupidity.

known, *a.* SYN.-accepted, acknowledged, admitted, certified, disclosed, established, familiar, learned, noted, prominent, proverbial, public, recognized, revealed.

L

label, *n.* SYN.-classification, description, identification, mark, marker, name, stamp, sticker, tag.

labor, *n.* SYN.-diligence, drudgery, effort, employment, endeavor, exertion, industry, striving, task, toil, travail, undertaking, work; childbirth, parturition. ANT.-idleness, indolence, leisure, recreation.

lacking, *a.* SYN.-deficient, destitute, inadequate, incomplete, insufficient, needed, scant, scanty, short. ANT.-adequate, ample, enough, satisfactory, sufficient.

lag, *n.* SYN.-cessation, retardation, slowdown, slowing, slowness.

lame, *a.* SYN.-crippled, defective, deformed, disabled, feeble, halt, hobbling, limping, maimed, unconvincing, unsatisfactory, weak. ANT.-agile, athletic, robust, sound, vigorous.

lament, *v.* SYN.-bemoan, bewail, deplore, grieve, mourn, repine, wail, weep.

land, *n.* SYN.-acreage, area, continent, country, domain, earth, estate, expanse, farm, field, ground, island, nation, plain, property, province, realm, region, soil, terrain, tract, turf.

land, *v.* SYN.-alight, arrive, berth, disembark, dock.

language, *n.* SYN.-cant, dialect, diction, idiom, jargon, lingo, phraseology, slang, speech, tongue, vernacular. ANT.-babble, drivel, gibberish, nonsense.

languish, *v.* SYN.-decline, deteriorate, droop, dwindle, fade, fail, flag, pine, shrink, shrivel, sink, waste, weaken, wilt, wither. ANT.-refresh, rejuvenate, renew, revive.

lapse, *n.* SYN.-backsliding, blunder boner, degeneration, error, mistake, slip.

larceny, *n.* SYN.-burglary, crime, depredation, embezzlement, fraud, pillage, plunder, robbery, theft, thievery.

large, *a.* SYN.-ample, big, capacious, colossal, considerable, cumbersome, enormous, extensive, extravagant, grand, great, huge, immense, lavish, massive, substantial, vast, wide. ANT.-little, mean, short, small, tiny.

largely, *a.* SYN.-chiefly, essentially, mainly, mostly, predominantly, primarily, principally.

last, *a.* SYN.-climactic, closing, concluding, crowning, decisive, ending, extreme, final, hindmost, latest, terminal, ultimate, utmost. ANT.-beginning, first, foremost, initial, opening.

lasting, *a.* SYN.-abiding, enduring permanent

late, *a.* SYN.-behind, belated, delayed, overdue, slow, tardy; advanced, contemporary, modern, new, recent. ANT.-early, timely.

latent, *a.* SYN.-concealed, dormant, hidden, inactive, potential, quiescent, secret, undeveloped, unseen. ANT.-conspicuous, evident, explicit, manifest, visible.

laugh, *n.* SYN.-amusement, cackle, chortle, chuckle, giggle, guffaw, jeer, merriment, mirth, mock, roar, scoff, snicker, titter.

laughable, *a.* SYN.-amusing, comic, comical, droll, funny, humorous, ludicrous.

launch, *v.* SYN.-begin, drive, inaugurate, introduce, originate, propel, start.

launched, *a.* SYN.-begun, driven, sent, started.

lavish, *a.* SYN.-excessive, extravagant, generous, improvident, plentiful, unstinting, wasteful.

lavish, *v.* SYN.-consume, dissipate, expend, misuse, profligate, scatter, spend, squander, waste. ANT.-accumulate, economize, preserve, save.

law, *n.* SYN.-act, code, constitution, decree, edict, enactment, injunction, order, ordinance, rule, ruling, statute.

lawful, *a.* SYN.-allowable, authorized, constitutional, enacted, legal, legalized, legitimate, permissible, permitted, rightful. ANT.-criminal, illegal, illegitimate, illicit, prohibited.

lawless, *a.* SYN.-barbarous, fierce, savage, tempestuous, uncivilized, violent, uncontrolled, untamed, wild.

lax, *a.* SYN.-careless, desultory, inaccurate, indifferent, neglectful, negligent, remiss, slack. ANT.-accurate, careful, meticulous.

lay, *a.* SYN.-earthly, laic, secular, temporal, worldly; amateur, beginner, novice, neophyte. ANT.-ecclesiastical; experienced, trained.

lay, *v.* SYN.-arrange, deposit, dispose, place, put, set. ANT.-disarrange, disturb, mislay, misplace, remove.

layman, *n.* SYN.-amateur, dilettante, nonprofessional, novice.

layout, *n.* SYN.-arrangement, blueprint, design, draft, organization, plan, scheme, strategy.

lazy, *a.* SYN.-idle, inactive, indifferent, indolent, inert, remiss, slothful, sluggish, supine, torpid. ANT.-active, alert, assiduous, diligent.

lead, *v.* SYN.-allure, beat, conduct,

control, convince, direct, entice, escort, excel, guide, induce, influence, manage, outstrip, persuade, pilot, precede, regulate, steer, supervise, surpass.

leader, *n.* SYN.-captain, chief, chieftain, commander, conductor, director, guide, head, manager, master, principal, ruler. ANT.-attendant, follower, servant, subordinate, underling.

leadership, *n.* SYN.-administration, authority, control, direction, guidance, influence, management, power, superiority

league, *n.* SYN.-alliance, association, brotherhood, club, coalition, combination, confederacy, entente, federation, fellowship, fraternity, partnership, union.

league, *v.* SYN.-band, combine, confederate, cooperate, unite.

lean, *v.* SYN.-bend, incline, list, sag, slant, slope, tend; depend, rely, trust. ANT.-erect, raise, rise, straighten.

leaning, *n.* SYN.-bent, bias, drift, inclination, partiality, penchant, predisposition, proclivity, proneness, propensity, tendency, trend. ANT.-aversion, deviation, disinclination.

leap, *v.* SYN.-bound, caper, clear, hop, hurdle, jump, spring, start, surmount, vault.

learn, *v.* SYN.-acquire, ascertain, determine, discover, get, master, memorize, understand, unearth.

learned, *a.* SYN.-able, academic, accomplished, adept, cultured, educated, enlightened, erudite, experience, expert, informed, intelligent, knowing, lettered, pedantic, professional, professorial, proficient, profound, sagacious, scholarly,

skilled, trained, wise. ANT.-foolish, illiterate, shallow, simple.

learning, *n.* SYN.-cognizance, education, erudition, information, knowledge, lore, scholarship, science, understanding, wisdom. ANT.-ignorance, illiteracy, misunderstanding, stupidity.

least, *a.* SYN.-infinitesimal, microscopic, minimal, minute, slightest, smallest, tiniest, trivial, unimportant.

leave, *v.* SYN.-abandon, abscond, depart, desert, embark, emigrate, flee, forsake, go, move, quit, relinquish, renounce, retire, vacate, withdraw. ANT.-abide, remain, stay, tarry.

lecture, *v.* SYN.-address, admonish, declaim, discourse, expound, harangue, preach, reason, reprimand, scold, speak, spout, talk, teach, upbraid.

led, *a.* SYN.-accompanied, escorted, guided, taken, taught.

legal, *a.* SYN.-allowable, authorized, constitutional, decreed, fair, forensic, just, lawful, legalized, legitimate, licit, permissible, right, rightful, sanctioned, sound, statutory, warranted. ANT.-criminal, illegal, illegitimate, illicit, prohibited.

legend, *n.* SYN.-allegory, chronicle, fable, fiction, myth, parable, saga, story, tradition. ANT.-fad, history.

legendary, *a.* SYN.-allegorical, apocryphal, celebrated, created, fabulous, famous, fanciful, historical, imaginary, immortal, invented, mythical, mythological, romantic, storied, traditional.

legible, *a.* SYN.-clear, comprehensible, conspicuous, distinct, intelligible, lucid, perceptible, plain, sharp, visible.

legitimate, *a.* SYN.-authentic, authorized, bona fide, correct, genuine, justifiable, lawful, legal, licit, logical, official, proper, proven, real, reasonable, regular, rightful, sanctioned, sensible, sincere, statutory, true, unadulterated, unaffected, valuable, veritable, warranted. ANT.-artificial, bogus, counterfeit, false, sham.

leisure, *n.* SYN.-calm, ease, freedom, intermission, pause, peace, quiet, recess, recreation, relaxation, repose, respite, rest, tranquility. ANT.-agitation, commotion, disturbance, motion, tumult.

leisurely, *a.* SYN.-dawdling, delaying, deliberate, dull, gradual, laggard, lethargic, premeditated, slow, slowly, sluggish. ANT.-fast, quick, rapid, speedy, swift.

lend, *v.* SYN.-accommodate, adjust, advance, allow, comply, confer, conform, contribute, entrust, furnish, give, grant, impart, loan, oblige, present, supply.

length, *n.* SYN.-dimension, distance, duration, expanse, interval, measure, period, range, reach, season, span, stretch.

lengthen, *v.* SYN.-attenuate, draw, elongate, extend, prolong, protract, stretch. ANT.-contract, shorten.

leniency, *n.* SYN.-charity, clemency, compassion, forgiveness, grace, indulgence, mercy, mildness, patience, pity, understanding. ANT.-cruelty, punishment, retribution, vengeance.

lenient, *a.* SYN.-clement, compassionate, forbearing, forgiving, humane, indulgent, kind, merciful, tender, tolerant. ANT.-brutal, cruel, pitiless, remorseless, unfeeling.

lessen, *v.* SYN.-abate, curtail, decline, decrease, deduct, degrade, diminish, dwindle, ease, fade, lighten, lower, reduce, shorten, shrink, subtract, truncate, wane. ANT.-amplify, enlarge, expand, grow, increase.

lessening, *a.* SYN.-abating, declining, decreasing, dwindling, ebbing, falling, reducing, shrinking, waning, weakening.

lesser, *a.* SYN.-diminutive, inferior, insignificant, minor, negligible, petty, secondary, trivial.

lesson, *n.* SYN.-assignment, drill, education, example, explanation, guide, instruction, lecture, model, schooling, study, teaching, tutoring.

let, *v.* SYN.-allow, approve, authorize, condone, consent, permit, tolerate.

lethargy, *n.* SYN.-apathy, daze, inactivity, indolence, languor, numbness, passivity, sloth, stupefaction, stupor, torpor. ANT.-activity, alertness, liveliness, readiness, wakefulness.

letter, *n.* SYN.-character, mark, sign, symbol, type; communication, dispatch, epistle, memorandum, message, missive, note, report, writ.

level, *a.* SYN.-aligned, balanced, equal, equivalent, even, flat, flush, horizontal, plane, smooth, stable, steady, uniform. ANT.-broken, hilly, irregular, sloping.

levy, *n.* SYN.-assessment, custom, duty, exaction, excise, impost, rate, tax, toll, tribute. ANT.-gift, remuneration, reward, wages.

lewd, *a.* SYN.-carnal, coarse, debauched, dirty, disgusting, dissolute, filthy, gross, impure, indecent, obscene, offensive, pornographic, prurient, ribald, smutty.

ANT.-decent, modest, pure, refined.

liability, n. SYN.-accountability, burden, debt, disadvantage, encumbrance, obligation, pledge, responsibility,

liable, a. SYN.-accountable, amenable, answerable, bound, exposed, likely, obliged, prone, responsible, sensitive, subject. ANT.-exempt, free, immune, independent, protected.

libel, n. SYN.-aspersion, backbiting, calumny, defamation, denigration, lie, scandal, slander, vilification. ANT.-applause, commendation, defense, flattery, praise.

liberal, a. SYN.-abundant, ample, bountiful, broad-minded, expanded, extensive, impartial, indulgent, large, left, progressive, radical, reform, sweeping, tolerant, unconventional, understanding, vast, wide. ANT.-confined, narrow, restricted.

liberate, v. SYN.-deliver, discharge, emancipate, free, loose, release, set free. ANT.-confine, imprison, oppress, restrict, subjugate.

liberated, a. SYN.-autonomous, discharged, dismissed, emancipated, exempt, free, freed, independent, loose, open, unconfined, unobstructed, unrestricted. ANT.-confined, restrained, restricted; blocked, impeded.

liberty, n. SYN.-autonomy, deliverance, freedom, holiday, immunity, independence, leave, license, leisure, permission, privilege, self-government, vacation. ANT.-captivity, imprisonment, submission; constraint.

library, n. SYN.-archives, books, collection, den, manuscripts, museum, studio, study.

license, n. SYN.-consent, excess, exemption, freedom, grant, immoderation, immunity, independence, latitude, liberation, liberty, permit, prerogative, privilege, right, sanction, unrestraint, warrant. ANT.-bondage, compulsion, constraint, necessity, servitude.

lie, n. SYN.-delusion, equivocation, fabrication, falsehood, fib, fiction, illusion, invention, prevarication, untruth. ANT.-axiom, canon, fact, truism.

lie, v. SYN.-deceive, distort, equivocate, exaggerate, falsify, fib, mislead, misrepresent, prevaricate.

life, n. SYN.-activity, animation, being, buoyancy, energy, entity, existence, growth, liveliness, mortality, spirit, vigor, vitality, vivacity. ANT.-death, demise, dullness, languor, lethargy.

lifeless, a. SYN.-dead, deceased, defunct, departed, dull, expired, extinct, gone, inactive, inanimate, inert, insensible, insipid, listless, passive, sluggish, spiritless, torpid, unconscious. ANT.-alive, animate, living, stirring.

lift, v. SYN.-elevate, exalt, heave, heighten, hoist, raise, uplift; recall, repeal, rescind, revoke. ANT.-depreciate, depress, lower.

light, a. SYN.-animated, blithe, buoyant, cheerful, elated, effervescent, lively, resilient, spirited, sprightly, vivacious. ANT.-dejected, depressed, despondent, hopeless, sullen.

light, n. SYN.-beam, brightness, dawn, flame, gleam, illumination, incandescence, lamp, luminosity, radiance, shine; enlightenment, insight, knowledge, understanding. ANT.-darkness, gloom, obscurity, shadow.

lighten, v. SYN.-allay, alleviate, cheer, console, ease, lessen, mitigate, reduce, unburden

like, a. SYN.-analogous, coincident, comparable, equal, equivalent, identical, indistinguishable, resembling, same, similar, uniform. ANT.-contrary, disparate, dissimilar, distinct, opposed.

like, v. SYN.-admire, approve, esteem, love; enjoy, fancy, relish, savor.

likely, a. SYN.-anticipated, apparent, appropriate, credible, encouraging, expected, feasible, hopeful, possible, promising, reasonable.

likeness, n. SYN.-affinity, analogy, congruence, correspondence, facsimile, image, parity, representation, resemblance, semblance, similarity, similitude. ANT.-difference, distinction, variance.

limit, n. SYN.-border, bound, boundary, confine, edge, end, extent, limitation, restraint, restriction, terminus. ANT.-boundlessness, endlessness, extension, infinity, vastness.

limitation, n. SYN.-barrier, check, condition, control, defect. deficiency, failing, fault, flaw, frailty, hindrance, inadequacy, obstruction, restriction, stipulation, stricture.

limp, a. SYN.-bending, feeble, flaccid, flimsy, frail, limber, pliable, pliant, relaxed, supple, yielding.

limpid, a. SYN.-clear, cloudless, crystalline, lucid, pure, transparent, unclouded. ANT.-cloudy; ambiguous, obscure, unclear, vague.

line, n. SYN.-arrangement, band, border, course, file, groove, limit, mark, path, queue, road, route rank, row, seam, stripe, streak, string, succession.

lineage, n. SYN.-ancestry, blood, breed, clan, descent, folk, line, nation, parentage, pedigree, people, race, species, stock, strain, tribe.

linger, v. SYN.-abide, amble, bide, dawdle, delay, drift, hesitate, lag, loiter, procrastinate, remain, rest, saunter, stay, stroll, tarry, wait. ANT.-act, expedite, hasten, leave.

link, n. SYN.-bond, connection, connective, coupler, juncture, loop, ring, splice, tie, union. ANT.-break, gap, interval, opening, split.

link, v. SYN.-adjoin, attach, combine, conjoin, connect, couple, join, loop, splice, tie, unite. ANT.-detach, disconnect, disjoin, separate.

lip, n. SYN.-brim, edge, flange, margin, portal, rim.

liquid, a. SYN.-flowing, fluent, fluid, juicy, liquor, molten, viscous, watery, wet. ANT.-congealed, gaseous, solid.

liquidate, v. SYN.-abolish, annihilate, assassinate, cancel, destroy, eliminate, eradicate, execute, obliterate, purge, reimburse, remove, repay.

list, n. SYN.-agenda, catalogue, directory, docket, index, muster, register, roll, roster, slate, tally.

list, v. SYN.-arrange, catalogue, enumerate, index, record, tabulate, tally; careen, incline, lean, tilt.

listen, v. SYN.-attend, hear, hearken, heed, learn, list, mark, mind, note, notice, obey, overhear. ANT.-disregard, ignore, reject, scorn.

listless, a. SYN.-apathetic, indifferent, indolent, languid, lethargic, passive, slow, sluggish, torpid.

literal, a. SYN.-accurate, complete, correct, exact, precise, true, verbatim, veritable.

literate, a. SYN.-educated, erudite, intelligent, learned, lettered, scholarly,

little, a. SYN.-diminutive, insignificant, miniature, minor, minute, paltry, petite, petty, puny, slight, small, tiny, trivial, wee; bigoted, mean, selfish, stingy. ANT.-big, enormous, huge, immense, large.

livelihood, n. SYN.-business, career, living, means, support, sustenance, vocation, work.

lively, a. SYN.-active, alive, animated, blithe, brisk, energetic, frolicsome, spirited, sprightly, spry, supple, vigorous, vivacious; bright, brilliant, clear, fresh, glowing, sparkling, vivid. ANT.-dull, insipid, listless, stale, vapid.

load, n. SYN.-burden, cargo, charge, encumbrance, obligation, onus, responsibility, trust, weight.

load, v. SYN.-burden, encumber, oppress, overload, recharge, resupply, stack, supply, tax, trouble, weigh. ANT.-alleviate, console, ease, lighten, mitigate.

loaf, v. SYN.-dawdle, idle, loiter, loll, lounge, relax

loathe, v. SYN.-abhor, abominate, despise, detest, dislike, hate. ANT.-admire, approve, cherish, like, love.

loathsome, a. SYN.-abominable, detestable, execrable, foul, hateful, odious, revolting, vile. ANT.-agreeable, commendable, delightful, pleasant.

locale, n. area, district, locality, place, region, site, spot, territory, vicinity.

locality, n. SYN.-area, district, environs, neighborhood, place, position, province, range, region, sec-

tion, sector, sphere, zone. ANT.-distance, remoteness.

locate, v. SYN.-discover, find, pinpoint, position, recover; dwell, inhabit, reside, settle.

location, n. SYN.-area, discovering, finding, locale, locality, place, point, position, region, site, situation, spot, station, vicinity, whereabouts.

lock, n. SYN.-bar, bolt, catch, clasp, closure, fastening, hook, latch, padlock; curl, plait, ringlet, tress, tuft.

lodge, n. SYN.-cabin, chalet, cottage, hostel, house, inn, resort, shelter; association, brotherhood, club, society.

lofty, a. SYN.-august, dignified, grand, grandiose, high, imposing, magnificent, majestic, noble, pompous, stately, sublime. ANT.-common, humble, lowly, ordinary, undignified.

logic, n. SYN.-deduction, discernment, induction, intellect, judgment, rationalism, reason, understanding.

logical, a. SYN.-cogent, coherent, conclusive, convincing, effective, efficacious, powerful, probable, rational, sound, strong, telling, valid, weighty. ANT.-counterfeit, null, spurious, void, weak.

loiter, v. SYN.-dally, dawdle, lag, linger, pause, remain, shuffle, tarry, trail, wait.

lone, a. SYN.-alone, apart, deserted, desolate, isolated, lonely, only, secluded, single, sole, solitary, unaided. ANT.-accompanied, attended, surrounded.

loneliness, n. SYN.-alienation, detachment, isolation, privacy, refuge, retirement, retreat, seclusion, solitude. ANT.-exposure, notoriety, publicity.

lonely, *a.* SYN.-abandoned, alone, deserted, desolate, forsaken, friendless, isolated, secluded. ANT.-accompanied, attended, surrounded.

long, *a.* SYN.-elongated, extended, extensive, lasting, lengthy, lingering, prolix, prolonged, protracted, tedious, wordy. ANT.-abridged, brief, concise, short, terse.

look, *v.* SYN.-anticipate, behold, discern, examine, eye, gaze, glance, hunt, inspect, observe, regard, scan, scrutinize, see, seek, stare, survey, view, watch, witness. ANT.-avert, hide, miss, overlook.

looks, *n.* SYN.-appearance, aspect, bearing, countenance, demeanor, features, manner.

loose, *a.* SYN.-careless, corrupt, detached, disengaged, dissolute, free, heedless, imprecise, indefinite, lax, limp, promiscuous, slack, unbound, unfastened, unrestrained, untied, vague, wanton. ANT.-fast, inhibited, restrained, tight.

lose, *v.* SYN.-drop, fail, forfeit, mislay, misplace, succumb, surrender, yield.

loser, *n.* SYN.-defeated, dispossessed, dud, failure, flop, prey, ruined, victim, washout.

lost, *a.* SYN.-adrift, astray, bewildered, condemned, confused, consumed, dazed, defeated, destroyed, distracted, doomed, forfeited, gone, missing, misspent, perplexed, preoccupied, squandered, used, vanquished, wasted. ANT.-anchored, found, located.

lot, *n.* SYN.-circumstance, consequence, destiny, fate, fortune, issue, outcome, portion, result;

acreage, parcel, plat, plot, tract.

loud, *a.* SYN.-blaring, booming, brash, clamorous, deafening, noisy, offensive, resonant, resounding, sonorous, stentorian, vociferous ANT.-dulcet, inaudible, quiet, soft, subdued.

lounge, *v.* SYN.-languish, loaf, loll, relax, rest, sprawl.

lousy, *a.* SYN.-bad, disliked, horrible, offensive, pedicular, undesirable, unwanted.

love, *n.* SYN.-adoration, affection, ardor, attachment, beloved, darling, devotion, endearment, fondness, passion, rapture. ANT.-aversion, dislike, enmity, hatred, indifference.

love, *v.* SYN.-adore, caress, cherish, embrace, fancy, hug, idolize, prize, treasure. ANT.-detest, loathe, spurn.

loveliness, *n.* SYN.-appeal, attractiveness, beauty, charm, comeliness, elegance, fairness, grace, handsomeness, pulchritude. ANT.-deformity, disfigurement, eyesore, homeliness, ugliness.

lovely, *a.* SYN.-beauteous, beautiful, charming, comely, elegant, fair, fine, handsome, pretty. ANT.-foul, hideous, homely, repulsive, unsightly.

loving, *a.* SYN.-affectionate, amorous, attentive, caring, close, concerned, considerate, devoted, familiar, generous, intimate, near, passionate, solicitous, tender, thoughtful. ANT.-ceremonious, conventional, distant, formal.

low, *a.* SYN.-abject, base, coarse, contemptible, crude, dejected, depressed, despicable, dishonorable, dispirited, groveling, ignoble, ignominious, inferior, lowly, mean, menial, plebeian, rude, servile, sordid, vile, vulgar. ANT.-teemed, exalted, honored, lofty, noble, righteous.

lower, *a.* SYN.-inferior, minor, poorer, secondary, subordinate. ANT.-better, greater, higher, superior.

lower, *v.* SYN.-abase, corrupt, debase, degrade, deprave, depress, impair, pervert, vitiate. ANT.-enhance, improve, raise, restore, vitalize.

lowly, *a.* SYN.-humble, ignoble, meek, menial, servile, unpretentious.

loyal, *a.* SYN.-ardent, attached, constant, dedicated, devoted, disposed, earnest, faithful, fond, inclined, prone, staunch, true, trustworthy, wedded. ANT.-detached, disinclined, indisposed, untrammeled.

loyalty, *n.* SYN.-allegiance, constancy, dependability, devotion, faith, faithfulness, fealty, fidelity, obedience, support. ANT.-disloyalty, falseness, perfidy, treachery.

lucid, *a.* SYN.-apparent, bright, brilliant, clear, cloudless, distinct, evident, intelligible, limpid, luminous, manifest, obvious, open, plain, radiant, rational, sane, shining, transparent; unmistakable, unobstructed, visible. ANT.-cloudy; ambiguous, obscure, unclear, vague.

lucky, *a.* SYN.-advantageous, auspicious, benign, favored, felicitous, fortuitous, happy, lucky, propitious, successful. ANT.-cheerless, condemned, ill-fated, persecuted, unlucky.

luminous, *a.* SYN.-bright, brilliant, clear, gleaming, lucid, lustrous, radiant, shining. ANT.-dark, dull, gloomy, murky, sullen.

lunacy, *n.* SYN.-craziness, delirium, dementia, derangement, frenzy, insanity, madness, mania, psychosis. ANT.-rationality, sanity, stability.

lure, *v.* SYN.-allure, attract, charm, draw, enchant, entrap, entice, fascinate, induce, lure, persuade, seduce, tempt. ANT.-alienate, contract, drive, propel.

lurk, *v.* SYN.-creep, crouch, hide, prowl, skulk, slink, sneak, steal.

luscious, *a.* SYN.-delectable, delicious, delightful, palatable, savory, sweet, tasty. ANT.-acrid, distasteful, nauseous, unpalatable, unsavory

lush, *a.* SYN.-dense, extensive, lavish, luxurious, opulent, ornate, profuse, rich.

lust, *n.* SYN.-appetite, aspiration, craving, desire, hungering, longing, passion, sensuality, urge, wish, yearning. ANT.-abomination, aversion, distaste, hate, loathing.

luster, *n.* SYN.-brightness, brilliance, brilliancy, effulgence, glory, gloss, polish, radiance, sheen, splendor. ANT.-darkness, dullness, gloom, obscurity.

lustful, *a.* SYN.-animal, base, carnal, corporeal, fleshly, gross, sensual, voluptuous, worldly, ANT.-exalted, intellectual, refined, spiritual, temperate.

lusty, *a.* SYN.-bold, energetic, hardy, healthy, hearty, robust, stout, strong, sturdy, vigorous, virile. ANT.-effeminate, emasculated, weak.

luxuriant, *a.* SYN.-abundant, ample, bountiful, copious, exuberant, fecund, fertile, fruitful, luxurious, opulent, ornate, plentiful, profuse, prolific, rich. ANT.-barren, sterile, unfruitful, unproductive.

luxurious, *a.* SYN.-affluent, bounteous, bountiful, lavish, opulent, ornate, plenteous plentiful, replete, rich, sumptuous. ANT.-deficient, insufficient, rare, scanty, scarce.

luxury, *n.* SYN.-abundance, affluence, fortune, money, opulence, plenty, possessions, riches, wealth. ANT.-indigence, need, poverty, want.

M

machine, *n.* SYN.-appliance, automaton, contrivance, device, implement, instrument, movement, organization, robot.

mad, *a.* SYN.-angry, crazy, delirious, demented, enraged, exasperated, furious, incensed, insane, lunatic, maniacal, provoked, wrathful. ANT.-calm, happy, healthy, pleased, sane, sensible.

made, *a.* SYN.-built, created, fashioned, formed, manufactured, shaped.

madly, *a.* SYN.-crazily, hastily, hurriedly, rashly, wildly.

madness, *n.* SYN.-craziness, delirium, dementia, derangement, frenzy, insanity, lunacy, mania, psychosis. ANT.-rationality, sanity, stability.

magic, *n.* SYN.-charm, conjuring, enchantment, hex, legerdemain, necromancy, occultism, sorcery, voodoo, witchcraft, wizardry.

magical, *a.* SYN.-astral, charmed, cryptic, enchanted, enchanting, entrancing, fascinating, miraculous, mysterious, mystical, mythical, spellbinding, spiritualistic, supernatural, uncanny.

magnanimous, *a.* SYN.-beneficent, charitable, exalted, forgiving, generous, giving, honorable, liberal, lofty, munificent, noble, openhanded, unselfish. ANT.-covetous, greedy, miserly, selfish, stingy.

magnetic, *a.* SYN. alluring, appealing, attractive, captivating, charming, fascinating, inviting, irresistible.

magnificent, *a.* SYN.-brilliant, dazzling, dignified, exalted, extraordinary, grand, imposing, lavish, luxurious, majestic, noble, splendid, stately

magnify, *v.* SYN.-amplify, augment, enhance, enlarge, exaggerate, expand, extend, grow, heighten, increase, intensify, overstate, stretch, wax. ANT.-belittle, depreciate, minimize, understate.

magnitude, *n.* SYN.-amplitude, bigness, bulk, consequence, dimensions, eminence, enormity, expanse, extent, greatness, importance, largeness, mass, quantity, significance, size, volume.

maim, *v.* SYN.-cripple, disable, disfigure, hurt, lame, mutilate, scar.

main, *a.* SYN.-cardinal, chief, dominant, essential, first, foremost, highest, leading, paramount, predominant, principal, significant. ANT.-auxiliary, minor, subordinate, subsidiary, supplemental.

mainly, *a.* SYN.-chiefly, essentially, largely, mostly, predominantly, primarily, principally.

maintain, *v.* SYN.-affirm, allege, assert, claim, contend, continue, declare; defend, hold, justify, keep, preserve, support, sustain, uphold, vindicate. ANT.-deny, discontinue, neglect, oppose, resist.

majestic, *a.* SYN.-august, dignified, exalted, grand, grandiose, high, imposing, lofty, magnificent, noble, pompous, regal, stately, sublime. ANT.-common, humble, lowly, ordinary, undignified.

make, v. SYN.-assemble, build, cause, compel, construct, create, establish, execute, fashion, form, gain, generate, manufacture, mold, plan, produce, shape. ANT.-break, demolish, destroy, undo, unmake.

makeshift, n. SYN.-alternative, equivalent, expedient, replacement, stopgap, substitute. ANT.-master, original, prime, principal.

malady, n. SYN.-ailment, complaint, disease, disorder, illness, infirmity, sickness. ANT.-health, healthiness, soundness, vigor.

malevolence, n. See **malice.**

malice, n. SYN.-animosity, enmity, grudge, hatred, ill will, malevolence, malignity, rancor, spite. ANT.-affection, kindness, love, toleration.

malicious, a. SYN.-bitter, evil-minded, hostile, malevolent, malignant, rancorous, spiteful, virulent, wicked. ANT.-affectionate, benevolent, benign, kind.

malign, v. SYN.-abuse, accuse, asperse, defame, disparage, ill-use, insult, libel, revile, scandalize, slander, traduce, vilify. ANT.-cherish, honor, praise, protect, respect.

malignant, a. SYN.-dangerous, destructive, growing, harmful, lethal, malicious, rancorous, vicious, virulent.

malleable, a. SYN.-flexible, impressionable, pliant, soft, supple, yielding. ANT.-hard, rigid, rough, tough, unyielding.

manage, v. SYN.-administer, arrange, command, conduct, contrive, control, direct, dominate, educate, engineer, govern, guide,

influence, lead, manipulate, officiate, oversee, pilot, regulate, rule, superintend, train. ANT.-abandon, follow, forsake, ignore, misdirect, misguide, submit.

manageable, a. SYN.-adaptable, compliant, controllable, docile, flexible, gentle, governable, humble, obedient, orderly, teachable, tractable.

manager, n. SYN.-administrator, coach, director, executive, handler, mentor, supervisor, trainer.

mandate, n. SYN.-command, decree, dictate, order, ordinance, regulation.

mandatory, a. SYN.-compulsory, imperative, obligatory, required, requisite.

maneuver, n. SYN.-action, design, execution, movement, operation, performance, plan, plot, proceeding, ruse, scheme, stratagem, tactics, trick. ANT.-cessation, inaction, inactivity, rest.

maneuver, v. SYN.-conspire, contrive, design, devise, intrigue, manage, manipulate, plan, plot, scheme, trick.

mania, n. SYN.-craze, enthusiasm, excitement, fad, frenzy, lunacy, madness, obsession.

manifest, a. SYN.-apparent, clear, distinct, evident, intelligible, lucid, obvious, open, plain, unmistakable, unobstructed, visible. ANT.-ambiguous, obscure, unclear, vague.

manifest, v. SYN.-confirm, declare, demonstrate, denote, designate, disclose, display, exhibit, indicate, prove, reveal, show, signify, specify. ANT.-conceal, distract, divert, falsify, mislead.

manipulate, v. SYN.-command, control, direct, govern, guide, handle, lead, manage, mold, shape.

manner, n. SYN.-custom, fashion, habit, method, mode, practice, style, way.

manners, n. SYN.-air, appearance, aspect, behavior, carriage, conduct, demeanor, deportment, look.

mansion, n. SYN.-castle, chateau, estate, manor, palace, residence, villa.

manufacture, v. SYN.-assemble, build, construct, fabricate, fashion, form, make, produce.

manuscript, n. SYN.-article, book, composition, document, essay, original, script, text, writing.

many, a. SYN.-divers, manifold, multifarious, multitudinous, numerous, several, sundry, various. ANT.-few, infrequent, meager, scanty, scarce.

map, n. SYN.-blueprint, chart, diagram, graph, outline, plan, plat, projection, sketch.

mar, v. SYN.-blemish, bruise, damage, deface, harm, hurt, injure, maim, ruin, scratch, spoil. ANT.-ameliorate, benefit, enhance, mend, repair.

marine, a. SYN.-maritime, nautical, naval, ocean, oceanic.

mark, n. SYN.-badge, brand, characteristic, distinction, emblem, feature, imprint, indication, label, property, scar, sign stain, stigma, symptoms, trace, trademark, trait, vestige.

mark, v. SYN.-brand, characterize, imprint, inscribe, label, tag; behold, descry, discover, distinguish, heed, notice, note, observe, perceive, recognize, regard, remark, see. ANT.-disregard, ignore, overlook, skip.

marriage, n. SYN.-espousal, matrimony, nuptials, union, wedding, wedlock. ANT.-celibacy, divorce, virginity.

marvelous, a. SYN.-astonishing, exceptional, extraordinary, peculiar, rare, remarkable, singular, uncommon, unusual, wonderful. ANT.-common, frequent, ordinary, usual.

masculine, a. SYN.-bold, hardy, lusty, male, manly, mannish, robust, strong, vigorous, virile. ANT.-effeminate, emasculated, feminine, unmanly, weak, womanish.

mask, v. SYN.-cloak, conceal, cover, disguise, hide, screen, secrete, suppress, veil, withhold. ANT.-disclose, display, divulge, expose, reveal, show, uncover.

mass, n. SYN.-accumulation, aggregate, body, bulk, chunk, collection, company, conglomerate, crowd, heap, hunk, mob, piece, pile, portion, rabble, section, stack. ANT.-intellect, mind, soul, spirit.

massacre, n. SYN.-atrocity, butchery, carnage, holocaust, killing, murder, pogrom, slaughter.

massacre, v. SYN.-annihilate, butcher, execute, exterminate, kill, liquidate, murder, slaughter, slay. ANT.-animate, protect, resuscitate, save, vivify.

masses, n. SYN.-crowd, mob, multitude, people, populace, proletariat, rabble.

massive, a. SYN.-bulky, burdensome, cumbersome, enormous, gigantic, heavy, huge, immense, imposing, impressive, monumental, ponderous, tremendous, weighty. ANT.-light, small.

master, n. SYN.-adept, authority, boss, chief, commander, employer, expert, head, leader, lord, maestro, manager, overseer, owner, proprietor, ruler, sage, teacher. ANT.-servant, slave.

mastery, *n.* SYN.-authority, command, control, domination, expertise, influence, jurisdiction, predominance, proficiency, skill, sovereignty, supremacy, sway, transcendence. ANT.-inferiority.

match, *v.* SYN.-balance, coordinate, equalize, equate, harmonize, liken, mate, pair, unite.

mate, *n.* SYN.-associate, buddy, colleague, companion, complement, comrade, consort, crony, counterpart, friend, partner, spouse. ANT.-adversary, enemy, stranger.

material, *a.* SYN.-bodily, corporeal, palpable, physical, real, sensible, solid, tangible; consequential, considerable, essential, germane, important, momentous, relevant, significant, substantial, weighty. ANT.-mental, metaphysical, spiritual; immaterial, insignificant.

material, *n.* SYN.-component, data, element, facts, figures, information, matter, stuff, substance; cloth, fabric, textile.

matrimony, *n.* SYN.-espousal, marriage, nuptials, union, wedding, wedlock. ANT.-celibacy, divorce, virginity.

matter, *n.* SYN.-element, material, stuff, substance, thing; affair, business, cause, concern, essence, focus, interest, occasion, situation, subject, theme, thing, topic, undertaking; consequence, difficulty, distress, importance, moment, perplexity, trouble. ANT.-immateriality, phantom, spirit.

mature, *a.* SYN.-adult, aged, complete, consummate, cultivated, developed, finished, full-grown, matured, mellow, old, ready, ripe, sophisticated. ANT.-crude, green, immature, raw, undeveloped.

mature, *v.* SYN.-age, culminate, develop, evolve, grow, mellow, perfect, ripen, season.

maxim, *n.* SYN.-adage, axiom, epithet, foundation, precept, principle, proverb, saying.

meager, *a.* SYN.-lacking, lean, scant, slight, stinted, wanting.

mean, *a.* SYN.-base, coarse, common, contemptible, despicable, low, malicious, mercenary, nasty, offensive, plebeian, selfish, shabby, sordid, stingy, treacherous, undignified, vile, vulgar. ANT.-admirable, dignified, exalted, generous, noble.

mean, *n.* SYN.-average, center, medium, middle, midpoint.

meander, *v.* SYN.-ramble, stroll, turn, twist, wander, wind.

meaning, *n.* SYN.-acceptation, connotation, drift, explanation, gist, implication, import, intent, interpretation, purport, purpose, sense, significance, signification.

meaningful, *a.* SYN.-consequential, explicit, important, material, pithy, profound, significant, substantial, useful.

meaningless, *a.* SYN.-insignificant, nonsensical, senseless, trivial, unimportant.

means, *n.* SYN.-agent, apparatus, approach, backing, channel, device, instrument, medium, method, mode, property, resources, substance, support, tool, utensil, vehicle, way, wealth. ANT.-hindrance, impediment, obstruction, preventive.

measure, *n.* SYN.-action, maneuver, move, procedure, proceeding; capacity, criterion, dimension, gauge, law, magnitude, mass, quantity, principle, proof, rule, size, standard, test, volume. ANT.-chance, fancy, guess, supposition.

meddle, v. SYN.-encroach, interfere, intervene, interpose, interrupt, intrude, monkey, pry, snoop, tamper.

mediocre, a. SYN.-average, common, fair, intermediate, mean, median, medium, middling, moderate, ordinary. ANT.-exceptional, extraordinary, outstanding.

meditate, v. SYN.-cogitate, consider, contemplate, deem, deliberate, muse, imagine, picture, plot, ponder, reason, recall, recollect, reflect, remember, speculate, study, think, weigh. ANT.-disregard, ignore, neglect, overlook.

meditation, n. SYN.-contemplation, examination, reflection, thought.

meek, a. SYN.-compliant, demur, docile, gentle; mild, passive, reserved, resigned, serene, shy, subdued, submissive, tame, timid, unassuming. ANT.-fierce, savage, spirited, wild; animated, exciting, lively, spirited.

meet, v. SYN.-assemble, collect, collide, confront, congregate, convene, converge, encounter, engage, face, find, greet, intersect. ANT.-cleave, disperse, part, scatter, separate.

melancholy, a. SYN.-dejected, depressed, despondent, disconsolate, dismal, dispirited, doleful, gloomy, glum, grave, moody, pensive, sad, somber, sorrowful, unhappy, wistful. ANT.-cheerful, happy, joyous, merry.

melodramatic, a. SYN.-affected, artificial, ceremonious, dramatic, emotive, histrionic, showy, stagy, theatrical. ANT.-modest, subdued,

unaffected, unemotional.

mellow, a. SYN.-aged, cultured, genial, gentle, good-natured, jovial, mature, quiet, peaceful, perfected, ripe, soft, sweet. ANT.-crude, green, immature, raw, undeveloped.

melodramatic, a. SYN.-artificial, exaggerated, overdone, overemotional, sensational, theatrical.

melody, n. SYN.-air, aria, ballad, composition, lyric, music, song, strain, tune.

melt, v. SYN.-decrease, disintegrate, dissolve, dwindle, fade, liquefy, soften, thaw, vanish.

member, n. SYN.-affiliate, component, constituent, element, ingredient, organ, part; faction, party, side. ANT.-entirety, whole.

memorable, a. SYN.-decisive, distinguished, eventful, exceptional, great, impressive, lasting, momentous, monumental, notable, noteworthy, outstanding, remarkable, significant, singular, unforgettable, unusual.

memorandum, n. SYN.-directive, letter, message, memo, missive, note, summary.

memorial, n. SYN.-commemoration, memento, monument, remembrance, souvenir.

memory, n. SYN.-consciousness, image, recall, recollection, remembrance, reminiscence, retrospection, vision. ANT.-forgetfulness, oblivion.

menace, n. SYN.-caution, danger, hazard, intimidation, peril, threat.

menace, v. SYN.-impend, intimidate, loom, portend, threaten.

mend, v. SYN.-ameliorate, amend, better, correct, improve, fix, patch, reconstruct, rectify, refit, reform, remedy, renew, repair, restore, sew. ANT.-deface, destroy, hurt, injure, rend.

menial, *a.* SYN.-abject, base, common, humble, low, mean, servile.

menial, *n.* SYN.-attendant, domestic, flunky, footman, hireling, lackey, minion, serf, servant.

mentality, *n.* SYN.-brain, comprehension, disposition, faculties, inclination, intellect, intelligence, intention, judgment, liking, mind, psyche, purpose, reason, understanding, will, wish, wit. ANT.-body, corporeality, materiality, matter.

mention, *v.* SYN.-cite, declare, disclose, discuss, divulge, impart, infer, intimate, introduce, notice, quote, remark, specify, state, suggest.

mercenary, *a.* SYN.-avaricious, corrupt, greedy, miserly, niggardly, parsimonious, penurious, selfish, sordid, stingy, tight, venal. ANT.-generous, honorable, liberal.

merchant, *n.* SYN.-businessman, dealer, exporter, importer, retailer, shopkeeper, storekeeper, trader, tradesman, wholesaler.

merciful, *a.* SYN.-clement, compassionate, forbearing, forgiving, gentle, gracious, humane, indulgent, kind, lenient, mild, tender, tolerant. ANT.-brutal, cruel, pitiless, remorseless, unfeeling.

merciless, *a.* SYN.-barbarous, bestial, brutal, brute, brutish, carnal, coarse, cruel, ferocious, gross, inhuman, pitiless, remorseless, rough, rude, ruthless, savage, sensual. ANT-civilized, courteous, gentle, humane, kind.

mercy, *n.* SYN.-charity, clemency, compassion, forgiveness, grace, leniency, mildness, pity. ANT.-cruelty, intolerance, punishment, ret-

ribution, selfishness, vengeance.

mere, *a.* SYN.-bare, insignificant, minor, scant, small.

merely, *a.* SYN.-but, exactly, hardly, just, only, solely.

merge, *v.* SYN.-amalgamate, blend, coalesce, combine, commingle, conjoin, consolidate, fuse, join, mingle, mix, unify, unite. ANT.-decompose, divide, disintegrate, separate.

merit, *n.* SYN.-credit desert, due, effectiveness, efficacy, entitlement, excellence, goodness, integrity, morality, probity, rectitude, value, virtue, worth. ANT.-corruption, fault, lewdness, sin, vice.

merit, *v.* SYN.-achieve, acquire, attain, deserve, earn, gain, get, justify, obtain, rate, warrant, win. ANT.-consume, forfeit, lose, spend, waste.

merited, *a.* SYN.-adequate, appropriate, condign, deserved, earned, fitting, proper, suitable. ANT.-improper, undeserved, unmerited.

merry, *a.* SYN.-blithe, cheerful, festive, gay, gleeful, hilarious, jolly, jovial, joyous, lively, mirthful, sprightly. ANT.-gloomy, melancholy, morose, sad, sorrowful.

mess, *n.* SYN.-chaos, clutter, confusion, congestion, difficulty, disorder, hodgepodge, jumble, melange, muddle, predicament, snag, unpleasantness, untidiness.

message, *n.* SYN.-annotation, comment, directive, information, letter, memorandum, missive, note, observation, remark, tidings.

messenger, *n.* SYN.-angel, bearer, courier, crier, emissary, envoy, herald, minister, prophet, runner.

messy, *a.* SYN.-dirty, disorderly, rumpled, sloppy, slovenly, untidy.

metaphor, *n.* SYN.-allegory, comparison, correlation, likening, resemblance, similarity, substitution. symbolism.

metaphorical, *a.* SYN.-allegorical, figurative, symbolic.

metaphysical, *a.* SYN.-abstract, mystical, spiritual, supernatural, transcendent.

mete, *v.* SYN.-allocate, allot, apportion, assign, deal, dispense, distribute, divide, dole, give, grant, measure, parcel. ANT.-confiscate, keep, refuse, retain, withhold.

method, *n.* SYN.-arrangement, design, fashion, manner, mode, order, plan, procedure, process, routine, style, system, technique, way. ANT.-confusion, disorder.

methodical, *a.* SYN.-accurate, careful, correct, definite, distinct, exact, orderly, regulated, strict, systematic, unequivocal; ceremonious, formal, precise, prim, rigid, stiff. ANT.erroneous, loose, rough, vague; careless, easy, informal.

mettle, *n.* SYN.-ardor, boldness, bravery, character, chivalry, courage, disposition, fearlessness, fortitude, intrepidity, nerve, pluck, prowess, resolution, spirit, temperament. ANT.-cowardice, fear, pusillanimity, timidity.

microscopic, *a.* SYN.-detailed, exact, infinitesimal, little, miniature, minute, particular, precise, small, tiny. ANT.-enormous, huge, large.

middle, *n.* SYN.-center, central, core, heart, intermediate, mean, median, midpoint, nucleus. ANT.-border, boundary, outskirts, periphery, rim.

midst, *n.* SYN.-center, core, heart, middle, midpoint, nucleus. ANT.-border, boundary, outskirts, periphery, rim.

might, *n.* SYN.-ability, dynamism, energy, force, intensity, potency, power, strength, vigor. ANT.-inability, weakness.

mighty, *a.* SYN.-firm, forceful, forcible, fortified, hale, hardy, impregnable, potent, powerful, robust, sinewy, strong, sturdy, tough. ANT.-brittle, delicate, feeble, fragile, insipid.

migrate, *v.* SYN.-emigrate, immigrate, leave, move.

mild, *a.* SYN.-bland, gentle, kind, meek, moderate, peaceful, soft, soothing, tender. ANT.-bitter, fierce, harsh, rough, severe.

militant, *a.* SYN.-aggressive, bellicose, belligerent, combative, contentious, firm, forceful, inflexible, obstinate, offensive, positive, quarrelsome, resolute, rigid, unbending.

militant, *n.* SYN.-activist, demonstrator, protester, radical.

mimic, *v.* SYN.-ape, copy, exaggerate, imitate, impersonate, mock, pantomime, parody, simulate. ANT.-alter, distort, diverge, invent.

mind, *n.* SYN.-brain, faculties, intellect, intelligence, judgment, memory, mentality, psyche, reason, recall, sense, soul, spirit, understanding, wit; belief, bias, disposition, inclination, intention, judgment, liking, proclivity, purpose, temper, will, wish, wont. ANT.-body, corporeality, materiality, matter.

mind, *v.* SYN.-attend, behave, heed, listen, mark, note, notice, obey, regard.

mindless, *a.* SYN.-asinine, brainless, careless, foolish, heedless, idiotic, inattentive, indifferent, oblivious, senseless, simple, stupid.

mingle, *v.* SYN.-amalgamate, blend, coalesce, combine, commingle, conjoin, consolidate, mix, merge, unify, unite. ANT.-analyze, decompose, disintegrate, separate.

miniature, *a.* SYN.-baby, diminutive, little, petite, small, tiny.

minimize, *v.* SYN.-contract, decrease, diminish, lessen, reduce.

minister, *n.* SYN.-chaplain, clergyman, cleric, curate, deacon, parson, pastor, preacher, prelate, priest, rector, vicar; ambassador, consul, diplomat, statesman.

minister, *v.* SYN.-aid, attend, comfort, heal, help, sustain, tend.

minor, *a.* SYN.-inconsequential, inferior, insignificant, lesser, lower, poorer, secondary, subordinate. ANT.-better, greater, higher, superior.

minute, *a.* SYN.-detailed, exact, fine, microscopic, miniature, particular, precise, tiny. ANT.-enormous, huge, large; general.

miraculous, *a.* SYN.-awesome, extraordinary, incredible, marvelous, metaphysical, phenomenal, preternatural, prodigious, spiritual, stupefying, superhuman, supernatural, unearthly, wondrous. ANT.-common, human, natural, physical, plain.

mirage, *n.* SYN.-apparition, delusion, dream, fantasy, hallucination, illusion, phantom, vision. ANT.-actuality, reality, substance.

mirror, *v.* SYN.-embody, epitomize, exemplify, illustrate, reflect, represent, symbolize, typify.

misbehave, *v.* SYN.-blunder, defy, disobey, fail, offend, rebel, sin, trespass.

miscarriage, *n.* SYN.-default, dereliction, failure, fiasco, malfunction, mistake, omission. ANT.-achievement, success, victory; sufficiency.

miscellaneous, *a.* SYN.-assorted, different, dissimilar, diverse, heterogeneous, indiscriminate, mixed, motley, odd, sundry, varied. ANT.-alike, classified, homogeneous, ordered, selected.

mischief, *n.* SYN.-damage, detriment, evil, fault, harm, hurt, ill, infliction, injury, malice, misconduct, misfortune, mishap, naughtiness, transgression, vandalism, wrong. ANT.-benefit, boon, favor, kindness.

misconception, *n.* SYN.-delusion, error, misapprehension, misinterpretation, mistake, misunderstanding.

miser, *n.* SYN.-cheapskate, skinflint, tightwad.

miserable, *a.* SYN.-afflicted, comfortless, disconsolate, distressed, forlorn, heartbroken, pitiable, sickly, suffering, tormented, troubled, wretched; abject, contemptible, despicable, low, mean, paltry, worthless. ANT.-contented, fortunate, happy; noble, significant.

miserly, *a.* SYN.-acquisitive, avaricious, greedy, niggardly, parsimonious, penurious, stingy, tight. ANT.-altruistic, bountiful, extravagant, generous, munificent.

misery, *n.* SYN.-agony, anguish, desolation, distress, grief, sadness, sorrow, suffering, torment, trial, tribulation, trouble, unhappiness, woe. ANT.-delight, elation, fun, joy, pleasure.

misfortune, *n.* SYN.-accident, adversity, affliction, calamity, catastrophe, disaster, distress, hardship, mishap, ruin, unpleasantness. ANT.-blessing, comfort, prosperity, success.

misgiving, *n.* SYN.-cynicism, distrust, doubt, mistrust, skepticism, suspicion.

misguided, *a.* SYN.-confused, deceived, delinquent, misled, mistaken, wayward.

mislead, *v.* SYN.-beguile, betray, cheat, deceive, defraud, delude, dupe, fool, misrepresent, outwit, trick, victimize.

misleading, *a.* SYN.-ambiguous, deceitful, deceptive, delusive, delusory, dubious, equivocal, fallacious, false, illusive, specious, unclear, vague. ANT.-authentic, genuine, honest, real, truthful.

misplace, *v.* SYN.-confuse, displace, disturb, lose, mislay, remove.

miss, *n.* SYN.-blunder, error, failure, fumble, mishap, mistake, slip.

missed, *a.* SYN.-desired, craved, gone, hidden, needed, neglected, strayed, mislaid, misplaced, unseen, wanted.

mistake, *n.* SYN.-blunder, error, fallacy, fault, inaccuracy, inadvertence, inattention, misapprehension, misconception, misprint, mistake, misunderstanding, neglect, omission, oversight, slip. ANT.-accuracy, precision, truth.

mistaken, *a.* SYN.-confounded, confused, deceived, deluded, duped, erroneous, faulty, fooled, imprecise, inaccurate, incorrect, misguided, misinformed, misled, untrue, wrong. ANT.-correct, right, true.

mistreat, *v.* SYN.-abuse, bully, harm, injure, maltreat, wrong.

mistress, *n.* SYN.-caretaker, concubine, courtesan, housekeeper, lover, manager, mother, paramour, wife.

misty, *a.* SYN.-dim, drizzly, foggy, hazy, murky, obscure, rainy, shrouded.

misuse, *v.* SYN.-abuse, asperse, defame, disparage, malign, misapply, misemploy, revile, scandalize, traduce, vilify. ANT.-cherish, honor, praise, protect, respect.

mitigate, *v.* SYN.-abate, allay, alleviate, assuage, diminish, extenuate, relieve, soften, solace, soothe. ANT.-aggravate, agitate, augment, increase, irritate.

mix, *v.* SYN.-alloy, amalgamate blend, combine, commingle, compound, concoct, confound, fuse, jumble, mingle; associate, consort, fraternize, join. ANT.-dissociate, divide, segregate, separate, sort.

mixture, *n.* SYN.-assortment, blend, combination, diversity, heterogeneity, medley, miscellany, multifariousness, variety, variousness. ANT.-homogeneity, likeness, monotony, sameness, uniformity.

mob, *n.* SYN.-bevy, crowd, crush, horde, host, masses, multitude, populace, press, rabble, swarm, throng.

mock, *a.* SYN.-counterfeit, fake, false, feigned, forged, fraudulent, pretended, sham.

mock, *v.* SYN.-caricature, challenge, dare, defy, deride, flout, gibe, imitate, jeer, mimic, ridicule, scoff, sneer, taunt. ANT.-compliment, flatter, laud, praise.

mockery, *n.* SYN.-banter, derision, gibe, irony, jeering, raillery, ridicule, sarcasm, satire, sneering.

model, *n.* SYN.-archetype, copy, example, ideal, guide, mold, pattern, prototype, specimen, standard, type. ANT.-imitation, production, reproduction.

moderate, *a.* SYN.-average, balanced, calm, careful, considered, cool, deliberate, disciplined, frugal, gentle, judicious, modest, reserved, restrained, tepid, tranquil.

moderate, *v.* SYN.-abate, appease, assuage, calm, decline, decrease, diminish, modulate, restrain; arbitrate, chair, preside, referee, regulate.

moderation, *n.* SYN.-balance, caution, constraint, continence, discretion, forbearance, restraint, temperance.

modern, *a.* SYN.-chic, contemporary, current, late, latest, new, novel, present, recent, stylish. ANT.-ancient, antiquated, bygone, old, past.

modest, *a.* SYN.-bashful, demure, diffident, humble, meek, moderate, proper, reasonable, reserved, restrained, retiring, shy, simple, unassuming, unpretentious, virtuous. ANT.-arrogant, bold, conceited, forward, immodest, ostentatious, proud.

modesty, *n.* SYN.-constraint, control, decency, diffidence, dignity, humility, inhibition, innocence, meekness, reserve, restraint, temperance.

modification, *n.* SYN.-adjustment, alteration, alternation, change, substitution, transformation, variation, variety. ANT.-monotony, stability, uniformity.

modify, *v.* SYN.-adjust, alter, change, convert, curb, exchange, limit, mitigate, qualify, shift, substitute, temper, transfigure, transform, vary. ANT.-retain; continue, establish, preserve, settle, stabilize.

mold, *v.* SYN.-arrange, cast, combine, compose, constitute, construct, convert, create, devise, fashion, forge, form, frame, influence, invent, make, organize, pattern, produce, shape, transfigure, transform. ANT.-destroy, disfigure, dismantle, misshape, wreck.

molest, *v.* SYN.-annoy, attack, bother, chafe, disturb, frighten, inconvenience, intrude, irk, irritate, meddle, pester, scare, tease, terrify, trouble, vex. ANT.-accommodate, console, gratify, soothe.

momentary, *a.* SYN.-brief, concise, curt, ephemeral, fleeting, laconic, meteoric, passing, pithy, quick, short, succinct, terse, transient. ANT.-extended, lengthy, long, prolonged, protracted.

momentous, *a.* SYN.-consequential, critical, decisive, grave, important, influential, material, pressing, prominent, relevant, significant, weighty. ANT.-insignificant, irrelevant, mean, petty, trivial.

monarch, *n.* SYN.-autocrat, despot, governor, king, lord, master, prince, ruler, sovereign.

monastery, *n.* SYN.-abbey, cloister, convent, hermitage, nunnery, priory, refuge, retreat. monopolize

monotonous, *a.* SYN.-boring, burdensome, dilatory, dreary, dull, humdrum, irksome, slow, sluggish, tardy, tedious, tiresome, uninteresting, wearisome. ANT.-amusing, entertaining, exciting, interesting, quick.

monster, *n.* SYN.-beast, brute, chimera, demon, fiend, freak, miscreant, monstrosity, villain, wretch.

monstrous, *a.* SYN.-abnormal, atrocious, colossal, dreadful, enormous, fantastic, frightful, gigantic, great, grotesque, hideous, horrible, large, massive, prodigious, repulsive, stupendous, unusual.

monument, *n.* SYN.-commemoration, landmark, masterpiece, memorial, remembrance, souvenir.

monumental, *a.* SYN.-classic, enormous, grand, great, immense, impressive, lofty, majestic, massive, memorable.

mood, *n.* SYN.-attitude, bent, caprice, disposition, humor, propensity, temper, temperament, tendency, whim.

mope, *v.* SYN.-brood, despair, fret, grieve, pine, sorrow, sulk.

moral, *a.* SYN.-chaste, courteous, decent, ethical, good, honorable, just, kindly, principled, proper, pure, respectable, right, righteous, scrupulous, trustworthy, truthful, virtuous. ANT.-amoral, libertine, licentious, sinful, unethical.

morale, *n.* SYN.-assurance, confidence, resolve, spirit.

morality, *n.* SYN.-chastity, decency, ethics, goodness, honesty, integrity, morals, probity, purity, rectitude, righteousness, virtue. ANT.-corruption, fault, lewdness, sin, vice.

morals, *n.* SYN.-belief, custom, dogma, mores, standards.

morbid, *a.* SYN.-aberrant, depressed, gloomy, gruesome, melancholic, morose, sullen; ailing, diseased, sickly, unhealthy.

morose, *a.* SYN.-crabbed, dejected, dour, downhearted, fretful, gloomy, glum, melancholy, moody, sad, sorrowful, sulky, surly, unhappy. ANT.-amiable, gay, joyous, merry, pleasant.

mortal, *a.* SYN.-deadly, destructive, fatal, final, killing, lethal, malignant, poisonous; ephemeral, frail, human, momentary, perishable,

temporal. ANT.-life-giving; divine, immortal.

mostly, *a.* SYN.-chiefly, customarily, especially, frequently, generally, often, particularly, regularly.

motherly, *a.* SYN.-devoted, gentle, kind, loving, maternal, protective, supporting, sympathetic, tender, watchful.

motion, *n.* SYN.-action, activity, change, gesture, move, movement, sign, stirring; plan, proposal, proposition, suggestion. ANT.-equilibrium, immobility, stability, stillness.

motivate, *v.* SYN.-arouse, begin, cause, encourage, goad, ignite, induce, instigate, prompt, start, whet.

motive, *n.* SYN.-cause, grounds, impulse, incentive, incitement, inducement, principle, purpose, reason, spur, stimulus.

motley, *a.* SYN.-assorted, diverse, heterogeneous, indiscriminate, miscellaneous, mixed, mottled, multicolored, sundry, varied, variegated. ANT.-alike, classified, homogeneous, ordered, selected.

motto, *n.* SYN.-adage, aphorism, axiom, credo, maxim, principle, rule, saying, sentiment, slogan, tenet, truism.

mount, *v.* SYN.-ascend, climb, grow, increase, rise, scale, tower; frame, secure, set. ANT.-descend, fall, sink.

mourn, *v.* SYN.-bemoan, bewail, deplore, grieve, lament, suffer, weep. ANT.-carouse, celebrate, rejoice, revel.

move, *v.* SYN.-actuate, advance, agitate, arouse, drive, excite, impel, impress, induce, influence, instigate, persuade, proceed, propel, propose, push, recommend, shift, stimulate, stir, suggest, sway, transfer. ANT.-deter. halt, rest, stay, stop.

moved, *a.* SYN.-carried, conveyed, departed, disturbed, excited, recommended, shifted, stimulated, taken, transferred.

movement, *n.* SYN.-action, activity, change, gesture, inclination, motion, move, progress, rhythm, tempo, tendency. ANT.-equilibrium, immobility, stability, stillness.

much, *a.* SYN.-abundant, ample, considerable, plentiful, profuse, substantial.

muddled, *a.* SYN.-addled, bewildered, confused, disconcerted, disordered, disorganized, indistinct, mixed, perplexed. ANT.-clear, lucid, obvious, organized, plain.

muddy, *a.* SYN.-blurred, cloudy, confused, dark, indistinct, indistinguishable, murky, obscure, unclear.

multitude, *n.* SYN.-army, crowd, host, legion, mob, throng. ANT.-few, handful, paucity, scarcity.

mundane, *a.* SYN.-earthly, laic, lay, normal, ordinary, practical, routine, secular, temporal, worldly. ANT.-ecclesiastical, religious, spiritual, unworldly.

municipality, *n.* SYN.-borough, city, community, district, town, village.

murder, *v.* SYN.-assassinate, butcher, destroy, execute, kill, mar, massacre, ruin, slaughter, slay, spoil. ANT.-animate, protect, resuscitate, save, vivify.

murky, *a.* SYN.-ambiguous, cloudy, dark, devious, dim, dusky, esoteric, gloomy, hazy, obscure, shadowy.

murmur, *n.* SYN.-complaint, grum-

ble, mumble, mutter, plaint, rumor, whimper.

murmur, *v.* SYN.-babble, complain, grouse, growl, grumble, moan, mumble, rumble, trickle, whisper.

museum, *n.* SYN.-archive, depository, gallery, library, treasury.

music, *n.* SYN.-air, consonance, harmonics, harmony, melody, song, symphony, tune.

muss, *n.* SYN.-chaos, clutter, confusion, disarry, disorder, disorganization, jumble, mess, muddle, turmoil.

muss, *v.* SYN.-crumple, disarrange, dishevel, disturb, jumble, ruffle, rumple, tousle.

must, *n.* SYN.-condition, contingency, demand, obligation, necessity, prerequisite, provision, requisite, requirement.

muster, *v.* SYN.-accumulate, amass, assemble, collect, congregate, convene, gather, marshal, summon. ANT.-disband, disperse, distribute, scatter, separate.

mute, *a.* SYN.-inarticulate, dumb, hushed, noiseless, peaceful, quiet, silent, still, taciturn, tranquil. ANT.-clamorous, loud, noisy, raucous.

mutiny, *n.* SYN.-agitation, commotion, coup, insurrection, overthrow, rebellion, revolt, revolution, sedition, uprising.

mutual, *a.* SYN.-collective, communal, common, correlative, interchangeable, joint, public, reciprocal, shared. ANT.-dissociated, separate, unrequited, unshared.

myriad, *a.* SYN.-endless, indefinite, innumerable, multiple, variable.

mysterious, *a.* SYN.-cabalistic, cryptic, dark, dim, enigmatic, esoteric, hidden, incomprehensible, inexplicable, inscrutable, mystical, obscure, occult, recondite, secret, strange. ANT.-clear, explained, obvious, plain, simple.

mystery, n. SYN.-cabal, conundrum, enigma, problem, puzzle, riddle, secret. ANT.-answer, clue, key, resolution, solution.

mystical, a. SYN.-abstruse, cabalistic, enigmatic, incomprehensible, mysterious.

mystique, n. SYN.-appearance, attitude, character, characteristics, demeanor, deportment, manner, nature, style.

myth, n. SYN.-allegory, chronicle, fable, fiction, legend, parable, saga. ANT.-fad, history.

N

nag, v. SYN.-aggravate, annoy, badger, bother, disturb, harass, harry, irritate, pester, plague, provoke, tantalize, taunt, tease, torment, vex, worry. ANT.-comfort, delight, gratify, please, soothe.

naive, a. SYN.-artless, callow, candid, fanciful, frank, guileless, ingenuous, innocent, instinctive, natural, open, provincial, romantic, simple, spontaneous, unaffected, unsophisticated. ANT.-crafty, cunning, sophisticated, worldly.

naked, a. SYN.-bare, defenseless, exposed, mere, nude, open, plain, simple, stripped, unclad, uncovered, unprotected; bald, barren, unfurnished. ANT.-clothed, covered, dressed; concealed; protected.

name, n. SYN.-appellation, denomination, designation, epithet, style, surname, title; acclaim, character, distinction, eminence, fame, honor, note, renown, reputation, repute. ANT.-misnomer, namelessness;

anonymity.

name, v. SYN.-address, appoint, baptize, call, characterize, christen, classify, denominate, entitle, enumerate, identify, indicate, label, mention, specify. ANT.-hint, miscall, misname.

named, a. SYN.-appointed, commissioned, delegated, designated, nominated, ordained, picked, selected.

nap, n. SYN.-catnap, doze, drowse, nod, repose, rest, sleep, slumber, snooze.

narrate, v. SYN.-declaim, deliver, describe, detail, enumerate, mention, recapitulate, recite, recount, rehearse, relate, repeat, tell.

narrative, n. SYN.-account, chronicle, description, detail, history, narration, recital, relation, story, yarn. ANT.-caricature, confusion, distortion, misrepresentation.

narrow, a. SYN.-close, confined, cramped, meager, slender, slim, spare, tight; bigoted, dogmatic, fanatical, illiberal, intolerant, narrow-minded, opinionated, parochial, prejudiced. ANT.-liberal, progressive, radical, tolerant.

nasty, a. SYN.-base, contemptible, defiled, despicable, disagreeable, disgusting, foul, gross, horrid, low, malicious, mean, nauseous, offensive, repellent, revolting, sordid, unpleasant, vile, vulgar. ANT.-admirable, amiable, attractive, decent, delightful, dignified, exalted, generous, nice, noble, pleasant.

nation, n. SYN.-commonwealth, community, country, domain, dominion, kingdom, nationality, people, populace, principality, realm, republic, state.

nationalism, n. SYN.-allegiance,

chauvinism, loyalty, provincialism, patriotism.

native, *a.* SYN.-aboriginal, congenital, domestic, endemic, fundamental, hereditary, inborn, indigenous, inherent, innate, natural, original.

natural, *a.* SYN.-actual, characteristic, common, congenital, crude, fundamental, general, genetic, genuine, ingenuous, inherent, innate, intrinsic, involuntary, native, normal, original, real, regular, simple, spontaneous, tangible, typical, unaffected, unconstrained, unfeigned, usual. ANT.-affected, artificial, embellished, forced, formal.

nature, *n.* SYN.-character; class, description, disposition, essence, individuality, kind, qualifications, reputation, repute, sort, standing, temperament.

nautical, *a.* SYN.-marine, maritime, naval, ocean, oceanic.

near, *a.* SYN.-adjacent, approaching, beside, bordering, close, coming, contiguous, expected, imminent, impending, neighboring, nigh, proximate; dear, familiar, intimate. ANT.-distant, far, removed.

neat, *a.* SYN.-clear, dapper, deft, exact, nice, orderly, precise, prim, smart, spruce, systematic, taut, tidy, trim, unadulterated, undiluted. ANT.-dirty, disheveled, sloppy, slovenly, unkempt.

necessary, *a.* SYN.-compulsory, essential, expedient, fundamental, indispensable, inevitable, needed, obligatory, requisite, unavoidable. ANT.-accidental, casual; contingent, nonessential, optional.

necessity, *n.* SYN.-compulsion. demand, exigency, fundamental, need, qualification, requirement, requisite, want. ANT.-choice, free-

dom, luxury, option, uncertainty.

need, *v.* SYN.-claim, covet, crave, demand, desire, lack, require, want, wish.

needless, *a.* SYN.-groundless, pointless, superfluous, unnecessary, useless.

negate, *v.* SYN.-annul, belie, cancel, contradict, impugn, repeal, retract.

neglect, *n.* SYN.-carelessness, default, dereliction, disregard, failure, heedlessness, indifference, negligence, omission, oversight, slight, thoughtlessness. ANT.-attention, care, diligence, watchfulness.

neglect, *v.* SYN.-affront, disregard, ignore, insult, omit, overlook, procrastinate, slight. ANT.-do, guard, perform, protect, satisfy.

negligence, *n.* SYN.-carelessness, default, dereliction, disregard, failure, heedlessness, neglect, nonchalance, omission, oversight, slight, thoughtlessness. ANT.-attention, care, diligence, watchfulness.

negligent, *a.* SYN.-careless, delinquent, derelict, desultory, heedless, imprudent, inaccurate, inattentive, lax, neglectful, remiss, thoughtless, unconcerned. ANT.-accurate, careful, meticulous, precise.

negotiate, *v.* SYN.-arbitrate, bargain, barter, conciliate, confer, consult, intercede, mediate, parley, referee.

neighbor, *n.* SYN.-acquaintance, associate, friend.

neighbor, *v.* SYN.-abut, adjoin, border, touch, verge.

neighborhood, *n.* SYN.-adjacency, block, district, environs, locality, nearness, vicinity. ANT.-distance, remoteness.

neighborly, *a.* SYN.-affable, amicable, companionable, congenial, friendly, genial, helpful, hospitable, kindly, sociable, social. ANT.-antagonistic, cool, distant, hostile, reserved.

nerve, *n.* SYN.-audacity, courage, fortitude, impudence, intrepidity, mettle, presumption, resolution, spirit, temerity.

nerves, *n.* SYN.-anxiety, apprehension, emotion, misgivings, strain, stress, tension.

nervous, *a.* SYN.-excitable, impatient, irritable, moody, restless, sensitive, tense, touchy, uneasy, unstable.

network, *n.* SYN.-arrangement, channels, complex, labyrinth, mesh, net, structure, system, tangle, web.

neurotic, *a.* SYN.-deranged, disturbed, erratic, irrational, troubled, unstable.

neutral, *a.* SYN.-detached, disinterested, impartial, inactive, indifferent, nonpartisan, unbiased.

new, *a.* SYN.-contemporary, current, fashionable, fresh, late, modern, newfangled, novel, original, recent, unique. ANT.-ancient, antiquated, archaic, obsolete, old.

news, *n.* SYN.-account, advice, copy, description, discovery, enlightenment, information, intelligence, message, narration, publication, report, tidings.

nice, *a.* SYN.-agreeable, amiable, considerate, courteous, cultured, genial, good, gracious, obliging, pleasant, pleasing, refined.

niche, *n.* SYN.-alcove, corner, cranny, cubbyhole, nook, recess.

nick, *n.* SYN.-dent, gouge, indentation, mar, notch, score, scrape, scratch.

niggardly, *a.* SYN.-avaricious, cheap, greedy, miserly, parsimonious, pe-nurious, stingy, tight. ANT.-altruistic, bountiful, extravagant, generous, munificent.

nimble, *a.* SYN.-active, agile, alert, bright, brisk, clever, flexible, lively, quick, spry, supple. ANT.-clumsy, heavy, inert, slow, sluggish.

noble, *a.* SYN.-courtly, cultivated, dignified, distinguished, elevated, eminent, exalted, grand, illustrious, imposing, impressive, lofty, lordly, majestic, refined, stately, virtuous. ANT.-base, low, mean, plebeian, vile.

nod, *v.* SYN.-acknowledge, assent, concur, consent, greet.

noise, *n.* SYN.-babel, clamor, cry, din, outcry, racket, row, sound, tumult, uproar. ANT.-hush, quiet, silence, stillness.

noisy, *a.* SYN.-cacophonous, clamorous, deafening, loud, resounding, sonorous, stentorian, vociferous ANT.-dulcet, inaudible, quiet, soft, subdued.

nonchalant, *a.* SYN.-aloof, apathetic, calm, casual, composed, detached, impassive, unconcerned. ANT.-active, attentive, emotional, enthusiastic.

nonconformist, *n.* dissenter, eccentric, maverick, radical, rebel.

nonexistent, *a.* SYN.-fictitious, imaginary, unreal.

nonsensical, *a.* SYN.-absurd, foolish, inconsistent, irrational, ludicrous, meaningless, preposterous, ridiculous, self-contradictory, silly, unreasonable. ANT.-consistent, rational, reasonable, sensible, sound.

normal, *a.* SYN.-common, conventional, customary, natural, ordinary, regular, steady, systematic, typical, uniform, unvaried, usual. ANT.-abnormal, erratic, exceptional.

rare, unusual.

nosy, *a.* SYN.-curious, inquiring, inquisitive, interrogative, meddling, peeping, peering, prying, searching, snoopy. ANT.-incurious, indifferent, unconcerned, uninterested.

notable, *a.* SYN.-celebrated, conspicuous, distinguished, eminent, famous, notable, remarkable, striking, unusual.

note, *n.* SYN.-indication, mark, sign, symbol, token; annotation, comment, letter, memorandum, message, observation, remark.

noted, *a.* SYN.-celebrated, distinguished, eminent, famous, glorious, illustrious, renowned, well-known. ANT.-hidden, ignominious, infamous, obscure, unknown.

notice, *n.* SYN.-alertness, attention, cognizance, heed, mindfulness, observance, watchfulness; advertisement, announcement, circular, declaration, notification, proclamation, sign, warning. ANT.-disregard, indifference, negligence, omission, oversight.

notice, *v.* SYN.-attend, behold, descry, distinguish, heed, mark, note, observe, perceive, recognize, regard, remark, see. ANT.-disregard, ignore, overlook, skip.

notify, *v.* SYN.-advise, announce, apprise, caution, communicate, convey, disclose, enlighten, inform, herald, mention, proclaim, reveal, telephone, tell, warn, write. ANT.-conceal, delude, distract, mislead.

notion, *n.* SYN.-assumption, belief, fancy, idea, impression, inkling, opinion, sentiment, thought, whim.

novel, *n.* SYN.-allegory, fiction, narrative, romance, story, tale. ANT.-fact, history, reality, truth, verity.

novice, *n.* SYN.-amateur, apprentice,

beginner, learner, neophyte. ANT.-adept, authority, expert, master, professional.

now, *n.* SYN.-immediate, present, promptly, soon, today.

nuance, *n.* SYN.-difference, gradation, shade, subtly, variation.

nude, *a.* SYN.-bare, exposed, naked, stripped, unclad, uncovered. ANT.-clothed, covered, dressed.

nudge, *v.* SYN.-bump, dig, jab, poke, tap, touch.

nuisance, *n.* SYN.-aggravation, annoyance, bother, irritation, pest, vexation.

nullify, *v.* SYN.-abolish, abrogate, annul, cancel, cross out, delete, eliminate, erase, expunge, invalidate, obliterate, quash, repeal, rescind, revoke. ANT.-confirm, enact, enforce, perpetuate

numb, *a.* SYN.-anesthetized, apathetic, callous, deadened, disinterested, lethargic, unfeeling.

number, *n.* SYN.-aggregate, amount, count, extent, enumeration, estimate, measure, portion, quantity, sum, total, volume. ANT.-nothing, nothingness, zero.

numerous, *a.* SYN.-divers, manifold, many. multifarious, multitudinous, several, sundry, various. ANT.-few, infrequent, meager, scanty, scarce.

nuptials, *n.* SYN.-espousal, marriage, matrimony, union, wedding, wedlock. ANT.-celibacy, divorce, virginity.

nurture, *v.* SYN.-cherish, feed, nourish, nurse, prize, sustain, treasure, value. ANT.-abandon, disregard, neglect, reject.

nutriment, *n.* SYN.-diet, edibles, feed, food, meal, provisions, rations, repast, sustenance, viands, victuals. ANT.-drink, hunger, starvation, want.

nymph, *n.* SYN.-dryad, fairy, goddess, mermaid, sprite.

O

oath, *n.* SYN.-affidavit, declaration, deposition, pledge, promise, testimony, vow.

obdurate, *a.* SYN.-callous, hard, impenitent, indurate, insensible, insensitive, tough, unfeeling. ANT.-compassionate, sensitive, soft, tender.

obedient, *a.* SYN.-compliant, deferential, dutiful, loyal, submissive, tractable, yielding. ANT.-insubordinate, intractable, obstinate, rebellious.

obese, *a.* SYN.-chubby, corpulent, fat, paunchy, plump, portly, pudgy, rotund, stocky, stout, thickset. ANT.-gaunt, lean, slender, slim, thin.

object, *n.* SYN.-article, particular, thing; aim, design, end, goal, intention, mark, objective, purpose. ANT.-shadow, spirit, vision; consequence, result.

object, *v.* SYN.-abominate, disagree, disapprove, oppose, protest, reject, remonstrate. ANT.-acquiesce, approve, assent, comply, concur.

objection, *n.* SYN.-challenge, difference, disagreement, dissent, dissentience, protest, remonstrance. ANT.-acceptance, agreement, assent, compliance.

objective, *n.* SYN.-aim, ambition, aspiration, craving, design, desire, end, goal, hope, intent, intention, object, passion, purpose.

obligate, *v.* SYN.-bind, commit, consign, entrust, force, oblige, pledge, relegate, trust. ANT.-free, loose, ne-

glect, release, renounce.

obligation, *n.* SYN.-accountability, bond, compulsion, contract, debt, duty, engagement, responsibility. ANT.-choice, exemption, freedom.

oblige, *v.* SYN.-coerce, compel, constrain, drive, enforce, force, impel; accommodate, aid, assist, favor, help, please. ANT.-allure, convince, exempt, induce, persuade; annoy, forsake.

obliterate, *v.* SYN.-annihilate, demolish, destroy, devastate, eradicate, exterminate, extinguish, ravage, raze, ruin, wreck. ANT.-construct, establish, make, preserve, save.

oblivious, *a.* SYN.-blind, ignorant, preoccupied, undiscerning, unmindful, unseeing. ANT.-aware, calculated, discerning, perceiving, sensible.

obnoxious, *a.* SYN.-annoying, disagreeable, displeasing, impertinent, insulting, nasty, odious, offensive

obscene, *a.* SYN.-coarse, dirty, disgusting, filthy, gross, impure, indecent, lewd, offensive, pornographic, smutty. ANT.-decent, modest, pure, refined.

obscure, *a.* SYN.-abstruse, ambiguous, cloudy, cryptic, dark, dim, dusky, enigmatic, indistinct, mysterious, unintelligible, vague. ANT.-bright, clear, distinct, lucid.

observance, *n.* SYN.-ceremony, formality, parade, pomp, protocol, rite, ritual, solemnity; awareness, cognizance, heed, notice, observation.

observant, *a.* SYN.-alert, assiduous, attentive, aware, careful, considerate, diligent, discerning, heedful, mindful, perceptive, sensitive, thoughtful, wakeful, wary, watchful. ANT.-apathetic, careless, inattentive, indifferent, oblivious, unaware.

observe, v. SYN.-behold, detect, discover, examine, eye, inspect, mark, note, notice, perceive, recognize, see, view, watch; celebrate, commemorate, honor, keep, solemnize; express, mention, remark, utter. ANT.-disregard, ignore, neglect, overlook.

obsession, n. SYN.-compulsion, craze, fascination, fixation, mania, passion.

obsolete, a. SYN.-ancient, antiquated, archaic, obsolescent, old, out-of-date, venerable. ANT.-current, extant, fashionable, modern, recent.

obstacle, n. SYN.-bar, barrier, block, check, difficulty, hindrance, impediment, obstruction, snag. ANT.-aid, assistance, encouragement, help.

obstinate, a. SYN.-contumacious, determined, dogged, firm, headstrong, immovable, inflexible, intractable, obdurate, pertinacious, stubborn, uncompromising, unyielding. ANT.-amenable, compliant, docile, submissive, yielding.

obstruct, v. SYN.-bar, barricade, block, clog, close, delay, impede, hinder, stop. ANT.-aid, clear, further, open, promote.

obtain, v. SYN.-acquire, assimilate, attain, collect, earn, get, glean, gather, procure, reap, recover, secure, win. ANT.-forego, forfeit, lose, miss, surrender.

obtuse, a. SYN.-blunt, boring, commonplace, dense, dull, slow, stupid, tedious. ANT.-animated, lively, sharp; clear, interesting.

obvious, a. SYN.-apparent, clear, conspicuous, distinct, evident, manifest, palpable, patent, plain, prominent, self-evident, unmistakable, visible. ANT.-abstruse, concealed, hidden, obscure.

occupation, n. SYN.-business, commerce, employment, engagement, enterprise, job, profession, trade, vocation, work. ANT.-avocation, hobby, pastime.

occupy, v. SYN.-absorb, busy, dwell, fill, have, hold, inhabit, keep, possess, remain. ANT.-abandon, release, relinquish.

occur, v. SYN.-appear, arise, bechance, befall, betide, chance, happen, transpire.

occurrence, n. SYN.-circumstance, episode, event, happening, incident, issue.

odd, a. SYN.-bizarre, curious, eccentric, peculiar, quaint, queer, singular, strange, unique, unusual. ANT.-common, familiar, normal, regular, typical.

odious, a. SYN.-abject, base, debased, depraved, despicable, foul, ignoble, loathsome, low, mean, obscene, revolting, sordid, vicious, vile, vulgar, wicked, worthless, wretched. ANT.-attractive, decent, honorable, laudable, upright.

odor, n. SYN.-aroma, fetidness, fragrance, fume, incense, perfume, redolence, scent, smell, stench, stink.

offend, v. SYN.-annoy, antagonize, bother, insult, slight.

offense, n. SYN.-aggression, affront, atrocity, crime, indignity, injustice, insult, outrage, misdeed, sin, transgression, trespass, vice, wrong. ANT.-gentleness, innocence, morality, right.

offensive, *a.* SYN.-disagreeable, disgusting, distressing, dreadful, foul, horrid, invidious, nauseous, nasty, repugnant, unpleasant.

offer, *n.* SYN.-bid, overture, proposal, proposition, suggestion, tender. ANT.-acceptance, denial, rejection, withdrawal.

offer, *v.* SYN.-advance, exhibit, extend, present, proffer, propose, sacrifice, tender, volunteer. ANT.-accept, receive, reject, retain, spurn.

offering, *n.* SYN.-alms, charity, contribution, donation, gift, present, sacrifice.

office, *n.* SYN.-building, cubicle, facility, site, station, suite; berth, incumbency, job, place, position, post, rank, situation, standing, status.

often, *adv.* SYN.-commonly, frequently, generally, recurrent, repeatedly. ANT.-infrequently, occasionally, rarely, seldom, sporadically.

old, *a.* SYN.-aged, ancient, antiquated, antique, archaic, elderly, obsolete, old-fashioned, senile, superannuated, venerable. ANT.-modern, new, young, youthful.

omen, *n.* SYN. augury, foretoken, gesture, indication, mark, portent, presage, sign, symbol, token, warning.

ominous, *a.* SYN.-dire, forbidding, foreboding, gloomy, grim, menacing, portentous, threatening.

omission, *n.* SYN.-default, deletion, failure, neglect, oversight. ANT.-attention, inclusion, insertion, notice.

omit, *v.* SYN.-cancel, delete, disregard, drop, eliminate, exclude, ignore, miss, neglect, overlook, skip.

ANT.-enter, include, insert, introduce, notice.

onslaught, *n.* SYN.-aggression, assault, attack, criticism, denunciation, invasion, offense. ANT.-defense, opposition, resistance, surrender, vindication.

open, *a.* SYN.-accessible, agape, ajar, available, candid, clear, disengaged, exposed, frank, free, honest, overt, passable, plain, public, unclosed, uncovered, unlocked, unobstructed, unoccupied, unrestricted.

open, *v.* SYN.-exhibit, expand, spread, unbar, unfasten, unfold, unlock, unseal. ANT.-close, conceal, hide, shut.

opening, *n.* SYN.-abyss, aperture, cavern, cavity, chasm, gap, gulf, hole, pore, slit, slot, void.

operate, *v.* SYN.-act, function, employ, interact, manage, manipulate, proceed, run, use, utilize.

operation, *n.* SYN.-action, agency, control, effort, enterprise, execution, handling, instrumentality, maneuver, manipulation, performance, proceeding, running, surgery, working. ANT.-cessation, inaction, inactivity, rest.

operative, *a.* SYN.-active, effective, serviceable, working. ANT.-dormant, inactive.

opinion, *n.* SYN.-belief, conviction, decision, feeling, idea, impression, judgment, notion, persuasion, sentiment, view. ANT.-fact, skepticism, misgiving, knowledge.

opinionated, *a.* SYN.-arrogant, authoritarian, bigoted, doctrinaire, dogmatic, domineering, magisterial, obstinate, overbearing, positive, stubborn. ANT.-fluctuating, indecisive, open-minded, questioning, skeptical.

opponent, *n.* SYN.-adversary, antagonist, challenger, competitor, contestant, enemy, foe, rival. ANT.-ally, comrade, confederate, teammate.

opportunity, *n.* SYN.-chance, contingency, freedom, fortune, happening, occasion, opening, possibility, probability. ANT.-disadvantage, hindrance, obstacle.

oppose, *v.* SYN.-argue, bar, combat, confront, contradict, counteract, debate, defy, deny, disapprove, hinder, mutiny, obstruct, protest, rebel, resist, thwart, withstand. ANT.-agree, cooperate, submit, succumb, support.

opposed, *a.* SYN.-adverse, antagonistic, contrary, hostile, opposite. ANT.-benign, favorable.

opposition, *n.* SYN.-conflict, contention, controversy, discord, encounter, fight, interference, struggle. ANT.-amity, concord, consonance, harmony.

oppress, *v.* SYN.-afflict, harass, harry, hound, persecute, plague, torment, torture, vex, worry. ANT.-aid, assist, comfort, encourage, support.

optimism, *n.* SYN.-anticipation, confidence, expectancy, expectation, faith, hope, trust. ANT.-despair, despondency, pessimism.

option, *n.* SYN.-alternative, choice, election, preference, selection.

opulence, *n.* SYN.-abundance, affluence, fortune, luxury, money, plenty, possessions, riches, wealth. ANT.-indigence, need, poverty, want.

oral, *a.* SYN.-literal, spoken, verbal, vocal. ANT.-documentary, recorded, written.

ordain, *v.* SYN.-appoint, cause, constitute, create, engender, fashion, form, formulate, generate, invent, make, originate, produce. ANT.-annihilate, demolish, destroy, disband, terminate.

ordeal, *n.* SYN.-affliction, examination, experiment, hardship, misery, misfortune, suffering, test, trial, tribulation, trouble. ANT.-alleviation, consolation.

order, *n.* SYN.-arrangement, class, method, plan, rank, regularity, sequence, series, succession, system; bidding, command, decree, dictate, injunction, instruction, mandate, requirement. ANT.-confusion, disarray, disorder, irregularity; consent, license, permission.

order, *v.* SYN.-bid, command, conduct, direct, govern, guide, instruct, manage, regulate, rule. ANT.-misdirect, misguide.

orderly, *a.* SYN.-arranged, methodical, neat, organized, systematic, tidy.

ordinary, *a.* SYN.-accustomed, common, conventional, customary, familiar, habitual, normal, plain, regular, typical, usual, vulgar. ANT.-extraordinary, marvelous, remarkable, strange, uncommon.

organization, *n.* SYN.-arrangement, method, mode, order, plan, process, regularity, rule, scheme, system. ANT.-chance, chaos, confusion, disarrangement, disorder, irregularity.

organize, *v.* SYN.-arrange, assort, classify, devise, place, plan, prepare, regulate, sort. ANT.-confuse, disorder, disturb, jumble, scatter.

origin, *n.* SYN.-beginning, birth, commencement, cradle, derivation, foundation, inception, source, spring, start. ANT.-end, harvest, issue, outcome, product.

original, *a.* SYN.-first, initial, primary, primeval, primordial, pristine; creative, fresh, inventive, new, novel. ANT.-derivative, later, modern., subsequent, terminal; banal, plagiarized, trite.

originate, *v.* SYN.-arise, begin, cause, commence, create, engender, establish, fashion, form, formulate, found, generate, inaugurate, initiate, institute, invent, make, organize, originate, produce, start; appoint, constitute, ordain. ANT.-annihilate, complete, demolish, destroy, disband, end, finish, terminate.

ornament, *n.* SYN.-adornment, decoration, embellishment, garnish, ornamentation.

ornate, *a.* SYN.-adorned, embellished, flashy, gaudy, lavish, showy, stylish, tawdry, trimmed

oscillate, *v.* SYN.-change, fluctuate, undulate, swing, vary, waver. ANT.-adhere, persist, resolve, stick.

ostentation, *n.* SYN.-boasting, display, flourish, pageantry, parade, pomp, show, vaunting. ANT.-humility, modesty, reserve, unobtrusiveness.

ostracize, *v.* SYN.-bar, blackball, except, exclude, expel, prevent, prohibit, restrain, shut out. ANT.-accept, admit, include, welcome.

oust, *v.* SYN.-banish, depose, discharge, dismiss, eject, evict, expel, overthrow, remove.

outline, *n.* SYN.-brief, contour, delineation, draft, figure, form, plan, profile, silhouette, sketch.

outrageous, *a.* SYN.-abominable, atrocious, disgraceful, exorbitant, heinous, infamous, notorious,

scandalous, shameless, shocking.

outsider, *n.* SYN.-alien, foreigner, immigrant, newcomer, stranger. ANT.-acquaintance, associate, countryman, friend, neighbor.

outspoken, *a.* SYN.-abrupt, bluff, blunt, brusque, candid, direct, frank, impertinent, impolite, insulting, plain, rough, rude, unceremonious. ANT.-polished, polite, suave, subtle, tactful.

overcast, *a.* SYN.-cloudy, dark, dim, murky, shadowy. ANT.-bright, clear, distinct, limpid, sunny.

overcome, *v.* SYN.-beat, conquer, crush, defeat, humble, master, quell, rout, subdue, subjugate, surmount, vanquish. ANT.-capitulate, cede, lose, retreat, surrender.

overload, *v.* SYN.-afflict, burden, encumber, load, oppress, tax, trouble, weigh. ANT.-alleviate, console, ease, lighten, mitigate.

overlook, *v.* SYN.-disregard, exclude, ignore, miss, neglect, omit, pass, pass over, skip. ANT.-enter, include, insert, introduce, notice.

overseer, *n.* SYN.-employer, foreman, head, leader, manager, master, owner, proprietor, superintendent, supervisor. ANT.-servant, slave; amateur.

oversight, *n.* SYN.-error, inadvertence, inattention, mistake, neglect, omission; charge, control, inspection, management, superintendence, supervision, surveillance. ANT.-attention, care, observation, scrutiny.

overturn, *v.* SYN.-destroy, overcome, replace, rout, ruin, supplant, upset. ANT.-conserve, maintain, preserve, uphold.

overthrow, *v.* SYN.-demolish, destroy, overcome, overturn, rout, ruin, supplant, upset, vanquish. ANT.-build, conserve, construct, preserve, uphold.

overwhelmed, *a.* SYN.-beaten crushed, extinguished, obliterated, ravaged, swamped; affected, impressed, moved, touched.

P

pacific, *a.* SYN.-calm, composed, dispassionate, imperturbable, peaceful, placid, quiet, serene, still, tranquil, undisturbed, unruffled. ANT.-excited, frantic, stormy, turbulent, wild.

pacify, *v.* SYN.-allay, alleviate, appease, assuage, calm, compose, lull, placate, quell, quiet, relieve, satisfy, soothe, still, tranquilize. ANT.-arouse, excite, incense, inflame.

packed, *a.* SYN.-crammed, filled, full, gorged, replete, satiated, soaked, stuffed, tamped. ANT.-depleted, devoid, empty, vacant; insufficient, lacking, partial.

pact, *n.* SYN.-accordance, agreement, bargain, compact, concord, concurrence, contract, covenant, stipulation, understanding, ANT.-difference, disagreement, discord, dissension, variance.

pageant, *n.* SYN.-array, celebration, display, exhibition, exposition, parade.

pain, *n.* SYN.-ache, agony, anguish, distress, grief, pang, paroxysm, suffering, throe, twinge. ANT.-comfort, ease, relief, happiness, pleasure. solace.

painful, *a.* SYN.-acrimonious, biting, bitter, caustic, distasteful, galling, grievous, harsh, poignant, sardonic, severe. ANT.-delicious, mellow, pleasant, sweet.

painting, *n.* SYN.-illustration, landscape, likeness, panorama, picture, portrait, portrayal, rendering, representation, scene, view.

pale, *a.* SYN.-anemic, ashen, blanched, haggard, pallid, sickly, wan.

pamper, *v.* SYN.-coddle, humor, indulge, spoil.

panic, *n.* SYN.-alarm, apprehension, dread, fear, fright, horror, terror, trembling. ANT.-calmness, composure, serenity, tranquility.

parable, *n.* SYN.-allegory, anecdote, fable, legend, narrative, story, tale, yarn.

parade, *n.* SYN.-cavalcade, ceremony, cortege, file, pageant, procession, review, train.

paradox, *n.* SYN.-ambiguity, contradiction, enigma, mystery, puzzle.

paradoxical, *a.* SYN.-ambiguous, contradictory, curious, discrepant, illogical, incompatible, incongruous, inconsistent, ironic, irreconcilable, obscure, puzzling, strange. ANT.-compatible, congruous, consistent, correspondent.

parallel, *a.* SYN.-akin, alike, allied, analogous, comparable, correlative, correspondent, corresponding, equal, like, similar. ANT.-different, dissimilar, divergent, incongruous, opposed.

parched, *a.* SYN.-arid, burned, dehydrated, desiccated, dry, thirsty, withered. ANT.-damp, moist.

pardon, *n.* SYN.-absolution, acquittal, amnesty, exoneration, forgiveness, remission. ANT.-conviction, penalty, punishment, sentence.

pardon, *v.* SYN.-absolve, acquit, condone, excuse, forgive, overlook, release, remit. ANT.-accuse, chastise, condemn, convict, punish.

park, *n.* SYN.-boulevard, common, esplanade, green, lawn, plaza, preserve, promenade, reservation, square, tract.

parley, *n.* SYN.-chat, colloquy, conference, conversation, dialogue, discourse, discussion, encounter, interview, meeting, negotiation, talk.

part, *n.* SYN.-allotment, apportionment, component, division, element, fragment, ingredient, member, moiety, piece, portion, scrap, section, segment, share; character, lines, role. ANT.-entirety, whole.

part, *v.* SYN.-break, cleave, detach, divide, separate, sever, sunder; allot, apportion, distribute, mete, parcel, share. ANT.-combine, convene, gather, join unite.

partake, *v.* SYN.-appropriate, cooperate, experience, participate, receive, share.

partiality, *n.* SYN.-affection, bent, bias, favoritism, fondness, inclination, leaning, predisposition, preference, prejudice, taste, tendency. ANT.-dislike, equality, fairness, impartiality, justice, proof, reason.

participation, *n.* SYN.-allotment, dividend, interest, quota, part, proportion; association, communion, encouragement, fellowship, intercourse, sacrament, sharing, union. ANT.-alienation, non participation.

particle, *n.* SYN.-atom, bit, corpuscle, crumb, grain, iota, jot, mite, scrap, shred, smidgen, speck. ANT.-aggregate, bulk, mass, quantity.

particular, *a.* SYN.-characteristic, distinctive, individual, peculiar, specific; singular, unusual; circumstantial, detailed, exact, min-

ute, specific; careful, choosy, fastidious, finicky, squeamish. ANT.-comprehensive, general, universal; ordinary; general, rough; undiscriminating.

particular, *n.* SYN.-circumstance, detail, feature, item, minutia, point, specification. ANT.-generality.

partisan, *n.* SYN.-adherent, attendant, devotee, disciple, follower, henchman, successor, supporter, votary. ANT.-chief, head, leader, master.

partner, *n.* SYN.-accomplice, ally, associate, attendant, cohort, colleague, companion, comrade, consort, crony, friend, mate, spouse. ANT.-adversary, enemy, stranger.

passable, *a.* SYN.-acceptable, admissible, average, fair, mediocre, marginal. ANT.-excellent, first-rate, worst.

passion, *n.* SYN.-affection, craving, desire, emotion, feeling, lust, sentiment, trepidation, turmoil. ANT.-calm, dispassion, indifference, restraint, tranquility.

passionate, *a.* SYN.-ardent, burning, excitable, fervent, fervid, fiery, glowing, hot, impetuous, impassioned, intense, irascible, moving, tempestuous, vehement. ANT.-apathetic, calm, cool, deliberate, quiet.

passive, *a.* SYN.-acquiescent, enduring, idle, inactive, inert, patient, quiet, relaxed, resigned, stoical, submissive. ANT.-active, aggressive, alert, dynamic, energetic, hostile, impatient.

pastime, *n.* SYN.-amusement, avocation, contest, diversion, fun, game, hobby match, merriment, play, recreation, sport. ANT.-business drudgery, hardship, labor, work.

patent, *a.* SYN.-apparent, clear, con-

spicuous, evident, indubitable,
manifest, obvious, open, overt,
unmistakable. ANT.-concealed, covert, hidden, obscure.

path, *n.* SYN.-avenue, channel,
course, passage, road, route,
street, thoroughfare, track, trail,
walk, way.

pathetic, *a.* SYN.-affecting, moving,
piteous, pitiable, poignant, sad,
touching. ANT.-comical, funny, ludicrous.

patience, *n.* SYN.-composure, endurance, forbearance, fortitude, long-
suffering, perseverance, resignation. ANT.-impatience, nervousness,
restlessness.

patient, *a.* SYN.-composed, forbearing, indulgent, long-suffering, passive, resigned, stoical, uncomplaining. ANT.-chafing, clamorous, high-
strung, hysterical, turbulent.

patron, *n.* SYN.-advocate, ally,
backer, benefactor, champion,
friend, helper, protector.

patronizing, *a.* SYN.-condescending,
contemptuous, disdainful, dispar-
aging, egotistic, overbearing, scornful.

pause, *v.* SYN.-delay, deliberate, demur, doubt, falter, hesitate, interrupt, reflect, rest, suspend, vacillate, waver. ANT.-continue, decide,
persevere, proceed.

pay, *n.* SYN.-allowance, compensation, consideration, earnings, fee,
payment, proceeds, recompense,
return, salary, stipend, wages.
ANT.-gift, gratuity, present.

peace, *n.* SYN.-calm, calmness,
hush, quiescence, quiet, quietude,
repose, serenity, silence, stillness,
tranquility; cease fire, disarma-
ment, treaty, truce. ANT.-agitation,
disturbance, excitement, noise,

tumult; hostility, war.

peaceful, *a.* SYN.-calm, gentle, mild,
pacific, placid, quiet, serene, still,
tranquil, undisturbed. ANT.-
agitated, disturbed, noisy, turbulent, violent.

peak, *n.* SYN.-acme, apex, climax,
consummation, crown, culmination, height, summit, top, zenith.
ANT.-anticlimax, base, depth, floor.

peculiar, *a.* SYN.-characteristic, distinctive, eccentric, exceptional, extraordinary, individual, odd, particular, rare, singular, special,
strange, striking, unusual. ANT.-
common, general, normal, ordinary.

peculiarity, *n.* SYN.-attribute, characteristic, feature, mark, property,
quality, trait.

pedantic, *a.* SYN.-academic, bookish, erudite, formal, learned,
scholarly, scholastic, theoretical.
ANT.-common-sense, ignorant,
practical, simple.

peevish, *a.* SYN.-fractious, fretful,
ill-natured, ill-tempered, irritable,
petulant, snappish, testy, touchy,
waspish. ANT.-affable, genial, good-
natured, good-tempered, pleasant.

penalty, *n.* SYN.-chastisement, fine,
forfeiture, punishment, retribution;
disadvantage, handicap. ANT.-com-
pensation, pardon, remuneration,
reward.

penance, *n.* SYN.-amends, atone-
ment, compensation, expiation,
mortification, purgation, reparation, repentance, restitution, suffering.

penetrating, *a.* SYN.-abstruse, deep,
discerning, perspicacious, profound, recondite, solemn. ANT.-
shallow, slight, superficial, trivial.

penitent, *a.* SYN.-apologetic, contrite, regretful, remorseful, repentant, sorrowful, sorry. ANT.-obdurate, remorseless.

pensive, *a.* SYN.-contemplative, dreamy, introspective, meditative, reflective, thoughtful. ANT.-heedless, inconsiderate, precipitous, rash, thoughtless.

people, *n.* SYN.-clan, community, folk, humanity, humankind, mankind, masses, multitude, nation, populace, proletariat, public, rabble, race, tribe.

perceive, *v.* SYN.-apprehend, comprehend, conceive, discern, note, notice, observe, recognize, see, understand. ANT.-ignore, miss, overlook.

perceptible, *a.* SYN.-appreciable, apprehensible, discernible, measurable, practical, reasonable, sensible, understandable. ANT.-absurd, impalpable, imperceptible, stupid.

perception, *n.* SYN.-apprehension, cognizance, comprehension, conception, discernment, insight, understanding. ANT.-ignorance, insensibility, misapprehension, misconception.

perceptive, *a.* SYN.-alert, astute, aware, cognizant, conscious, discerning, keen, mindful, observant, sensitive, shrewd, wise. ANT.-oblivious, unaware.

perfect, *a.* SYN.-absolute, blameless, complete, consummate, downright, entire, excellent, faultless, finished, full, holy, ideal, immaculate, pure, sinless, superlative, supreme, unqualified, utter, whole. ANT.-blemished, defective, deficient, faulty, imperfect, incomplete, lacking.

perfection, *n.* SYN.-accuracy, completion, consummation, fulfillment, ideal, paragon, precision, realiza-

tion, standard, ultimate.

perform, *v.* SYN.-accomplish, achieve, act, complete, discharge, do, entertain, execute, finish, fulfill, impersonate, play, pretend, render, transact.

performance, *n.* SYN.-accomplishment, act, demonstration, entertainment, exhibition, play, production, show, spectacle.

perfunctory, *a.* SYN.-artificial, careless, cursory, dull, mechanical, stiff. ANT.-easy, heartfelt, natural, unrestrained.

peril, *n.* SYN.-danger, hazard, jeopardy, risk. ANT.-defense, immunity, protection, safety.

perilous, *a.* SYN.-critical, dangerous, hazardous, insecure, menacing, precarious, risky, threatening, unsafe. ANT.-firm, protected, safe, secure.

period, *n.* SYN.-age, date, duration, epoch, era, interim, season, span, spell, term, time.

periphery, *n.* SYN.-border, boundary, extremity, frontier, limit, outpost, perimeter.

perish, *v.* SYN.-cease, decay, decease, depart, die, expire. ANT.-begin, flourish, grow, live, survive.

permanent, *a.* SYN.-abiding, changeless, constant, durable, enduring, fixed, indestructible, lasting, stable, unchangeable. ANT.-ephemeral, temporary, transient, transitory, unstable.

permeate, *v.* SYN.-fill, infiltrate, penetrate, pervade, run through, saturate.

permissible, *a.* SYN.-admissible, allowable, fair, probable, tolerable, warranted. ANT.-inadmissible, irrelevant, unsuitable.

permission, *n.* SYN.-approval, authority, authorization, consent, grace, grant, leave, liberty, license, permit, sanction. ANT.-denial, opposition, prohibition, refusal.

permit, v. SYN.-allow, authorize, give, grant, indulge, let, sanction, suffer, tolerate, yield. ANT.-forbid, object, protest, refuse, resist.

permitted, a. SYN.-allowed, authorized, granted, legalized, licensed, sanctioned.

perpetrate, v. SYN.-commit, do, execute, perform. ANT.-fail, miscarry, neglect.

perpetual, a. SYN.-ceaseless, continual, endless, eternal, everlasting, infinite, timeless, undying. ANT. ephemeral, finite, mortal, temporal, transient.

perpetually, adv. SYN.-always, constantly, continually, eternally, ever, evermore, forever, incessantly, unceasingly. ANT.-fitfully, never, occasionally, rarely, sometimes.

perplex, v. SYN.-bewilder, confound, confuse, dumfound, mystify, nonplus, puzzle. ANT.-clarify, explain, illumine, instruct, solve.

perplexed, a. SYN.-bewildered, confused, deranged, disconcerted, disordered, disorganized, indistinct, mixed, muddled. ANT.-clear, lucid, obvious, organized, plain.

perplexing, a. SYN.-complex, complicated, intricate, involved. ANT.-plain, simple, uncompounded.

persecute, v. SYN.-afflict, annoy, badger, harass, harry, hound, oppress, pester, plague, torment, torture, vex, worry. ANT.-aid, assist, comfort, encourage, support.

persevere, v. SYN.-abide, continue, endure, last, press, persist, strive. ANT.-desist, discontinue, vacillate, waver.

perseverance, n. SYN.-constancy, determination, fortitude, industry, persistence, persistency, pertinacity, resolution, steadfastness, tenacity. ANT.-cessation, idleness, laziness, rest, sloth.

persist, v. SYN.-abide, continue, endure, last, persevere, remain. ANT.-cease, desist, discontinue, vacillate, waver.

persistence, n. SYN.-constancy, endurance, grit, perseverance, pluck, resolve, tenacity,

persistent, a, SYN.-constant, dogged, enduring, fixed, immovable, indefatigable, lasting, obstinate, persevering, perverse, steady, stubborn. ANT.-hesitant, unsure, vacillating, wavering.

persuade, v. SYN.-allure, coax, convince, entice, exhort, incite, induce, influence, prevail upon, urge, win over. ANT.-coerce, compel, deter, dissuade, restrain.

persuasion, n. SYN.-belief, conviction, decision, feeling, idea, impression, judgment, notion, opinion, sentiment, view. ANT.-fact, skepticism, misgiving, knowledge.

pertain, v. SYN.-apply, bear, concern, include, involve, refer, relate.

pertinent, a. SYN.-applicable, apposite, appropriate, apropos, apt, fit, germane, material, related, relating, relevant. ANT.-alien, extraneous, foreign, unrelated.

perturb, v. SYN.-annoy, agitate, bewilder, bother, confound, disturb, irritate, perplex, pester, worry.

pervade, v. SYN.-diffuse, fill, infiltrate, penetrate, permeate, run through, saturate.

perverse, a. SYN.-contrary, disobedient, forward, fractious, intractable, obstinate, peevish, perverted, petulant, sinful, stubborn, ungovernable, untoward, wicked. ANT.-agreeable, docile, obliging, tractable.

perverted, *a.* SYN.-corrupt, degenerate, depraved, deviated, distorted, kinky, lascivious, sick, twisted, unnatural, warped.

pesky, *a.* SYN.-annoying, disturbing, irritating, irksome, nagging, provoking, troublesome, unpleasant, vexing.

pessimistic, *a.* SYN.-cynical, despairing, fatalistic, foreboding, gloomy, hopeless, morbid, morose, sullen, troubled.

pester, *v.* SYN.-annoy. bother, chafe, disturb, irk, irritate, tease, trouble, vex. ANT.-accommodate, console, gratify, soothe.

petite, *a.* SYN.-baby, diminutive, inconsequential, little, tiny, small, trifling, trivial, unimportant.

petition, *n.* SYN.-appeal, entreaty, invocation, plea, prayer, request, suit, supplication.

petrify, *v.* SYN.-fossilize, harden, ossify, solidify; benumb, frighten, paralyze, scare, startle, terrify,

petty, *a.* SYN.-frivolous, insignificant, paltry, small, trifling, trivial, unimportant. ANT.-important, momentous, serious, weighty.

petulant, *a.* SYN.-fretful, irritable, peevish, testy, touchy. ANT.-affable, genial, good-natured, good-tempered, pleasant.

phase, *n.* SYN.-level, procedure, stage, step.

phenomenon, *n.* SYN.-happening, incident, marvel, miracle, occurrence, wonder.

philanthropy, *n.* SYN.-altruism, beneficence, benevolence, charity, generosity, humanity, kindness,

liberality, magnanimity. ANT.-malevolence, selfishness, unkindness.

philosophic, *a.* SYN.-pensive, profound, rational, reflective, thoughtful.

phlegmatic, *a.* SYN.-cold, cool; frigid, passionless, stoical, unfeeling. ANT.-hot, torrid; ardent, passionate.

phobia, *n.* SYN.-apprehension, anxiety, aversion, avoidance, concern, dread, fear, trepidation.

phony, *a.* SYN.-affected, artificial, assumed, bogus, counterfeit, ersatz, fake, feigned, fictitious, sham, spurious, synthetic, unreal. ANT.-genuine, natural, real, true.

phrase, *n.* SYN.-clause, excerpt, expression, idiom, maxim, slogan, term, word.

physical, *a.* SYN.-bodily, carnal, corporal, corporeal, material, natural, somatic, tangible, visible. ANT.-mental, spiritual.

pick, *v.* SYN.-accumulate, acquire, choose, collect, criticize, cull, get, elect, opt, pluck, reap, select. ANT.-refuse, reject.

picky, *a.* SYN.-aesthetic, choosy, cultivated, discerning, discriminating, fastidious, particular, selective

picture, *n.* SYN.-appearance, cinema, drawing, effigy, engraving, etching, film, illustration, image, landscape, likeness, painting, panorama, photograph, portrait, portrayal, print, rendering, representation, resemblance, scene, sketch, view.

picturesque, *a.* SYN.-charming, colorful, impressive, interesting, pictorial, striking

piece, *n.* SYN.-amount, bit, fraction, fragment, morsel, part, portion, scrap, section, share. ANT.-all, entirety, sum, total, whole.

piety, n. SYN.-devotion, devoutness, faith. grace, godliness, homage, sanctity.

pigment, n. SYN.-color, dye, hue, paint, shade, stain, tincture, tinge, tint. ANT.-achromatism, paleness, transparency.

piker, n. SYN.-cheapskate, miser, skinflint, tightwad.

pilfer, v. SYN.-appropriate, cop, embezzle, filch, rob, steal, swindle, swipe.

pillage, n. SYN.-booty, destruction, plunder, spoils,

pillage, v. SYN.-despoil, loot, plunder, ravage, rob, sack.

innacle, n. SYN.-apex, crest, crown, head, summit, top, zenith; ornament, steeple, turret. ANT.-base, bottom, foot, foundation.

pious, a. SYN.-blessed, consecrated, devout, divine, hallowed, holy, religious, sacred, saintly, spiritual. ANT.-evil, profane, sacrilegious, secular, worldly.

pirate, n. SYN.-criminal, marauder, robber, swindler, thief.

pirate, v. SYN.-adopt, appropriate, confiscate, overcharge, plagiarize, steal, usurp

pitch, v. SYN.-cast, fling, hurl, propel, throw, thrust, toss. ANT.-draw, haul, hold, pull, retain.

pitfall, n. SYN.-ambush, scam, snare, scheme, stratagem, trap, trick, wile.

pitiable, a. SYN.-contemptible, insignificant, pathetic, piteous, poignant, sad. ANT.-comical, funny, ludicrous.

pitiful, a. SYN.-afflicted, depressing, dismal, distressed, miserable, mournful, pathetic, sorrowful, suffering, tearful, touching.

pity, n. SYN.-charity, commiseration, compassion, condolence, mercy, understanding, sympathy. ANT.-brutality, cruelty, hardness, inhumanity, ruthlessness.

placate, v. SYN.- appease, assuage, calm, mollify, pacify, satisfy, soothe.

place, v. SYN.-arrange, deposit, dispose, lay, locate, put, set. ANT.-disarrange, disturb, mislay, misplace, remove.

placid, a. SYN.-calm, composed, dispassionate, imperturbable, pacific, peaceful, quiet, serene, still, tranquil, undisturbed, unruffled. ANT.-excited, frantic, stormy, turbulent, wild.

plagiarize, v. SYN.-adopt, appropriate, copy, duplicate, filch, pilfer, steal.

plague, v. SYN.-aggravate, annoy, badger, bother, chafe, disturb, gall, harass, harry, irritate, nag, pester, vex.

plain, a. SYN.-even, flat, level, smooth; apparent, clear, distinct, evident, manifest, obvious, palpable, visible; candid, frank, modest, open, simple, sincere, unpretentious; absolute, unqualified. ANT.-abrupt, broken, rough, undulatory, uneven; abstruse, ambiguous, enigmatical, obscure; adorned, embellished, feigned, insincere.

plan, n. SYN.-delineation, design, draft, drawing, method, outline, plat, plot, scheme, sketch; intent, intention, objective, purpose, system. ANT.-result; accident, chance, confusion, disorder.

plan, v. SYN.-contrive, delineate, design, devise, intend, outline, plot, prepare, project, scheme, sketch.

platitude, n. SYN.-banality, bromide,

cliché, inanity, motto, saying, truism

plausible, *a.* SYN.-believable, credible, feasible, possible, practicable, probable, reasonable. ANT.-impossible, impracticable, visionary.

play, *n.* SYN.-amusement, diversion, entertainment, fun, game, pastime, recreation, romp, sport. ANT.-boredom, labor, toil, work.

play, *v.* SYN.-caper, frolic, gamble, gambol, revel, romp, sport, stake, toy, wager; execute, perform; act, impersonate, pretend.

plea, *n.* SYN.-appeal, entreaty, invocation, overture, petition, prayer, request, suit, supplication.

plead, *v.* SYN.-appeal, ask, beg, beseech, entreat, implore, petition, supplicate; argue, defend, discuss, rejoin. ANT.-deny, deprecate, refuse.

pleasant, *a.* SYN.-acceptable, agreeable, amiable, charming, gratifying, pleasing, pleasurable, suitable, welcome. ANT.-disagreeable, obnoxious, offensive, unpleasant.

please, *v.* SYN.-appease, beguile, captivate, charm, delight, enchant, enrapture, gratify, satisfy, suffice. ANT.-annoy, displease, dissatisfy.

pleasing, *a.* SYN.-agreeable, delightful, engaging, gentle, honeyed, luscious, mellifluous, melodious, saccharine, sugary, sweet, winning, ANT.-acrid, bitter, offensive, repulsive, sour.

pleasure, *n.* SYN.-amusement, comfort, delight, enjoyment, felicity, gladness, gratification, happiness, joy. ANT.-affliction, pain, suffering, trouble, vexation.

pledge, *n.* SYN.-agreement, assurance, assuredness, certainty, contract. conviction, guarantee, oath,

pact, security, surety, promise, word, vow; assertion, declaration, statement.

pledge, *v.* SYN.-consign, entrust, relegate, trust; bind, commit, guarantee, obligate, promise, swear, vouch, vow. ANT.-fail, miscarry, neglect; mistrust, release, renounce; free, loose.

plentiful, *a.* SYN.-abundant, ample, bounteous, bountiful, copious, luxurious, plenteous profuse, replete. ANT.-deficient, insufficient, rare, scanty, scarce.

pliable, *a.* SYN.-compliant, ductile, elastic, flexible, limber, lithe, pliant, resilient, supple, tractable. ANT.-brittle, hard, rigid, stiff, unbending.

plight, *n.* SYN.-danger, difficulty, dilemma, fix, peril, predicament, scrape, situation, strait. ANT.-calmness, comfort, ease, satisfaction.

plot, *n.* SYN.-cabal, conspiracy, design, intrigue, machination, plan, scheme, stratagem; chart, diagram, graph, sketch.

plotting, *n.* SYN.-artfulness, contrivance, cunning, design, planning, scheming. ANT.-candor, sincerity.

ploy, *n.* SYN.-antic, artifice, deception, device, fraud, guile, hoax, imposture, ruse, stratagem, stunt, subterfuge, trick, wile. ANT.-candor, exposure, honesty, openness, sincerity.

plump, *a.* SYN.-chubby, corpulent, fat, obese, paunchy, portly, pudgy, rotund, stocky, stout, thickset. ANT.-gaunt, lean, slender, slim, thin.

plunge, *v.* SYN.-bound, dash, descend, dive, fall, immerse, jump, leap, lunge, plummet, submerge, surge. ANT.-extricate, raise, rescue.

poignant, *a.* SYN.-affecting, heart-rending, impressive, moving, pitiable, sad, tender, touching. ANT.-animated, enlivening, exhilarating, removed.

point, *v.* SYN.-aim, direct, indicate, level, train. ANT.-deceive, distract, misdirect, misguide.

pointed, *a.* SYN.-acute, cutting, keen, sharp; acrid, biting, bitter, pungent; penetrating, piercing, severe, shrill. ANT.-bland, blunt, gentle.

poise, *n.* SYN.-balance, calmness, carriage, composure, equanimity, equilibrium, self-possession. ANT.-agitation, anger, excitement, rage, turbulence.

poise, *v.* SYN.-balance, dangle, hang, hover, ready, suspend.

poison, *v.* SYN.-contaminate, corrupt, infect, pollute, taint. ANT.-disinfect, purify.

polished, *a.* SYN.-courtly, cultivated, cultured, diplomatic, genteel, glib, polite, refined, suave, urbane, well-bred; glossy, shiny, sleek, slick, smooth. ANT.-boorish, bluff, coarse, crude, rude, vulgar; harsh, rough, rugged.

polite, *a.* SYN.-accomplished, civil, considerate, courteous, cultivated, genteel, refined, urbane, well-bred, well-mannered. ANT.-boorish, impertinent, rude, uncivil, uncouth.

pollute, *v.* SYN.-befoul, contaminate, corrupt, defile, infect, poison, sully, taint. ANT.-disinfect, purify.

pomp, *n.* SYN.-affectation, display, flourish, ostentation, pageantry, parade, show, splendor, vaunting, vanity. ANT.-humility, modesty, reserve, unobtrusiveness.

pompous, *a.* SYN.-arrogant, condescending, contemptuous, haughty, proud, superior.

ponder, *v.* SYN.-cogitate, contemplate, deliberate, meditate, muse, reflect, study, think, weigh.

poor, *a.* SYN.-destitute, impecunious, indigent, needy, penniless, poverty-stricken; bad, deficient, inferior, scanty, shabby, unfavorable, wrong. ANT.-affluent, opulent, rich, wealthy; ample, good, right, sufficient.

popular, *a.* SYN.-common, familiar, favorite, general, prevailing, prevalent. ANT.-esoteric, exclusive, restricted, unpopular.

portal, *n.* SYN.-doorway, entrance, entry, gate, inlet, opening. ANT.-departure, exit.

portion, *n.* SYN.-bit, division, fragment, parcel, part, piece, section, segment, share. ANT.-bulk, whole.

portray, *v.* SYN.-delineate, depict, describe, draw, paint, picture, represent, sketch. ANT.-caricature, misrepresent, suggest.

position, *n.* SYN.-locality, place, site, situation, station; caste, condition, place, rank, standing, status; berth, incumbency, job, office, post, situation; attitude, bearing, pose, posture.

positive, *a.* SYN.-assured, certain, definite, fixed, indubitable, inevitable, secure, sure, undeniable, unquestionable. ANT.-doubtful, probable, questionable, uncertain.

possess, *v.* SYN.-control, have, hold, occupy, own; affect, obtain, seize. ANT.-abandon, lose, renounce, surrender.

possessions, *n.* SYN.-belongings, effects, estate, goods, property, stock, wares, wealth. ANT.-deprivation, destitution, poverty, privation, want.

possible, *a.* SYN.-credible, feasible, likely, plausible, practicable, practical, probable. ANT.-impossible, impracticable, visionary.

possibility, *n.* SYN.-chance, contingency, opening, opportunity. ANT.-disadvantage, hindrance, obstacle.

post, *n.* SYN.-locality, place, site, situation, station; berth, incumbency, job, office, position, situation.

postpone, *v.* SYN.-defer, delay, interrupt, pause, stay, suspend. ANT.-continue, maintain, persist, proceed.

postulate, *n.* SYN.-adage, aphorism, apothegm, axiom, byword, fundamental, maxim, principle, proverb, saw, saying, theorem, truism.

posture, *n.* SYN.-attitude, carriage, demeanor, presence, pose, stance.

potency, *n.* SYN.-ability, capability, competency, effectiveness, efficacy, efficiency, power, strength. ANT.-inability, ineptitude, wastefulness.

pound, *v.* SYN.-beat, belabor, buffet, conquer, dash, defeat, hit, knock, overpower, overthrow, pummel, punch, rout, smite, strike, subdue, thrash, thump, vanquish; palpitate, pulsate, pulse, throb. ANT.-defend, shield, stroke, fail, surrender.

poverty, *n.* SYN.-destitution, indigence, necessity, need, penury, privation, want. ANT.-abundance, affluence, plenty, riches, wealth.

power, *n.* SYN.-ability, authority, capability, cogency, command, competency, control, dominion, energy, faculty, force, influence, might, predominance, potency, sovereignty, strength, sway, talent, validity, vigor. ANT.-debility, disablement, fatigue, impotence, incapacity, inaptitude, weakness.

powerful, *a.* SYN.-athletic, cogent, concentrated, firm, forceful, forcible, fortified, hale, hardy, impregnable, mighty, potent, robust, sinewy, strong, sturdy, tough. ANT.-brittle, delicate, feeble, fragile, insipid.

practical, *a.* SYN.-aware, cognizant, discreet, intelligent, judicious, prudent, reasonable, sagacious, sage, sensible, sober, sound, wise. ANT.-absurd, impalpable, imperceptible, stupid, unaware.

practice, *n.* SYN.-custom, drill, exercise, habit, manner, training, usage, use, wont. ANT.-disuse, idleness, inexperience, speculation, theory.

pragmatic, *a,* SYN.-intelligent, logical, practical, rational, realistic, sensible, utilitarian.

praise, *n.* SYN.-acclaim, adulation, applause, approval, commendation, compliment, eulogy, flattery, laudation. ANT.-abuse, censure, condemnation, disapproval.

praise, *v.* SYN.-acclaim, applaud, commend, compliment, eulogize, extol, flatter, glorify, laud. ANT.-censure, condemn, criticize, disparage, reprove.

prayer, *n.* SYN.-appeal, entreaty, invocation, petition, plea, request, suit, supplication.

preach, *v.* SYN.-discourse, exhort, harangue, lecture, moralize, sermonize, teach.

preamble, *n.* SYN.-beginning, forward, introduction, preface, prelude, prologue, start. ANT.-completion, conclusion, end, epilogue, finale.

precarious, *a.* SYN.-critical, dangerous, hazardous, insecure, menacing, perilous, risky, threatening, unsafe. ANT.-firm, protected, safe, secure.

precept, n. SYN.-belief, creed, doctrine, dogma, teaching, tenet. ANT.-conduct, deed, performance, practice.

precious, a. SYN.-costly, expensive, valuable; dear, esteemed; profitable. ANT.-cheap, mean, poor; trashy, worthless.

precise, a. SYN.-accurate, ceremonious, correct, definite, distinct, exact, formal, prim, rigid, stiff, strict, unequivocal. ANT. careless, easy, erroneous, informal, loose, rough, vague.

preclude, v. SYN.-bar, ban eliminate, forestall, hinder, impede, obstruct, obviate, omit, prevent, thwart. ANT.-aid, encourage, expedite, permit, promote.

preclusion, n. SYN.-exception, exclusion, omission. ANT.-inclusion.

predicament, n. SYN.-condition, difficulty, dilemma, fix, impasse, plight, scrape, situation, strait. ANT.-calmness, comfort, ease, satisfaction.

predilection, n. SYN.- affection, attachment, bent, bias, desire, disposition, inclination, leaning, penchant, preference. ANT.-apathy, aversion, distaste, nonchalance, repugnance.

predominant, a. SYN.-cardinal, chief, foremost, highest, leading, main, overwhelming, paramount, principal, supreme. ANT.-auxiliary, minor, subordinate, subsidiary, supplemental.

preference, n. SYN.-alternative, choice, disposition, election, favorite, fondness, liking, option, partiality, predisposition, predilection, selection.

prejudice, n. SYN.-bias, bigotry, disposition, partiality, preconception, predisposition, slant. ANT.-fairness, impartiality, proof, reason.

prejudiced, a. SYN.-bigoted, disposed, dogmatic, fanatical, illiberal, intolerant, narrow-minded. ANT.-liberal, progressive, radical, tolerant.

premeditated, a. SYN.-contemplated, deliberate, designed, intended, intentional, studied. ANT.-accidental, fortuitous.

premeditation, n. SYN.-deliberation, forecast, forethought, intention. ANT.-accident, extemporization, hazard, impromptu.

premise, n. SYN.-assumption, base, basis, foundation, ground, groundwork, postulate, presumption, presupposition, principle, support, underpinning. ANT.-conclusion, derivative, implication, superstructure, trimming.

preoccupied, a. SYN.-abroad, absent, absent-minded, abstracted, away, departed, distracted, inattentive. ANT.-attending, present; attentive, watchful.

prepare, v. SYN.-concoct, condition, contrive, equip, fit, furnish, get ready, make ready, predispose, provide, qualify, ready.

preposterous, a. SYN.-absurd, foolish, inconsistent, irrational, nonsensical, ridiculous, self-contradictory, silly, unreasonable. ANT.-consistent, rational, reasonable, sensible, sound.

prerogative, n. SYN.-authority, grant, liberty, license, privilege, right. ANT.-encroachment, injustice, violation, wrong.

present, n. SYN.-boon, donation, gift, grant, gratuity, largess; instant, moment, now, today.

present, *v.* SYN.-advance, exhibit, extend, introduce, offer, proffer, propose, sacrifice, submit, tender, volunteer. ANT.-accept, receive, reject, retain, spurn.

presentation, *n.* SYN.-award. contribution, donation, gift, grant, present, remembrance; demonstration, display, exhibition, exposition, performance, show, unveiling.

presented, *a.* SYN.-bestowed, conferred, given.

preserve, *v.* SYN.-conserve, defend, guard, keep, maintain, protect, rescue, safeguard, save, secure, spare, uphold. ANT.-abandon, abolish, destroy, impair, injure.

preside, *v.* SYN.-arbitrate, chair, control, direct, lead, moderate, referee, regulate, umpire.

press, *v.* SYN.-crowd, drive, force, impel, propel, push, shove; hasten, pressure, promote, urge. ANT.-drag, falter, halt, pull, retreat; ignore, oppose.

pressing, *a.* SYN.-cogent, compelling, critical, crucial, exigent, impelling, imperative, important, importunate, insistent, instant, necessary, serious, urgent. ANT.-insignificant, petty, trifling, trivial, unimportant.

pressure, *n.* SYN.-compression, force; constraint, influence; compulsion, exigency, hurry, press, stress, urgency. ANT. ease, lenience, recreation, relaxation.

prestige, *n.* SYN.-fame, name, renown, reputation, standing, status.

presume, *v.* SYN.-apprehend, assume, believe, conjecture, deduce, guess, imagine, speculate, suppose, surmise, think. ANT.-ascertain, conclude, demonstrate, know, prove.

presumption, *n.* SYN.-audacity, boldness, effrontery, impertinence, impudence, insolence, rudeness, sauciness. ANT.-diffidence, politeness, subserviency, truckling.

pretend, *v.* SYN.-act, affect, assume, feign, imitate, profess, sham, simulate. ANT.-display, exhibit, expose, reveal.

pretense, *n.* SYN.-affectation, cloak, disguise, excuse, garb, mask, pretension, pretext, semblance, show, simulation, subterfuge. ANT.-actuality, fact, reality, sincerity, truth.

pretty, *a.* SYN.-attractive, beauteous, beautiful, charming, comely, elegant, fair, fine, handsome, lovely. ANT.-foul, hideous, homely, repulsive, unsightly.

prevalent, *a.* SYN.-common, customary, efficacious, familiar, frequent, general, ordinary, popular, regular, superior, universal, usual. ANT.-exceptional, extraordinary, odd, rare, scarce, singular.

prevent, *v.* SYN.-arrest, block, forestall, frustrate, hinder, impede, obstruct, obviate, preclude, stop, thwart. ANT.-aid, encourage, expedite, permit, promote.

previous, *a.* SYN.-aforesaid, antecedent, anterior, foregoing, former, preceding, prior. ANT.-consequent, following, later, subsequent, succeeding.

price, *n.* SYN.-charge, cost, expenditure, expense, payment, value, worth.

pride, *n.* SYN.-arrogance, conceit, haughtiness, self-esteem, self-respect, superciliousness, vainglory, vanity. ANT.-humility, lowliness, meekness, modesty, shame.

prim, *a.* SYN.-decorous, demur, formal, orderly, precise, stiff, tidy, trim.

primary, *a.* SYN.-beginning, earliest, first, initial, original, prime, primeval, primitive, pristine; chief, foremost. ANT.-hindmost, last, latest; least, subordinate.

prime, *a.* SYN.-beginning, best, chief, choice, earliest, first, fundamental, original, primary, principal, top.

primitive, *a.* SYN.-aboriginal, ancient, antiquated, crude, early, old, primary, primeval, primordial, pristine, raw, rough, simple, undeveloped. ANT.-civilized, late, modern, modish, sophisticated.

princely, *a.* SYN.-abundant, ample, generous, grand, lavish, liberal, luxurious, noble, profuse, regal, stately, sumptuous.

principal, *a.* SYN.-cardinal, chief, essential, first, foremost, highest, leading, main, paramount, predominant, supreme. ANT.-auxiliary, minor, subordinate, subsidiary, supplemental.

principal, *n.* SYN.-chief, commander, dean, director, head, leader, master; asset, capital, equipment, property. ANT.-follower, subordinate, underling; base, bottom, foot.

principle, *n.* SYN.-axiom, canon, formula, guide, law, maxim, method, order, precept, regulation, rule, standard, statute, system. ANT.-chance, deviation, exception, hazard, irregularity.

prior, *a.* SYN.-aforesaid, foregoing, former, past, preceding, previous. ANT.-consequent, following, later, subsequent, succeeding.

privacy, *n.* SYN.-isolation, retreat, seclusion, solitude, withdrawal.

private, *a.* SYN.-clandestine, concealed, confidential, covert, exclu-

sive, hidden, isolated, latent, masked, personal, remote, secret, separate, special, surreptitious, unknown. ANT.-conspicuous, disclosed, exposed, known, obvious.

privilege, *n.* SYN.-advantage, exemption, favor, immunity, liberty, license, prerogative, right, sanction. ANT.-disallowance, inhibition, prohibition, restriction.

prize, *n.* SYN.-accolade, award, bonus, booty, bounty, compensation, honor, plunder, premium, recompense, remuneration, reward. ANT,-assessment, charge, earnings, punishment, wages.

prize, *v.* SYN.-appreciate, cherish, esteem, treasure, value.

probable, *a.* SYN.-conceivable, feasible, inclined, liable, likely, possible, prone.

probe, *v.* SYN-ask, explore, extend, inquire, investigate, penetrate, query, question, reach, search, seek, stretch.

problem, *n.* SYN.-difficulty, dilemma, enigma, issue, obstacle, predicament, puzzle, riddle.

procedure, *n.* SYN.-course, deed, fashion, form, habit, maneuver, manner, method, mode, operation, plan, practice, process, style, system, way.

proceed, *v.* SYN.-advance, arise, continue, emanate, further, improve, issue, progress, rise, thrive. ANT.-hinder, oppose, retard, retreat, withhold.

proceeding, *n.* SYN.-affair, business, deal, deed, gathering, meeting, negotiation, occurrence, transaction.

procession, *n.* SYN.-cavalcade, cortege, file, parade, retinue, sequence, succession, train.

proclaim, *v.* SYN.-affirm, announce,

assert, aver, broadcast, declare, express, make known, profess, promulgate, protest, state, tell. ANT.-conceal, repress, suppress, withhold.

procure, v. SYN.-acquire, attain, buy, earn, gain, get, obtain, purchase, secure. ANT.-dispose of, sell, vend.

prodigal, a. SYN.-abundant, bountiful, copious, extravagant, lavish, plentiful, profligate, profuse, reckless, wasteful.

prodigal, n. SYN.-carouser, playboy, spendthrift, wastrel

prodigious, a. SYN.-amazing, astonishing, astounding, enormous, huge, immense, marvelous, monstrous, monumental, remarkable, stupendous, vast. ANT.-commonplace, insignificant, small.

prodigy, n. SYN.-curiosity, marvel, spectacle, wonder.

produce, n. SYN.-crop, fruit, harvest, proceeds, product, reaping, result, store, vegetables, yield.

produce, v. SYN.-bear, breed, conceive, exhibit, fabricate, fashion, generate, hatch, make, manufacture, procreate, show, supply, yield; accomplish, cause, effect, occasion, originate. ANT.-consume, destroy, reduce, waste; conceal, hide.

productive, a. SYN.-bountiful, fecund, fertile, fruitful, luxuriant, plenteous, prolific, rich, teeming. ANT.-barren, impotent, sterile, unproductive.

profane, v. SYN.-debauch, defile, deflower, desecrate, dishonor, infringe, invade, pollute, ravish, transgress, violate,

profess, v. SYN.-affirm, announce, assert, aver, broadcast, declare,

express, make known, proclaim, promulgate, protest, state, tell. ANT.-conceal, repress, suppress, withhold.

profession, n. SYN.-avocation, business, calling, career, employment, occupation, vocation, work; allegation, assertion, claim, contention, declaration, statement, vow.

professional, a. SYN.-adept, competent, efficient, expert, learned, licensed, proficient, skilled, trained.

proficient, a. SYN.-able, accomplished, adept, clever, competent, cunning, expert, ingenious, practiced, skilled, skillful, versed. ANT.-awkward, bungling, clumsy, inexpert, untrained.

profit, n. SYN.-advantage, avail, benefit, emolument, gain, improvement, service, use. ANT.-damage, detriment, loss, ruin, waste.

profitable, a. SYN.-advantageous, beneficial, favorable, lucrative, productive, remunerative, valuable.

profligate, a. SYN.-contaminated, corrupt, corrupted, crooked, debased, depraved, dishonest, impure, putrid, spoiled, tainted, unsound, venal, vitiated.

profound, a. SYN.-abstruse, deep, intellectual, intense, penetrating, recondite, solemn, wise. ANT.-shallow, slight, superficial, trivial.

profuse, a. SYN.-abundant, copious, excessive, extravagant, exuberant, immoderate, improvident, lavish, luxuriant, overflowing, plentiful, prodigal, wasteful. ANT.-economical, meager, poor, skimpy, sparse.

profusion, n. SYN.-abundance, excess, extravagance, immoderation, intemperance, superabundance, superfluity, surplus. ANT.-dearth, deficiency, lack, paucity, want.

program, *n.* SYN.-agenda, bulletin, calendar, curriculum, plan, presentation, schedule.

progress, *n.* SYN.-advance, advancement, betterment, course, development, growth, improvement, proceeding, progression. ANT.-decline, delay, regression, relapse, retrogression.

progress, *v.* SYN.-advance, augment, elevate, enlarge, further, improve, increase, proceed, promote, rise, thrive. ANT.-hinder, oppose, retard, retreat, withhold.

progression, *n.* SYN.-arrangement, chain, following, gradation, order, sequence, series, string, succession.

prohibit, *v.* SYN.-ban, debar, enjoin, forbid, halt, hinder, impede, inhibit, interdict, obstruct, prevent, restrain. ANT.-allow, permit, sanction, tolerate.

project, *n.* SYN.-aim, contrivance, design, device, intention, plan, proposal, proposition, scheme. ANT.-accomplishment, performance, production.

project, *v.* SYN.-brew, concoct, contemplate, contrive, devise, forecast, frame, plan.

prolific, *a.* SYN.-bountiful, fecund, fertile, fruitful, luxuriant, plenteous, productive, rich, teeming. ANT.-barren, impotent, sterile, unproductive.

prolong, *v.* SYN.-drag, draw, extend, lengthen, protract, stretch. ANT.-abbreviate, contract, curtail, shorten.

prominent, *a.* SYN.-celebrated, conspicuous, distinguished, eminent, famous, illustrious, influential, noteworthy, outstanding, remarkable, renowned. ANT.-common,

humble, low, ordinary, vulgar.

promiscuous, *a.* SYN.-careless, confused, garbled, immoral, indiscriminate, licentious, loose, mixed,

promise, *n.* SYN.-agreement, assurance, bestowal, contract, covenant, engagement, fulfillment, guarantee, oath, pledge, undertaking, vow.

promote, *v.* SYN.-advance, advocate, aid, assist, back, champion, encourage, facilitate, forward, foster, patronize, support, urge. ANT.-demote, discourage, hinder, impede, obstruct.

prompt, *a.* SYN.-exact, precise, punctual, timely. ANT.-dilatory, late, slow, tardy.

prompt, *v.* SYN.-arouse, cause, coach, create, cue, effect, evoke, help, incite, induce, inspire, instigate, make, occasion, originate, provoke, remind, suggest.

promptly, *adv.* SYN.-directly, forthwith, immediately, instantaneously, instantly, now, quickly, presently, rapidly, straight-away. ANT.-distantly, hereafter, later, shortly, sometime.

promulgate, *v.* SYN.-affirm, announce, assert, aver, broadcast, declare, express, make known, proclaim, profess, state, tell. ANT.-conceal, repress, suppress, withhold.

proof, *n.* SYN.-confirmation, corroboration, demonstration, evidence, experiment, test, testimony, trial, verification. ANT.-failure, fallacy, invalidity.

propaganda, *n.* SYN.-advertising, broadcasting, inducement, influence, notice, persuasion, promotion, publicity.

propagate, *v.* SYN.-bear, beget, breed, conceive, engender, generate, procreate.

propel, *v.* SYN.-actuate, agitate, drive, impel, induce, instigate, move, persuade, push, shift, stir, transfer. ANT.-deter. halt, rest, stay, stop.

propensity, *n.* SYN.-bent, bias, capacity, drift, inclination, leaning, predisposition, proclivity, proneness, talent, tendency, trend. ANT.-aversion, deviation, disinclination.

proper, *a.* SYN.-appropriate, befitting, conventional, correct, decent, fit, formal, legitimate, meet, respectable, right, seemly, suitable.

property, *n.* SYN.-belongings, commodities, effects, estate, goods, merchandise, possessions, stock, wares, wealth; attribute, characteristic, peculiarity, quality, trait. ANT.-deprivation, destitution, poverty, privation, want.

prophesy, *v.* SYN.-anticipate, augur, divine, envision, forecast, foresee, predict.

prophet, *n.* SYN.-astrologer, clairvoyant, economist, forecaster, fortuneteller, medium, meteorologist, oracle, palmist, seer, soothsayer, sorcerer, wizard.

proponent, *n.* SYN.-advocate, champion, defender, patron, promoter, supporter.

proportion, *n.* SYN.-balance, dimensions, distribution, equilibrium, extent, part, percentage, piece, portion, ratio, share, size, symmetry.

proposal, *n.* SYN.-bid, motion, offer, overture, plan, proposition, suggestion, tender. ANT.-acceptance, denial, rejection, withdrawal.

propose, *v.* SYN.-design, intend, move, offer, present, proffer, propound, purpose, suggest, tender.

ANT.-effect, fulfill, perform.

propound, *v.* SYN.-adduce, advance, advise, allege, elevate, forward, further, offer, promote, propose, submit, suggest. ANT.-hinder, oppose, retard, retreat, withhold.

proprietor, *n.* SYN.-employer, head, leader, master, manager, overseer, owner. ANT.-employee. helper, laborer, servant, slave, worker.

propriety, *n.* SYN.-aptness, congruity, decency, decorum, dignity, etiquette, fitness, modesty, protocol, seemliness.

prosper, *v.* SYN.-achieve, burgeon, flourish, flower, gain, grow, increase, prevail, succeed, thrive, win. ANT.-fail, miscarry, miss.

prosperous, *a.* SYN.-affluent, ample, bountiful, copious, exorbitant, luxurious, opulent, plentiful, rich, sumptuous, wealthy, well-to-do. ANT.-beggarly, destitute, indigent, needy, poor.

protect, *v.* SYN.-defend, guard, keep, maintain, preserve, safeguard, save, secure, uphold. ANT.-abandon, abolish, destroy, impair, injure.

protection, *n.* SYN.-bulwark, defense, fence, guard, refuge, safeguard, security, shelter, shield.

protest, *n.* SYN.-challenge, demonstration, disagreement, dissent, dissentience, objection, remonstrance, revolt, riot. ANT.-acceptance, agreement, assent, compliance.

protest, *v.* SYN.-complain, demonstrate, demur, disagree, disapprove, object, oppose, rebel, reject, remonstrate, riot. ANT.-acquiesce, approve, assent, comply, concur.

prototype, *n.* SYN.-archetype, example, illustration, instance,

model, pattern, sample, specimen.
ANT.-concept, precept, principle,
rule.

protract, *v.* SYN.-distend, distort,
elongate, expand, extend, lengthen,
spread, strain, stretch. ANT.-con-
tract, loosen, shrink, slacken,
tighten.

proud, *a.* SYN.-arrogant, conceited,
disdainful, egotistical, haughty, imposing, lofty, magnificent, majestic,
overbearing, stately, supercilious,
vain, vainglorious. ANT.-ashamed,
humble, lowly, meek.

prove, *v.* SYN.-affirm, confirm, corroborate, demonstrate, document,
establish, justify, manifest, substantiate, test, try, validate, verify.
ANT.-contradict, disprove, refute.

proverb, *n.* SYN.-adage, aphorism,
apothegm, axiom, byword, maxim,
motto, platitude, saw, saying.

provide, *v.* SYN.-accommodate, afford, assist, endow, equip, fit, furnish, give, help, oblige, outfit, produce, supply, yield. ANT.-denude,
despoil, divest, strip.

provident, *a.* SYN.-careful, economical, frugal, niggardly, saving,
sparing, thrifty. ANT.-extravagant,
improvident, lavish, prodigal,
wasteful.

provincial, *a.* SYN.-awkward, boorish, bucolic, callow, coarse, crude,
ignorant, rough, rustic, simple,
unpolished, unrefined, unsophisticated

provision, *n.* SYN.-accumulation, arrangement, fund, hoard, plan,
preparation, reserve, stock, store,
supply; condition, requirement,
stipulation.

provoke, *v.* SYN.-agitate, arouse,
awaken, cause, disquiet, disturb,
encourage, excite, foment, goad,

incite, induce, instigate, irritate,
rouse, stimulate, stir up, urge.
ANT.-allay, calm, pacify, quell,
quiet.

prowess, *n.* SYN.-boldness, bravery,
chivalry, courage, fearlessness,
fortitude, intrepidity, mettle, resolution. ANT.-cowardice, fear, pusillanimity, timidity.

proxy, *n.* SYN.-agent, alternate,
deputy, lieutenant, representative,
substitute, understudy. ANT.-head,
master, principal, sovereign.

prudence, *n.* SYN.-care, caution,
heed, vigilance, wariness, watchfulness. ANT.-abandon, carelessness, recklessness.

prudent, *a.* SYN.-aware, cognizant,
comprehending, conscious, discreet, intelligent, judicious, perceiving, practical, reasonable,
sagacious, sage, sensible, sentient,
sober, sound, wise. ANT.-absurd,
impalpable, imperceptible, stupid,
unaware.

prying, *a.* SYN.-curious, inquiring,
inquisitive, interrogative, meddling,
nosy, peeping, peering, searching,
snoopy. ANT.-incurious, indifferent,
unconcerned, uninterested.

psychic, *a.* SYN.-extrasensory,
mental, mystic, telepathic, supernatural.

psychosis, *n.* SYN.-delirium, dementia, derangement, frenzy, insanity,
lunacy, madness, mania. ANT.-ra-
tionality, sanity, stability.

publication, *n.* SYN.-advertisement,
airing, announcement, broadcast,
disclosure, dissemination, notification, statement.

publish, *v.* SYN.-advertise, air, announce, broadcast, declare, disclose, disseminate, divulge, issue,
proclaim.

pull, v. SYN.-allure, attract, drag, draw, entice, haul, induce, lure, persuade, tow, tug. ANT.-drive, propel, push, repel.

pulsate, v. SYN.-beat, buffet, palpitate, pound, pulse, throb, thump, vibrate.

punctual, a. SYN.-exact, nice, precise, prompt, ready, timely. ANT.-dilatory, late, slow, tardy.

punish, v. SYN.-castigate, chastise, correct, discipline, pummel, reprove, strike. ANT.-acquit, exonerate, free, pardon, release.

punishment, n. SYN.-chastisement, correction, discipline, fine, forfeiture, penalty, retribution. ANT.-chaos, confusion, turbulence.

puny, a. SYN.-decrepit, delicate, enervated, exhausted, faint, feeble, forceless, impaired, infirm, languid, powerless, weak. ANT.-forceful, lusty, stout, strong, vigorous.

purchase, v. SYN.-acquire, buy, get, obtain, procure. ANT.-dispose of, sell, vend.

pure, a. SYN.-chaste, clean, clear, genuine, guiltless, immaculate, innocent, modest, sincere, spotless, unadulterated, undefiled, untainted; virginal; absolute, bare, sheer, utter. ANT.-foul, polluted, sullied, tainted, tarnished; corrupt, defiled.

purified, a. SYN.-clarified, clean, cleansed, distilled, pure, purged, refined, sweet. ANT.-boorish, coarse, crude, rude, vulgar.

purify, v. SYN.-clean, cleanse, disinfect, filter, mop, refine, rinse, scrub, sweep, wash. ANT.-dirty, pollute, soil, stain, sully.

purpose, n. SYN.-aim, aspiration, design, drift, end, expectation, goal, intent, intention, object, objective.

ANT.-accident, fate, hazard.

pursue, v. SYN.-chase, endeavor, follow, hunt, maintain, persist, proceed, seek, track, trail. ANT.-abandon, disregard, elude, escape, evade, flee, ignore.

push, v. SYN.-crowd, drive, force, impel, jostle, press, propel, shove; hasten, promote, urge. ANT.-drag, falter, halt, pull, retreat; ignore, oppose.

put, v. SYN.-deposit, establish, install, lay, plant, set, situate.

puzzle, n. SYN.-conundrum, enigma, mystery, problem, riddle. ANT.-answer, clue, key, resolution, solution.

puzzle, v. SYN.-bewilder, confound, confuse, dumfound, mystify, nonplus, perplex. ANT.-clarify, explain, illumine, instruct, solve.

q

quack, n. SYN.-charlatan, fake, impostor, phony, pretender, rogue, swindler.

quaint, a. SYN.-curious, cute, eccentric, odd, peculiar, queer, strange, unusual, whimsical. ANT.-common, familiar, normal, ordinary, usual.

qualified, a. SYN.-able, capable, clever, competent, efficient, fitted, skillful. ANT.-inadequate, incapable, incompetent, unfitted.

quality, n. SYN.-attribute, characteristic, distinction, feature, peculiarity, property, trait; caliber, grade, value. ANT.-being, essence, nature, substance.

quantity, n. SYN.-aggregate, amount, content, extent, measure, number, portion, sum, volume. ANT.-nothing, nothingness, zero.

quarrel, n. SYN.-affray, altercation,

argument, bickering, contention, disagreement, dispute, feud, spat, squabble, wrangle. ANT.-agreement, friendliness, harmony, peace, reconciliation.

queer, a. SYN.-curious, droll, eccentric, odd, peculiar, quaint, singular, strange, unusual, whimsical. ANT.-common, familiar, normal, ordinary, usual.

quest, n. SYN.-examination, exploration, inquiry, interrogation, investigation, query, question, research, scrutiny, search. ANT.-disregard, inactivity, inattention, negligence.

question, v. SYN.-ask, challenge, dispute, doubt, examine, inquire, interrogate, pump, query, quiz. ANT.-accept, answer, reply, respond, state.

quick, a. SYN.-active, brisk, excitable, fast, hasty, impatient, irascible, lively, nimble, precipitate, rapid, sharp, speedy, swift, testy, touchy; acute, clever, discerning, keen, sensitive, shrewd. ANT.-slow, sluggish; dull, inattentive, unaware.

quicken, v. SYN.-accelerate, dispatch, expedite, facilitate, forward, hasten, hurry, push, rush, speed. ANT.-block, hinder, impede, retard, slow.

quiet, a. SYN.-calm, gentle, hushed, meek, mild, modest, motionless, passive, patient, peaceful, placid, quiescent, silent, still, tranquil, undisturbed. ANT.-agitated, disturbed, loud, perturbed, strident.

quiet, n. SYN.-calm, calmness, hush, peace, quiescence, quietude, repose, rest, serenity, silence, stillness, tranquility. ANT.-agitation, commotion, disturbance, excitement, noise, tumult.

quiet, v. SYN.-allay, alleviate, appease, assuage, calm, compose, lull, pacify, placate, quell, relieve, satisfy, soothe, still, tranquilize. ANT.-arouse, excite, incense, inflame.

quirk, n. SYN.-caprice, characteristic, flavor, idiosyncrasy, irregularity, oddity, peculiarity, style, temperament, whim.

quit, v. SYN.-abandon, cease, depart, desist, discontinue, leave, relinquish, resign, stop, surrender, withdraw. ANT.-continue, endure, occupy, persist, stay.

quiver, v. SYN.-quake, shake, shiver, shudder, tremble, tremor.

quiz, v. SYN.-ask, examine, inquire, interrogate, pump, query, question. ANT.-answer, reply, respond, state.

quote, v. SYN.-adduce, cite, extract, paraphrase, plagiarize, recite, repeat. ANT.-contradict, misquote, refute, retort.

R

rabble, n. SYN.-crowd, masses, mob, people, populace, proletariat.

race, n. SYN.-ancestry, clan, culture, family, folk, lineage, nation, people, stock, strain, tribe.

racket, n. SYN.-cacophony, clamor, clatter, din, noise, pandemonium, row, rumpus, sound, tumult, uproar. ANT.-hush, quiet, silence, stillness.

racy, a. SYN.-erotic, indecent, lewd, risqué, suggestive.

radiance, n. SYN.-brightness, brilliance, brilliancy, effulgence, luster, splendor. ANT.-darkness, dullness, gloom, obscurity.

radiant, a. SYN.-brilliant, bright, dazzling, effulgent, glorious, gorgeous, grand, illustrious, magnificent, resplendent, shining, showy, splendid, sumptuous, superb. ANT.-dull, mediocre, modest, ordinary, unimpressive.

radical, *a.* SYN.-basic, complete, constitutional, extreme, fundamental, inherent, innate, insurgent, intrinsic, natural, organic, original, total, thorough, ultra, uncompromising. ANT.-conservative, moderate, superficial; extraneous.

rage, *n.* SYN.-anger, animosity, choler, fury, indignation, ire, passion, resentment, temper, wrath. ANT.-conciliation, forbearance, patience, peace, self-control.

raging, *a.* SYN.-acute, boisterous, extreme, fierce, forceful, furious, impetuous; intense, passionate, powerful, raving, severe, turbulent, vehement, violent, wild. ANT.-calm, feeble, gentle, quiet, soft.

raid, *n.* SYN.-assault, attack, foray, incursion, invasion.

rain, *v.* SYN.-deluge, drench, drizzle, drop, fall, mist, patter, pour, shower, storm.

raise, *v.* SYN.-elevate, erect, exalt, heave, heighten, hoist, lift, uplift; breed, cultivate, grow, produce; gather, levy, muster. ANT.-abase, depreciate, depress, destroy, lower.

ram, *v.* SYN.-bump, butt, collide, crash, cram, hit, jam, pound, stuff.

ramble, *v.* SYN.-deviate, digress, err, range, roam, rove, saunter, stray, stroll, traipse, wander. ANT.-halt, linger, settle, stay, stop.

rampant, *a.* SYN.-frantic, furious, raging, tumultuous, turbulent, uncontrolled, violent, widespread, wild.

rancor, *n.* SYN.-animosity, enmity, grudge, ill-will, malevolence, mal-

ice, malignity, spite. ANT.-affection, kindness, love, toleration.

random, *a.* SYN.-accidental, aimless, casual, chance, haphazard, indiscriminate, unplanned, unpredictable,

rank, *n.* SYN.-blood, class, degree, dignity, distinction, eminence, estate, grade, quality, standing, station, status; fetid, foul, gamy, malodorous, nasty, putrid, rancid, reeking, smelly, stinking. ANT.-disrepute, shame, stigma; clean, pleasant, sweet.

rapid, *a.* SYN.-expeditious, fast, fleet, hasty, lively, precipitate, quick, speedy, swift. ANT.-slow, sluggish.

rapture, *n.* SYN.-blessedness, bliss, blissfulness, delight, ecstasy, exaltation, felicity, happiness, joy, pleasure, satisfaction, transport, trance. ANT.-grief, misery, sorrow, woe, wretchedness.

rare, *a.* SYN.-choice, exceptional, incomparable, infrequent, occasional, precious, scarce, singular, strange, uncommon, unique, unusual. ANT.-abundant, commonplace, customary, frequent, numerous, ordinary, usual, worthless.

rascal, *n.* SYN.-beggar, bum, cad, charlatan, knave, rake, reprobate, rogue, scalawag, scamp, sneak, scoundrel, tramp, villain, wastrel, wretch,

rash, *a.* SYN.-blind, careless, hasty, headlong, heedless, impetuous, impulsive, oblivious, passionate, quick, undiscerning, unmindful, unseeing. ANT.-aware, calculated, cautious, discerning, perceiving, reasoning, sensible.

rate, *v.* SYN.-appraise, assess, classify, evaluate, grade, judge, rank, value.

ratify, *v.* SYN.-approve, authorize, confirm, endorse, sanction.

rational, *a.* SYN.-calm, circumspect, cool, discerning, intelligent, judicious, logical, prudent, reasonable, sane, sensible, sober, sound, wise. ANT.-absurd, foolish; irrational, insane.

rationale, *n.* SYN.-aim, argument, basis, design, excuse, explanation, ground, intelligence, justification, motive, purpose, reason, rationalization, sake.

ravage, *v.* SYN.-annihilate, demolish, despoil, destroy, devastate, exterminate, extinguish, pillage, plunder, ransack, ruin, sack, strip, waste. ANT.-accumulate, economize, preserve, save.

ravish, *v.* SYN.-debauch, defile, desecrate, dishonor, pollute, profane, violate.

raw, *a.* SYN.-coarse, crass, crude, green, harsh, ill-prepared, rough, uncouth, unfinished, unpolished, unrefined. ANT.-finished, well-prepared; cultivated, refined.

raze, *v.* SYN.-annihilate, demolish, destroy, devastate, eradicate, exterminate, extinguish, obliterate, ravage, ruin, wreck. ANT.-construct, establish, make, preserve, save.

reach, *v.* SYN.-approach, arrive, attain, extend, overtake, stretch, touch. ANT.-fail, fall short, miss.

react, *v.* SYN.-answer, counter, counteract, experience, feel, rejoin, reply, respond, retort. ANT.-disregard, ignore, overlook.

reaction, *n.* SYN.-answer, backlash, feedback, rejoinder, reply, response, retort.

ready, *a.* SYN.-aged, available, complete, consummate, convenient, finished, full-grown, handy, mature, matured, mellow, prepared, ripe, seasonable, steeled. ANT.-crude, green, immature, raw, undeveloped.

ready, *v.* SYN.-condition, equip, fit, furnish, get ready, make ready, predispose, prepare, provide, qualify.

real, *a.* SYN.-actual, authentic, certain, genuine, positive, substantial, true, veritable. ANT.-apparent, fictitious, imaginary, supposed, unreal.

realize, *v.* SYN.-appreciate, apprehend, comprehend, conceive, discern, grasp, know, learn, perceive, see, understand. ANT.-ignore, misapprehend, mistake, misunderstand.

realm, *n.* SYN.-area, circle, domain, kingdom, orbit, province, sphere

reap, *v.* SYN.-acquire, gain, garner, gather, get, glean, harvest, obtain, pick, receive. ANT.-lose, plant, sow, squander.

reaping, *n.* SYN.-crop, harvest, proceeds, produce, product, result, yield.

rear, *v.* SYN.-bear, beget, breed, conceive, engender, foster, generate, nurture, procreate, propagate, raise, train.

reason, *n.* SYN.-aim, argument, basis, cause, design, ground, motive, purpose, sake; intelligence, mind, rationality, sense, understanding.

reason, *v.* SYN.-argue, conclude, deduce, deliberate, discuss, infer, judge, reflect. ANT.-bewilder, confuse, guess.

reasonable, *a.* SYN.-appreciable, apprehensible, perceptible; alive, awake, aware, cognizant, comprehending, conscious, discreet, intelligent, judicious, perceiving, practical, prudent, sagacious, sage, sensible, sentient, sober, sound, wise. ANT.-absurd, impalpable, imperceptible, stupid, unaware.

rebel, *v.* SYN.-defy, mutiny, oppose, resist, revolt, strike.

rebellion, *v.* SYN.-coup, insurrection, mutiny, overthrow, revolt, revolution, uprising.

rebellious, *a.* SYN. defiant, disobedient, insubordinate, undutiful, unruly. ANT.-compliant, dutiful, unruly. ANT.-compliant, dutiful, obedient, submissive.

rebuild, *v.* SYN.-reconstruct, reestablish, rehabilitate, renew, renovate, repair, restore.

rebuke, *v.* SYN.-censure, chide, reprimand, reprove, scold, upbraid.

rebuttal, *n.* SYN.-answer, defense, rejoinder, reply, response, retort; ANT.-argument, inquiry, questioning, summoning;

recall, *v.* SYN.-recollect, remember, remind, reminisce. ANT.-disregard, forget, ignore, overlook.

recede, *v.* SYN.-abate, decline, decrease, drop, ebb, lessen, retreat, subside.

receive, *v.* SYN.-accept, admit, entertain, gain, get, inherit, shelter, take, welcome. ANT.-bestow, discharge, give, impart, reject, turn away.

recent, *a.* SYN.-fresh, late, modern, new, newfangled, novel, original. ANT.-ancient, antiquated, archaic, obsolete, old.

recitation, *n.* SYN.-address, discourse, interpretation, lecture, monologue, narration, reading, soliloquy, speech, recital.

recite, *v.* SYN.-declaim, deliver, describe, detail, enumerate, mention,

narrate, recapitulate, recount, rehearse, relate, repeat, tell.

reckless, *a.* SYN.-careless, heedless, imprudent, inattentive, inconsiderate, indiscreet, neglectful, negligent, remiss, thoughtless, unconcerned, ANT.-accurate, careful, meticulous, nice.

reckon, *v.* SYN.-assess, consider, estimate, evaluate, judge, weigh.

recognize, *v.* SYN.-acknowledge, apprehend, avow, concede, confess, identify, own, perceive, recollect, remember. ANT.-disown, forget, ignore, overlook, renounce, repudiate.

recollection, *n.* SYN.-memory, remembrance, reminiscence, retrospection. ANT.-forgetfulness, oblivion.

recommend, *v.* SYN.-advise, allude, counsel, hint, imply, insinuate, intimate, offer, propose, refer, suggest. ANT.-declare, demand, dictate, insist.

recommendation, *n.* SYN.-advice, caution, counsel, exhortation, instruction, suggestion, warning.

reconsider, *v.* SYN.-analyze, consider, ponder, review, revise. ANT.-ignore, reject.

record, *n.* SYN.-account, achievement, archive, career, chronicle, document, history, mark, memorandum, memorial, minute, note, report, register, trace, vestige,

recount, *v.* SYN.-describe, narrate, recite, relate, report, tell.

recover, *v.* SYN.-cure, rally, recuperate, restore, revive; recapture, recoup, redeem, regain, repossess, retrieve. ANT.-regress, relapse, revert, weaken; forfeit, lose.

recreation, *n.* SYN.-amusement, diversion, entertainment, fun, game, pastime, play, sport. ANT.-boredom, labor, toil, work.

rectify, v. SYN.-amend, correct, mend, reform, right. ANT.-aggravate, ignore, spoil.

recuperate, v. SYN.-heal, rally, recover, restore, revive; recapture, recoup, redeem, regain, repossess, retrieve. ANT.-regress, relapse, revert, weaken; forfeit, lose.

redeemer, n. SYN.-deliverer, liberator, protector, rescuer.

reduce, v. SYN.-abate, assuage, curtail, decline, decrease, deduct, diminish, lessen, lower, moderate, shorten, subtract, suppress. ANT.-amplify, enlarge, increase, intensify, revive.

refined, a. SYN.-courtly, cultivated, cultured, genteel, polished, polite, well-bred; clarified, purified. ANT.-boorish, coarse, crude, rude, vulgar.

refinement, n. SYN.-breeding, civilization, cultivation, culture, education, enlightenment. ANT.-boorishness, ignorance, illiteracy, vulgarity.

reflect, v. SYN.-apprehend, cogitate, consider, contemplate, deliberate, imagine, meditate, muse, opine, picture, ponder, reason, recall, recollect, reckon, regard, remember, speculate, suppose, think. ANT.-conjecture, forget, guess.

reflection, n. SYN.-cogitation, conception, consideration, contemplation, deliberation, fancy, idea, imagination, impression, judgment, meditation, memory, notion, opinion, recollection, regard, retrospection, sentiment, thought, view.

reform, v. SYN.-ameliorate, amend, better, change, correct, help, improve, mend, rectify, renew, right.

ANT.-aggravate, corrupt, damage, debase, ignore, impair, spoil.

refrain, v. SYN.-abstain, desist, forbear, withhold. ANT.-continue, indulge, persist.

refreshing, a. SYN.-modern, new, novel, recent; artless, brisk, cool, fresh, green, inexperienced, natural, raw. ANT.-decayed, faded, hackneyed, musty, stagnant.

refuge, n. SYN.-asylum, harbor, haven, retreat, sanctuary, shelter. ANT.-danger, exposure, hazard, jeopardy, peril.

refuse, v. SYN.-decline, deny, rebuff, reject, repudiate, spurn, withhold. ANT.-accept, grant, welcome.

refute, v SYN.-confute, controvert, disprove, rebut. ANT.-accept, affirm, confirm, establish, prove.

regain, v. SYN.-recapture, recoup, recover, redeem, repossess, retrieve. ANT.-forfeit, lose.

regal, a. SYN.-courtly, dignified, grand, imperial, kingly, lordly, majestic, monarchal, noble, princely, royal, ruling, sovereign, stately, supreme. ANT.-common, humble, low, plebeian, proletarian, servile, vulgar.

regard, n. SYN.-affection, attention, care, concern, consideration, esteem, liking, notice, observation. ANT.-antipathy, disgust, disaffection, neglect.

regard, v SYN.-esteem, honor, respect, value; behold, contemplate, look, mark, notice, observe, see, view, watch; account, believe, deem, hold, imagine, reckon, suppose, think. ANT.-insult, mock; ignore, neglect, overlook.

region, n. SYN.-area, belt, locale, locality, location, place, sector, site, situation, spot, station, vicinity, zone.

regret, *n.* SYN.-compunction, contrition, grief, penitence, qualm, remorse, repentance, self-reproach, sorrow. ANT.-complacency, impenitence, obduracy, self-satisfaction.

regular, *a.* SYN.-customary, methodical, natural, normal, orderly, ordinary, periodical, steady, systematic, uniform, unvaried. ANT.-abnormal, erratic, exceptional, rare, unusual.

regulation, *n.* SYN.-canon, control, correction, discipline, guide, law, order, principle, punishment, regulation, restraint, rule, self-control, standard, statute. ANT.-chaos, confusion, turbulence.

rehabilitate, *v.* SYN.-cure, heal, rebuild, reconstruct, recover, reestablish, refresh, rejuvenate, renew, reinstate, renovate, repair, replace, restore, return, revive

reiterate, *v.* SYN.-cite, copy, duplicate, iterate, quote, recapitulate, recite, relate, repeat, reproduce.

reject, *v.* SYN.-decline, deny, discard, eliminate, exclude, rebuff, refuse, repudiate, spurn. ANT.-accept, grant, welcome.

rejection, *n.* SYN.-challenge, disagreement, dissent, dissentience, noncompliance, nonconformity, objection, protest, remonstrance, variance. ANT.-acceptance, agreement, assent, compliance.

relate, *v* SYN.-describe, narrate, recite, recount, rehearse, repeat, report, tell; ally, associate, connect, correlate, link, pertain, refer.

relation, *n.* SYN.-alliance, association, coalition, combination, compact, confederacy, connection, covenant, dependence, entente, federation, league, marriage, part-

nership, treaty, union. ANT.-divorce, schism, separation.

relationship, *n.* SYN.-affinity, alliance, association, bond, conjunction, connection, link, tie, union. ANT.-disunion, isolation, separation.

relatives, *n.* SYN.-clan, blood, family, kin, kindred, kinsfolk, people, race, relations, tribe. ANT.-disconnection, foreigners, strangers.

relaxed, *a.* SYN.-casual, cozy, gratifying, informal, nonchalant, offhand, pleasing, restful, unconcerned, unpremeditated. ANT. formal, planned, pretentious.

release, *v.* SYN.-deliver, discharge, emancipate, fire, free, lay off, let go, liberate, loose, set free, terminate, unloose, unfetter, untie. ANT.-confine, imprison, oppress, restrict, subjugate.

relent, *v.* SYN.-abdicate, accede, acquiesce, capitulate, cede, quit, relinquish, resign, submit, succumb, surrender, waive, yield. ANT.-assert, resist, strive, struggle.

relevant, *a.* SYN.-applicable, apposite, appropriate, apropos, apt, fit, germane, material, pertinent, related, relating, to the point. ANT.-alien, extraneous, foreign, unrelated.

reliable, *a.* SYN.-certain, dependable, safe, secure, sure, tried, trustworthy, trusty. ANT.-dubious, fallible, questionable, uncertain, unreliable.

reliance, *n.* SYN.-belief, confidence, constancy, conviction, credence, dependence, faith, fidelity, hope, loyalty, trust. ANT.-doubt, incredulity, mistrust, skepticism; infidelity.

relief, *n.* SYN.-aid, assistance, back

ing, furtherance, help, succor, support. ANT.-antagonism, counteraction, defiance, hostility, resistance.

relieve, v. SYN.-abate, allay, alleviate, assuage, comfort, diminish, ease, extenuate, lighten, mitigate, soften, solace, soothe. ANT.-aggravate, agitate, augment, increase, irritate.

religion, n. SYN.-belief, creed, doctrine, dogma, faith, persuasion, tenet; constancy, fidelity, loyalty. ANT.-doubt, incredulity, mistrust, skepticism; infidelity.

religious, a. SYN.-devout, divine, godly, holy, pietistic, pious, reverent, sacred, sanctimonious, spiritual, theological. ANT.-atheistic, impious, profane, secular, skeptical.

religiousness, n. SYN.-ardor, consecration, dedication, devotion, devoutness, fidelity, loyalty, piety, zeal. ANT.-alienation, apathy, aversion, indifference, unfaithfulness.

relinquish, v. SYN.-abandon, acquiesce, capitulate, cede, renounce, resign, sacrifice, submit, surrender, yield. ANT.-conquer, overcome, resist, rout.

relish, v. SYN.-anticipate, appreciate, enjoy, fancy, like, prefer.

reluctance, n. SYN.-abhorrence, antipathy, aversion, disinclination, distaste, dread, hatred, loathing, repugnance, repulsion. ANT.-affection, attachment, devotion, enthusiasm.

reluctant, a. SYN.-averse, disinclined, hesitant, loath, slow, unwilling. ANT.-disposed, eager, inclined, ready, willing.

remain, v. SYN.-abide, continue, dwell, endure, halt, last, rest, stay, survive, tarry, wait. ANT.-depart,

go, leave; dissipate, finish, terminate.

remains, n. SYN.-balance, relics, remainder, residue, rest, surplus.

remark, n. SYN.-annotation, assertion, comment, declaration, observation, statement, utterance.

remark, v. SYN.-aver, comment, express, mention, note, observe, state, utter. ANT.-disregard, ignore.

remarkable, a. SYN.-arresting, commanding, exciting, imposing, impressive, majestic, moving, overpowering, splendid, stirring, striking, thrilling, touching. ANT.-commonplace, ordinary, regular, unimpressive.

remedy, n. SYN.-antidote, cure, help, medicant, restorative; redress, relief, reparation.

remedy, v. SYN.-ameliorate, better, correct, cure, fix, heal, improve, mend, patch, rectify, refit, reform, repair, restore. ANT.-deface, destroy, hurt, injure, rend.

remember, v SYN.-mind, recall, recollect, remind, reminisce. ANT.-disregard, forget, ignore, overlook.

remembrance, n. SYN.-commemoration, memento, memorial, monument, recollection, reminiscence, souvenir, token.

remonstrate, v. SYN.-complain, grouch, grumble, lament, murmur, protest, regret, repine, whine. ANT.-applaud, approve, praise, rejoice.

remorse, n. SYN.-contrition, grief, penitence, regret, repentance, self-reproach, sorrow. ANT.-impenitence, obduracy, self-satisfaction.

remote, a. SYN.-distant, far, faraway, removed; aloof, cold, reserved, stiff, unfriendly. ANT.-close, near, nigh; cordial, friendly.

remove, v. SYN.-dislodge, displace,

move, shift, transfer, transport; discharge, dismiss, eject, oust, vacate; extract, withdraw. ANT.-leave, remain, stay; retain.

renounce, v. SYN.-abandon, deny, disavow, disclaim, disown, forego, forsake, quit, reject, relinquish, resign, retract, revoke, sacrifice. ANT.-acknowledge, assert, defend, maintain, recognize, uphold.

renovate, v. SYN.-rebuild, reconstruct, reestablish, refresh, rehabilitate, renew, repair, restore.

renown, n. SYN.-acclaim, distinction, eminence, fame, honor, luster, notability, reputation. ANT.-disgrace, disrepute, obscurity.

renowned, a. SYN.-celebrated, distinguished, eminent, famous, glorious, illustrious, noted, well-known. ANT.-hidden, ignominious, infamous, obscure, unknown.

repair, v. SYN.-amend, correct, darn, fix, mend, patch, refit, redress, remedy, renew, renovate, restore, retrieve, tinker. ANT.-break, destroy, harm.

repay, v. SYN.-avenge, compensate, indemnify, pay, recompense, refund, reimburse, retaliate, settle.

repeal, v. SYN.-abolish, abrogate, annul, cancel, eliminate, expunge, invalidate, nullify, obliterate, quash, rescind, revoke. ANT.-confirm, enact, enforce, perpetuate

repeat, v SYN.-cite, copy, duplicate, iterate, quote, recapitulate, recite, rehearse, reiterate, relate, reproduce.

repentance, n. SYN.-contrition, grief, penitence, regret, remorse, self-reproach, sorrow. ANT.-impenitence, obduracy, self-satisfaction.

repentant, a. SYN.-contrite, penitent, regretful, remorseful, sorrow-

ful, sorry. ANT.-obdurate, remorseless.

repine, v. SYN.-complain, grouch, grumble, lament, murmur, protest, regret, remonstrate, whine. ANT.-applaud, approve, praise, rejoice.

replace, v. SYN.-displace, reinstate, restore, return, substitute, supplant.

replica, n. SYN.-copy, duplicate, exemplar, facsimile, imitation, Photostat, reproduction, transcript. ANT.-original, prototype.

reply, n. SYN.-answer, defense, rebuttal, rejoinder, response, retort. ANT.-inquiry, questioning, summoning; argument.

reply, v. SYN.-answer, react, rebut, rejoin, respond. ANT.-disregard, ignore, overlook.

report, v. SYN.-advertise, announce, declare, give out, herald, make known, notify, proclaim, promulgate, publish. ANT.-bury, conceal, stifle, suppress, withhold.

repose, n. SYN.-calm, calmness, hush, peace, quiescence, quiet, quietude, rest, serenity, silence, stillness, tranquility. ANT.-agitation, disturbance, excitement, noise, tumult.

represent, v. SYN.-depict, describe, draw, paint, picture, portray, sketch. ANT.-caricature, misrepresent, suggest.

representation, n. SYN.-drawing, effigy, engraving, etching, illustration, image, landscape, likeness, painting, panorama, photograph, picture, portrait, portrayal, print, rendering, resemblance, scene, sketch, view.

representative, n. SYN.-agent, ambassador, delegate, deputy, emissary, envoy, legislator, proxy.

repress, v. SYN.-bridle, check, constrain, curb, hinder, hold back, inhibit, limit, restrain, stop, suppress. ANT.-aid, encourage, incite, loosen.

reprimand, v. SYN.-admonish, berate, blame, censure, lecture, rate, rebuke, reprehend, scold, upbraid, vituperate. ANT.-approve, commend, praise.

reproduction, n. SYN.-copy, duplicate, exemplar, facsimile, imitation, Photostat, replica, transcript. ANT.-original, prototype.

repugnance, n. SYN.-abhorrence, antipathy, aversion, disgust, disinclination, dislike, distaste, dread, hatred, loathing, repulsion, reluctance. ANT.-affection, attachment, devotion, enthusiasm.

repulsive, a. SYN.-deformed, despicable, disgusting, hideous, homely, horrid, nauseating, offensive, plain, repellent, repugnant, revolting, ugly, uncomely, vile. ANT.-attractive, beautiful, fair, handsome, pretty.

reputation, n. SYN.-character, description, estimation, individuality, kind, nature, repute, sort, standing.

repute, n. SYN.-character, class, disposition, esteem, estimation, fame, honor, name, nature, reputation, sort, standing.

request, v SYN.-appeal, ask, beg, beseech, desire, entreat, implore, importune, petition, pray, seek, sue, supplicate. ANT.-demand, require.

require, v SYN.-ask, claim, command, demand, exact, lack, necessitate, need, order, prescribe, want.

requisite, a. SYN.-basic, essential, fundamental, important, indispen-

sable, intrinsic, necessary, needed, vital. ANT.-expendable, extrinsic, optional, peripheral.

rescind, v. SYN.-abolish, abrogate, annul, cancel, delete, eliminate, expunge, invalidate, nullify, quash, repeal, revoke. ANT.-confirm, enact, enforce, perpetuate

rescue, v. SYN.-deliver, free, liberate, recover, retrieve, save,

research, n. SYN.-exploration, interrogation, inquiry, investigation, query, quest, question, scrutiny. ANT.-disregard, inactivity, inattention, negligence.

resemblance, n. SYN.-analogy, correspondence, likeness, parity, similarity, similitude. ANT.-difference, distinction, variance.

reserve, n. SYN.-accumulation, fund, hoard, provision, stock, store, supply.

reserved, a. SYN.-aloof, cautious, cold, demure, diffident, distant, modest, remote, reserved, retiring, stiff, unfriendly. ANT.-audacious, close, cordial, friendly.

residence, n. SYN.-abode, base, castle, domicile, dwelling, estate, habitat, hearth, home, house, hovel, manor, palace, quarters, seat, shack.

resign, v. SYN.-abandon, depart, discontinue, give up, leave, quit, relinquish, stop, surrender, withdraw. ANT.-continue, endure, occupy, persist, stay.

resignation, n. SYN.-composure, endurance, forbearance, fortitude, long-suffering, patience, perseverance. ANT.-impatience, nervousness, restlessness, unquiet.

resigned, a. SYN.-composed, forbearing, indulgent, long-suffering, passive, patient, stoical, uncomplaining. ANT.-chafing, clamorous, high-strung, hysterical, turbulent.

resist, v. SYN.-attack, confront, defy, hinder, impede, obstruct, oppose, repel, repulse, thwart, withstand. ANT.-accede, allow, cooperate, relent, yield.

resolution, n. SYN.-courage, decision, determination, firmness, fortitude, persistence, resolve, steadfastness. ANT.-inconstancy, indecision, vacillation.

resolve, n. See **resolution.**

resolve, v. SYN.-adjudicate, conclude, decide, determine, end, fix, settle, terminate. ANT.-doubt, hesitate, suspend, vacillate, waver.

respect, v. SYN.-admire, consider, heed, honor, regard, revere, reverence, value, venerate. ANT.-abuse, despise, disdain, neglect, scorn.

respectable, a. SYN.-adequate, befitting, decent, decorous, fit, fitting, proper, seemly, suitable, tolerable. ANT.-coarse, gross, indecent, reprehensible, vulgar.

respond, v. SYN.-answer, react, rejoin, reply. ANT.-disregard, ignore, overlook.

response, n. SYN.-answer, defense, rebuttal, rejoinder, reply, retort. ANT.-inquiry, questioning, summoning; argument.

responsibility, n. SYN.-accountability, amenability, burden, capability, duty, liability, obligation, reliability, trust, trustworthiness.

responsible, a. SYN.-accountable, amenable, answerable, bound, capable, dependable, liable, obligated, reliable, stable, trusty, trustworthy. ANT.-exempt, free, immune; careless, negligent.

rest, n. SYN.-calm, ease, leisure, peace, quiet, relaxation, repose, sleep, slumber, tranquility; cessation, intermission, pause, respite; balance, remainder, remains, residue, surplus. ANT.-agitation, commotion, disturbance, motion, tumult.

restless, a. SYN.-active, agitated, disquieted, disturbed, irresolute, roving, sleepless, transient, uneasy, unquiet, wandering. ANT.-at ease, peaceable, quiet, tractable.

restore, v. SYN.-cure, heal, rebuild, reconstruct, recover, reestablish, refresh, rehabilitate, reinstate, rejuvenate, renew, renovate, repair, replace, return, revive.

restrain, v. SYN.-bridle, check, constrain, curb, hinder, hold back, inhibit, limit, repress, stop, suppress. ANT.-aid, encourage, incite, loosen.

restraint, n. SYN.-control, discipline, order, regulation, self-control; correction, punishment. ANT.-chaos, confusion, turbulence.

restrict, v. SYN.-circumscribe, confine, contain, control, hamper, impede, inhibit, limit, regulate, restrain, suppress, tether.

result, n. SYN.-conclusion, consequence, determination, effect, end, eventuality, issue, resolution, resolve.

retain, v. SYN.-hold, keep, maintain, preserve, save.

retaliation, n. SYN.-reprisal, requital, retribution, revenge, vengeance, vindictiveness. ANT.-mercy, pardon, reconciliation, remission, forgiveness.

retard, v. SYN.-arrest, delay, detain, hamper, hinder, impede, slow, stay. ANT.-expedite, hasten, precipitate, quicken.

retort, *n.* SYN.-answer, defense, rebuttal, rejoinder, reply, response. ANT.-inquiry, questioning, summoning; argument.

retribution, *n.* SYN.-punishment, reparation, reprisal, retaliation, reward, revenge. ANT.-mercy, pardon, forgiveness.

return, *v.* SYN.-go back, recur, retreat, revert; repay, replace, requite, restore. ANT.-appropriate, keep, retain, take.

reveal, *v.* SYN.-betray, disclose, discover, divulge, expose, impart, show, uncover. ANT.-cloak, conceal, cover, hide, obscure.

revelation, *n.* SYN.-apparition, dream, ghost, hallucination, mirage, phantasm, phantom, prophecy, specter, vision. ANT.-reality, substance, verity.

revenge, *n.* SYN.-reparation, reprisal, requital, retaliation, retribution, vengeance, vindictiveness. ANT.-mercy, pardon, reconciliation, remission, forgiveness.

revenge, *v.* SYN.-avenge, requite, retaliate, vindicate. ANT.-forgive, pardon, pity, reconcile.

revere, *v.* SYN.-adore, esteem, honor, venerate, worship. ANT.-despise, hate, ignore.

reverence, *n.* SYN.-adoration, deference, dignity, esteem, homage, honor, praise, respect, worship. ANT.-contempt, derision, disgrace, dishonor, reproach.

reverse, *v.* SYN.-annul, countermand, invert, overthrow, overturn, repeal, rescind, revoke, subvert, transpose, turn about, unmake, upset. ANT.-affirm, confirm, endorse, maintain, stabilize, vouch.

revert, *v.* SYN.-go back, repay, replace, restore, retreat, return. ANT.-keep, retain.

review, *n.* SYN.-commentary, criticism, critique, examination, inspection, reconsideration, retrospect, retrospection, revision, survey, synopsis; digest, journal, periodical.

review, *v.* SYN.-analyze, consider, criticize, discuss, edit, examine, inspect, reconsider, revise, survey. ANT.-ignore, reject.

revision, *n.* SYN.-amendment, change, correction, remedy.

revoke, *v.* SYN.-abolish, abrogate, annul, cancel, delete, eliminate, erase, expunge, invalidate, nullify, obliterate, quash, repeal, rescind. ANT.-confirm, enact, enforce, perpetuate

revolting, *a.* SYN.-abominable, detestable, execrable, foul, hateful, loathsome, odious, vile. ANT.-agreeable, commendable, delightful, pleasant.

revolution, *n.* SYN.-coup, insurrection, mutiny, overthrow, rebellion, revolt, uprising.

revolve, *v.* SYN.-circle, gyrate, rotate, spin, turn, twirl, wheel, whirl. ANT.-proceed, stop, stray, travel, wander.

reward, *n.* SYN.-award, bonus, bounty, compensation, premium, prize, recompense, remuneration, requital. ANT.-assessment, charge, earnings, punishment, wages.

rich, *a.* SYN.-abundant, affluent, ample, bountiful, copious, costly, exorbitant, luxurious, opulent, plentiful, prosperous, sumptuous, wealthy, well-to-do; fecund, fertile, fruitful, luxuriant, prolific. ANT.-beggarly, destitute, indigent, needy, poor; barren, sterile, unfruitful, unproductive.

riddle, n. SYN.-conundrum, enigma, mystery, problem, puzzle. ANT.-answer, clue, key, resolution, solution.

ridicule, n. SYN.-banter, derision, gibe, irony, jeering, mockery, raillery, sarcasm, satire, sneering.

right, a. SYN.-accurate, appropriate, correct, direct, erect, ethical, fair, fit, just, lawful, legitimate, proper, real, seemly, straight, suitable, true, upright. ANT.-bad, false, improper, wrong.

right, n. SYN.-authority, grant, liberty, license, prerogative, privilege; equity, honor, justice, propriety, virtue. ANT.-encroachment, injustice, violation, wrong.

righteous, a. SYN.-chaste, decent, ethical, good, honorable, just, moral, pure, right, scrupulous, virtuous. ANT.-amoral, libertine, licentious, sinful, unethical.

rigid, a. SYN.-austere, harsh, inflexible, rigorous, severe, stern, stiff, strict, stringent, unbending, unyielding. ANT.-compassionate, lax, lenient, mild, yielding; elastic, flexible, resilient, supple.

rigorous, a. SYN.-arduous, burdensome, cruel, difficult, hard, harsh, jarring, onerous, rough, rugged, severe, stern, strict, stringent, tough, unfeeling. ANT.-easy, effortless, facile; simple; gentle, lenient, tender.

rim, n. SYN.-border, boundary, brim, brink, edge, fringe, frontier, limit, margin, outskirts, termination, verge. ANT.-center, core, interior, mainland.

ring, v. SYN.-circle, confine, encircle, encompass, loop, surround; chime, clap, clang, peal, resound, strike, toll.

rinse, v. SYN.-bathe, clean, dip, soak, wash.

rip, v. SYN.-disunite, lacerate, rend, rive, sever, split, sunder, tear. ANT.-join, mend, repair, sew, unite.

ripe, a. SYN.-aged, complete, consummate, finished, full-grown, mature, matured, mellow, ready, seasonable. ANT.-crude, green, immature, raw, undeveloped.

rise, v. SYN.-adduce, advance, climb, elevate, further, improve, mount, proceed, progress, promote, scale, soar, thrive. ANT.-descend, fall, hinder, retard, retreat, sink.

risk, n. SYN.-danger, hazard, jeopardy, peril. ANT.-defense, immunity, protection, safety.

risk, v. SYN.-endanger, expose, hazard, jeopardize, peril; speculate, venture. ANT.-insure, protect, secure.

risky, a. SYN.-critical, dangerous, hazardous, insecure, menacing, ominous, perilous, precarious, threatening, unsafe. ANT.-firm, protected, safe, secure.

rite, n. SYN.-act, ceremony, custom, formality, liturgy, practice, protocol, ritual, system.

ritual, n. SYN.-ceremony, form, formality, observance, parade, pomp, protocol, rite, solemnity.

rival, n. SYN.-adversary, antagonist, competitor, contestant, enemy, foe, opponent. ANT.-ally, comrade, confederate, teammate.

rivalry, n. SYN.-adversary, antagonist, competition, contention, dispute, opposition, struggle.

road, n. SYN.-boulevard, drive, highway, parkway, roadway, street, thoroughfare, turnpike.

roam, v. SYN.-drift, meander, ramble, range, rove, stray, wander.

ANT.-halt, linger, settle, stay, stop.
rob, v. SYN.-burglarize, cheat, defraud, despoil, fleece, loot, pilfer, pillage, plunder, sack, steal, strip.
robber, n. SYN.-burglar, cheat, pirate, plunderer, raider, swindler, thief, thug.
robbery, n. SYN.-burglary, depredation, larceny, pillage, plunder, theft.
robust, a. SYN.-hale, healthy, hearty, sound, strong, well. ANT.-delicate, diseased, frail, infirm.
rock, n. SYN.-boulder, gravel, jewel, pebble, stone.
rogue, n. SYN.-cheat, criminal, knave, outlaw, rascal, scamp, scoundrel.
role, n. SYN.-character, function, lines, impersonation, part, performance.
romantic, a. SYN.-dreamy, extravagant, fanciful, fantastic, fictitious, ideal, idealistic, imaginative, maudlin, mawkish, picturesque, poetic, sentimental. ANT.-factual, literal, matter-of-fact, practical, prosaic.
room, n. SYN.-abode, apartment, chamber, cubicle, dormitory, flat, garret, hotel, inn, motel, niche, office; latitude, leeway, scope, space, vastness.
roomy, a. SYN.-ample, broad, capacious, extensive, large, spacious, vast, wide. ANT.-confined, cramped, limited, narrow.
root, n. SYN.-ancestor, base, basis, bottom, foundation, ground, groundwork, substructure, support, underpinning.
roster, n. SYN.-catalogue, document, index, list, register, roll, scroll.
rot, v. SYN.-decay, decompose, disintegrate, putrefy, spoil, waste. ANT.-

flourish, grow, increase, luxuriate, rise.
rotten, a. SYN.-bad, decayed, defective, depraved, disgusting, filthy, offensive, putrid, putrefied, rancid, rank, spoiled,
rotate, v. SYN.-circle, circulate. invert, revolve, spin, turn, twirl, twist, wheel, whirl. ANT.-arrest, fix, stand, stop.
rotund, a. SYN.-bulbous, chubby, plump, round.
rough, a. SYN.-blunt, brusque, churlish, coarse, craggy, crude, cursory, gruff, harsh, imperfect, incomplete, irregular, jagged, rude, rugged, scabrous, scratchy, severe, stormy, tempestuous, turbulent, uncivil, uneven, unfinished, unpolished, violent; approximate, imprecise, inexact. ANT.-calm, civil, courteous, even, fine, finished, gentle, level, mild, placid, polished, refined sleek, slippery, smooth, tranquil, unruffled.
round, a, SYN.-bulbous, chubby, circular, complete, curved, cylindrical, entire, globular, plump, rotund, spherical.
roundabout, a. SYN.-circuitous, crooked, cunning, devious, distorted, indirect, tortuous, tricky, wandering, winding. ANT.-direct, honest, straight, straightforward.
rouse, v. SYN.-anger, aggravate, annoy, animate, awaken, excite, incite, irk, provoke, startle, stimulate, urge.
rout, v. SYN.-beat, conquer, crush, defeat, humble, master, overcome, quell, subdue, subjugate, surmount, vanquish. ANT.-capitulate, cede, lose, retreat, surrender.
route, n. SYN.-avenue, channel, course, passage, path, road, street,

thoroughfare, track, trail, walk, way.

routine, *n.* SYN.-act, custom, fashion, habit, norm, practice, procedure, system, usage, use, wont.

rove, *v.* SYN.-explore, meander, range, roam, wander.

rowdy, *n.* SYN.-bully, rascal, ruffian, thug.

royal, *a.* SYN.-courtly, dignified, grand, imperial, kingly, lordly, majestic, monarchal, noble, princely, regal, ruling, sovereign, stately, supreme. ANT.-common, humble, low, plebeian, proletarian, servile, vulgar.

rub, *v.* SYN.-brush, burnish, chafe, clean, massage, polish, scour, scrub, shine.

rude, *a.* SYN.-blunt, boorish, coarse, crude, discourteous, fierce, gruff, harsh, ignorant, illiterate, impolite, impudent, inclement, insolent, primitive, raw, rough, saucy, savage, surly, tumultuous, uncivil, unpolished, untaught, violent, vulgar. ANT.-calm, civil, courtly, dignified, genteel, mild, noble, peaceful, polished, stately.

ruffle, *v.* SYN.-agitate, anger, annoy, bother, disturb, fret, harass, irritate, rumple, torment, tousle, upset.

rugged, *a.* SYN.-craggy, harsh, irregular, jagged, rough, scabrous, severe, stormy, tempestuous, turbulent, uneven, violent. ANT.-even, fine, finished, level, polished, refined, sleek, slippery, smooth.

ruin, *v.* SYN.-annihilate, bankrupt, demolish, destroy. devastate, drain, fleece, obliterate, ravage, raze, sabotage, vandalize, wreck. ANT.-construct, establish, make, preserve, save.

ruinous, *a.* SYN.-baneful, deadly, deleterious, destructive, detrimental, devastating, fatal, injurious, noxious, pernicious. ANT.-beneficial, constructive, creative, profitable, salutary.

rule, *n.* SYN.-axiom, canon, formula, guide, law, maxim, method, order, precept, principle, propriety, regulation, standard, statute, system; authority, control, direction, dominion, government, jurisdiction, mastery, reign, sovereignty, sway. ANT.-chance, deviation, exception, hazard, irregularity; anarchy, chaos, misrule.

rule, *v.* SYN.-command, control, direct, dominate, govern, manage, regulate, superintend. ANT.-abandon, follow, forsake, ignore, submit.

rumor, *n.* SYN.-chatter, fabrication, gossip, hearsay, news, scandal, slander.

run, *v.* SYN.-bound, dart, dash, escape, go, hurry, jog, move, race, rush, scramble, scurry, sprint, trot.

rupture, *v.* SYN.-break, burst, crack, crush, demolish, destroy, fracture, rack, rend, shatter, smash. ANT.-join, mend, renovate, repair, restore.

rural, *a.* SYN.-agrarian, agricultural, bucolic, pastoral, rustic, suburban.

ruse, *n.* SYN.-artifice, deception, device, fraud, guile, hoax, imposture, ploy, stratagem, stunt, subterfuge, trick, wile. ANT.-candor, exposure, honesty, openness, sincerity.

rush, *v.* SYN.-accelerate, expedite, hasten, hurry, precipitate, quicken, speed. ANT.-delay, detain, hinder, retard, tarry.

rustic, *a.* SYN.-boorish, bucolic, coarse, country, homely, pastoral, plain, rural, simple, uncouth, unsophisticated. ANT.-cultured, elegant, polished, refined, urbane.

ruthless, *a.* SYN.-barbarous, bestial, brutal, brute, brutish, carnal, coarse, cruel, ferocious, fierce, gross, inhuman, merciless, remorseless, rough, rude, savage, sensual. ANT-civilized, courteous, gentle, humane, kind.

S

sabotage, *v.* SYN.-attack, damage, destroy, subvert, undermine, vandalize.

sacrament, *n.* SYN.-association, ceremony, communion, covenant, fellowship, intercourse, observance, participation, pledge, rite, union. ANT.-alienation, non participation.

sacred, *a.* SYN.-blessed, consecrated, devout, divine, hallowed, holy, pious, religious, saintly, scriptural, spiritual. ANT.-evil, profane, sacrilegious, secular, worldly.

sacrifice, *n.* SYN.-atonement, forfeiture, offering, penance, reparation, tribute.

sacrifice, *v.* SYN.-forfeit, forgo, relinquish, renounce, surrender.

sad, *a.* SYN.-cheerless, dejected, depressed, despondent, disconsolate, dismal, doleful, downcast, gloomy, lugubrious, melancholy, mournful, somber, sorrowful. ANT.-cheerful, glad, happy, joyous, merry.

sadness, *n.* SYN.-blues, dejection, depression, despondency, gloom, grief, melancholy, sorrow,

safe, *a.* SYN.-certain, dependable, harmless, protected, reliable, secure, snug, trustworthy. ANT.-dangerous, hazardous, insecure, peril-

ous, unsafe.

safeguard, *n.* SYN.-bulwark, defense, guard, protection, refuge, security, shelter, shield.

safety, *n.* SYN.-asylum, protection, refuge, sanctuary, security, shelter.

sagacity, *n.* SYN.-discretion, erudition, foresight, information, insight, intelligence, judgment, knowledge, learning, prudence, reason, sageness, sense, wisdom. ANT.-foolishness, ignorance, imprudence, nonsense, stupidity.

sage, *n.* SYN.-disciple, intellectual, learner, philosopher, pupil, savant, scholar, student. ANT. dolt, dunce, fool, idiot, ignoramus.

saint, *n.* SYN.-altruist, believer, example, ideal, martyr, paragon.

salary, *n.* SYN.-compensation, earnings, fee, pay, payment, recompense, stipend, wages. ANT.-gift, gratuity, present.

sale, *n.* SYN.-barter, commerce, deal, marketing, selling, trade, transaction,

salient, *a.* SYN.-clear, conspicuous, distinguished, manifest, noticeable, obvious, projecting, prominent, protruding, striking, visible. ANT.-common, hidden, inconspicuous, obscure.

salutary, *a.* SYN.-advantageous, beneficial, good, helpful, profitable, serviceable, useful, wholesome. ANT.-deleterious, destructive, detrimental, harmful, injurious.

salve, *n.* SYN.-balm, cream, emollient, lubricant, ointment, unguent.

same, *a.* SYN.-coincident, equal, equivalent, identical, indistinguishable, like, similar. ANT.-contrary, disparate, dissimilar, distinct, opposed.

sample, *n.* SYN.-case, example, illustration, instance, model, pattern, prototype, specimen.

sanction, *n.* SYN.-approbation, approval, assent, commendation, consent, endorsement, praise, support. ANT.-censure, reprimand, reproach, stricture.

sanction, *v.* SYN.-allow, authorize, give, grant, let, permit, suffer, tolerate, yield. ANT.-forbid, object, protest, refuse, resist.

sanctuary, *n.* SYN.-asylum, church, cover, harbor, haven, protection, refuge, retreat, safety, security, shelter, shrine, temple. ANT.-danger, exposure, hazard, jeopardy, peril.

sane, *a.* SYN.-intelligent, logical, lucid, normal, rational, reasonable, sensible, sound.

sarcasm, *n.* SYN.-asperity, banter, bitterness, contempt, derision, irony, lampooning, mockery, ridicule, satire,

sarcastic, *a.* SYN.-acrimonious, biting, caustic, cutting, derisive, ironic, sardonic, satirical, sneering, taunting. ANT.-affable, agreeable, amiable, pleasant.

sardonic, *a.* SYN.-acrimonious, bitter, caustic, cruel, fierce, harsh, relentless, ruthless, severe. ANT.-delicious, mellow, pleasant, sweet.

satiate, *v.* SYN.-accomplish, cloy, deluge, fulfill, glut, gratify, inundate, meet, oversupply, satisfy.

satire, *n.* SYN.-banter, cleverness, fun, humor, irony, mockery, ridicule, sarcasm, wit, witticism. ANT.-commonplace, platitude, sobriety, solemnity, stupidity.

satirical, *a.* SYN.-acrimonious, biting, caustic, cutting, derisive, ironic, sarcastic, sardonic, sneering, taunting. ANT.-affable, agree-

able, amiable, pleasant.

satisfactory, *a.* SYN.-adequate, ample, commensurate, enough, fitting, sufficient, suitable. ANT.-deficient, lacking, scant.

satisfy, *v.* SYN.-appease, compensate, content, fulfill, gratify, please, remunerate, satiate, suffice. ANT.-annoy, displease, dissatisfy, frustrate, tantalize.

saturate, *v.* SYN.-fill, impregnate, overfill, penetrate, permeate, pervade, soak.

sauciness, *n.* SYN.-audacity, boldness, effrontery, impertinence, impudence, insolence, presumption, rudeness. ANT.-diffidence, politeness, subserviency, truckling.

savage, *a.* SYN.-barbarous, bestial, brutal, brute, brutish, carnal, coarse, cruel, ferocious, gross, inhuman, merciless, remorseless, rough, rude, ruthless, sensual. ANT-civilized, courteous, gentle, humane, kind.

save, *v.* SYN.-conserve, defend, guard, keep, maintain, preserve, protect, rescue, safeguard, secure, spare, uphold. ANT.-abandon, abolish, destroy, impair, injure.

savings, *n.* SYN.-accumulation, assets, cache, hoard, investment, property, reserve, resources, security.

savor, *v.* SYN.-appreciate, enjoy, like, relish, sample, sip, taste.

savory, *a.* SYN.-appetizing, aromatic, agreeable, delectable, delicious, delightful, luscious, hearty, palatable, tasty. ANT.-acrid, distasteful, nauseous, unpalatable, unsavory

say, *v.* SYN.-articulate, converse, declare, discourse, express, harangue, speak, talk, tell, utter. ANT.-be silent, hush, refrain.

saying, *n.* SYN.-adage, aphorism, apothegm, byword, maxim, motto, proverb, saw.

scamper, *v.* SYN.-dash, hasten, hurry, run, speed, sprint.

scan, *v.* SYN.-browse, consider, examine, inspect, peruse, scrutinize, skim, study, survey.

scandal, *n.* SYN.-abasement, chagrin, disgrace, dishonor, disrepute, humiliation, ignominy, mortification, odium, opprobrium, shame. ANT.-dignity, glory, honor, praise, renown.

scandalize, *v.* SYN.-abuse, asperse, defame, disparage, ill-use, malign, revile, traduce, vilify. ANT.-cherish, honor, praise, protect, respect.

scandalous, *a.* SYN.-abusive, damning, discreditable, disgraceful, dishonorable, disreputable, false, ignominious, infamous, gossiping, libelous, malicious, outrageous, shameful, slanderous, sordid. ANT. teemed, honorable, renowned, respectable.

scanty, *a.* SYN.-inadequate, insufficient, lean, little, meager, paltry, scarce, sparse.

scar, *n.* SYN.-blemish, defect, disfigurement, flaw, mark.

scarce, *a.* SYN.-choice, exceptional, incomparable, infrequent, occasional, precious, rare, singular, uncommon, unique, unusual. ANT.-abundant, commonplace, customary, frequent, numerous, ordinary, usual, worthless.

scare, *v.* SYN.-affright, alarm, appall, daunt, dismay, frighten, horrify, intimidate, startle, terrify, terrorize. ANT.-allay, compose, embolden, reassure, soothe.

scared, *a.* SYN.-afraid, apprehensive, fainthearted, fearful, frightened,

terrified, timid, timorous. ANT.-assured, bold, composed, courageous, sanguine.

scatter, *v.* SYN.-broadcast, diffuse, dispel, disperse, disseminate, dissipate, separate, sprinkle, strew, throw. ANT.-accumulate, amass, assemble, collect, gather.

scenery, *n.* SYN.-countryside, landscape, panorama, spectacle, view, vista.

scenic, *a.* SYN.-beautiful, breathtaking, dramatic, picturesque, pretty, spectacular, unspoiled.

scent, n, SYN.-aroma, fetidness, fragrance, fume, incense, odor, perfume, redolence, smell, stench, stink.

schedule, *n.* SYN.-agenda, calendar, catalogue, inventory, plan, program, record, register, roll, timetable.

scheme, *v.* SYN.-contrive, design, devise, outline, plan, plot, prepare, project, sketch.

scheme, *n.* SYN.-arrangement, artfulness, cabal, conspiracy, contrivance, cunning, design, diagram, intrigue, machination, outline, pattern, plan, planning, plotting, program, project, sketch, stratagem, system. ANT.-candor, result, sincerity.

scheming, *a.* SYN.-crafty, crooked, deceitful, devious, dishonest, foxy, perverse, planning, plotting, sly, treacherous, underhanded, unfaithful.

scholar, *n.* SYN.-disciple, intellectual, learner, pupil, sage, savant, student. ANT. dolt, dunce, fool, idiot, ignoramus.

scholarly, *a.* SYN.-academic, bookish, erudite, formal, learned, pedantic, scholastic, theoretical. ANT.-

common-sense, ignorant, practical, simple.

scholarship, n. SYN.-cognizance, comprehension, erudition, information, knowledge, learning, lore, understanding, wisdom. ANT.-ignorance, illiteracy, misunderstanding, stupidity.

school, n. SYN.-academy, conservatory, institution.

science, n. SYN.-discipline, enlightenment, knowledge, learning, scholarship. ANT.-ignorance, nascence, superstition.

scold, v. SYN.-admonish, berate, blame, censure, chide, lecture, rate, rebuke, reprehend, reprimand, upbraid, vituperate. ANT.-approve, commend, praise.

scoot, v. SYN.-bustle, dart, hasten, hurry, rush, speed.

scope, n. SYN.-amount, area, compass, degree, expanse, extent, length, magnitude, measure, range, reach, size, stretch.

scorch, v. SYN.-blister, burn, char, scald, sear, singe. ANT.-extinguish, put out, quench.

scorn, n. SYN.-contempt, contumely, derision, detestation, disdain, hatred, loathing. ANT.-awe, esteem, regard, respect, reverence.

scoundrel, n. SYN.-blackguard, cad, knave, rascal, rogue, scamp, villain.

scrap, v. SYN.-discard, dismiss, eliminate, exclude, reject; bicker, clash, conflict, fight, feud, quarrel, squabble.

scream, v. SYN.-cry, howl, shout, shriek, yell.

screen, v. SYN.-cloak, conceal, cover, hide, protect, shelter, shield, shroud, veil; choose, eliminate, select, sift.

scrimp, v. SYN.- conserve, curtail, economize, limit, pinch, save, skimp, squeeze, tighten.

scrub, v. SYN.-brush, clean, cleanse, mop, rub, scour, wash. ANT.-dirty, pollute, soil, stain, sully.

scruple, n. SYN.-compunction, doubt, hesitation, misgiving, reluctance, uncertainty, uneasiness.

scrupulous, a. SYN.-accurate, careful, cautious, conscientious, exact, particular, precise, strict.

scrutinize, v. SYN.-analyze, appraise, assess, audit check, contemplate, criticize, dissect, evaluate, examine, inspect, notice, question, review, scan, survey, view, watch. ANT.-approve, disregard, neglect, overlook.

search, n. SYN.-examination, exploration, inquiry, investigation, pursuit, quest. ANT.-abandonment, cession, resignation.

search, v. SYN. examine, explore, ferret, hunt, investigate, look, probe, ransack, rummage, scour, scrutinize, seek.

searching, a. SYN.-curious, inquiring, inquisitive, nosy, peeping, peering, prying, seeking, snoopy. ANT.-incurious, indifferent, unconcerned, uninterested.

seasoned, a. SYN.-experienced, established, mature, practiced, settled, skilled, versed.

secede, v. SYN.-depart, leave, retire, retreat, withdraw.

secluded, a. SYN.-alone, deserted, desolate, isolated, lone, lonely, only, single, sole, solitary, unaided. ANT.-accompanied, attended, surrounded.

seclusion, n. SYN.-isolation, insulation, loneliness, quarantine, retirement, segregation, separation, solitude, withdrawal. ANT.-association, communion, connection, fellowship, union.

secondary, *a.* SYN.-dependent, derived, indirect, inferior, lesser, lower, poorer, subordinate, subsequent, subsidiary. ANT.-better, greater, higher, superior.

secrecy, *n.* SYN.-concealment, confidence, hiding, mystery, privacy, seclusion, stealth, solitude.

secret, *a.* SYN.-clandestine, concealed, covert, hidden, latent, mystical, private, secluded, secretive, shrouded, surreptitious, unknown, veiled. ANT.-conspicuous, disclosed, exposed, known, obvious.

secrete, *v.* SYN.-cloak, conceal, cover, curtain, disguise, envelop, hide, mask, protect, screen, shield, shroud, veil. ANT.-bare, divulge, expose, reveal, unveil.

section, *n.* SYN.-district, division, domain, dominion, land, place, province, quarter, region, territory.

secular, *a.* SYN.-earthly, laic, lay, mundane, profane, temporal, worldly. ANT.-ecclesiastical, religious, spiritual, unworldly.

secure, *a.* SYN.-assured, certain, definite, fixed, indubitable, inevitable, positive, sure, undeniable, unquestionable. ANT.-doubtful, probable, questionable, uncertain.

secure, *v.* SYN.-achieve, acquire, attain, earn, gain, get, obtain, procure, receive. ANT. -forfeit, leave, lose, renounce, surrender.

security, *n.* SYN.-assurance, bail, bond, earnest, guarantee, guaranty, pawn, pledge, surety, token, warrant.

seduce, *v.* SYN.-allure, attract, bait, beguile, deceive, delude, dupe, en-

tice, induce, lure, pervert, stimulate, tempt, trick, violate.

see, *v.* SYN.-behold, contemplate, descry, discern, distinguish, espy, glimpse, inspect, look at, notice, observe, perceive, scan, scrutinize, view, watch, witness.

seek, *v.* SYN.-ask, attempt, endeavor, ferret, hunt, investigate, look, probe, pursue, rummage, scour, scrutinize, search, try.

seem, *v.* SYN.- appear, look, resemble, suggest. ANT.-be, exist.

segment, *n.* SYN.-allotment, apportionment, division, fragment, moiety, part, piece, portion, scrap, section, share. ANT.-entirety, whole.

segregate, *v.* SYN.-detach, divide, insulate, isolate, separate, sever, split.

seize, *v.* SYN.-apprehend, arrest, capture, catch, check, clutch, confiscate, detain, grab, grasp, grip, hinder, hold, interrupt, obstruct, restrain, retain snatch, stop, take, withhold. ANT.-activate, discharge, free, liberate, release.

seldom, *a.* SYN.-hardly, infrequently, occasionally, rarely.

select, *a.* SYN.-best, choice, chosen, cream, elite, exceptional, pick, picked, preferred.

select, *v.* SYN.-choose, cull, elect, opt, pick, prefer, winnow. ANT.-refuse, reject.

selection, *n.* SYN.-alternative, choice, decision, election, option, preference.

selfish, *a.* SYN. egoistic, illiberal, mercenary, narrow, parsimonious, self-centered, self-seeking, stingy, ungenerous. ANT.-altruistic, charitable, liberal, magnanimous.

sell, *v.* SYN.-barter, liquidate, market, merchandise, peddle, trade, vend.

send, *v.* SYN.-cast, discharge, dispatch, emit, impel, propel, ship, throw, transmit. ANT.-bring, get, hold, receive, retain.

senior, *n.* SYN.-ancestor, elder, master, older, patiarch, superior.

seniority, *n.* SYN.-age, dotage, precedence, priority, senescence, senility, senior, rank. ANT.-childhood, infancy, junior, youth.

sensation, *n.* SYN.-apprehension, feeling, image, impression, perception, sense, sensibility. ANT.-apathy, insensibility, stupor, torpor.

sensational, *a.* SYN.-astonishing, breathtaking, dramatic, incredible, moving, spectacular, startling, thrilling.

sense, *n.* SYN.-connotation, drift, explanation, gist, implication, import, intent, interpretation, meaning, purport, purpose, significance, signification.

senseless, *a.* SYN.-brainless, crass, dense, dull, dumb, foolish, obtuse, stupid, witless. ANT.-alert, bright, clever, discerning, intelligent.

sensibility, *n.* SYN.-appreciation, awareness, judgment, perceptiveness, rapport, sensitivity, understanding.

sensible, *v.* SYN.-alive, appreciable, apprehensible, awake, aware, cognizant, comprehending, conscious, perceiving, perceptible, sentient; discreet, intelligent, judicious, practical, prudent, reasonable, sagacious, sage, sober, sound, wise. ANT.-absurd, impalpable, imperceptible, stupid, unaware.

sensitive, *a.* SYN.-delicate, impressionable, nervous, perceptive, prone, responsive, sentient, susceptible, sympathetic, tender, tense, touchy. ANT.-callous, dull, hard, indifferent, insensitive.

sensitivity, *n.* SYN.-awareness, consciousness, sensibility, sympathy.

sensual, *a.* SYN.-carnal, earthy, lascivious, lecherous, lewd, licentious, moving, pleasing, sensory, sensuous, sexual, stimulating, stirring, voluptuous, wanton. ANT.-abstemious, ascetic, chaste, continent, virtuous.

sentence, *n.* SYN.-decree, decision, dictum, edict, judgment, order, pronouncement.

sentence, *v.* SYN.-blame, censure, confine, convict, condemn, damn, denounce, incarcerate, imprison, judge, punish. ANT.-absolve, acquit, exonerate, pardon.

sentient, *a.* SYN.-aware cognizant, conscious, feeling, rational, reasoning, sensitive.

sentiment, *n.* SYN.-affection, emotion, feeling, impression, opinion, passion, sensibility, tenderness. ANT.-coldness, imperturbability, insensibility.

sentimental, *a.* SYN.-dreamy, extravagant, fanciful, ideal, idealistic, imaginative, maudlin, mawkish, picturesque, poetic, romantic. ANT.-factual, literal, matter-of-fact, practical, prosaic.

sentinel, *n.* SYN.-guard, lookout, sentry, scout, watch.

separate, *v.* SYN.-disconnect, divide, isolate, part, sever, split, sunder. ANT.-combine, gather, join unite.

separation, *n.* SYN.-alienation, insulation, isolation, quarantine, seclusion, segregation, solitude, withdrawal. ANT.-association, communion, connection, fellowship, union.

sequel, *n.* SYN.-continuation, epilogue, installment, postscript, supplement.

sequence, *n.* SYN.-arrangement, chain, classification, continuity, distribution, flow, following, gradation, order, placement, progression, series, string, succession, train.

serene, *a.* SYN.-calm, composed, dispassionate, imperturbable, pacific, peaceful, placid, quiet, still, tranquil, undisturbed, unruffled. ANT.-excited, frantic, stormy, turbulent, wild.

serenity, *n.* SYN.-calm, calmness, hush, peace, quiescence, quiet, quietude, repose, rest, silence, stillness, tranquility. ANT.-agitation, disturbance, excitement, noise, tumult.

series, *n.* SYN.-arrangement, chain, following, gradation, order, progression, sequence, string, succession, train.

serious, *a.* SYN.-alarming, critical, dangerous, earnest, grave, great, important, momentous, risky, sedate, sober, solemn, staid, weighty. ANT.-informal, relaxed, small, trifling, trivial.

sermon, *n.* SYN.-discourse, guide, homily, lesson, lecture, message, oration, speech, talk.

servant, *n.* SYN.-aid, aide, attendant, domestic, helper, hireling, menial, orderly, retainer.

serve, *v.* SYN.-administer, aid, assist, attend, benefit, cater, contribute, distribute, enlist, follow, forward, help, obey, oblige, promote, purvey, succor, work; provide, satisfy, suffice, supply. ANT.-command, dictate, direct, rule.

service, *n.* SYN.-aid, assistance, attendance, co-operation, duty, help, ministration, use, value; ceremony, rite, sermon, worship.

servile, *a.* SYN.-abject, base, contemptible, despicable, dishonorable, groveling, ignoble, ignominious, low, lowly, mean, menial, sordid, vile, vulgar. ANT.-teemed, exalted, honored, lofty, noble, righteous.

servitude, *n.* SYN.-apprenticeship, bondage, captivity, confinement, imprisonment, serfdom, slavery, subjugation, thralldom, vassalage. ANT.-freedom, liberation.

session, *n.* SYN.-assembly, conference, confrontation, congress, council, encounter, gathering, meeting, parley, rally.

set, *v.* SYN.-arrange, deposit, lay, place, put. ANT.-disarrange, disturb, mislay, misplace, remove.

setback, *n.* SYN.-blow, calamity, check, delay, difficulty, hindrance, misfortune, mishap, reversal, shock.

setting, *n.* SYN.-arena, atmosphere, backdrop, circumstances, context, environment, milieu, perspective, position, scene, stage, surroundings, viewpoint.

settle, *v.* SYN.-adjudicate, conclude, confirm, decide, determine, end, judge, resolve, terminate. ANT.-doubt, hesitate, suspend, vacillate, waver.

settlement, *n.* SYN.-agreement, close, completion, conclusion, decision, deduction, end, finale, issue, judgment, termination. ANT.-beginning, commencement, inception, prelude, start.

sever, *v.* SYN.-chop, cut, divide, part, separate, split, sunder. ANT.-combine, convene, gather, join unite.

severe, *a.* SYN.-acute, arduous, distressing, exacting, extreme, hard, harsh, intense, relentless, rigid, rigorous, sharp, stern, stringent, unmitigated, unyielding, violent. ANT.-considerate, genial, indulgent, merciful, yielding.

shabby, *a.* SYN.-deficient, inferior, mean, paltry, poor, ragged, scanty, seedy, threadbare, worn. ANT.-ample, good, new, opulent.

shack, *n.* SYN.-hovel, hut, shanty, shed.

shade, *n.* SYN.-amount, cast, color, complexion, hint, hue, obscurity, pigment, shadow, stain, tinge, tint, trace, variation. ANT.-achromatism, paleness, transparency.

shadowy, *a.* SYN.-dark, dim, dismal, gloomy, mournful, murky, obscure, somber, sorrowful, unilluminated; evil, sinister, sullen, wicked; hidden, mystic, occult, secret. ANT.-bright, clear, light, lucid, pleasant.

shake, *v.* SYN.-agitate, flutter, jar, jolt, quake, quaver, quiver, rock, shiver, shudder, sway, totter, tremble, vibrate, waver.

shaky, *a.* SYN.-dubious, faltering, insecure, loose, precarious, questionable, rickety, tentative, tenuous, uncertain, unreliable, unsteady, unsound, unstable, vacillating.

shallow, *a.* SYN.-cursory, exterior, flimsy, frivolous, imperfect, inconsequential, slight, superficial, trite. ANT.-abstruse, complete, deep, profound, thorough.

sham, *n.* SYN.-counterfeit, cover, fabrication, fake, forgery, fraud, imitation, pretense.

shame, *n.* SYN.-abasement, chagrin, disgrace, dishonor, disrepute, humiliation, ignominy, mortification, odium, opprobrium, scandal. ANT.-dignity, glory, honor, praise, renown.

shameful, *a.* SYN.-discreditable, disgraceful, dishonorable, disreputable, humiliating, immoral, ignominious, indecent, lewd, mortifying, obscene, odious, outrageous, scandalous, vulgar. ANT. teemed, honorable, renowned, respectable.

shameless, *a.* SYN.-audacious, blatant, bold, brazen, corrupt, depraved, forward, immodest, incorrigible, insolent, unabashed, unashamed. ANT.-modest, principled, proper.

shape, *n.* SYN.-appearance, build, cast, configuration, contour, cut, figure, form, frame, guise, image, mold, outline, pattern. ANT.-contortion, deformity, distortion, mutilation.

shape, *v.* SYN.-arrange, combine, compose, constitute, construct, create, devise, fashion, forge, form, frame, invent, make, mold, organize, produce. ANT.-destroy, disfigure, dismantle, misshape, wreck.

share, *n.* SYN.-allotment, allowance, bit, division, fragment, parcel, part, piece, portion, section, segment. ANT.-bulk, whole.

share, *v.* SYN.-accord, allot, apportion, appropriate, assign, bestow, cooperate, dispense, distribute, divide, give, parcel, partake, participate, partition, portion. ANT.-aggregate, amass, combine, condense.

shared, *a.* SYN.-common, communal, correlative, interchangeable, joint, mutual, reciprocal. ANT.-dissociated, separate, unrequited, unshared.

sharp, *a.* SYN.-acrid, acute, biting,

bitter, cutting, keen, penetrating, piercing, pointed, pungent, severe, shrill; astute, clever, cunning, quick, shrewd, wily, witty. ANT.-bland, blunt, gentle, shallow, stupid.

shatter, v. SYN.-break, burst, crack, demolish, destroy, fracture, pound, rack, rend, rupture, smash. ANT.-join, mend, renovate, repair, restore.

shattered, a. SYN.-broken, crushed, destroyed, flattened, fractured, reduced, rent, ruptured, smashed, wrecked. ANT.-integral, repaired, united, whole.

shed, v. SYN.-cast, discard, drop, emit, molt, radiate, scatter, spread.

sheer, a. SYN.-delicate, fine, flimsy, gossamer, thin, transparent; absolute, downright, pure, simple, utter; abrupt, precipitous, steep.

shelter, n. SYN.-asylum, cover, harbor, haven, protection, refuge, retreat, safety, sanctuary, security. ANT.-danger, exposure, hazard, jeopardy, peril.

shelter, v. SYN.-clothe, cover, defend, envelop, fortify, guard, protect, safeguard, shield. ANT.-bare, expose, reveal.

shelve, v. SYN.-delay, postpone, scrap, suspend.

shield, v. SYN.-cloak, clothe, conceal, cover, curtain, disguise, envelop, guard, hide, mask, protect, screen, shroud, veil. ANT.-bare, divulge, expose, reveal, unveil.

shift, v. SYN.-alter, change, convert, modify, transfigure, transform, vary, veer. ANT.-continue, establish, preserve, settle, stabilize.

shiftless, a. SYN.-idle, indolent, lazy, sluggish, useless, worthless.

shifting, a. SYN.-changeable, fickle,

fitful, inconstant, unstable, vacillating, variable, wavering. ANT.-constant, stable, steady, unchanging, uniform.

shifty, a. SYN.-artful, capricious, conniving, deceitful, deceptive, guileful, questionable, sly, treacherous, tricky, undependable, unreliable.

shine, v. SYN.-beam, blaze, flash, flicker, glare, gleam, glimmer, glisten, glitter, glow, radiate, scintillate, shimmer, sparkle, twinkle; brush, buff, burnish, clean, polish, wax.

shining, a. SYN.-brilliant, bright, dazzling, effulgent, glorious, gorgeous, grand, illustrious, magnificent, radiant, resplendent, showy, splendid, sumptuous, superb. ANT.-dull, mediocre, modest, ordinary, unimpressive.

ship, v. SYN.-consign, dispatch, forward, remit, send, transport

shirk, v. SYN.-avoid, disdain, disregard, dodge, duck, evade, ignore, malinger, neglect, shun, sidestep, slack.

shock, v. SYN.-alarm, amaze, astonish, astound, disconcert, dumbfound, flabbergast, startle, stun, surprise, take aback. ANT.-admonish, caution, forewarn, prepare.

shocked, a. SYN.-aghast, appalled, astonished, astounded, awed, bewildered, dumbfounded, offended, overwhelmed, startled, stunned, upset.

shocking, a. SYN.-appalling, dreadful, fearful, frightful, gruesome, hideous, horrible, horrid, severe, terrible. ANT.-happy, joyous, pleasing, safe, secure.

shoddy, a. SYN.-defective, deficient, inferior, faulty, flawed, imperfect,

mediocre, poor, second-rate, substandard.

short, *a.* SYN.-dumpy, dwarfed, little, low, pudgy, small, squat, undersized; abrupt, brief, compendious, concise, curt, laconic, succinct, summary, terse; deficient,
inadequate, insufficient, lacking,
limited. ANT.-abundant, ample, big,
extended, protracted.

shorten, *v.* SYN.-abbreviate, abridge,
condense, contract, curtail, diminish, lessen, limit, reduce, restrict.
ANT.-elongate, extend, lengthen.

shortsighted, *a.* SYN.- expedient,
improvident, impulsive, incautious,
heedless, mindless, rash, reckless,
thoughtless, unmindful, unthink-
ing.

shout, *v.* SYN.-bellow, call, call out,
cry, cry out, holler, scream, vociferate, yell. ANT.-intimate, whisper,
write.

show, *n.* SYN.-array, display, exhibition, exposition; demonstration,
flourish, ostentation, parade, spectacle, splurge; entertainment,
movie, performance, production.

show, *v.* SYN.-demonstrate, disclose,
display, evidence, exhibit, expose,
indicate, manifest, parade, present,
prove, reveal, unfold, verify; conduct, direct, guide, inform, instruct, teach, usher. ANT. conceal,
confuse, hide.

showy, *a.* SYN.-affected, artificial,
ceremonious, dramatic, flashy,
gaudy, histrionic, melodramatic,
ostentatious, pretentious, stagy,
superficial, tawdry, theatrical. ANT.-
modest, subdued, unaffected, unemotional.

shred, *n.* SYN.-bit, crumb, fragment,
ort, particle, piece, scrap, snip,
tatter.

shred, *v.* SYN.-lacerate, rend, rip,
rive, sever, slit, split, sunder, tear.
ANT.-join, mend, repair, sew, unite.

shrewd, *a.* SYN.-artful, astute, calcu-
lating, clever, crafty, cunning, foxy,
furtive, guileful, insidious, intelligent, keen, perceptive, quick,
sharp, sly, stealthy, subtle, surreptitious, tricky, underhanded,
wily. ANT.-candid, frank, ingenuous, open, sincere.

shriek, *n.* SYN.-cry, howl, scream,
screech, squawk.

shrill, *a.* SYN.-acute, cutting; biting,
penetrating, piercing, sharp. ANT.-
bland, blunt, gentle.

shrine, *n.* SYN.-column, crypt, mausoleum, memorial, monolith,
monument, obelisk, statue.

shrink, *v.* SYN.-cringe, flinch, recoil,
wince, withdraw; decrease, dimin-
ish, dwindle, lessen, reduce,
shrivel.

shrivel, *v.* SYN.-abate, contract, decline, dry, parch, shrink, wilt,
wither, wizen. ANT.-refresh, rejuvenate, renew.

shun, *v.* SYN.-avert, avoid, disregard,
dodge, eschew, elude, evade, forbear, forestall, ignore, reject, scorn,
slight, snub, spurn. ANT.-confront,
encounter, face, meet, oppose.

shut, *v.* SYN.-close, conclude, fasten,
lock, secure, seal. ANT.-open.

shy, *a.* SYN.-bashful, cautious,
chary, demure, diffident, fearful,
modest, reserved, retiring, sheepish, shrinking, timorous, wary.
ANT.-audacious, bold, brazen, forward, immodest.

sick, *a.* SYN.-ailing, diseased, ill, indisposed, infirm, morbid, un-
healthy, unwell. ANT.-healthy, robust, sound, strong, well.

sicken, *v.* SYN.-appall, disgust, displease, horrify, nauseate, offend, outrage, repel, repulse, revolt, shock. ANT.-approve, charm, delight, like, please.

sickly, *a.* SYN.-debilitated, delicate, feeble, frail, fragile, infirm, puny, unhealthy, weak.

sickness, *n.* SYN.-ailment, complaint, disease, disorder, illness, infirmity, malady. ANT.-health, healthiness, soundness, vigor.

sidestep, *v.* SYN.-avoid, bypass, circumvent, dodge, elude, evade, skirt.

siege, *n.* SYN.-assault, attack, blockade, invasion, offensive, onslaught, raid, strike.

sight, *n.* SYN.-display, scene, spectacle, view, vision.

sign, *n.* SYN.-beacon, clue, emblem, foreboding, gesture, hint, indication, mark, note, omen, premonition, portent, proof, signal, suggestion, symbol, symptom, token.

signal, *n.* SYN.-alarm, beacon, call, flag, impulse, warning, wave. ANT.-calm, inactivity, quiet, security, tranquillity.

significance, *n.* SYN.-connotation, drift, explanation, gist, implication, import, intent, interpretation, meaning, purport, purpose, sense, signification.

significant, *a.* SYN.-critical, grave, important, indicative, material, momentous, telling, weighty. ANT.-insignificant, irrelevant, meaningless, negligible, unimportant.

signify, *v.* SYN.-denote, designate, disclose, imply, indicate, intimate, manifest, reveal, show, specify. ANT.-conceal, distract, divert, falsify, mislead.

silence, *n.* SYN.-hush, quiet, quietude, serenity, stillness, tranquil-

ity. ANT.-noise, tumult.

silent, *a.* SYN.-calm, dumb, hushed, mute, noiseless, peaceful, quiet, still, taciturn, tranquil. ANT.-clamorous, loud, noisy, raucous.

silly, *a.* SYN.-absurd, asinine, brainless, crazy, foolish, idiotic, irrational, nonsensical, preposterous, ridiculous, senseless, simple, witless. ANT.-judicious, prudent, sagacious, sane, wise.

similar, *a.* SYN.-akin, alike, allied, analogous, comparable, correlative, correspondent, corresponding, like, parallel. ANT.-different, dissimilar, divergent, incongruous, opposed.

similarity, *n.* SYN.-analogy, correspondence, likeness, parity, resemblance, similitude. ANT.-difference, distinction, variance.

simile, *n.* SYN.-association, comparison, connection, kinship, parity, relationship, similarity.

simmer, *v.* SYN.-boil, bubble, fret, fume, rage, seeth, stew, worry.

simper, *v.* SYN.-grimace, smile, smirk.

simple, *a.* SYN. easy, effortless, elementary, facile, mere, pure, single, uncompounded, unmixed; artless, frank, homely, humble, naive, natural, open, plain, unsophisticated; asinine, credulous, foolish, silly. ANT.-adorned, artful, complex, intricate, wise.

simpleton, *n.* SYN.-clod, dolt, dope, dunce, fool, idiot.

simplify, *v.* SYN.-aid, ease, encourage, facilitate, promote

simply, *a.* SYN.-absolutely, directly, easily, frankly, honestly, merely, openly, plainly, purely, sincerely, utterly.

simulate, *v.* SYN.-ape, copy, counterfeit, duplicate, feign, imi-

tate, impersonate, mimic, mock.
ANT.-alter, distort, diverge, invent.
sin, *n.* SYN.-crime, evil, guilt, iniquity, offense, transgression, ungodliness, vice, wickedness, wrong.
ANT.-goodness, innocence, purity,
righteousness, virtue.
sincere, *a.* SYN.-candid, earnest,
frank, genuine, heartfelt, honest,
open, straightforward, true, truthful, unfeigned, upright. ANT.-affected, dishonest, hypocritical, insincere, untruthful.
sincerity, *n.* SYN.-candor, fairness,
frankness, honesty, integrity, justice, openness, rectitude, responsibility, trustworthiness, uprightness. ANT.-cheating, deceit, dishonesty, fraud, trickery.
sinful, *a.* SYN.-bad, corrupt, dissolute, immoral, indecent, licentious,
profligate, unprincipled, vicious,
wicked. ANT.-chaste, high-minded,
noble, pure, virtuous.
sing, *v.* SYN.-carol, chant, croon,
hum, intone, lilt, warble.
singe, *v.* SYN.-burn, char, scorch,
sear. ANT.-extinguish, put out,
quench.
single, *a.* SYN.-alone, distinct, distinctive, exclusive, individual, lone,
only, particular, separate, singular,
sole, solitary, special, specific,
unattached, unwed, unique. ANT.-
common, general, ordinary, universal.
singly, *a.* SYN.-apart, independently,
individually, separately.
singular, *a.* SYN.-choice, curious,
distinctive, exceptional, extraordinary, individual, matchless, odd,
particular, peculiar, rare, remarkable, special, strange, striking, uncommon, unequaled, unique, unusual. ANT.-common, general, nor-

mal, ordinary.
sinister, *a.* SYN.-bad, base, dire,
evil, foreboding, malevolent, menacing, ominous, perverse, threatening, unlucky, wicked. ANT.-beneficent, desirable, encouraging, favorable, fortunate, good, lucky.
sinless, *a.* SYN.-blameless, clean,
faultless, innocent, pure, spotless,
untainted, virtuous.
sip, *v.* SYN.-drink, imbibe, partake,
sample, savor, taste.
sire, *v.* SYN.-beget, breed, create, engender, father, generate, originate,
procreate, produce, propagate.
ANT.-abort, destroy, extinguish, kill,
murder.
site, *n.* SYN.-locale, locality, location,
place, plat, plot, position, section,
spot, station.
situated, *a.* SYN.-entrenched, established, fixed, located, placed,
placement, positioned.
situation, *n.* SYN.-case, circumstance, condition, employment,
job, plight, predicament, post,
rank, standing, state, station,
status.
size, *n.* SYN.-amount, amplitude,
area, bigness, bulk, dimensions,
expanse, extent, greatness, largeness, magnitude, mass, proportions, scope, stature, volume.
skeptic, *n.* SYN.-agnostic, cynic, deist, doubter, freethinker, infidel,
non-believer, questioner, unbeliever. ANT.-adorer, believer, follower, worshiper.
skepticism, *n.* SYN.-ambiguity, distrust, doubt, incredulity, scruple,
suspicion, unbelief, uncertainty.
ANT.-belief, certainty, conviction,
determination, faith.
sketch, *n.* SYN.-blueprint, chart,
contour, delineation, description,

sketch

sketch 216 **slight**

draft, drawing, illustration, image,
likeness, outline, plan, portrayal,
profile, rendering, representation,
scene, silhouette, view.

sketch, *v.* SYN.-chart, compose, delineate, depict, draft, draw, formulate, outline, picture, portray, represent, trace, write.

skill, *n.* SYN.-ability, adroitness,
cleverness, cunning, deftness,
dexterity, facility, ingenuity, knack,
readiness, skillfulness, ANT.-awk-
wardness, clumsiness, inability,
ineptitude.

skilled, *a.* See **skillful.**

skillful, *a.* SYN.-able, accomplished,
adept, clever, competent, cunning,
expert, ingenious, practiced, proficient, skilled, versed. ANT.-awk-
ward, bungling, clumsy, inexpert,
untrained.

skimpy, *a.* SYN.-deficient, lacking,
inadequate, insufficient, scant,
scarce, short.

skinflint, *n.* SYN.-cheapskate,
hoarder, miser, piker, tightwad.

skirmish, *n.* SYN.-assault, attack,
battle, clash, conflict, encounter,
engagement, fight, offensive.

skittish, *a.* SYN.-excitable, high-
strung, jittery, jumpy, nervous,
restless

slack, *a.* SYN.-baggy, disorderly,
limp, loose, negligent, relaxed, remiss, slovenly, unbound, unfastened, unkempt, untied. ANT.-tight,
restrained.

slacken, *v.* SYN.-abate, decrease,
diminish, lessen, mitigate, weaken.

slake, *v.* SYN.-allay, appease, gratify,
mollify, placate, please, sate,
satiate, satisfy.

slander, *n.* SYN.-aspersion, backbiting, calumny, defamation, libel,
scandal, vilification. ANT.-applause,

commendation, defense, flattery,
praise.

slang, *n.* SYN.-argot, cant, jargon,
lingo, patter.

slant, *n.* SYN.-grade, incline, pitch,
slope; bent, bias, inclination, judgment, leaning, opinion, prejudice.

slant, *v.* SYN.-incline, lean, skew,
tilt; color, distort, misconstrue,
misinterpret, misrepresent, prejudice.

slap, *v.* SYN.-buffet, hit, pat, punch,
smack, spank, strike, whack.

slash, *v.* SYN.-cut, gash, sever, slice;
abridge, curtail, decrease, diminish, lessen, lower, reduce.

slate, *n.* SYN.-ballot, line-up, list,
roll, roster, ticket.

slattern, *n.* SYN.-harlot, hooker,
hussy, prostitue, strumpet, tramp,
trollop, whore.

slaughter, *n.* SYN.-bloodshed, butchery, carnage, massacre, murder,
pogrom, slaying.

slaughter, *v.* SYN.-assassinate,
butcher, devastate, execute, kill,
massacre, murder, slay. ANT.-ani-
mate, protect, resuscitate, save,
vivify.

slavery, *n.* SYN.-bondage, captivity,
confinement, imprisonment, serfdom, servitude, thralldom, vassalage. ANT.-freedom, liberation.

sleazy, *a.* SYN.-base, cheap, flimsy,
shoddy, tacky, trashy.

sleek, *a.* SYN.-glossy, polished, silky,
slick, smooth. ANT.-harsh, rough,
rugged.

sleep, *n.* SYN.-catnap, doze, drowse,
nap, nod, repose, rest, slumber,
snooze, trance.

slender, *a.* SYN.-lean, skinny, slight,
slim, spare, thin. ANT.-broad,
bulky, fat, thick, wide.

slight, *a.* SYN.-delicate, emaciated,

flimsy, frail, insignificant, lean, paltry, petty, scrawny, skinny, slender, slim, spare, superficial, thin, trifling, unimportant. ANT.-broad, bulky, fat, thick, wide.

slight, *n.* SYN.-affront, disdain, contempt, disregard, insult, neglect, scorn.

slightly, *a.* SYN.-barely, hardly, inconsiderably, lightly, little, scarcely,

slink, *v.* SYN.-cower, lurk, prowl, skulk, sneak, steal.

slip, *n.* SYN.-blunder, error, fallacy, fault, inaccuracy, indiscretion, lapse, mistake, misstatement. ANT.-accuracy, precision, truth.

slogan, *n.* SYN.-axiom, device, legend, motto, trademark.

slope, *n.* SYN.-bank, bending, grade, inclination. incline, leaning, ramp

slothful, *a.* SYN.-idle, inactive, indolent, inert, lazy, slow, sluggish, supine, torpid. ANT.-active, alert, assiduous, diligent.

slow, *a.* SYN.-dawdling, delaying, deliberate, dull, gradual, laggard, leisurely, sluggish, tired. ANT.-fast, quick, rapid, speedy, swift.

sluggish, *a.* See **slow, slothful.**

slumber, *n.* SYN.-inactivity, quiescence, repose, rest, sleep.

slumber, *v.* SYN.-catnap, doze, drowse, nap, nod, repose, rest, sleep, snooze.

sly, *a.* SYN.-artful, astute, clandestine, covert, crafty, cunning, foxy, furtive, guileful, insidious, shrewd, stealthy, subtle, surreptitious, tricky, underhanded, wily. ANT.-candid, frank, ingenuous, open, sincere.

small, *a.* SYN.-diminutive, insignificant, little, miniature, minute, petty, puny, slight, tiny, trivial,

wee. ANT.-big, enormous, huge, immense, large.

smart, *a.* SYN.-adroit, adept, alert, astute, bright, clever, discerning, enlightened, ingenious, intellectual, intelligent, knowledgeable, quick, quick-witted, sharp, talented, well-informed, witty. ANT.-awkward, bungling, clumsy, dull, foolish, slow, stupid.

smart, *n.* SYN.-affront, bite, burn, hurt, insult, prick, sting, wound.

smash, *v.* SYN.-break, burst, crack, crush, demolish, destroy, fracture, pound, rack, rend, rupture, shatter. ANT.-join, mend, renovate, repair, restore.

smell, *n.* SYN.-aroma, fetidness, fragrance, fume, incense, odor, perfume, redolence, scent, stench, stink.

smolder, *v.* SYN.-burn, fester, fret, fume, stew, seethe, smoke.

smooth, *a.* SYN.-diplomatic, even, flat, glib, level, plain, polished, sleek, slick, suave, urbane. ANT.-bluff, blunt, harsh, rough, rugged.

smother, *v.* SYN.-choke, drench, gag, quench, stifle, throttle.

smug, *a.* SYN.-complacent, conceited, egotistical, satisfied, self-righteous, snobbish.

snag, *n.* SYN.-adversity, complication, barrier, difficulty, hindrance, obstacle, pitfall, problem.

snare, *v.* SYN.-capture, catch, enmesh, entangle, grasp, grip, seize, trap. ANT.-liberate, lose, release.

snatch, *v.* SYN.-grab, grasp, nab, pluck, seize, steal, swipe.

sneak, *v.* SYN.-creep, lurk, prowl, skulk, slink.

sneer, *v.* SYN.-deride, flout, gibe, jeer, mock, scoff, scorn, taunt. ANT.-compliment, flatter, laud, praise.

sneering, *n.* SYN.-derision, gibe, jeering, mockery, raillery, ridicule, sarcasm.

snob, *n.* SYN.- elitist, egotist, pretender, showoff, upstart

snoopy, *a.* SYN.-curious, inquiring, inquisitive, interrogative, meddling, nosy, peeping, peering, prying, searching. ANT.-incurious, indifferent, unconcerned, uninterested.

snub, *v.* SYN.-disdain, disregard, humiliate, ignore, neglect, slight.

snug, *a.* SYN.-close, comfortable, compact, cozy, constricted, homey, intimate, secure, tight. ANT.-lax, loose, open.

soar, *v.* SYN.-flit, float, flutter, fly, glide, hover, mount, sail. ANT.-descend, fall, plummet, sink.

sober, *a.* SYN.-calm, composed, controlled, earnest, grave, rational, restrained, sedate, serious, solemn, somber, sound, staid, steady, subdued, temperate. ANT.-boisterous, informal, joyful.

sobriety, *n.* SYN.-abstention, abstinence, continence, forbearance, moderation, self-denial, temperance. ANT.-excess, gluttony, greed, intoxication, self-indulgence.

social, *a.* SYN.-affable, civil, communicative, congenial, friendly, gregarious, hospitable, outgoing, pleasant, sociable. ANT.-antisocial, disagreeable, hermitic, inhospitable.

soft, *a.* SYN.-compassionate, flexible, gentle, lenient, malleable, meek, mellow, mild, subdued, supple, tender, yielding. ANT.-hard, rigid, rough, tough, unyielding.

soil, *n.* SYN.-dirt, earth, ground, land, loam.

soil, *v.* SYN.-befoul, blemish, spot,

stain, sully, tarnish. ANT.-clean, cleanse.

solace, *n.* SYN.-alleviate, comfort, consolation, contentment, ease, relief, soothe, succor. ANT.-affliction, discomfort, misery, suffering, torment, torture.

sole, *a.* SYN.-alone, deserted, desolate, isolated, lonely, secluded, unaided, lone, only, single, solitary. ANT.-accompanied, attended, surrounded.

solemn, *a.* SYN.-august, awe-inspiring, ceremonious, earnest, formal, grave, imposing, impressive, majestic, reverential, ritualistic, sedate, serious, sober, staid. ANT.-boisterous, informal, joyful, ordinary.

solicitude, *n.* SYN.-anxiety, care, caution, circumspection, compassion, concern, consideration, thoughtfulness, regard, wariness, worry. ANT.-disregard, indifference, neglect.

solid, *a.* SYN.-compact, dependable, firm, fixed, genuine, hard, reliable, sound, stable, substantial, unbroken, whole. ANT.-counterfeit, divided, elastic, flimsy, frail.

solitary, *a.* SYN.-alone, deserted, desolate, isolated, lone, lonely, only, secluded, single, sole, unaided. ANT.-accompanied, attended, surrounded.

solitude, *n.* SYN.-alienation, asylum, concealment, isolation, loneliness, privacy, refuge, retirement, retreat, seclusion. ANT.-exposure, notoriety, publicity.

somber, *a.* SYN.-bleak, cheerless, dark, dismal, doleful, dreary, dull, funereal, gloomy, melancholy, morose, sad, sullen. ANT.-cheerful, gay, joyous, lively.

song, n. SYN.-air, aria, lyric, melody, music, strain, tune.

soon, adv. SYN.-beforehand, betimes, early, easily, readily, shortly, speedily. ANT.-belated, late, over-due, tardy.

soothe, v. SYN.-cheer, comfort, console, encourage, gladden, mitigate, relieve, soften, solace, sympathize. ANT.-antagonize, aggravate, depress, dishearten.

soothing, a. SYN.-benign, calm, comforting, docile, gentle, mild, peaceful, placid, relaxed, serene, soft, tame, tractable. ANT.-fierce, harsh, rough, savage, violent.

sophisticated, a. SYN.-artificial, blasé, complex, cultivated, cultured, mature, practical, precious, refined, worldly, worldly-wise. ANT.-crude, ingenuous, naive, simple, uncouth.

sorcery, n. SYN.-alchemy, black art, conjuring, enchantment, legerdemain, magic, necromancy, voodoo, witchcraft, wizardry.

sordid, a. SYN.-abject, base, debased, depraved, despicable, foul, ignoble, loathsome, low, mean, obscene, odious, revolting, vicious, vile, vulgar, wicked, worthless, wretched. ANT.-attractive, decent, honorable, laudable, upright.

sorrow, n. SYN.-affliction, anguish, distress, grief, heartache, lamentation, misery, mourning, sadness, tribulation, woe. ANT.-comfort, consolation, happiness, joy, solace.

sorry, a. SYN.-afflicted, beggarly, contemptible, grieved, hurt, mean, pained, paltry, pitiable, pitiful, poor, sad, shabby, sorrowful, vexed, vile, worthless, wretched; contrite, penitent, remorseful, repentant. ANT.-cheerful, delighted, impenitent, splendid; unrepentant.

sort, n. SYN.-category, character, class, description, kind, nature, type. ANT.-deviation, eccentricity, monstrosity, peculiarity.

sound, a. SYN.-binding, dependable, healthy, hearty, legal, orthodox, powerful, proper, prudent, rational, reasonable, reliable, robust, sane, stable, strong, valid, vigorous, weighty. ANT.-counterfeit, null, spurious, void, weak.

sound, n. SYN.-din, intonation, noise, note, resonance, timbre, tone, vibration. ANT.-hush, quiet, silence, stillness.

sound, v. SYN.-articulate, echo, enunciate, pronounce, reverberate, say, shout, utter.

sour, a. SYN.-acid, acrimonious, bitter, glum, morose, peevish, rancid, sharp, sullen, tart. ANT.-genial, kindly, sweet, wholesome.

source, n. SYN.-agent, beginning, cause, determinant, incentive, inducement, motive, origin, principle, reason. ANT.-consequence, effect, end, result.

sovereignty, n. SYN.-authority, command, control, dominion, influence, power, predominance, sway.

spacious, a. SYN.-ample, broad, capacious, extensive, large, roomy, vast, wide. ANT.-confined, cramped, limited, narrow.

sparkle, v. SYN.-flicker, gleam, glimmer, glisten, glitter, glow, radiate, shimmer, shine, twinkle.

sparse, a. SYN.-barren, deficient, lean, meager, scanty.

speak, v. SYN.-articulate, converse, declare, discourse, express, harangue, lecture, say, talk, tell, utter. ANT.-be silent, hush, refrain.

special, *a.* SYN.-distinctive, exceptional, extraordinary, individual, particular, peculiar, uncommon, unusual. ANT.-broad, comprehensive, general, prevailing, widespread.

specific, *a.* SYN.-definite, explicit, limited, precise; categorical, characteristic, especial, peculiar. ANT.-general, generic, vague.

species, *n.* SYN.-class, division, family, genus, kind, order, variety, sort.

specify, *v.* SYN.-appoint, call, categorize, choose, classify, denominate, differentiate, distinguish, entitle, identify, mention, name, stipulate. ANT.-hint, miscall, misname.

specimen, *n.* SYN.-example, illustration, model, pattern, prototype, sample.

spectacle, *n.* SYN.-array, display, exhibition, exposition; demonstration, flourish, ostentation, parade, show, splurge.

speculate, *v.* SYN.-apprehend, assume, believe, conjecture, deduce, guess, imagine, presume, suppose, surmise, think. ANT.-ascertain, conclude, demonstrate, know, prove.

speech, *n.* SYN.-conversation, dialogue, discourse, discussion, lecture, report, talk. ANT.-correspondence, meditation, silence, writing.

speed, *v.* SYN.-accelerate, dispatch, expedite, facilitate, forward, hasten, hurry, push, quicken, rush. ANT.-block, hinder, impede, retard, slow.

spend, *v.* SYN.-circulate, consume, deplete, disburse, dispense, pass, pay, squander

spherical, *a.* SYN.-bulbous, circular, curved, cylindrical, globular, plump, rotund, round.

spirit, *n.* SYN.-apparition, ghost, phantom, soul, specter; courage, enthusiasm, fortitude, liveliness, temper, verve, vigor, vitality, zeal. ANT.-body, flesh, substance; languor, listlessness.

spirited, *a.* SYN.-active, alive, animated, blithe, lively, sprightly, vivacious.

spiritual, *a.* SYN.-divine, ethereal, ghostly, holy, immaterial, incorporeal, religious, sacred, supernatural, unearthly, unworldly. ANT.-carnal, corporeal, material, mundane, physical.

spiteful, *a.* SYN.-disagreeable, ill-natured, malicious, surly, vengeful, vicious. ANT.-peaceful, placid.

splendid, *a.* SYN.-brilliant, bright, dazzling, effulgent, glorious, gorgeous, grand, illustrious, magnificent, radiant, resplendent, shining, showy, sumptuous, superb. ANT.-dull, mediocre, modest, ordinary, unimpressive.

splendor, *n.* SYN.-brightness, brilliance, brilliancy, effulgence, grandeur, luster, magnificence, radiance. ANT.-darkness, dullness, gloom, obscurity.

split, *v.* SYN.-cleave, rend, rip, rive, sever, shred, slit, sunder, tear. ANT.-join, mend, repair, sew, unite.

spoil, *v.* SYN.-decay, decompose, disintegrate, putrefy, rot, ruin, waste. ANT.-flourish, grow, rise.

spoken, *a.* SYN.-literal, oral, phonetic, told, uttered, verbal, vocal. ANT.-documentary, recorded, written.

spontaneous, *a.* SYN.-automatic, extemporaneous, impulsive, instinctive, offhand, voluntary, willing. ANT.-compulsory, forced, planned, prepared, rehearsed.

sport, *n.* SYN.-amusement, contest, diversion, fun, game, match, merriment, pastime, play, recreation. ANT.-business drudgery, hardship, labor, work.

sport, *v.* SYN.-caper, frolic, gamble, gambol, play, revel, romp, stake, wager

spread, *v.* SYN.-air, broadcast, distribute, exhibit, expand, extend, open, scatter, smear, unfold, unfurl. ANT.-close, conceal, shut.

sprightly, *a.* SYN.-animated, blithe, buoyant, cheerful, effervescent, elated, gay, light, lively, resilient, spirited, vivacious. ANT.-dejected, depressed, despondent, hopeless, sullen.

spur, *n.* SYN.-cause, impulse, incentive, incitement, inducement, motive, principle, purpose, reason, stimulus. ANT.-action, attempt, deed, effort, result.

squabble, *v.* SYN.-altercate, argue, bicker, contend, contest, debate, disagree, discuss, dispute, quarrel, wrangle. ANT.-agree, allow, assent, concede.

squalid, *a.* SYN.-dirty, filthy, foul, grimy, mean, muddy, nasty, pitiful, shabby, soiled, wretched. ANT.-clean, neat, presentable; pure, wholesome.

squander, *v.* SYN.-dissipate, lavish, misuse, waste, wear out. ANT.-accumulate, economize, preserve, save.

stable, *a.* SYN.-constant, durable, enduring, established, firm, fixed, immovable, immutable, lasting, permanent, secure, staunch, steadfast, steady, unwavering. ANT.-changeable, erratic, irresolute, vacillating, variable.

staff, *n.* SYN.-assistants, cadre, crew, employees, force, help, helpers, organization, personnel.

staid, *a.* SYN.-demure, grave, modest, sedate, serious, sober, solemn. ANT.-boisterous, informal, joyful, ordinary.

stain, *v.* SYN.-befoul, blemish, blight, defile, discolor, disgrace, soil, spot, sully, tarnish; color, dye, tinge, tint. ANT.-bleach, cleanse, decorate, honor, purify.

stale, *a.* SYN.-banal, common, dry, dull, flat, insipid, musty, old, trite.

stand, *v.* SYN.-abide, bear, continue, endure, suffer, sustain, tolerate; halt, pause, remain, rest, stay, stop. ANT.-advance, progress, run, submit, yield.

standard, *n.* SYN.-criterion, gauge, law, measure, norm, rule, test, touchstone. ANT.-chance, fancy, guess, supposition.

start, *n.* SYN.-beginning, commencement, genesis, inception, opening, origin, outset, source. ANT.-close, completion, consummation, end, termination.

start, *v.* SYN.-arise, begin, commence, establish, found, inaugurate, initiate, institute, organize, originate. ANT.-complete, end, finish, terminate.

startle, *v.* SYN.-alarm, amaze, astonish, astound, disconcert, dumbfound, flabbergast, frighten, panic, scare, shock, stun, surprise, terrify. ANT.-admonish, caution, forewarn, prepare.

starved, *a.* SYN.-craving, famished, hungry, ravenous, voracious. ANT.-full, gorged, sated, satiated, satisfied.

state, *n.* SYN.-case, circumstance,

condition, plight, predicament, situation; commonwealth, community, kingdom, nationality, people, realm.

state, *v.* SYN.-affirm, assert, avow, claim, declare, explain, express, propound, recite, recount, say, specify, tell, utter. ANT.-conceal, deny, imply, retract.

stately, *a.* SYN.-courtly, dignified, grand, imperial, kingly, lordly, majestic, monarchal, noble, princely, regal, royal, ruling, sovereign, supreme. ANT.-common, humble, low, plebeian, proletarian, servile, vulgar.

statement, *n.* SYN.-allegation, announcement, assertion, communication, declaration, mention, proposition, report, thesis.

station, *n.* SYN.-level, location, occupation, office, order, place, position, post, rank, spot, standing.

statuesque, *a.* SYN.-august, beautiful, dazzling, divine, elegant, exquisite, gorgeous, graceful, grand, impressive, radiant, stately, venerable.

status, *n.* SYN.-caste, class, condition, estate, grade, incumbency, job, office, place, position, post, quality, rank, situation, standing, station.

statute, *n.* SYN.-act, decree, edict, law, ordinance.

stay, *v.* SYN.-abide, arrest, check, delay, halt, hinder, linger, obstruct, remain, sojourn, stand, tarry, wait. ANT.-advance, expedite, hasten, leave, progress.

steadfast, *a.* SYN.-authoritative, constant, dependable, dogmatic, fast, firm, fixed, inflexible, reliable, secure, solid, stable, steady, unswerving, unyielding. ANT.-inse-

cure, loose, unstable, unsteady.

steal, *v.* SYN.-burglarize, embezzle, loot, pilfer, pillage, plagiarize, plunder, purloin, rob, snatch, swipe. ANT.-buy, refund, repay, restore, return.

steep, *a.* SYN.-abrupt, hilly, precipitous, sharp, sheer, sudden. ANT.-flat, gradual, level.

steer, *v.* SYN.-direct, conduct, control, escort, guide, lead, manage, regulate.

stench, *n.* SYN.-aroma, fetidness, fragrance, fume, incense, odor, perfume, redolence, scent, smell, stink.

stern, *a.* SYN.-absolute, austere, dogmatic, exacting, hard, harsh, intense, relentless, rigid, rigorous, severe, sharp, stringent, unmitigated, unyielding. ANT.-considerate, genial, indulgent, merciful, yielding.

stiff, *a.* SYN.-constrained, formal, inflexible, obstinate, prim, resolved, rigid, severe, stern, stilted, strict, stringent, unbending, unyielding; abrupt, awkward, clumsy, crude. ANT.-compassionate, lax, lenient, mild, yielding; elastic, flexible, resilient, supple.

stigma, n, SYN.-brand, mark, scar, stain, stigmata, trace, vestige.

still, *a.* SYN.-hushed, motionless, noiseless, peaceful, placid, quiescent, quiet, silent, tranquil, undisturbed; calm, silent. ANT.-loud, strident.

stimulate, *v.* SYN.-agitate, arouse, disquiet, excite, incite, irritate, provoke, rouse, stir up. ANT.-allay, calm, pacify, quell, quiet.

stimulus, *n.* SYN.-arousal, encouragement, goad, incentive, instigation, motive, provocation, spur, stimulant. ANT.-depressant, discouragement, dissuasion, response.

stingy, *a.* SYN.-acquisitive, avaricious, greedy, miserly, niggardly, parsimonious, penurious, tight. ANT.-altruistic, bountiful, extravagant, generous, munificent.

stock, *n.* SYN.-accumulation, fund, goods, hoard, inventory, merchandise, provision, reserve, store, supplies, supply.

stock, *v.* SYN.-equip, fill, furnish, have, replenish, retain, save, store, supply. ANT.-deplete, drain, empty, exhaust.

stoical, *a.* SYN.-calm, composed, forbearing, impassive, passive, patient, resigned, serene, uncomplaining. ANT.-chafing, clamorous, hysterical, turbulent.

stone, *n.* SYN.-boulder, gravel, jewel, pebble, rock.

stop, *v.* SYN.-abstain, arrest, bar, cease, check, close, cork, desist, discontinue, end, halt, hinder, impede, interrupt, obstruct, plug, seal, terminate. ANT.-begin, proceed, promote, speed, start.

storm, *n.* SYN.-blizzard, cloudburst, cyclone, downpour, hurricane, squall, tempest, tornado.

stormy, *a.* SYN.-blustery, gusty, inclement, roaring, rough, tempestuous, turbulent, windy. ANT.-calm, clear, peaceful, quiet, tranquil.

story, *n.* SYN.-account, anecdote, chronicle, fable, fabrication, falsehood, fiction, history, narration, narrative, novel, report, tale, yarn.

stout, *a.* SYN.-chubby, corpulent, fat, obese, paunchy, plump, portly, pudgy, rotund, stocky, thickset. ANT.-gaunt, lean, slender, slim, thin.

straight, *a.* SYN.-direct, erect, fair, honest, honorable, just, right, square, unbent, undeviating, unswerving, upright, vertical. ANT.-bent, circuitous, crooked; dishonest, winding.

strain, *n.* SYN.-ancestry, breed, extraction, kind, sort, species, stock, subspecies, variety; effort, exertion, force, pressure; bruise, injury, sprain, twist, wrench; anxiety, pressure, stress, tension.

strange, *a.* SYN.-abnormal, bizarre, curious, eccentric, extraordinary, foreign, grotesque, irregular, odd, mysterious, peculiar, queer, singular, surprising, uncommon, unusual. ANT.-common, conventional, familiar, ordinary, regular.

stranger, *n.* SYN.-alien, foreigner, immigrant, interloper, intruder, newcomer, outsider. ANT.-acquaintance, associate, countryman, friend, neighbor.

strategy, *n.* SYN.-approach, method, plan, procedure, scheme, system, tactics.

stray, *v.* SYN.-deviate, digress, err, ramble, range, roam, rove, saunter, stroll, traipse, wander. ANT.-halt, linger, settle, stay, stop.

stream, *v.* SYN.-abound, come, emanate, flow, gush, issue, run, spout, spurt; abound.

street, *n.* SYN.-avenue, boulevard, court, lane, passage, path.

strength, *n.* SYN.-durability, force, fortitude, intensity, lustiness, might, potency, power, stamina, stoutness, sturdiness, toughness, vigor. ANT.-feebleness, frailty, infirmity, weakness.

strengthen, *v.* SYN.-approve, confirm, encourage, fix, fortify, hearten, intensify, ratify, reinforce, sanction, temper, toughen.

stress, *n.* SYN.-accent, compulsion, constraint, distress, exigency, force, hurry, importance, influence, press, pressure, significance, strain, tension, urgency. ANT. ease, lenience, recreation, relaxation.

stretch, *v.* SYN.-distend, distort, elongate, expand, extend, lengthen, protract, spread, strain. ANT.-contract, loosen, shrink, slacken, tighten.

strict, *a.* SYN.-austere, critical, demanding, exacting, harsh, rigorous, rough, rugged, severe, stringent. ANT.-gentle, melodious, mild, smooth, soft.

strife, *n.* SYN.-battle, clash, combat, conflict, fight, struggle.

strike, *v.* SYN.-beat, clout, cuff, hit, knock, pound, pummel, punch, slap, smite; boycott, picket, quit, stop.

striking, *a.* SYN.-affecting, arresting, august, commanding, exciting, forceful, grandiose, imposing, impressive, majestic, moving, overpowering, remarkable, splendid, stirring, thrilling, touching. ANT.-commonplace, ordinary, regular, unimpressive.

stringent, *a.* SYN.-forcible, harsh, rigorous, rough, rugged, severe, strict. ANT.-gentle, melodious, mild, smooth, soft.

strive, *v.* SYN.-aim, attempt, endeavor, try, struggle, undertake. ANT.-abandon, neglect.

stroll, *v.* SYN.-amble, meander, ramble, roam, saunter, walk.

strong, *a.* SYN.-athletic, cogent, concentrated, enduring, firm, forceful, forcible, fortified, hale, hardy, impregnable, mighty, potent, powerful, robust, sinewy, sturdy, tough.

ANT.-brittle, delicate, feeble, fragile, insipid.

struggle, *n.* SYN.-battle, combat, conflict, contest, encounter, fight, fray, skirmish, strife. ANT.-agreement, concord, peace, truce.

struggle, *v.* SYN.-battle, brawl, combat, conflict, contend, dispute, encounter, fight, scuffle, skirmish.

stubborn, *a.* SYN.-contumacious, determined, dogged, firm, headstrong, immovable, inflexible, intractable, obdurate, obstinate, pertinacious, uncompromising, unyielding. ANT.-amenable, compliant, docile, submissive, yielding.

student, *n.* SYN.-disciple, learner, observer, pupil, scholar.

study, *v.* SYN.-cogitate, contemplate, examine, investigate, learn, master, meditate, muse, ponder, reflect, scrutinize, weigh.

stuff, *n.* SYN.-items, material, matter, substance, thing. ANT.-immateriality, phantom, spirit.

stuff, *v.* SYN.-cram, fill, glut, gorge, occupy, pervade, sate, satiate, satisfy. ANT.-deplete, drain, empty, exhaust, void.

stumble, *v.* SYN.-blunder, drop, fall, falter, hesitate, sink, topple, trip, tumble. ANT.-arise, ascend, climb, mount, soar.

stun, *v.* SYN.-amaze, astound, dumbfound, flabbergast, shock, startle, surprise, take aback. ANT.-admonish, caution, forewarn, prepare.

stunning, *a.* SYN.-astonishing, astounding, beautiful, charming, dazzling, exquisite, gorgeous, marvelous, remarkable, shocking, staggering, striking.

stupid, *a.* SYN.-addled, brainless, crass, dense, dull, dumb, foolish,

obtuse, senseless, witless. ANT.-
alert, bright, clever, discerning, intelligent.

stupor, *n.* SYN.-daze, drowsiness, insensibility, languor, lethargy,
numbness, stupefaction, torpor.
ANT.-activity, alertness, liveliness,
readiness, wakefulness.

sturdy, *a.* SYN.-enduring, firm, formidable, fortified, hard, hardy, impregnable, mighty, potent, powerful, robust, sinewy, stout, strong,
tough. ANT.-brittle, delicate, feeble,
fragile, insipid.

suave, *a.* SYN.-courtly, cultured, elegant, genteel, glib, polished, refined, smooth, sophisticated, urbane.

subdue, *v.* SYN.-beat, conquer,
crush, defeat, humble, master,
overcome, quell, rout, subjugate,
surmount, vanquish. ANT.-capitu-
late, cede, lose, retreat, surrender.

subject, *n.* SYN.-citizen, dependent,
inferior, liegeman, subordinate,
vassal; argument, case, matter,
object, patient, point, theme, thesis, topic.

sublime, *a.* SYN.-elevated, exalted,
glorious, grand, high, lofty, majestic, noble, raised, splendid, supreme. ANT.-base, ignoble, low, ordinary, ridiculous.

submerge, *v.* SYN.-absorb, bury, dip,
dunk, engage, engross, immerse,
plunge, sink. ANT.-elevate, recover,
uplift.

submissive, *a.* SYN.-compliant,
deferential, dutiful, obedient, tractable, yielding. ANT.-insubordinate,
intractable, obstinate, rebellious.

submit, *v.* SYN.-abdicate, accede,
acquiesce, capitulate, cede, quit,
relent, relinquish, resign, succumb, surrender, waive, yield.

ANT.-assert, resist, strive, struggle.

subordinate, *a.* SYN.-following, inferior, lesser, lower, minor, poorer,
secondary. ANT.-better, greater,
higher, superior.

subordinate, *n.* SYN.-aide, assistant,
citizen, dependent, helper, inferior,
liegeman, subject, underling, vassal.

substantial, *a.* SYN.-abundant, ample, considerable, plentiful; actual,
concrete, corporeal, material,
physical, tangible, visible; firm,
large, sound, strong; affluent, important, influential, rich, wealthy.

substantiate, *v.* SYN.-attest,
authenticate, confirm, corroborate,
validate, verify.

substitute, *n.* SYN.-agent, alternate,
deputy, double, lieutenant, proxy,
representative, stand-in, surrogate,
understudy; equivalent, expedient,
makeshift. ANT.-head, master,
principal, sovereign.

substitution, *n.* SYN.-alteration, alternation, change, modification,
variation, variety, vicissitude. ANT.-
monotony, stability, uniformity.

subterfuge, *n.* SYN.-alibi, disguise,
evasion, excuse, pretense, pretext.
ANT.-actuality, fact, reality, sincerity, truth.

subtract, *v.* SYN.-decline, decrease,
deduct, diminish, lessen, reduce,
remove, shorten, wane. ANT.-am-
plify, enlarge, expand, grow, increase.

succeed, *v.* SYN.-achieve, flourish,
gain, prevail, prosper, thrive, win;
ensue, follow, inherit, supersede,
supplant. ANT.-fail, miscarry, miss;
anticipate, precede.

successful, *a.* SYN.-auspicious,
flourishing, fortunate, lucky, prosperous, triumphant.

succession, *n.* SYN.-arrangement, chain, following, gradation, order, progression, sequence, series, string, train.

succinct, *a.* SYN.-brief, compendious, concise, curt, fleeting, laconic, momentary, passing, pithy, short, terse, transient. ANT.-extended, lengthy, long, prolonged, protracted.

succor, *n.* SYN.-aid, assistance, comfort, consolation, relief, solace, support. ANT.-affliction, discomfort, misery, suffering, torment, torture.

sudden, *a.* SYN.-abrupt, hasty, immediate, instantaneous, rapid, unexpected. ANT.-anticipated, gradual, slowly.

sue, *v.* SYN.-appeal, beg, claim, demand, entreat, indict, litigate, petition, plead, pray, prosecute, solicit.

suffer, *v.* SYN.-bear, endure, feel, stand, sustain, tolerate, undergo; allow, indulge, let, permit, tolerate. ANT.-banish, discard, exclude, overcome.

suffering, *n.* SYN.-ache, agony, anguish, distress, misery, pain, throe, torment, torture, woe. ANT.-comfort, ease, mitigation, relief.

sufficient, *a.* SYN.-adequate, ample, commensurate, enough, fitting, satisfactory, suitable. ANT.-deficient, lacking, scant.

suggest, *v.* SYN.-advise, allude, counsel, hint, imply, insinuate, intimate, offer, propose, recommend, refer. ANT.-declare, demand, dictate, insist.

suggestion, *n.* SYN.-admonition, advice, caution, counsel, exhortation, hint, information, instruction, intelligence, notification, recommendation, warning.

suitable, *a.* SYN.-acceptable, agree-able, amiable, gratifying, pleasant, pleasing, pleasurable, welcome. ANT.-disagreeable, obnoxious, offensive, unpleasant.

sullen, *a.* SYN.-dour, fretful, gloomy, glum, moody, morose, sulky, surly. ANT.-amiable, gay, joyous, merry, pleasant.

sum, *n.* SYN.-aggregate, entirety, total, whole. ANT.-fraction, ingredient, part, sample.

sum, *v.* SYN.-add, affix, append, attach, augment, increase, total. ANT.-deduct, detach, reduce, remove, subtract.

summarize, *v.* SYN.-abridge, abstract, outline, part, recap. ANT.-add, replace, restore, return, unite.

summit, *n.* apex, crest, crown, head, pinnacle, top, zenith. ANT.-base, bottom, foot, foundation.

sundry, *a.* SYN.-different, divers, few, miscellaneous, several, unlike, various. ANT.-alike, congruous, identical, same, similar.

sunny, *a.* SYN.-bright, clear, cloudless, fair. ANT.-cloudy, foul, overcast.

superb, *a.* SYN.-beautiful, elegant, excellent, impressive, grand, magnificent, marvelous, splendid.

superficial, *a.* SYN.-cursory, exterior, flimsy, frivolous, imperfect, shallow, slight. ANT.-abstruse, complete, deep, profound, thorough.

superintend, *v.* SYN.-command, control, direct, dominate, govern, manage, regulate, rule. ANT.-abandon, follow, forsake, ignore.

superiority, *n.* SYN.-advantage, edge, lead, mastery, supremacy. ANT.-handicap, weakness.

supernatural, *a.* SYN.-marvelous, metaphysical, miraculous, other-worldly, preternatural, spiritual, superhuman, unearthly. ANT.-common, human, natural, physical, plain.

supervise, v. SYN.-boss, command, control, direct, dominate, govern, manage, oversee, regulate, rule, superintend. ANT.-abandon, forsake, ignore.

supervision, n. SYN.-charge, control, direction, inspection, instruction, management, oversight, superintendence, surveillance. ANT.-attention, care, observation, scrutiny .

supplant, v. SYN.-overcome, overthrow, overturn, remove, replace, rout, ruin, uproot, upset, vanquish. ANT.-build, conserve, construct, preserve, uphold.

supple, a. SYN.-compliant, ductile, elastic, flexible, lithe, pliable, pliant, resilient, tractable. ANT.-brittle, hard, rigid, stiff, unbending.

supply, n. SYN.-accumulation, fund, hoard, provision, reserve, stock, store.

supply, v. SYN.-endow, equip, fit, fit out furnish, provide. ANT.-denude, despoil, divest, strip.

support, n. SYN.-base, basis, brace, buttress, foundation, groundwork, prop, stay; aid, assistance, backing, comfort, encouragement, favor, help, patronage, succor; livelihood, living, maintenance, subsistence; confirmation, evidence. ANT.-attack, enmity, opposition.

support, v. SYN.-advocate, assist, back, bear, brace, encourage, foster, further, help, keep, maintain, preserve, prop, sustain, uphold, ANT.-abandon, betray, destroy, discourage, oppose.

supporter, n. SYN.-adherent, apologist, apostle, attendant, devotee,

disciple, follower, henchman, partisan, successor, votary. ANT.-chief, head, leader, master.

suppose, v. SYN.-apprehend, assume, believe, conjecture, deduce, guess, imagine, presume, speculate, surmise, think. ANT.-ascertain, conclude, demonstrate, know, prove.

supremacy, n. SYN.-ascendancy, domination, mastery, predominance, sovereignty, sway, transcendence. ANT.-inferiority.

supreme, a. SYN.-cardinal, chief, foremost, highest, leading, main, paramount, predominant, principal. ANT.-auxiliary, minor, subordinate, subsidiary, supplemental.

sure, a. SYN.-assured, certain, definite, fixed, indubitable, inevitable, positive, secure, undeniable, unquestionable. ANT.-doubtful, probable, questionable, uncertain.

surly, a. SYN.-disagreeable, dour, ill-natured, quarrelsome, rude, spiteful, sullen, vicious. ANT.-friendly, pleasant.

surplus, n. SYN. abundance, excess, extra, extravagance, overs, profusion, remains, superabundance, superfluity, . ANT.-dearth, deficiency, lack, paucity, want.

surprise, n. SYN.-amazement, astonishment, awe, bewilderment, wonder, wonderment. ANT.-apathy, expectation, indifference.

surprise, v. SYN.-alarm, amaze, astonish, astound, disconcert, dumbfound, flabbergast, shock, startle, stun, take aback. ANT.-admonish, caution, forewarn, prepare.

surrender, v. SYN.-abandon, acquiesce, capitulate, cede, relinquish, renounce, resign, sacrifice, submit, yield. ANT.-conquer, overcome, resist, rout.

surround, *v.* SYN.-bound, circumscribe, confine, enclose, encompass, envelop, fence, limit. ANT.-develop, distend, enlarge, expand, expose, open.

survey, *n.* SYN.-critique, examination, inspection, outline, poll, review, study.

survey, *v.* SYN.-examine, inspect, observe, scan, scrutinize, view, watch.

survive, *v.* SYN.-endure, last, persevere, persist, outlast, outlive, remain, weather.

suspect, *v.* SYN.-distrust, doubt, hesitate, mistrust, question, waver, wonder. ANT.-believe, confide, decide, rely on, trust.

suspend, *v.* SYN.-adjourn, defer, delay, discontinue, interrupt, postpone, stay; balance, dangle, hang, poise, swing. ANT.-continue, maintain, persist, proceed, prolong.

suspense, *n.* SYN.-apprehension, doubt, hesitation, indecision, irresolution, uncertainty, vacillation, wavering.

suspicion, *n.* SYN.-distrust, doubt, hesitation, incredulity, misgiving, mistrust, skepticism, unbelief, uncertainty. ANT.-belief, certainty, conviction, determination. faith.

suspicious, *a.* SYN.-distrustful, doubtful, dubious, peculiar, questionable, shady, skeptical, strange, suspect, untrustworthy, unusual, wary.

sustain, *v.* SYN.-advocate, back, encourage, foster, further, help, keep, maintain, preserve, prop, support, uphold, ANT.-abandon, betray, destroy, discourage, oppose.

sustenance, *n.* SYN.-diet, edibles, fare, feed, food, meal, nutriment,

provisions, rations, repast, subsistence, viands, victuals. ANT.-drink, hunger, starvation, want.

swap, *v.* SYN.-barter, exchange, interchange, switch, trade.

swarm, *n.* SYN.-bevy, crowd, flock, horde, host, mass, multitude, pack, throng.

sway, *n.* SYN.-authority, control, dominion, influence, mastery, power.

sway, *v.* SYN.-actuate, affect, bias, control, direct, dominate, govern, impel, incite, influence, prevail, rule; fluctuate, oscillate, swing, wave.

swear, *v.* SYN.-affirm, assert, aver, declare, maintain, promise, protest, state, testify. ANT.-contradict, demur, deny, dispute, oppose.

sweeping, *a.* SYN.-broad, exaggerated, extravagant, expanded, extensive, large, vast, wide; liberal, tolerant. ANT.-confined, narrow, restricted.

sweet, *a.* SYN.-agreeable, delightful, engaging, gentle, honeyed, luscious, mellifluous, melodious, pleasing, saccharine, sugary, winning, ANT.-acrid, bitter, offensive, repulsive, sour.

swell, *v.* SYN.-balloon, bloat, bulge, dilate, enlarge, expand, grow, increase, inflate.

swift, *a.* SYN.-abrupt, expeditious, fast, fleet, quick, rapid, speedy, sudden, unexpected. ANT.-slow, sluggish.

swindle, *n.* SYN.-cheat, chicanery, deceit, deception, duplicity, fraud, guile, imposition, imposture, trick. ANT.-fairness, honesty, integrity, sincerity.

swindle, *v.* SYN.-bilk, cheat, circumvent, deceive, defraud, dupe, fool, gull, hoax, hoodwink, outwit, trick, victimize.

switch, *v.* SYN.-alter, exchange, rearrange, replace, shift, substitute.

syllabus, *n.* SYN.-abridgement, brief, condensation, digest, outline, summary, synopsis.

symbol, *n.* SYN.-character, emblem, mark, representation, sign, token.

symbolic, *a.* SYN.-characteristic, illustrative, indicative, representative, typical.

sympathetic, *a.* SYN.-affable, benevolent, benign, compassionate, forbearing, gentle, good, humane, indulgent, kind, kindly, merciful, tender, thoughtful. ANT.-cruel, inhuman, merciless, severe, unkind.

sympathize, *v.* SYN.-cheer, comfort, commiserate, console, empathize, encourage, gladden, solace, soothe. ANT.-antagonize, aggravate, depress, dishearten.

sympathy, *n.* SYN.-affinity, agreement, commiseration, compassion, concord, condolence, congeniality, empathy, harmony, pity, tenderness, warmth. ANT.-antipathy, harshness, indifference, malevolence, unconcern.

synonymous, *a.* SYN.-corresponding, equivalent, identical, like, same.

synopsis, *n.* SYN.-See **syllabus.**

synthetic, *a.* SYN.-artificial, bogus, counterfeit, ersatz, fake, feigned, fictitious, phony, sham, spurious, unreal. ANT.-genuine, natural, real, true.

system, *n.* SYN.-arrangement, method, mode, order, organization, plan, process, regularity, rule, scheme. ANT.-chance, chaos, confusion, disarrangement, disorder, irregularity.

T

tact, *n.* SYN.-acumen, address, adroitness, dexterity, diplomacy, discrimination, finesse, knack, perception, poise, prudence, refinement, savoir faire, skill. ANT.-awkwardness, blunder, incompetence, rudeness, vulgarity.

tactful, *a.* SYN.-adroit, attentive, careful, concerned, delicate, diplomatic, discreet, discriminating, gentle, judicious, politic. ANT.-boorish, churlish, coarse, gruff, rude.

tactless, *a.* SYN.-clumsy, crude, discourteous, gruff, hasty, impolite, imprudent, rough, stupid.

tainted, *a.* SYN.-contaminated, corrupt, corrupted, debased, depraved, impure, poisoned, profligate, putrid, spoiled, unsound, venal, vitiated.

take, *v.* SYN.-accept, adopt, appropriate, assume, capture, catch, choose, claim, clasp, clutch, confiscate, demand, ensnare, espouse, gain, get, grasp, grip, obtain, purloin, receive, remove, require, seize, select steal; bear, endure, stand, tolerate; bring, carry, convey, escort; attract, captivate, charm, delight, interest.

tale, *n.* SYN.-account, anecdote, chronicle, exaggeration, fable, fabrication, fiction, narration, narrative, novel, story, yarn.

talent, *n.* SYN.-ability, aptitude, capability, cleverness, endowment, faculty, genius, gift, knack, skill. ANT.-incompetence, ineptitude, stupidity.

talented, *a.* SYN.-able, adroit, apt, bright, clever, dexterous, ingenious, quick, quick-witted, sharp, skillful, smart, witty. ANT.-awkward, bungling, clumsy, dull, foolish, slow, stupid, unskilled.

talk, n. SYN.-chatter, conference, conversation, dialogue, discourse, discussion, gossip, lecture, report, rumor, speech. ANT.-correspondence, meditation, silence, writing.

talk, v. SYN.-argue, blab, chat, comment, confer, consult, converse, declaim, deliberate, discourse, discuss, gossip, harangue, jabber, lecture, mutter, plead, prattle, preach, rant, reason, speak, spout, tattle.

talkative, a. SYN.-chattering, chatty, communicative, garrulous, glib, loquacious, verbose, voluble. ANT.-laconic, reticent, silent, taciturn, uncommunicative.

tall, a. SYN.-elevated, high, lofty, towering; exaggerated, outlandish, unbelievable. ANT.-small, stunted, tiny; actual, honest, true.

tame, a. SYN.-docile, domestic, domesticated, gentle, meek, subdued, submissive; dull, flat, insipid, tedious. ANT.-fierce, savage, spirited, wild; animated, exciting, lively, spirited.

tangible, a. SYN.-corporeal, manifest, material, palpable, perceptible, physical, real, sensible, substantial. ANT.-mental, metaphysical, spiritual.

tarnish, v. SYN.-blemish, blight, defile, discolor, disgrace, soil, spot, sully, stain. ANT.-cleanse, honor, purify.

tart, a. SYN.-acrid, acrimonious, biting, bitter, caustic, distasteful, galling, grievous, harsh, painful, poignant, pungent, sardonic, severe, sour. ANT.-delicious, mellow, pleasant, sweet.

taste, n. SYN.-flavor, relish, savor, tang; discernment, disposition, inclination, judgment, liking, predilection, sensibility, zest. ANT.-antipathy, disinclination, indelicacy, insipidity.

taught, a. SYN.-directed, educated, instructed, trained.

taunt, v. SYN.-badger, deride, flout, gibe, harass, harry, jeer, mock, sneer, torment, worry. ANT.-compliment, flatter, laud, praise.

taunting, a. SYN.-biting, caustic, contemptuous, cutting, derisive, insulting, rude, sarcastic, scornful, sneering. ANT.-affable, agreeable, amiable, pleasant.

taut, a. SYN.-contracted, firm, stretched, tense, tight. ANT.-lax, loose, open, relaxed, slack.

tax, n. SYN.-assessment, custom, duty, exaction, excise, impost, levy, rate, toll, tribute; burden, encumber, strain. ANT.-gift, remuneration, reward, wages.

tax, v. SYN.-appraise, assess, calculate, compute, evaluate, levy, reckon; burden, demand, encumber.

teach, v. SYN.-educate, inculcate, inform, instill, instruct, school, train, tutor. ANT.-misguide, misinform.

tear, v. SYN.-cleave, disunite, lacerate, rend, rip, rive, sever, shred, slit, split, sunder, wound. ANT.-join, mend, repair, sew, unite.

tease, v. SYN.-aggravate, annoy, badger, bother, disturb, harass, harry, irritate, molest, nag, pester, plague, provoke, tantalize, taunt, torment, vex, worry. ANT.-comfort, delight, gratify, please, soothe.

tedious, a. SYN.-boring, burdensome, dilatory, dreary, dull, humdrum, irksome, monotonous, slow, sluggish, tardy, tiresome, uninteresting, wearisome. ANT.-amusing, entertaining, exciting, interesting, quick.

tedium, *n.* SYN.-boredom, doldrums, dullness, ennui, monotony, weariness. ANT.-activity, excitement, motive, stimulus.

telepathy, *n.* SYN.- insight, premonition, prescience.

tell, *v.* SYN.-acquaint, announce, apprise, betray, communicate, confess, describe, direct, disclose, divulge, express, inform, instruct, mention, narrate, notify, order, publish, recount, rehearse, relate, report, request, reveal, speak, state, utter; discern, discover, distinguish, recognize.

temerity, *n.* SYN.-audacity, boldness, foolhardiness, precipitance, rashness, recklessness. ANT.-caution, hesitation, prudence, timidity, wariness.

temper, *n.* SYN.-anger, choler, fury, ire, irritation, passion, petulance, rage, resentment, wrath. ANT.-conciliation, forbearance, patience, peace, self-control.

temperament, *n.* SYN.-character, constitution, disposition, humor, mood, nature, temper.

temperance, *n.* SYN.-abstention, abstinence, continence, fasting, forbearance, moderation, self-denial, sobriety. ANT.-excess, gluttony, greed, intoxication, self-indulgence.

tempest, *n.* SYN.-blast, gale, gust, hurricane, squall, storm, wind.

temporal, *a.* SYN.-earthly, laic, lay, mundane, profane, secular, worldly. ANT.-ecclesiastical, religious, spiritual, unworldly.

temporary, *a.* SYN.-brief, ephemeral,

evanescent, fleeting, momentary, short-lived, transient. ANT.-abiding, immortal, lasting, permanent, timeless.

temptation, *n.* SYN.-appeal, enticement, fascination, inducement, lure, stimulus.

tenacity, *n.* SYN.-cohesion, obstinance, perseverance, persistence, persistency, pertinacity, steadfastness. ANT.-cessation, idleness, laziness, rest, sloth.

tend, *v.* SYN.-accompany, attend, escort, follow, guard, protect, serve, watch.

tendency, *n.* SYN.-aim, bent, bias, drift, inclination, leaning, predisposition, proclivity, proneness, propensity, trend. ANT.-aversion, deviation, disinclination.

tender, *a.* SYN.-affectionate, compassionate, considerate, delicate, gentle, kind, mild, moderate, soft, soothing, sympathetic, sweet. ANT.-bitter, fierce, harsh, rough, severe.

tenderness, *n.* SYN.-commiseration, compassion, condolence, empathy, endearment, fondness, kindness, love, pity, sweetness, sympathy, warmth. ANT.-hatred, indifference, repugnance.

tenet, *n.* SYN.-belief, concept, creed, doctrine, dogma, opinion, precept, principle, teaching. ANT.-conduct, deed, performance, practice.

tense, *a.* SYN.-agitated, excited, nervous, strained. ANT.- caim, composed, relaxed.

term, *n.* SYN.-boundary, duration, interval, limit, period, time; condition, expression, name, phrase, word.

terminal, *a.* SYN.-concluding, conclusive, decisive, ending, eventual, extremity, final, last, latest, limit, terminus, ultimate. ANT.-first, inaugural, incipient, original, rudimentary.

terminate, *v.* SYN.-abolish, cease, close, complete, conclude, end, expire, finish, stop. ANT.-begin, commence, establish, initiate, start.

terms, *n.* SYN.-agreement, conditions, details, particulars, settlement, understanding.

terrible, *a.* SYN.-appalling, awful, dire, dreadful, fearful, frightful, gruesome, hideous, horrible, horrid, severe, shocking. ANT.-happy, joyous, pleasing, safe, secure.

terrify, *v.* SYN.-affright, alarm, daunt, frighten, horrify, intimidate, scare, startle, terrorize. ANT.-allay, compose, embolden, reassure, soothe.

territory, *n.* SYN.-country, district, division, domain, dominion, land, place, province, quarter, region, section.

terror, *n.* SYN.-alarm, consternation, dismay, dread, fear, fright, horror, panic. ANT.-assurance, calm, peace, security.

terse, *a.* SYN.-brief, compact, concise, condensed, incisive, neat, pithy, succinct, summary. ANT.-lengthy, prolix, verbose, wordy.

test, *v.* SYN.-analyze, assay, examine, experiment, inspect, prove, try, verify.

testimony, *n.* SYN.-attestation, confirmation, declaration, evidence, proof, witness. ANT.-argument, contradiction, disproof, refutation.

testy, *a.* SYN.-choleric, churlish, fractious, ill-natured, ill-tempered, irritable, peevish, petulant, snappish, touchy, waspish. ANT.-affable, genial, good-natured, good-tem-

pered, pleasant.

theatrical, *a.* SYN.-affected, artificial, ceremonious, dramatic, histrionic, melodramatic, showy, stagy. ANT.-modest, subdued, unaffected, unemotional.

theft, *n.* SYN.-burglary, depredation, larceny, pillage, plunder, robbery.

theme, *n.* SYN.-composition, essay, motive, subject, text, thesis, topic.

theory, *n.* SYN.-conjecture, doctrine, hypothesis, opinion, postulate, presupposition, speculation. ANT.-fact, practice, proof, verity.

therefore, *adv.* SYN.-accordingly, consequently, hence, so, then, thence.

thick, *a.* SYN.-abundant, close, compact, compressed, concentrated, crowded, heavy; dull, dense, obtuse, slow, stupid; guttural, husky, indistinct, muffled. ANT.-dispersed, dissipated, sparse, thin; clever, quick; clear, distinct.

thin, *a.* SYN.-attenuated, diaphanous, diluted, emaciated, fine, flimsy, gaunt, gauzy, gossamer, lank, lean, meager, narrow, rare, scanty, scrawny, skinny, slender, slight, slim, spare, tenuous. ANT.-broad, bulky, fat, thick, wide.

think, *v.* SYN.-apprehend, believe, cogitate, conceive, consider, contemplate, deem, deliberate, esteem, imagine, judge, meditate, muse, opine, picture, ponder, reason, recall, reckon, recollect, reflect, regard, remember, speculate, suppose; devise, intend, mean, plan, purpose. ANT.-conjecture, forget, guess.

thorough, *a.* SYN.-accurate, attentive, complete, careful, detailed, painstaking, perfect, persevering, thoroughgoing, total, unbroken, uncompromising, undivided. ANT.-imperfect, lacking, superficial, unfinished.

thought, n. SYN.-cogitation, conception, consideration, contemplation, deliberation, fancy, idea, imagination, impression, judgment, meditation, memory, notion, opinion, recollection, reflection, regard, retrospection, sentiment, view.

thoughtful a. SYN.-attentive, careful, cautious, concerned, considerate, heedful, provident, prudent: contemplative, dreamy, introspective, meditative, pensive, reflective. ANT.-heedless, inconsiderate, precipitous, rash, thoughtless.

thoughtless, a. SYN.-careless, desultory, heedless, imprudent, inaccurate, inattentive, inconsiderate, indiscreet, lax, neglectful, negligent, reckless, remiss, unconcerned. ANT.-accurate, careful, meticulous, nice.

threatening, a. SYN.-approaching, dangerous, grave, imminent, impending, menacing, nigh, ominous, serious, troublesome. ANT.-afar, distant, improbable, remote, retreating.

thrifty, a. SYN.-economical, frugal, parsimonious, provident, saving, sparing, stingy, temperate. ANT.-extravagant, intemperate, self-indulgent, wasteful.

throb, v. SYN.-beat, palpitate, pound, pulsate, pulse, thump, vibrate. ANT.-defend, shield, stroke, fail, surrender.

throng, n. SYN.-bevy, crowd, crush, horde, host, masses, mob, multitude, populace, press, rabble, swarm.

throw, v. SYN.-cast, fling, hurl, pitch, propel, thrust, toss. ANT.-

draw, haul, hold, pull, retain.

thrust, v. SYN.-drive, force, impel, propel. ANT.-drag, falter, halt, pull, retreat.

thwart, v. SYN.-baffle, block, check, circumvent, defeat, disappoint, foil, frustrate, hinder, impede, obstruct, outwit, prevent, restrain, stop. ANT.-accomplish, fulfill, further, promote.

tidings, n. SYN.-greetings, information, intelligence, message, news, report.

tidy, a. SYN.-neat, orderly, precise, spruce, trim. ANT.-dirty, disheveled, sloppy, slovenly, unkempt.

tie, n. SYN.-accord, agreement, alliance, association, bond, conjunction, connection, connective, juncture, link, pact, relationship, union. ANT.-disunion, isolation, separation.

tie, v. SYN.-attach, bind, connect, engage, fasten, fetter, join, link, oblige, restrain, restrict. ANT.-free, loose, unfasten, untie.

tight, a. SYN.-close, compact, constricted, contracted, firm, narrow, snug, stretched, taut, tense; closefisted, niggardly, parsimonious, penny-pinching, stingy. ANT.-lax, loose, open, relaxed, slack.

time, n. SYN.-age, date, duration, epoch, era, interim, period, season, span, spell, tempo, term.

timid, a. SYN.-afraid, apprehensive, bashful, coy, diffident, fainthearted, fearful, frightened, humble, recoiling, scared, sheepish, shy, timorous. ANT.-adventurous, assured, bold, composed, courageous, daring, fearless, gregarious, outgoing, sanguine.

tiny, a. SYN.-diminutive, insignificant, little, miniature, minute,

petty, puny, slight, small, trivial,
wee. ANT.-big, enormous, huge,
immense, large.

tire, v. SYN.-bore, exhaust, fatigue,
jade, tucker, wear out, weary. ANT.-
amuse, invigorate, refresh, restore,
revive.

tired, a. SYN.-exhausted, fatigued,
spent, wearied, weary, worn. ANT.-
fresh, hearty, invigorated, rested.

title, n. SYN.-appellation, denomination, designation, epithet, name;
claim, due, privilege, right.

toil, n. SYN.-drudgery, effort, labor,
slave, travail, work. ANT.-ease, leisure, play, recreation, vacation.

tolerant, a. SYN.-broad, compassionate, forbearing, forgiving, humane, kind, lenient, liberal, long-
suffering, merciful, patient, understanding. ANT.-confined, narrow,
restricted.

tolerate, v. SYN.-abide, allow, bear,
brook, endure, permit, stand. ANT.-
forbid, prohibit; protest.

toll, n. SYN.-assessment, exaction,
excise, impost, levy, tax, tribute;
burden, damage, destruction,
losses, sacrifice, strain. ANT.-gift,
remuneration, reward, wages.

too, adv. SYN.-also, besides, furthermore, in addition, likewise,
moreover, similarly.

tool, n. SYN.-agent, apparatus, device, instrument, means, medium,
utensil. ANT.-hindrance, impediment, obstruction, preventive.

top, n. SYN.-apex, chief, crest,
crown, head, pinnacle, summit,
zenith. ANT.-base, bottom, foot,
foundation.

topic, n. SYN.-discourse, issue,
matter, point, subject, theme, thesis.

torment, n. SYN.-ache, agony, an-

guish, distress, misery, pain, suffering, throe, torture, woe. ANT.-
comfort, ease, mitigation, relief.

torment, v. SYN.-aggravate, annoy,
badger, bother, disturb, harass,
harry, haze, irritate, molest, nag,
pain, persecute, pester, plague,
provoke, tantalize, taunt, tease,
trouble, vex, worry. ANT.-comfort,
delight, gratify, please, soothe.

torpor, n. SYN.-apathy, daze, insensibility, languor, lethargy, numbness, stupefaction, stupor. ANT.-
activity, alertness, liveliness, readiness, wakefulness.

torrid, a. SYN.-burning, hot, scalding, scorching, steaming, swelter-
ing, tropical,; ardent, fervent, fiery,
hot-blooded, impetuous, intense,
passionate. ANT.-cold, cool, freezing, frigid; apathetic, impassive,
indifferent, passionless, phlegmatic.

torture, n. SYN.-ache, anguish, agony, distress, misery, pain, suffering, throe, torment, woe. ANT.-com-
fort, ease, mitigation, relief.

torture, v. SYN.-badger, harass,
harry, hound, oppress, persecute,
plague, torment. ANT.-aid, assist,
comfort, encourage, support.

toss, v. SYN.-cast, fling, hurl, pitch,
propel, throw, thrust. ANT.-draw,
haul, hold, pull, retain.

total, a. SYN.-all, complete, concluded, consummated, detailed,
ended, entire, finished, full, perfect, thorough, unbroken, undivided, whole. ANT.-imperfect, lacking, unfinished.

total, n. SYN.-aggregate, amount,
collection, conglomeration, entirety, sum, whole. ANT.-element,
ingredient, part, particular, unit.

total, v. SYN.-add, calculate, count,

figure, sum.

touching, *a.* SYN.-affecting, heart-rending, impressive, moving, pitiable, poignant, sad, tender; adjacent, adjunct, bordering, tangent. ANT.-animated, enlivening, exhilarating, removed.

touchy, *a.* SYN.-choleric, excitable, fiery, hasty, hot, irascible, irritable, peevish, petulant, snappish, testy. ANT.-agreeable, calm, composed, tranquil.

tough, *a.* SYN.-cohesive, firm, hardy, stout, strong, sturdy, tenacious; difficult, formidable, hard, laborious, troublesome, trying; callous, incorrigible, obdurate, stubborn, vicious. ANT.-brittle, fragile, frail; easy, facile; compliant, forbearing, submissive.

toughness, n, SYN.-durability, fortitude, might, potency, power, stamina, stoutness, strength, sturdiness. ANT.-feebleness, frailty, infirmity, weakness.

tour, *v.* SYN.-go, journey, ramble, roam, rove, travel, trek, visit. ANT.-stay, stop.

tow, *v.* SYN.-drag, draw, haul, pull, tow, tug.

train, *v.* SYN.-direct, educate, inform, instill, instruct, school, teach, tutor; aim, level, point. ANT.-misdirect, misguide.

training, *n.* SYN.-cultivation, development, drill, education, exercise, instruction, knowledge, learning, lesson, operation, schooling, study, tutoring.

trait, *n.* SYN.-attribute, characteristic, feature, mark, peculiarity, property, quality.

traitorous, *a.* SYN.-apostate, disloyal, faithless, false, perfidious, recreant, treacherous, treasonable.

ANT.-constant, devoted, loyal, true.

tramp, *n.* SYN.-beggar, bum, hobo, rover, vagabond, vagrant, wanderer. ANT.-gentleman, laborer, worker.

tranquil, *a.* SYN.-appease, calm, collected, composed, dispassionate, imperturbable, pacific, peaceful, placid, quiet, sedate, serene, still, undisturbed, unmoved, unruffled. ANT.-excited, frantic, stormy, turbulent, wild.

tranquility, *n.* SYN.-calm, calmness, hush, peace, quiescence, quiet, quietude, repose, rest, serenity, silence, stillness. ANT.-agitation, disturbance, excitement, noise, tumult.

transact, *v.* SYN.-carry on, conduct, execute, manage, negotiate, perform, treat.

transaction, *n.* SYN.-affair, business, deal, deed, negotiation, occurrence, proceeding.

transfer, *v.* SYN.-assign, consign, convey, dispatch, relegate, remove, send, transmit, transplant, transport.

transform, *v.* SYN.-alter, change, convert, modify, remodel, shift, transfigure, vary, veer. ANT.-retain; continue, establish, preserve, settle, stabilize.

transient, *a.* SYN.-brief, ephemeral, evanescent, fleeting, momentary, short-lived, temporary. ANT.-abiding, immortal, lasting, permanent, timeless.

translate, *v.* SYN.-decipher, decode, elucidate, explain, explicate, interpret, render. ANT.-confuse, distort, falsify, misconstrue, misinterpret.

transmit, *v.* SYN.-convey, disclose, divulge, impart, inform, notify, relate, reveal, send, tell. ANT.-conceal, hide, withhold.

transparent, *a.* SYN.-clear, crystalline, limpid, lucid, thin, translucent; evident, explicit, manifest, obvious, open. ANT.-muddy, opaque, thick, turbid; ambiguous, questionable.

transpire, *v.* SYN.-bechance, befall, betide, chance, happen, occur, take place.

transport, *v.* SYN,-bear, carry, convey, move, remove, shift, transfer; enrapture, entrance, lift, ravish, stimulate.

trap, *n.* SYN.-ambush, artifice, bait, intrigue, lure, net, pitfall, ruse, snare, stratagem, trick, wile.

travel, *v.* SYN.-go, journey, ramble, roam, rove, tour. ANT.-stay, stop.

treachery, *n.* SYN.-collusion, conspiracy, deception, dishonesty, disloyalty, intrigue, machination, perfidy, plot, subversion, treason, violation.

treason, *n.* SYN.-betrayal, cabal, collusion, combination, conspiracy, intrigue, machination, plot, subversion, treachery.

treasure, *v.* SYN.-adore, appreciate, cherish, hold dear, prize, protect, value. ANT.-dislike, disregard, neglect.

treat, *v.* SYN.-apply, conduct, employ, handle, manage, manipulate, use. ANT.-ignore, neglect.

treaty, *n.* SYN.-alliance, association, coalition, compact, confederacy, covenant, entente, federation, league, marriage, partnership, union. ANT.-divorce, schism, separation.

tremble, *v.* SYN.-agitate, flutter, quake, quaver, quiver, shake, shiver, shudder, vibrate, waver.

trespass, *v.* SYN.-encroach, infringe, intrude, invade, penetrate, violate. ANT.-abandon, evacuate, relinquish, vacate.

trial, *n.* SYN.-examination, experiment, proof, test; attempt, effort, endeavor, essay; affliction, hardship, misery, misfortune, ordeal, suffering, tribulation, trouble. ANT.-alleviation, consolation.

trick, *n.* SYN.-antic, artifice, cheat, deception, device, fraud, guile, hoax, imposture, ploy, ruse, stratagem, stunt, subterfuge, wile. ANT.-candor, exposure, honesty, openness, sincerity.

tricky, *a.* SYN.-artful, covert, crafty, cunning, foxy, furtive, guileful, shrewd, sly, stealthy, subtle, surreptitious, underhanded, wily. ANT.-candid, frank, ingenuous, open, sincere.

trifling, *a.* SYN.-frivolous, immaterial, insignificant, paltry, petty, slight, small, trivial, unimportant, worthless. ANT.-important, momentous, serious, weighty.

trim, *v.* SYN.-adorn, beautify, bedeck, decorate, embellish, garnish, gild, ornament. ANT.-deface, deform, disfigure, mar, spoil.

trip, *n.* SYN.-cruise, expedition, jaunt, journey, passage, pilgrimage, safari, tour, travel, vacation, voyage.

trite, *a.* SYN.-banal, common, hackneyed, ordinary, stale, stereotyped. ANT.-fresh, modern, momentous, novel, stimulating.

triumph, *n.* SYN.-achievement, conquest, jubilation, ovation, victory. ANT.-defeat, failure.

trivial, *a.* SYN.-frivolous, insignificant, paltry, petty, small, trifling, unimportant. ANT.-important, momentous, serious, weighty.

trouble, n. SYN.-affliction, annoyance, anxiety, bother, calamity, care, disorder, distress, disturbance, embarrassment, grief, hardship, irritation, misery, pain, problem, sorrow, torment, woe, worry; effort, exertion, labor, toil.

trouble, v. SYN.-agitate, annoy, bother, chafe, disturb, inconvenience, interrupt, irk, irritate, molest, pester, tease, vex, worry. ANT.-accommodate, console, gratify, pacify, settle, soothe.

troublesome, a. SYN.-annoying, arduous, bothersome, burdensome, difficult, distressing, disturbing, irksome, laborious, tedious, trying, vexatious. ANT.-accommodating, amusing, easy, gratifying, pleasant.

true, a. SYN.-accurate, actual, authentic, correct, exact, genuine, real, veracious, veritable; constant, faithful, honest, loyal, reliable, sincere, steadfast, trustworthy. ANT.-counterfeit, erroneous, false, fictitious, spurious; faithless, false, fickle, inconstant.

trust, n. SYN.-confidence, constancy, credence, dependence, faith, fidelity, loyalty, reliance. ANT.-doubt, incredulity, infidelity, mistrust, skepticism.

trust, v. SYN.-believe, commit, confide, credit, depend on, entrust, esteem, hope, reckon on, rely on. ANT.-doubt, impugn, question, suspect.

trustworthy, a. SYN.-dependable, honest, honorable, reliable, safe, secure, sure, tried, trusty. ANT.-dubious, fallible, questionable, uncertain, unreliable.

truth, n. SYN.-accuracy, actuality, authenticity, correctness, exactness, fact, honesty, rightness, truthfulness, veracity, verisimilitude, verity. ANT.-falsehood, falsity, fiction, lie, untruth.

truthful, a. SYN.-accurate, candid, correct, exact, frank, honest, open, reliable, sincere, true, veracious. ANT.-deceitful, misleading, sly.

try, v. SYN.-aim, aspire, attempt, design, endeavor, intend, mean, strive, struggle, undertake; afflict, prove, test, torment, trouble. ANT.-abandon, decline, ignore, neglect, omit; comfort, console.

trying, a. SYN.-annoying, bothersome, distressing, disturbing, irksome, troublesome, vexatious. ANT.-accommodating, amusing, easy, gratifying, pleasant.

tumult, n. SYN.-chaos, clamor, commotion, confusion, din, disarray, disorder, jumble, noise, racket, row, stir, turmoil, uproar. ANT.-certainty, order, peace, tranquility.

tune, n. SYN.-air, harmony, melody, strain.

turbulent, a. SYN.-blustery, gusty, roaring, rough, stormy. tempestuous, windy. ANT.-calm, clear, peaceful, quiet, tranquil.

turmoil, n. SYN.-agitation, chaos, commotion, confusion, disarrangement, disarray, disorder, ferment, jumble, stir, tumult. ANT.-certainty, order, peace, tranquility.

turn, v. SYN.-circle, circulate. invert, revolve, rotate, spin, twirl, twist, wheel, whirl; avert, deflect, deviate, divert, swerve; alter, change, transmute. ANT.-arrest, fix, stand, stop; continue, proceed; endure, perpetuate.

twist, v. SYN.-bend, bow, crook, curve, deflect, lean, revolve, rotate, spin, turn, twirl, whirl; influence, mold. ANT.-break, resist, stiffen, straighten.

type, n. SYN.-emblem, mark, sign, symbol; category, character, class, description, exemplar, kind, model, nature, pattern, sort, stamp. ANT.-deviation, eccentricity, monstrosity, peculiarity.

typical, a. SYN.-common, customary, familiar, habitual, normal, ordinary, plain, regular, usual. ANT.-extraordinary, marvelous, remarkable, strange, uncommon.

tyrant, n. SYN.-autocrat, despot, dictator, oppressor, persecutor.

U

ugly, a. SYN.-deformed, hideous, homely, plain, repellent, repulsive, uncomely; disagreeable, ill-natured, spiteful, surly, vicious. ANT.-attractive, beautiful, fair, handsome, pretty.

ultimate, a. SYN.-extreme, final, last, latest, terminal, utmost. ANT.-beginning, first, foremost, initial, opening.

unadulterated, a. SYN.-clean, clear, genuine, immaculate, pure, spotless, undefiled, untainted. ANT.-foul, polluted, sullied, tainted, tarnished.

unassuming, a. SYN.-compliant, humble, lowly, meek, modest, plain, simple, submissive, unostentatious, unpretentious. ANT.-arrogant, boastful, haughty, proud, vain.

uncertain, a. SYN.-ambiguous, dim, hazy, indefinite, indistinct, obscure, unclear, undetermined, unsettled, vague. ANT.-clear, explicit, lucid, precise, specific.

uncertainty, n. SYN.-ambiguity,

distrust, doubt, hesitation, incredulity, scruple, skepticism, suspense, suspicion, unbelief, uncertainty. ANT.-belief, certainty, conviction, determination. faith.

uncompromising, a. SYN.-dogged, firm, headstrong, immovable, inflexible, intractable, obdurate, obstinate, pertinacious, stubborn, unyielding. ANT.-amenable, compliant, docile, submissive, yielding.

unconcern, n. SYN.-apathy, disinterestedness, impartiality, indifference, insensibility, neutrality. ANT.-affection, ardor, fervor, passion.

unconditional, a. SYN.-absolute, actual, complete, entire, perfect, pure, ultimate, unqualified, unrestricted. ANT.-accountable, conditional, contingent, dependent, qualified.

uncouth, a. SYN.-awkward, clumsy, coarse, crass, crude, discourteous, harsh, ill-mannered, rough, rude, unfinished, unpolished, unrefined, vulgar. ANT.-cultivated, refined.

uncover, v. SYN.-disclose, discover, divulge, expose, impart, reveal, show. ANT.-cloak, conceal, cover, hide, obscure.

under, prep. SYN.-below, beneath, under, underneath. ANT.-above, over.

undergo, v. SYN.-bear, brave, encounter, endure, experience, stand, suffer, sustain, tolerate. ANT.-banish, discard, exclude, overcome.

understand, v. SYN.-appreciate, apprehend, comprehend, conceive, discern, grasp, know, learn, perceive, realize, see. ANT.-ignore, misapprehend, mistake, misunderstand.

understanding, n. SYN.-accordance, agreement, bargain, coincidence, compact, concord, concurrence, contract, covenant, harmony, pact, stipulation, unison. ANT.-difference, disagreement, discord, dissension, variance.

understudy, *n.* SYN.-alternate, proxy, representative, substitute. ANT.-principal.

undertaking, *n.* SYN.-attempt, effort, endeavor, essay, experiment, trial. ANT.-inaction, laziness, neglect.

undivided, *a.* SYN.-all, complete, entire, intact, integral, perfect, total, whole. ANT.-deficient, incomplete, partial.

undying, *a.* SYN.-ceaseless, deathless, endless, eternal, everlasting, immortal, infinite, perpetual, timeless. ANT. ephemeral, finite, mortal, temporal, transient.

unearthly, *a.* SYN.-metaphysical, other-worldly, preternatural, spiritual, supernatural. ANT.-common, human, natural, physical, plain.

uneducated, *a.* SYN.-ignorant, illiterate, uncultured, uninformed, unlearned, unlettered, untaught. ANT.-cultured, educated, erudite, informed, literate.

unemployed, *a.* SYN.-dormant, idle, inactive, indolent, inert, lazy, slothful, unoccupied. ANT.-active, employed, industrious, occupied, working.

unexpected, *a.* SYN.-abrupt, sudden, unforeseen. ANT.-anticipated, gradual, slowly.

unfasten, *v.* SYN.-free, loosen, open, unbar, unlock, untie. ANT.-bar, close, fasten, lock, shut.

unfavorable, *a.* SYN.-adverse, antagonistic, contrary, counteractive, disastrous, hostile, opposed, opposite, unlucky. ANT.-benign, favor-

able, fortunate, lucky, propitious.

unfold, *v.* SYN.-amplify, develop, elaborate, enlarge, evolve, expand, open. ANT.-compress, contract, restrict.

uniform, *a.* SYN.-methodical, orderly, periodical, regular, steady, systematic, unvaried. ANT.-abnormal, erratic.

uninteresting, *a.* SYN.-boring, burdensome, dreary, dull, humdrum, monotonous, tedious, tiresome. ANT.-amusing, entertaining, exciting, interesting, quick.

union, *n.* SYN.-agreement, alliance, amalgamation, coalition, combination, concert, concord, concurrence, confederacy, fusion, harmony, incorporation, joining, league, marriage, solidarity, unanimity, unification. ANT.-disagreement, discord, division, schism, separation.

unique, *a.* SYN.-choice, distinctive, exceptional, matchless, peculiar, rare, singular, sole, solitary, uncommon, unequaled. ANT.-common, commonplace, frequent, ordinary, typical.

unison, *n.* SYN.-accordance, agreement, coincidence, concord, concurrence, harmony, understanding. ANT.-difference, disagreement, discord, dissension, variance.

unite, *v.* SYN.-amalgamate, associate, attach, blend, combine, conjoin, connect, consolidate, embody, fuse, join, link, merge, unify. ANT.-disconnect, disrupt, divide, separate, sever.

universal, *a.* SYN.-broad, common, familiar, frequent, general, omnipotent, omnipresent, ordinary, popular, prevalent, ubiquitous, usual, vast. ANT.-exceptional, extraordinary, odd, scarce.

unlawful, *a.* SYN.-criminal, illegal, illegitimate, illicit, outlawed, prohibited. ANT.-honest, lawful, legal, permitted.

unlike, *a.* SYN.-different, dissimilar, distinct, divergent, diverse, incongruous, opposite, variant; divers, miscellaneous, sundry, various. ANT.-alike, congruous, identical, same, similar.

unlimited, *a.* SYN.-boundless, endless, eternal, illimitable, immeasurable, immense, infinite, interminable, unbounded, vast. ANT.-bounded, circumscribed, confined, finite, limited.

unobstructed, *a.* SYN.-clear, free, immune loose, open, unconfined, unfastened, unrestricted. ANT.-blocked, clogged, confined, impeded, restrained, restricted.

unsafe, *a.* SYN.-chancy, critical, dangerous, hazardous, insecure, menacing, perilous, precarious, risky, threatening. ANT.-firm, protected, safe, secure.

unselfish, *a.* SYN.-beneficent, bountiful, generous, giving, liberal, magnanimous, munificent, openhanded. ANT.-covetous, greedy, miserly, selfish, stingy.

unsophisticated, *a.* SYN.-artless, candid, frank, ingenuous, innocent, naive, natural, open, simple. unlearned, untutored. ANT.-crafty, cunning, sophisticated, worldly.

unstable, *a.* SYN.-capricious, changeable, fickle, fitful, inconstant, restless, unreliable, variable. ANT.-constant, reliable, stable, steady, trustworthy.

untainted, *a.* SYN.-clean, clear, genuine, immaculate, spotless, pure, unadulterated. ANT.-foul, polluted, sullied, tainted, tarnished.

untamed, *a.* SYN.-barbarous, boisterous, extravagant, fierce, foolish, frenzied, giddy, impetuous, irregular, mad, outlandish, rash, reckless, rough, rude, savage, stormy, tempestuous, turbulent, uncivilized, uncultivated, undomesticated, wanton, wayward, wild. ANT.-calm, civilized, gentle, placid, quiet.

unusual, *a.* SYN.-aberrant, abnormal, capricious, devious, eccentric, irregular, unnatural, variable. ANT.-fixed, methodical, ordinary, regular, usual.

unyielding, *a.* SYN.-constant, fast, firm, inflexible, secure, solid, stable, steadfast, steady, unswerving. ANT.-slow, sluggish; insecure, loose, unstable, unsteady.

upbraid, *v.* SYN.-admonish, berate, blame, censure, lecture, rebuke, reprehend, reprimand, scold, vituperate. ANT.-approve, commend, praise.

uphold, *v.* SYN.-advocate, bolster, defend, endorse, help, maintain, protect, safeguard, screen, shield, support, sustain. ANT.-assault, attack, deny, submit.

upright, *a.* SYN.-erect, straight, unbent, vertical; direct, fair, honest, honorable, just, right, square, undeviating, unswerving. ANT.-bent, crooked; circuitous, devious, dishonest, fraudulent, winding.

upset, *v.* SYN.-annoy, bother, disturb, harass, haunt, inconvenience, molest, perplex, pester, plague, tease, trouble, worry. ANT.-gratify, please, relieve, soothe.

urge, *n.* SYN.-appetite, aspiration, craving, desire, hunger, hungering,

longing, lust, wish, yearning. ANT.-
abomination, aversion, distaste,
hate, loathing.
urge, *v.* SYN.-allure, coax, entice,
exhort, incite, induce, influence,
persuade, prevail upon. ANT.-co-
erce, compel, deter, dissuade, restrain.
urgency, *n.* SYN.-compulsion, crisis,
emergency, exigency, press,
pressure, stress.
urgent, *a.* SYN.-cogent, compelling,
critical, crucial, exigent, impelling,
imperative, important, importunate, insistent, instant, necessary,
pressing, serious. ANT.-insignifi-
cant, petty, trifling, trivial, unimportant.
use, *n.* SYN.-custom, habit, manner,
practice, training, usage, wont.
ANT.-disuse, idleness, inexperience,
speculation, theory.
use, *v.* SYN.-apply, avail, consume,
employ, exercise, exert, exhaust,
expend, exploit, handle, manage,
manipulate, operate, practice,
treat, utilize; accustom, familiarize,
inure, train. ANT.-ignore, neglect,
overlook, waste.
useful, *a.* SYN.-advantageous, beneficial, funcional, good, handy, helpful, serviceable, utilitarian, workable. ANT.-deleterious, destructive,
detrimental, harmful, injurious.
usefulness, *n.* SYN.-advantage, application, edge, gain, merit, utility,
value, worthiness. ANT.-cheapness,
uselessness, valueless.
useless, *a.* SYN.-abortive, empty,
fruitless, futile, idle, ineffectual,
obsolete, pointless, unavailing, un-
usable, valueless, vain, vapid,
worthless. ANT.-effective, potent,
profitable.
usual, *a.* SYN.-accustomed, common,

customary, every-day, familiar,
general, habitual, normal, ordinary. ANT.-abnormal, exceptional,
extraordinary, irregular, rare.
usurp, *v.* SYN.-adopt, appropriate,
assume, confiscate, expropriate,
occupy, take. ANT.-reject, repel,
surrender.
utensil, *n.* SYN.-apparatus, appliance, device, gadget, instrument,
tool.
utilize, *v.* SYN.-apply, avail, employ,
occupy, use. ANT.-banish, discard,
discharge, reject.
utter, *a.* SYN.-absolute, complete,
entire, total, unconditional. ANT.-in-
complete, inconsiderable, meager,
paltry.
utter, *v.* SYN.-announce, orate, proclaim, say, speak, state, talk, verbalize, vocalize

V

vacant, *a.* SYN.-bare, barren, blank,
empty, unoccupied, vacuous, void.
ANT.-busy, employed, engaged, full,
replete.
vacate, *v.* SYN.-abandon, abdicate,
abjure, desert, forsake, leave, quit,
relinquish, renounce, resign, surrender, waive. ANT.-defend, maintain, uphold; stay, support.
vacillate, *v.* SYN.-change, fluctuate,
hesitate, oscillate, totter, undulate,
vary, waver. ANT.-adhere, decide,
persist, resolve, stick.
vacillating, *a.* SYN.-fluctuating, inconsistent, irreconcilable, irresolute, unsteady, wavering. ANT.-con-
sistent, sure.
vacuity, *n.* SYN.-blank, emptiness,
idleness, insignificance, nothingness, stupidity, unimportance,
vacuum, void.

vacuous, a. SYN.-barren, blank, empty, vacant.

vagabond, n. SYN.-beggar, mendicant, nomad, pauper, ragamuffin, rascal, scrub, starveling, tatterdemalion, tramp, wanderer, wretch.

vagrant, n. SYN.-beggar, bum, hobo, rover, tramp, vagabond, wanderer. ANT.-gentleman, laborer, worker.

vague, a. SYN.-ambiguous, dim, hazy, indefinite, indistinct, obscure, uncertain, unclear, undetermined, unsettled. ANT.-clear, explicit, lucid, precise, specific.

vain, a. SYN.-abortive, bootless, empty, fruitless, futile, idle, ineffectual, pointless, unavailing, useless, valueless, vapid, worthless; conceited, proud, vainglorious. ANT.-effective, potent, profitable; meek, modest.

vainglory, n. SYN.-boastfulness, conceit, haughtiness, pomp, pride, self-esteem, self-respect, vainglory, vanity. ANT.-humility, lowliness, meekness, modesty, shame.

valiant, a. SYN.-adventurous, audacious, brave, bold, chivalrous, courageous, daring, dauntless, fearless, gallant, heroic, intrepid, valorous. ANT.-cowardly, cringing, fearful, timid, weak.

valid, a. SYN.-binding, cogent, conclusive, convincing, effective, efficacious, legal, logical, powerful, sound, strong, telling, weighty. ANT.-counterfeit, null, spurious, void, weak.

validate, v. SYN.-authenticate, certify, confirm, document, endorse, notarize, prove, sanction, substantiate, verify

valuable, a. SYN.-costly, dear, esteemed, expensive, precious, profitable, use. ANT.-cheap, mean, poor, trashy, worthless.

valuation, n. SYN.-appraisal, assessment, consideration, estimate, estimation, guess, judgment, opinion, theory.

value, n. SYN.-excellence, merit, price, usefulness, utility, worth, worthiness. ANT.-cheapness, uselessness, valueless.

value, v. SYN.-appraise, appreciate, cherish, esteem, hold dear, prize, treasure. ANT.-dislike, disregard, neglect.

vandalism, n. SYN.-damage, destruction, ruin, waste, wreckage.

vanish, v. SYN.-disappear, disintegrate, disperse, dissipate, dissolve, evaporate, fade, scatter, vaporize.

vanity, n. SYN.-conceit, egotism, haughtiness, pride, self-esteem, vainglory, vanity. ANT.-diffidence, humility, meekness, modesty.

vanquish, v. SYN.-beat, conquer, crush, defeat, humble, master, overcome, quell, rout, subdue, subjugate, surmount. ANT.-capitulate, cede, lose, retreat, surrender.

variable, a. SYN.-changeable, fickle, fitful, inconstant, shifting, unstable, vacillating, wavering. ANT.-constant, stable, steady, unchanging, uniform.

variant, a. SYN.-changing, contrary, different, differing, dissimilar, divergent, diverse, fickle, incongruous, inconstant, restless, unlike. ANT.-alike, congruous, identical, same, similar; constant.

variation, n. SYN.-alteration, alternation, change, modification, mutation, substitution, variety, vicissitude. ANT.-monotony, stability, uniformity.

variety, n. SYN.-assortment, change, difference, dissimilarity, diversity, heterogeneity, medley, miscellany, mixture, multifariousness, variety; breed, kind, sort, stock, strain, subspecies. ANT.-homogeneity, likeness, monotony, sameness, uniformity.

various, *a.* SYN.-divers, miscellaneous, several, sundry. ANT.-same, singular.

vary, *v.* SYN.-alter, change, convert, modify, remodel, shift, transfigure, transform. ANT.-retain; continue, establish, preserve, settle, stabilize.

vassalage, *n.* SYN.-bondage, serfdom, servitude, slavery, thralldom. ANT.-freedom, liberation.

vast, *a.* SYN.-big, capacious, colossal, extensive, great, huge, immense, large, wide. ANT.-little, mean, short, small, tiny.

vehement, *a.* SYN.-ardent, burning, fervent, fervid, fiery, impetuous, passionate. ANT.-apathetic, calm, cool, deliberate, quiet.

veil, *v.* SYN.-cloak, conceal, cover, curtain, disguise, envelop, guard, hide, mask, protect, screen, shield, shroud. ANT.-bare, divulge, expose, reveal, unveil.

venerate, *v.* SYN.-admire, adore, appreciate, approve, esteem, respect, revere, worship. ANT.-abhor, despise, dislike.

vengeance, *n.* SYN.-reprisal, requital, retaliation, retribution, revenge, vindictiveness. ANT.-mercy, pardon, reconciliation, remission, forgiveness.

vent, *v.* SYN.-breathe, discharge, eject, emanate, emit, expel, express, hurl, shed, shoot, spurt, utter, verbalize.

venture, *v.* SYN.-brave, dare, hazard, jeopardy, peril, risk. ANT.-defense, immunity, protection, safety.

verbal, *a.* SYN.-literal, oral, spoken, vocal. ANT.-documentary, recorded, written.

verbose, *a.* SYN.-chattering, chatty, garrulous, glib, loquacious, talkative, voluble. ANT.-laconic, reticent, silent, taciturn, uncommunicative.

verbosity, *n.* SYN.-long-windiness, redundancy, talkativeness, verboseness, wordiness. ANT.-conciseness, laconism, terseness.

verification, *n.* SYN.-confirmation, corroboration, demonstration, proof, testimony. ANT.-failure, fallacy, invalidity.

verify, *v.* SYN.-ascertain, conclude, confirm, corroborate, define, determine, substantiate; acknowledge, assure, establish, settle.

veritable, *a.* SYN.-accurate, actual, authentic, correct, exact, genuine, real, true, veracious. ANT.-counterfeit, erroneous, false, fictitious, spurious.

vertical, *a.* SYN.-erect, perpendicular, plumb, straight, upright. ANT.-horizontal, inclined, level, oblique, prone.

vex, *v.* SYN.-aggravate, anger, annoy, bother, chafe, disturb, embitter, exasperate, harass, inflame, irritate, nettle, pester, plague, provoke. ANT.-appease, palliate soften, soothe.

vexation, *n.* SYN.-annoyance, chagrin, exasperation, irritation, mortification, pique. ANT.-appeasement, comfort, gratification, pleasure.

vibrate, *v.* SYN.-agitate, flutter, quake, quaver, quiver, shake, shiver, shudder, sway, tremble, waver.

vice, *n.* SYN.-corruption, crime, depravity, evil, immorality, iniquity, offense, sin, transgression, ungodliness, wickedness, wrong. ANT.-goodness, innocence, purity, righteousness, virtue.

vicinity, *n.* SYN.-area, district, environs, locality, neighborhood; adjacency, closeness, nearness, propinquity, proximity. ANT.-distance, remoteness.

victory, *n.* SYN.-accomplishment, achievement, attainment, conquest, mastery, overthrow, success, triumph. ANT.-defeat, failure.

view, *n.* SYN.-observation, outlook, panorama, perspective, prospect, range, scene, regard, review, sight, survey, vista; belief, conception, impression, judgment, opinion, sentiment.

view, *v.* SYN.-behold, discern, examine, eye, gaze, glance, inspect, look, observe, regard, scan, see, stare, survey, watch, witness. ANT.-avert, hide, miss, overlook.

viewpoint, *n.* SYN.-angle, aspect, attitude, outlook, perspective, pose, position, posture, slant, stand, standpoint.

vigilant, *a.* SYN.-alert, anxious, attentive, careful, cautious, circumspect, observant, wakeful, wary, watchful. ANT.-careless, inattentive, lax, neglectful, oblivious.

vigor, *n.* SYN.-endurance, energy, enthusiasm, health, liveliness, potency, power, spirit, stamina, strength, temper, verve, vitality, zeal. ANT.-languor, listlessness.

vigorous, *a.* SYN.-active, alert, animated, blithe, bright, brisk, clear, effective, energetic, forceful, fresh, frolicsome, glowing, lively, spirited, sprightly, striking, strong, supple, vivacious, vivid. ANT.-dull, insipid, listless, stale, vapid.

vile, *a.* SYN.-abject, base, debased, depraved, despicable, foul, ignoble, loathsome, low, mean, obscene, odious, revolting, sordid, vicious, vulgar, wicked, worthless, wretched. ANT.-attractive, decent, laudable; honorable, upright.

vilify, *v.* SYN.-abuse, asperse, assail, criticize, defame, denounce, disparage, ill-use, impugn, malign, revile, scandalize, traduce. ANT.-cherish, honor, praise, protect, respect.

villainous, *a.* SYN.-bad, baleful, base, deleterious, evil, immoral, iniquitous, noxious, pernicious, sinful, unsound, unwholesome, wicked. ANT.-excellent, good, honorable, moral, reputable.

vindicate, *v.* SYN.-absolve, acquit, assert, clear, defend, excuse, exonerate, justify, support, uphold. ANT.-abandon, accuse, blame, convict.

violate, *v.* SYN.-break, defile, debauch, deflower, desecrate, dishonor, disobey, infringe, invade, pollute, profane, ravish, transgress.

violence, *n.* SYN.-brutality, clash, coercion, compulsion, commotion, disorder, disturbance, energy, force, fury, injury, intensity, might, outrage, passion, potency, power, severity, strength, vehemence, vigor. ANT.-feebleness, frailty, gentleness, impotence, mildness, persuasion, respect, weakness.

violent, *a.* SYN.-boisterous, fierce, forceful, furious, impetuous, passionate, powerful, raging, raving, turbulent, vehement, wild; acute, extreme, intense, severe. ANT.-calm, feeble, gentle, quiet, soft.

virgin, *a.* SYN.-chaste, guiltless, innocent, pure, undefiled. ANT.-defiled, sullied, tainted.

virtue, *n.* SYN.-chastity, goodness, integrity, morality, probity, purity, rectitude, virginity; effectiveness, efficacy, excellence, force, merit, power, strength, worth. ANT.-corruption, lewdness, sin, vice; fault.

virtuous, *a.* SYN.-chaste, decent, ethical, good, honorable, just, moral, pure, right, righteous, scrupulous. ANT.-amoral, libertine, licentious, sinful, unethical.

visible, *a.* SYN.-apparent, clear, distinct, evident, intelligible, lucid, manifest, obvious, open, plain, unobstructed. ANT.-ambiguous, obscure, unclear, vague.

vision, *n.* SYN.-apparition, daydream, dream, ghost, hallucination, mirage, phantasm, phantom, prophecy, revelation, specter. ANT.-reality, substance, verity.

visionary, *a.* SYN.-exemplary, fancied, faultless, ideal, imaginary, perfect, supreme, unreal, utopian. ANT.-actual, faulty, imperfect, material, real.

vital, *a.* SYN.-active, alive, animate, animated, energetic, lively, living, spirited, sprightly, vigorous, vivacious; basic, cardinal, critical, essential, fundamental, imperative, indispensable, necessary, paramount, urgent. ANT.-inanimate, inert, lifeless; nonessential, unimportant.

vitality, *n.* SYN.-animation, ardor, buoyancy, enthusiasm, life, liveliness, spirit, vigor, vivacity, zeal. ANT.-death, demise, dullness, languor, lethargy.

vitiate, *v.* SYN.-abase, adulterate, alloy, corrupt, debase, defile, degrade, deprave, depress, pervert.

ANT.-enhance, improve, raise, restore, vitalize.

vitiated, *a.* SYN.-contaminated, corrupted, crooked, debased, depraved, dishonest, impure, profligate, putrid, spoiled, tainted, venal, vitiated.

vivid, *a.* SYN.-animated, bright, brilliant, clear, expressive, fresh, graphic, intense, lively, lucid, striking. ANT.-dull, dim, dreary, dusky, vague.

vocation, *n.* SYN.-business, employment, engagement, enterprise, job, occupation, profession, trade, work. ANT.-avocation, hobby, pastime.

void, *a.* SYN.-bare, barren, blank, empty, unoccupied, vacant, vacuous. ANT.-busy, employed, engaged, full, replete.

volatile, *a.* SYN.-animated, blithe, cheerful, effervescent, elated, hopeful, jocund, light, lively, resilient, spirited, sprightly, vivacious; changeable, ephemeral, transient. ANT.-dejected, depressed, despondent, hopeless, sullen; constant, sure, unchanging.

volition, *n.* SYN.-choice, decision, desire, determination, intention, preference, resolution, taste, testament, will, wish. ANT.-coercion, compulsion, disinterest, indifference.

volume, *n.* SYN.-amount, bulk, capacity, cube, extent, magnitude, mass, measure, quantity, size; book, edition, encyclopedia, manuscript, tome; amplification, loudness, intensity.

voluntary, *a.* SYN.-automatic, extemporaneous, impulsive, instinctive, offhand, spontaneous, willing. ANT.-compulsory, forced, planned, prepared, rehearsed.

volunteer, v. SYN.-contribute, donate, enlist, offer, proffer, propose, propound, render, submit, suggest, tender. ANT.-rejection, withdrawal.

vulgar, a. SYN.-common, familiar, general, ordinary, plebeian, popular; base, coarse, gross, impolite, indecent, low, nasty, obscene, odious, ribald, rude, tasteless, unrefined. ANT.-esoteric, select; aristocratic, polite, refined.

W

wages, n. SYN.-compensation, earnings, pay, payment, recompense, salary, stipend. ANT.-gift, gratuity, present.

wait, v. SYN.-abide, bide, delay, linger, remain, rest, stay, tarry; await, expect, watch; attend, minister, serve. ANT.-act, expedite, hasten, leave.

wander, v. SYN.-deviate, digress, err, ramble, range, roam, rove, saunter, stray, stroll, traipse. ANT.-halt, linger, settle, stay, stop.

want, v. SYN.-covet, crave, desire, lack, long for, need, require, wish.

wariness, n. SYN.-care, caution, heed, prudence, vigilance, watchfulness. ANT.-abandon, carelessness, recklessness.

warm, a. SYN.-amiable, amicable, ardent, cordial, eager, earnest, enthusiastic, friendly, gracious, hearty, sincere, sociable. ANT.-aloof cool, reserved, taciturn.

warn, v. SYN.-admonish, advise, alert, apprise, caution, counsel, inform, notify.

warning, n. SYN.-admonition, advice, caution, indication, information, notice, portent, sign.

wary, a. SYN.-alert, alive, awake, aware, careful, heedful, mindful, observant, thoughtful, vigilant, watchful. ANT.-apathetic, indifferent, oblivious, unaware.

wash, v. SYN.-bathe, clean, cleanse, launder, rinse, scrub, wet. ANT.-dirty, foul, soil, stain.

waste, a. SYN.-abandoned, bare, barren, bleak, deserted, desolate, devastated, extra, forlorn, forsaken, lonely, ravaged, ruined, solitary, uninhabited, useless, wild. ANT.-attended, cultivated, fertile.

waste, v. SYN.-consume, corrode, decay, despoil, destroy, devastate, diminish, dissipate, dwindle, lavish, misuse, pillage, plunder, ravage, ruin, sack, scatter, spend, squander, strip, wear out, wither. ANT.-accumulate, economize, preserve, save.

watch, v. SYN.-behold, discern, distinguish, espy, inspect, look at, observe, perceive, scan, scrutinize, view, witness.

waver, v. SYN.-distrust, doubt, falter, flicker, hesitate, mistrust, quiver, question, suspect, sway, tremble, vacillate. ANT.-believe, confide, decide, rely on, trust.

wavering, a. SYN.-changeable, fickle, fitful, inconstant, shifting, unstable, vacillating, variable. ANT.-constant, stable, steady, unchanging, uniform.

wax, v. SYN.-accrue, amplify, augment, enhance, enlarge, expand, extend, grow, heighten, increase, intensify, magnify, multiply, raise. ANT.-atrophy, contract, decrease, diminish, reduce.

way, n. SYN.-avenue, channel, course, passage, path, road, route, street, thoroughfare, track, trail, walk; fashion, form, habit, manner, method, mode, plan, practice, procedure, process, style, system.

weak, *a.* SYN.-bending, debilitated, decrepit, delicate, feeble, fragile, frail, impotent, infirm, illogical , inadequate, ineffective, irresolute, lame, pliable, pliant, poor, tender, vacillating, vague, wavering, yielding; assailable, defenseless, exposed, vulnerable. ANT.-potent, powerful, robust, strong, sturdy.

weakness, *n.* SYN.-disability, handicap, impotence; inability, incapacity. ANT.-ability, capability, power, strength.

wealth, *n.* SYN.-abundance, affluence, fortune, luxury, money, opulence, plenty, possessions, riches. ANT.-indigence, need, poverty, want.

wealthy, *a.* SYN.-affluent, luxurious, opulent, plentiful, prosperous, rich, sumptuous, well-to-do. ANT.-beggarly, destitute, indigent, needy, poor.

wearied, *a.* SYN.-bored, dim, drained, faded, faint, feeble, languid, pale. ANT.-conspicuous, glaring; strong, vigorous; brave, forceful.

weary, *a.* SYN.-bored, exhausted, faint, fatigued, jaded, spent, tired, wearied, worn. ANT.-fresh, hearty, invigorated, rested.

weary, *v.* SYN.-annoy, distress, exhaust, fatigue, harass, irk, jade, tire, tucker, vex, wear out. ANT.-amuse, invigorate, refresh, restore, revive.

wedlock, *n.* SYN.-espousal, marriage, matrimony, nuptials, union. ANT.-celibacy, divorce, virginity.

weigh, *v.* SYN.-consider, contemplate, deliberate, examine, meditate, ponder, reflect, study. ANT.-ignore, neglect, overlook.

weight, *n.* SYN.-burden, gravity, heaviness, load, pressure; emphasis, import, importance, influence, significance, stress, value. ANT.-buoyancy, levity, lightness; insignificance, triviality.

well, *a.* SYN.-hale, happy, healthy, hearty, sound; beneficial, convenient, expedient, good, profitable. ANT.-depressed, feeble, infirm, weak.

whim, *n.* SYN.-caprice, fancy, humor, impulse, inclination, notion, quirk, thought, urge, vagary, whimsy.

whole, *a.* SYN.-all, complete, entire, intact, integral, perfect, total, undivided, unimpaired; hale, healed, healthy, sound, well. ANT.-defective, deficient, imperfect, incomplete, partial.

wholesome, *a.* SYN.-hale, healthy, hearty, robust, sound, strong, well; hygienic, salubrious, salutary. ANT.-delicate, diseased, frail, infirm; injurious, noxious.

wicked, *a.* SYN.-bad, baleful, base, deleterious, evil, immoral, iniquitous, malevolent, malicious, noxious, pernicious, sinful, unsound, unwholesome, villainous, virulent. ANT.-benevolent, excellent, good, honorable, kind, moral, reputable.

wide, a, SYN.-broad, expanded, extensive, large, sweeping, vast. ANT.-confined, narrow, restricted.

wild, *a.* SYN.-barbarous, boisterous, fierce, outlandish, rude, savage, stormy, tempestuous, uncivilized, undomesticated, untamed; deserted, desolate, rough, uncultivated, waste; extravagant, foolish, frantic, frenzied, giddy, impetuous, irregular, mad, rash, reckless, turbulent, wanton, wayward. ANT.-civilized, gentle; calm, placid, quiet.

willful, *a.* SYN.-contemplated, deliberate, designed, intended, intentional, premeditated, studied, voluntary. ANT.-accidental, fortuitous.

will, *n.* SYN.-choice, decision, desire, determination, intention, pleasure, preference, resolution, testament, volition, wish. ANT.-coercion, compulsion, disinterest, indifference.

win, *v.* SYN.-achieve, gain, prevail, prosper, succeed, thrive. ANT.-fail, miscarry, miss.

wind, *n.* SYN.-blast, breeze, draft, gale, gust, hurricane, squall, storm, tempest, zephyr.

wisdom, *n.* SYN.-discretion, erudition,. foresight, information, insight, intelligence, judgment, knowledge, learning, prudence, reason, sagacity, saneness, sense. ANT.-foolishness, ignorance, imprudence, nonsense, stupidity.

wise, a, SYN.-deep, discerning, enlightened, erudite, informed, intelligent, knowing, learned, penetrating, profound, sagacious, scholarly, sound; advisable, expedient, prudent. ANT.-foolish, shallow, simple.

wish, *n.* SYN.-aspiration, craving, desire, hungering, longing, yearning. ANT.-abomination, aversion, distaste, hate, loathing.

wish, *v.* SYN.-covet, crave, desire, hanker, hunger, long, thirst, want, yearn. ANT.-decline, despise, reject, repudiate, scorn.

wit, *n.* SYN.-comprehension, intellect, intelligence, mind, perspicacity, reason, sagacity, sense, un-

derstanding; banter, cleverness, fun, humor, irony, pleasantry, raillery, sarcasm, satire, witticism. ANT.-commonplace, platitude, sobriety, solemnity, stupidity.

witchcraft, *n.* SYN.-black art, conjuring, enchantment, legerdemain, magic, necromancy, sorcery, voodoo, wizardry.

withdraw, *v.* SYN.-depart, give up, go, leave, quit, relinquish, renounce, retire, vacate. ANT.-abide, remain, stay, tarry.

wither, *v.* SYN.-decline, droop, dry, fail, languish, sear, shrink, shrivel, sink, waste, weaken, wilt, wizen. ANT.-refresh, rejuvenate, renew, revive.

withhold, *v.* SYN.-abstain, desist, forbear, refrain, restrain. ANT.-continue, indulge, persist.

witness, *n.* SYN.-attestation, confirmation, declaration, evidence, proof, testimony. ANT.-argument, contradiction, disproof, refutation.

witty, *a.* SYN.-amusing, bright, clever, comical, droll, funny, humorous, ingenious, quick, quick-witted, sharp, smart. ANT.-dull, foolish, melancholy, sad, serious, sober, solemn, stupid.

wonder, *n.* SYN.-curiosity, marvel, miracle, phenomenon, prodigy, rarity, spectacle; admiration, amazement, astonishment, awe, bewilderment, curiosity, surprise, wonderment. ANT.-familiarity, triviality; apathy, expectation, indifference.

word, *n.* SYN.-account, assertion, assurance, commitment, declaration, expression, guarantee, name, news, phrase, pledge, promise, report, statement, tidings, utterance.

work, *n.* SYN.-achievement, business, drudgery, effort, employment, labor, occupation, opus, performance, production; task, toil, travail. ANT.-ease, leisure, play, recreation, vacation.

worldly, a. SYN.-base, carnal, corporeal, fleshly, gross, lustful, sensual; cultured, discriminating, sophisticated, urbane. ANT.-exalted, spiritual, temperate.

worn, a. SYN.-exhausted, fatigued, jaded, spent, tired, wearied; frayed, tattered, threadbare, shabby. ANT.-fresh, hearty, invigorated, rested; new, unused.

worry, n. SYN.-anxiety, apprehension, concern, disquiet, fear, misgiving, trouble, uneasiness. ANT.-contentment, equanimity, peace, satisfaction.

worry, v. SYN.-annoy, bother, disturb, gall, harass, harry, haze, irritate, pain, persecute, tease, torment, trouble, vex; care, chafe, fidget, fret, fume, fuss. ANT.-comfort, console, solace.

worship, v. SYN.-adore, deify, honor, idolize, respect, revere, reverence, venerate. ANT.-blaspheme, curse, despise, loathe, scorn.

worth, n. SYN.-excellence, merit, price, usefulness, utility, value, virtue, worthiness. ANT.-cheapness, uselessness, valueless.

worthless, a. SYN.-abortive, empty, fruitless, futile, ineffectual, irrelevant, pointless, unavailing, unnecessary, useless, vain, valueless, vapid. ANT.-effective, potent, profitable.

wound, v. SYN.-abuse, cut, damage, disfigure, harm, hurt, injure, maim; affront, dishonor, insult, wrong. ANT.-benefit, help, preserve; compliment, praise.

wrap, v. SYN.-cloak, clothe, cover, envelop, shield, shroud, veil. ANT.-bare, expose, reveal.

wrath, n. SYN.-anger, choler, fury, indignation, ire, passion, rage, resentment, temper. ANT.-conciliation, forbearance, patience, peace, self-control.

wreck, v. SYN.-annihilate, demolish, destroy, devastate, eradicate, exterminate, extinguish, obliterate, ravage, raze, ruin. ANT.-construct, establish, make, preserve, save.

wretched, a. SYN.-comfortless, disconsolate, distressed, forlorn, heartbroken, miserable, pitiable; abject, beggarly, contemptible, despicable, low, mean, paltry, pitiful, poor, shabby, sorry, vile, worthless. ANT.-contented, fortunate, happy; noble, significant.

writer, n. SYN.-author, artist, composer, essayist, reporter.

wrong, a. SYN.-amiss, askew, awry, erroneous, fallacious, false, faulty, inaccurate, incorrect, mistaken, imprecise, untrue; improper, inappropriate, unsuitable; aberrant, bad, criminal, evil, immoral, iniquitous, reprehensible. ANT.-correct, right, true; suitable; proper.

Y

yearning, n. SYN.-appetite, aspiration, craving, desire, hungering, longing, lust, urge. ANT.-abomination, aversion, distaste, hate, loathing.

yield, n. SYN.-crop, fruit, harvest, proceeds, produce, product, profit, reaping, result.

yield, v. SYN.-afford, bear, bestow, breed, generate, impart, pay, produce, supply; accord, allow, concede, grant, permit; abdicate, accede, acquiesce, capitulate, cede, quit, relent, relinquish, resign, submit, succumb, surrender, waive. ANT.-deny, dissent, oppose, refuse; assert, resist, strive, struggle.

yielding, *a.* SYN.-compliant, deferential, dutiful, obedient, submissive, tractable. ANT.-insubordinate, intractable, obstinate, rebellious.

yokel, *n.* SYN.-boor, bumpkin, hayseed, hick, klutz.

young, *a.* See **youthful.**

youthful, *a.* SYN.-adolescent, boyish, callow, childish, childlike, girlish, immature, inexperienced, juvenile, puerile, young. ANT.-aged, elderly, mature, old, senile.

Z

zeal, *n.* SYN.-ardor, devotion, earnestness, enthusiasm, excitement, fanaticism, fervency, fervor, intensity, vehemence. ANT.-apathy, detachment, ennui, indifference, unconcern.

zealous, *a.* SYN.-ardent, eager, enthusiastic, fervent, fervid, fiery, impassioned, intense, keen, passionate, vehement. ANT.-apathetic, cool, indifferent, nonchalant.

zenith, *n.* SYN.-acme, apex, climax, consummation, culmination, height, peak, summit. ANT.-anticlimax, base, depth, floor.

zone, *n.* SYN.-belt, climate, locality, region, sector, tract.